America Now

Short Readings from Recent Periodicals

America Now

Short Readings from Recent Periodicals

Seventh Edition

Edited by

ROBERT ATWAN

Director, The Blue Hills Writing Institute at Curry College
Series Editor, *The Best American Essays*

Exercises prepared with the assistance of

Maria Halovanic
Boston University
Andrew Michael Knoll
Boston University
Timothy Walsh

Bedford/St. Martin's   Boston ♦ New York

For Bedford / St. Martin's

Senior Developmental Editor: Ellen Thibault
Senior Production Editor: Karen S. Baart
Production Supervisor: Andrew Ensor
Senior Marketing Manager: Karita dos Santos
Associate Editor: Christina Gerogiannis
Editorial Assistant: Stephanie Naudin
Assistant Production Editor: Kristen Merrill
Copyeditor: Lisa Wehrle
Text Design: Jean Hammond
Cover Design: Hannus Design
Composition: Pine Tree Composition, Inc.
Printing and Binding: Haddon Craftsmen, Inc., an R.R. Donnelley &
    Sons Company

President: Joan E. Feinberg
Editorial Director: Denise B. Wydra
Editor in Chief: Karen S. Henry
Director of Marketing: Karen Melton Soeltz
Director of Editing, Design, and Production: Marcia Cohen
Managing Editor: Elizabeth M. Schaaf

Library of Congress Control Number: 2006940478

Manufactured in the United States of America.

1 0 9 8 7
f e d c b a

For information, write: Bedford/St. Martin's, 75 Arlington Street,
Boston, MA 02116   (617-399-4000)

ISBN-10:   0–312–45709–X
ISBN-13:   978–0–312–45709–9

Acknowledgments

*Acknowledgments and copyrights appear at the back of the book on pages 437–40,
which constitute an extension of the copyright page. It is a violation of the law to re-
produce these selections by any means whatsoever without the written permission of
the copyright holder.*

About the Editor

Robert Atwan is director of The Blue Hills Writing Institute at Curry College and the series editor of the annual *Best American Essays*, which he founded in 1985. His essays, reviews, and critical articles have appeared in the *New York Times*, the *Los Angeles Times*, the *Atlantic Monthly*, *Iowa Review*, *Denver Quarterly*, *Kenyon Review*, *River Teeth*, and many other publications. For Bedford/ St. Martin's, he has also edited *Ten on Ten: Major Essayists on Recurring Themes* (1992), *Our Times*, Fifth Edition (1998), and *Convergences*, Second Edition (2005). He has coedited (with Jon Roberts) *Left, Right, and Center: Voices from Across the Political Spectrum* (1996), and is coeditor with Donald McQuade of *The Writer's Presence*, Fifth Edition (2005).

Preface for Instructors

People write for many reasons, but one of the most compelling is to express their views on matters of current public interest. Browse any newsstand, library magazine rack, or Web page and you'll find an abundance of articles and opinion pieces responding to current issues and events. Too frequently, students see the writing they do in a composition class as having little connection with real-world problems and issues. *America Now*, with its provocative professional and student writing—all very current opinion essays drawn from a range of periodicals—shows students that by writing on the important issues of today, they can influence campus and public discourse and truly make a difference.

The seventh edition of *America Now* offers a generous sampling of timely and provocative material. *America Now* is designed to immerse introductory writing students in the give-and-take of public dialogue and to stimulate thinking, discussion, and composition. Its overriding instructional principle—which guides everything from the choice of readings and topics to the design of questions—is that participation in informed discussion will help generate and enrich student writing. The book systematically encourages its users to view reading, thinking, discussion, and writing as closely interrelated activities. It assumes that (1) attentive reading and reflection will lead to informed discussion; (2) participation in open and informed discussion will result in a broadening of viewpoints; (3) an awareness of different viewpoints will stimulate further reflection and renewed discussion; and (4) this process in turn will lead to thoughtful papers. The book's general introduction, "The Persuasive Writer," takes the student through the process and offers some useful guidelines for engaging in productive discussion and advice on forming and expressing opinions along with two annotated student essays that serve as models of effective opinion writing. Instructors may also find helpful my essay "Writing and the Art of Discussion," which can be found in the instructor's manual and at the book's companion Web site.

New to This Edition

Following is a brief overview of the seventh edition of *America Now*. For a more in-depth description of the book, see "Using *America Now*" beginning on page ix of this preface.

Forty-five readings and **twenty-seven visual texts**—all new and *very* current. Drawn from more than forty recent periodicals, including seventeen student newspapers, each reading is not only new to this edition but has appeared within a year or two of the book's publication. With over half of its selections published in 2006, *America Now* is the most current short essay reader available. Some of the readings you will find in the seventh edition are Jhumpa Lahiri and Henry Louis Gates Jr. on identity, Camille Paglia on plastic surgery, The Sims inventor Will Wright on video games and violence, and Senator John McCain on torture.

Seven new issues of current interest. Seven of the twelve thematic chapters have been updated to reflect the changing interests of students over the past two years. Sure to spark lively discussion and writing, these new topics are social networking online (Facebook), DNA and identity, language and technology, gaming and violence, consumerism and sweatshops, science and "intelligent design," and torture.

New advice on the visual expression of opinion. Because we live in an increasingly visual culture, the book's introduction now offers a section on expressing opinions visually—with striking examples from photojournalism, cartoons, and opinion advertisements.

New annotations of student writing. To highlight models of persuasive writing, I have annotated a section of a student paper in each chapter. My comments point out some of the most effective strategies of the student writers in the book and offer advice for structuring sentences, stating a main point, using analogies, shaping arguments, presenting examples and evidence, calling for action, and more.

Even more "Student Writer at Work" interviews. This edition includes ten brief, inspiring interviews in which student authors in the book explain how—and why—they express their opinions in writing. Body image, Muslim identity, and questions surrounding genetics and race are just a handful of the topics covered in this feature.

An updated companion Web site (bedfordstmartins.com/americanow) provides students with access to the Read/Hear/See It Now links referenced throughout the book, annotated research links for each chapter, electronically scored *ESL and Developmental Quizzes* for each chapter, and links to every online newspaper, magazine, and journal in *America Now*. The site also includes an online version of the book's **instructor's manual.**

Using America Now

Professional and Student Writing from a Wide Variety of Sources

The book's selections by professional writers are drawn from recent periodicals, ranging from journals such as the *Columbia Journalism Review* to influential general magazines such as the *New Yorker*. As would be expected in a collection that focuses heavily on social trends and current events, *America Now* features several newspapers and news-oriented magazines: the *Boston Globe*, the *New York Times*, the *Wall Street Journal*, the *Philadelphia Inquirer*, the *Los Angeles Times*, *Newsweek*, and the *New York Times Magazine*. With its additional emphasis on public discourse, this collection also draws on some of America's leading political magazines, including *Reason*, the *New Republic*, *Townhall.com*, and the *Weekly Standard*. Also represented are magazines that appeal primarily to specialized audiences, such as the *Chronicle of Higher Education*, *Adbusters*, *DoubleTake*, and *Wired*. In general, the reading illustrate the variety of personal, informative, and persuasive writing read daily by millions of Americans. The readings are kept short (many under three pages, and some no longer than a page) to hold student interest and to serve as models for the student's own writing. To introduce a more in-depth approach to various topics, the book includes a few longer essays in the final chapters.

America Now also features eighteen published student selections—essays and cartoons—from online college newspapers. These recent works reveal student writers confronting in a public forum the same topics and issues that challenge some of our leading social critics and commentators, and they show how student writers can enter into and influence public discussion. In this way, the student selections in *America Now*—complemented by Student Writer at Work interviews—encourage students to see writing as a form of personal and public empowerment.

Timely Topics for Discussion and Debate

Student essays not only make up a large percentage of the readings in this book, they also shape the volume's contents. As we monitored the broad spectrum of online college newspapers—and reviewed several hundred student essays—we gradually found the most commonly discussed campus issues and topics. Issues such as those mentioned on page viii of this preface have provoked so much recent student response that they could have resulted in several single-topic collections. Many college papers do not restrict themselves to news items and editorial opinion but make room for personal essays as well. Some popular student topics are gender, cultural identity, and body image, all of which are reflected in the book's table of contents.

To facilitate group discussion and in-class work, *America Now* features twelve bite-sized units. These tightly focused chapters permit instructors to cover a broad range of themes and issues in a single semester. Each can be conveniently handled in one or two class periods. In general, the chapters move from accessible, personal topics (for example, body image, identity, and gender) to more public issues (science, religion, and torture), thus accommodating instructors who prefer to start with personal writing and gradually progress to exposition, analysis, and argument.

Since composition courses naturally emphasize issues revolving around language and the construction of meaning, *America Now* also includes two chapters designed to encourage students to examine the powerful influence of words and symbols. Language issues also surface in many readings throughout the book.

For instructors who want to concentrate on developing argumentation skills, the book arranges several controversial topics into **Paired Readings, Campus Debates,** and **Opposing Views.** Paired Readings offer linked perspectives on plastic surgery; a Campus Debate in the book's introduction presents two student opinions on how to approach the issue of date rape; and Opposing Views feature differing opinions on the ethics of sweatshop labor and on creationism and evolution.

The Visual Expression of Opinion

America Now encourages students to pay close attention to the persuasive power of language and images. Reflecting the growing presence of advertising in public discussion, among the book's images are recent opinion advertisements (or "Op-Ads"). These pieces, which focus on racial profiling and cultural identity, encourage students to uncover the visual and verbal strategies of various advocacy groups trying to influence the consciousness and ideology of large audiences.

To demonstrate the persuasive power of the image, the book also features several other kinds of visual texts. Iconic photos include Joe

Rosenthal's World War II "Flag Raising at Iwo Jima" and Thomas E. Franklin's famous 9/11 image, "Three Firefighters Raising the Flag." Numerous cartoons comment on a variety of topics such as gender, politics, foreign policy, immigration, stem cell research, and creationism. Another assortment of visual selections, titled "America Then," provides students with historical perspectives on "America Now." These images show that many of the issues we deal with today have roots in the past. They include a 1904 automobile ad that illustrates a trend toward conspicuous consumption, a cluster of 1925 photos from the "Scopes Monkey Trial" documenting the trial of a Tennessee teacher who dared to teach evolution, a 1947 Charles Atlas ad offering a perspective on male body image, and a 1976 video game that sparked censorship and controversy on the relationship between gaming and violence.

The Instructional Apparatus: Before, During, and After Reading

The apparatus of *America Now* supports both discussion-based instruction and more individualized approaches to reading and writing. Taking into account the increasing diversity of students (especially the growing number of nonnative speakers) in today's writing programs, the apparatus offers extensive help with college-level vocabulary and features a "Words to Learn" list preceding each selection. This vocabulary list with brief definitions will allow students to spot ahead of time some of the words they may find difficult; encountering the word later in context will help lock it in memory. It's unrealistic, however, to think students will acquire a fluent knowledge of new words by memorizing a list. Therefore, the apparatus following each selection includes additional exercises under the headings "Vocabulary/Using a Dictionary" and "Responding to Words in Context." These sets of questions introduce students to prefixes, suffixes, connotations, denotations, tone, and etymology.

To help promote reflection and discussion, the book includes a prereading assignment for each main selection. The questions in "Before You Read" provide students with the opportunity to explore a few of the avenues that lead to fruitful discussion and interesting papers. A full description of the advantages gained by linking reading, writing, and classroom discussion can be found in my introduction to the instructor's manual.

Along with the discussion of vocabulary, incrementally structured questions follow individual selections. Picking up on the vocabulary lists preceding each selection, another question set, "Responding to

Words in Context," supplements the "Vocabulary/Using a Dictionary" questions and asks students to use what they have learned from the dictionary exercises and vocabulary lists. Following the vocabulary questions, the "Discussing Main Point and Meaning" and "Examining Sentences, Paragraphs, and Organization" questions help to guide students step by step through the reading process, culminating in the set of "Thinking Critically" questions. As instructors well know, beginning students can sometimes be too trusting of what they see in print, especially in textbooks. Therefore, the "Thinking Critically" questions invite students to take a more skeptical attitude toward their reading and to form the habit of challenging a selection from both analytical and experiential points of view. The selection apparatus concludes with "In-Class Writing Activities," which emphasize freewriting exercises and collaborative projects.

In addition to the selection apparatus, *America Now* contains end-of-chapter questions designed to stimulate further discussion and writing. The chapter apparatus approaches the reading material from topical and thematic angles, with an emphasis on group discussion. The introductory comments to each chapter highlight the main discussion points and the way selections are linked together. These points and linkages are then reintroduced at the end of the chapter through three sets of interlocking study questions and tasks: (1) a suggested topic for discussion, (2) questions and ideas to help students prepare for class discussion, and (3) several writing assignments that ask students to move from discussion to composition—that is, to develop papers out of the ideas and opinions expressed in class discussion and debate. Instructors with highly diverse writing classes may find "Topics for Cross-Cultural Discussion" a convenient way to encourage an exchange of perspectives and experiences that could also generate ideas for writing. Located on the book's Web site (bedfordstmartins.com/americanow) are **ESL and Developmental Quizzes** that test vocabulary and comprehension skills. Electronic scoring, which can be monitored by instructors, offers immediate feedback.

The Instructor's Manual

Maria Halovanic of Boston University, Timothy Walsh, and the late Andrew Michael Knoll of Boston University prepared the instructor's manual, bringing to the task valuable classroom experience at all levels of composition instruction. The manual contains an essay for each chapter, offering suggestions for teaching the selections together and separately, plus suggested answers and possible discussion topics based on every question posed in the text. Anyone using *America Now* should be sure to consult the manual before designing a syllabus, framing a discussion topic, or even assigning individual selections. Liz deBeer of Rutgers University also contributed a helpful essay on designing student panels ("Forming Forums"), along with advice on using the book's apparatus in both developmental and mainstream composition classes that is available at the book's companion Web site.

Acknowledgments

While putting together the seventh edition of *America Now*, I was fortunate to receive the assistance of many talented individuals. In addition to their work on the instructor's manual, Maria Halovanic, Timothy Walsh, and Andrew Michael Knoll offered many useful suggestions for the book's instructional apparatus.

To revise a text is to entertain numerous questions: What kind of selections work best in class? What types of questions are most helpful? How can reading, writing, and discussion be most effectively intertwined? This edition profited immensely from the following instructors who generously took the time to respond to the sixth edition: Kaye Falconer, Bakersfield College; Nancy Freiman, Milwaukee Area Technical College; Terry Meier, Bakersfield College; Marty Price, Mississippi State University; Ann Spurlock, Mississippi State University; and Frances Whitney, Bakersfield College.

I'd also like to acknowledge instructors who have reviewed previous editions, and whose ideas and suggestions continue to inform the book: Kim M. Baker, Roger Williams University; Kevin Ball, Youngstown State University; Deborah Biorn, St. Cloud State University; Joan Blankmann, Northern Virginia Community College; Diane Bosco, Suffolk County Community College; Mikel Cole, University of Houston–Downtown; Steven Florzcyk, the State University of New York–New Paltz; Andrea Germanos, Saint Augustine College; Kim Halpern, Pulaski Technical College; Jessica Harvey, Alexandria Technical College; Chris Hayes, University of Georgia; Sharon Jaffee, Santa Monica College; Patricia W. Julius, Michigan State University; Jessica Heather Lourey, Alexandria Technical College; Brian Ludlow, Alfred University; Sherry Manis, Foothill College; Melody Nightingale, Santa Monica College; Kimme Nuckles, Baker College; Michael Orlando, Bergen Community College; David Pryor, University of the Incarnate Word; Hubert C. Pulley, Georgia Southern University;

Sherry Robertson, Pulaski Technical College; Lynn Sabas, Saint Augustine College; Jennifer Satterlee, Parkland College; Andrea D. Shanklin, Howard Community College; Linda Weiner, the University of Akron; and Martha Anne Yeager-Tobar, Cerritos College.

Other people helped in various ways. I'm indebted to Barbara Gross of Rutgers University, Newark, for her excellent work in preparing the Instructor's Manual for the first edition. Two good friends, Charles O'Neill and Jack Roberts, both of St. Thomas Aquinas College, went over my early plans for the book and offered many useful suggestions.

As always, it was a pleasure to work with the superb staff at Bedford/St. Martin's. Jane Betz, my editor on the first edition, shaped the book in lasting ways and helped with the planning of the revision. Of all the people acknowledged, I owe the most gratitude to this edition's senior developmental editor, Ellen Thibault. Her insightful suggestions, remarkable good sense, and uncanny ability to keep track of so many minute details made this collection a pleasure to work on from start to finish. Ellen is also responsible for the student interviews that are such an important feature of this edition. Christina Gerogiannis, associate editor, and Stephanie Naudin, editorial assistant, researched images and readings for the book, contacted the students profiled in the book, and worked energetically on the book's Web site and instructor's manual. Jason Reblando cleared text and art permissions under a tight schedule. Karen Baart guided the book through production with patience and care, staying on top of many details, and Elizabeth Schaaf managed the production process with great attentiveness. I was fortunate to receive the careful copyediting of Lisa Wehrle. In the advertising and promotion department, Tom Macy and Angela Dambrowski deserve warm thanks for their work, as does senior marketing manager Karita dos Santos.

I am grateful to Charles H. Christensen, the retired president of Bedford/St. Martin's, for his generous help and thoughtful suggestions throughout the life of this book. Finally, I especially want to thank Bedford's president, Joan E. Feinberg, who conceived the idea for *America Now* and who continues to follow it closely through its various editions, for her deep and abiding interest in college composition. It is a great pleasure and privilege to work with her.

Robert Atwan

Contents

1   Body Image: Is It a Serious Issue?   47

Opinion polls regularly show that most Americans are discontented with their appearance. Does our body image seriously determine our self-esteem? Do we spend too much time fretting about our hair, our skin, our weight, our height, our abs, the shape of our nose? A prominent author and linguistics professor asks, "What is it about mothers and hair?" as she reflects on how "women in our society are judged by appearance." ... Is it dangerous to take our body image too seriously? inquires a University of Texas student. ... Cosmetic surgery is drastically narrowing our sense of human beauty, maintains one of our major cultural critics. ... Though he despises the whole idea of plastic surgery, a newspaper reporter offers some arguments in its favor. ... A popular 1947 advertisement links huge muscles with self-esteem, violence, and sex appeal.

2   Social Networking: How Is Facebook Changing Student Life?   83

How are recent Web sites like Facebook and MySpace changing student life? Is the recent surge in the popularity of "Me Media" an indication of serious community expansion or a distracting form of current egomania? Why are these sites so addictive? A college communications professor is concerned that Facebook is another "digital distraction" and a misuse of a school's information technology policies. . . . Facebook is distracting, a Mississippi State University student admits, but where else can you find the unlimited "free discourse" that Facebook permits?

3   Cultural Identities: Can We Live Dual Lives?   101

Many of us feel the pressure of living double lives as we try to juggle a mixture of heritages, backgrounds, and loyalties. What are the difficulties and how can they be resolved? A Pulitzer Prize–winning Indian American author experiences "the intense pressure to be two things, loyal to the old world and fluent in the new." . . . Why do assimilated Asian American students and those who cling to their ethnic heritage discriminate against each other? wonders a University of California (Irvine) freshman. . . . An advertisement for the American Indian College Fund stresses the importance of tribal colleges for preserving Native American identity. . . . The constant mistake of confusing Islam with its cultural and political representations frustrates a University of Chicago Muslim student.

4   Can Genetics Explain Who We Are?   130

What do recent DNA tests tell us about the origins of human life?
How did different races come into existence? How did they spread
throughout the globe? What does genetic testing tell us about our
personal racial makeup? A *National Geographic* writer traces the
trail of our DNA to "pinpoint humanity's ancestral home." . . . One
of the nation's most distinguished African American writers and
scholars uses a combination of genealogy and genetics to discover
his complex roots. . . . A groundbreaking book and television miniseries of the 1970s traces a family's history and examines the impact
of slavery. . . . A Pennsylvania State University staff writer reports on
what happens when college students voluntarily take DNA tests
to determine their roots. . . . In an editorial, the *New York Times*
maintains that the DNA tests of college students prove to them that
"race and ethnicity are more fluid and complex" than they previously imagined.

5   Gender Differences: How Real Are They?   162

Do males and females behave as though they come from different planets? Can gender differences be overcome so that true equality can exist between the sexes? Who gets shortchanged more by our educational system—boys or girls? Is one sex smarter than the other? A popular comic strip team succinctly depicts what happens when guys hang out and when girls hang out. . . . A columnist famous for her exceptional IQ comes up with some answers to the question Who's smarter, men or women? . . . The controversy sparked by a college president's remarks over women in the sciences tells us more about restrictions on academic discourse than about gender disparities, maintains a prominent Harvard psychology professor. . . . Another psychology professor reports on her long-term study showing why young women today dramatically outperform young men in college. . . . Could single-sex classrooms help improve our damaged educational system? asks a Tufts University columnist.

6   Do Words Matter?   203

Do our word choices make any significant differences? Can words create hostile environments all by themselves? Can they have far-reaching political consequences? Who decides which words are offensive? Is it permissible for some groups to use words that are forbidden to others? One of the nation's most prominent word-watchers reports on why the term *climate change* may be replacing *global warming*. . . . A noted news magazine columnist take us on a guided tour of today's most fashionable euphemisms. . . . How would the Statue of Liberty welcome today's immigrants? A cartoonist provides an idea. . . . "I'll do my part in educating you," claims an Emory University student as she offers a list of definitions for a wide range of sex and gender distinctions that people too often overlook. . . . An essayist carefully considers the best word to describe her condition: Crippled? Disabled? Handicapped? . . . Why don't we have a word for the space between each finger and toe? wonders a linguist who's traced many handy words that appear in other languages but not English.

7   The American Language Today: How Is It Changing?   239

What are some of the factors currently transforming the English language? How is technology altering the way we write and spell? Now that e-mail communication and online meetings demand more writing, is our grammar betraying us? What are the most effective educational methods for helping writing students to understand the differences between the informal language of home and the Standard English needed for academic communication? An essayist examines the linguistic repercussions of text messaging. . . . How did Americans communicate news and information quickly before the Internet was invented? A 1940s ad promotes the "revolutionary" technology of the telegram. . . . If you want to find dates online, poor grammar and usage may be a liability, writes a Michigan State University student. . . . Red-ink corrections are counterproductive, advises an educational researcher, who suggests that the best way to teach young students Standard English is by showing them how to "code-switch between the language of the home and the language of the school."

8   Video Games: How Are They Transforming the Culture?   276

Are today's video games expanding the human imagination or are they a worthless addiction? Is it a proven case that violent games lead to violent behavior? A prominent creator of numerous bestselling games says it's time to stop condemning games and recognize the many ways they benefit our culture and intellect. . . . Our nation must examine the ways violent video games "affect the civility and safety of our children and of our society," argues a conservative columnist and concerned mother. . . . If video games are making us more violent, why has violent crime in America—especially among teenagers—sharply declined over the past decade? wonders a student at the University of Connecticut. . . . A 1970s movie poster shows that censorship has long plagued the video game.

9   Do We Need an Ethics of Buying?   300

Have you ever bought something you didn't need? Have you ever bought something you really couldn't afford? What about something that you knew was counterfeit or was produced by the labor of exploited workers? Do Americans need to act more responsibly as consumers? Do we need to develop an ethics of consumption? One of the nation's leading environmental writers browses an upscale catalogue that contains "the essential secret of American consumer life." . . . An anti-consumer magazine invites us to celebrate "Buy Nothing Day." . . . The business of counterfeit or pirated goods is costing the world far more than money, reports a major women's magazine. . . . After succumbing to a knock-off Coach purse, a Louisiana State student confronts her guilty conscience. . . . The Manifesto of the United Students Against Sweatshops demands that colleges "adopt strong codes of conduct that protect workers' rights." . . . . But what would happen to the poorest workers in developing nations if sweatshops were abolished? asks a Columbia University student who views sweatshops as a necessary stage of economic progress. . . . An ad for one of the first automobiles suggests a trend toward what economist Thorstein Veblen called "conspicuous consumption" in 1899.

10   The News Media: Are Opinions Replacing Facts?   341

Do the American media now rely on opinions more than facts? Are Americans more persuaded by the expression of subjective opinions than by the presentation of objective information? The president of a major TV network worries about what happens to truthful reporting when opinion dominates. . . . Going against the grain, a veteran journalist maintains that subjectivity will improve our newspapers and not interfere with factual accuracy. . . . It's commonly said that in a democracy we all have the right to an opinion, but perhaps today the

As views of life and perspectives on the world, will religion and science always be at odds? Are they mutually exclusive, or can science
and religion find common ground? Can religion find room in a science
curriculum and vice versa? An America Then feature looks at the historical 1925 trial that pitted evolutionary science against the teachings
of the Bible and made headlines throughout the nation. . . . In a *USA
Today* debate, two teams of experts propose two different views: One
believes that it is educationally healthy to challenge Darwin's theories
in science classrooms, while the other believes that promoting intelligent design as an equivalent theory will jeopardize both a student's
scientific education and our national interests. . . . What happens
when students who believe in creationism are also working toward
university degrees in science? An Auburn University reporter profiles
one such student. . . . A *Doonesbury* comic strip imagines a seriously
ill creationist seeking the best scientific treatment in a doctor's office.

12   Torture: Can It Ever Be Justified?   392

Has the war on terror redefined the acceptable treatment of enemy
prisoners? Is torture permitted to extract information that might save
thousands of civilian lives? Is the "ticking bomb" rationale for torture justified? Even if the torture of terrorists could give us a significant advantage, we still must refrain from the practice, argues a University of Illinois columnist. . . . A popular and prominent senator
explains why torture can never be permitted. . . . All well and good,
claims a controversial political commentator, but just suppose there
really is a ticking bomb, what then? . . . If we grant that in rare cases
some degree of torture might be necessary to save scores of lives,
where would it stop? asks a columnist concerned about the "slippery
slope" as she weighs the arguments advanced in the previous essays.

America Now

Short Readings from Recent Periodicals

The Persuasive Writer: Expressing Opinions with Clarity, Confidence, and Civility

It is not possible to extricate yourself from the questions in which your age is involved.

−Ralph Waldo Emerson, "The Fortune of the Republic" (1878)

What Is America Now?

America Now collects very recent essays and articles that have been carefully selected to encourage reading, provoke discussion, and stimulate writing. The philosophy behind the book is that interesting, effective writing originates in public dialogue. The book's primary purpose is to help students proceed from class discussions of reading assignments to the production of complete essays that reflect an engaged participation in those discussions.

The selections in *America Now* come from two main sources — from popular, mainstream periodicals and from college newspapers available on the Internet. Written by journalists and columnists, public figures and activists, as well as by professors and students from all over the country, the selections illustrate the types of material read by millions of Americans every day. In addition to magazine and newspaper writing, the book features a number of recent opinion advertisements (what I call "Op-Ads" for short). These familiar forms of "social marketing" are often sponsored by corporations or nonprofit organizations and advocacy groups to promote policies, programs, and ideas such as gun control, family planning, literacy, civil rights, or conservation. Such advertising texts allow one to pinpoint and discuss specific techniques of verbal and visual persuasion that are critical in the formation of public opinion.

1

I have gathered the selections into twelve units that cover today's most widely discussed issues and topics: media bias, science and religion, racial conflict, gender differences, consumption and marketing, torture, video game violence, and so on. As you respond to the readings in discussion and writing, you will be actively taking part in some of the major controversies of our time. Although I have tried in this new edition of *America Now* to represent as many viewpoints as possible on a variety of controversial topics, it's not possible in a collection of this scope to include under each topic either a full spectrum of opinion or a universally satisfying balance of opposing opinions. For some featured topics, an entire book would be required to represent the full spectrum of opinion; for others, a rigid pro-con, either-or format could distort the issue and perhaps overly polarize student responses to it. Selections within a unit usually illustrate the most commonly held opinions on a topic so that readers will get a reasonably good sense of how the issue has been framed and the public discourse and debate it has generated. But if a single opinion isn't immediately or explicitly balanced by an opposite opinion, or if a view seems unusually idiosyncratic, that in no way implies that it is somehow editorially favored or endorsed. Be assured that questions following *every* selection will encourage you to analyze and critically challenge whatever opinion or perspective is expressed in that selection.

Participation is the key to this collection. I encourage you to view reading and writing as a form of participation. I hope you will read the selections attentively, think about them carefully, be willing to discuss them in class, and use what you've learned from your reading and discussion as the basis for your papers. If you do these things, you will develop three skills necessary for successful work in college and beyond: the ability to read critically, to discuss topics intelligently, and to write persuasively. These skills are also sorely needed in our daily lives as citizens. A vital democracy depends upon them. The reason democracy is hard, said the Czech author and statesman Vaclav Havel, is that it requires the participation of everyone.

America Now invites you to see reading, discussion, and writing as closely related activities. As you read a selection, imagine that you have entered into a discussion with the author. Take notes as you read. Question the selection. Challenge its point of view or its evidence. Compare your experience with the author's. Consider how different economic classes or other groups are likely to respond. Remember, just because something appears in a newspaper or book doesn't make it true or accurate. Form the habit of challenging what you read. Don't be persuaded by an opinion simply because it appears in print or because you believe you should accept it. Trust your own observations and experiences. Though logicians never say so, personal experiences and keen observations often form the basis of our most convincing arguments.

When your class discusses a selection, be especially attentive to what others think of it. It's always surprising how two people can read the same article and reach two entirely different interpretations. Observe the range of opinion. Try to understand why and how people arrive at different conclusions. Do some seem to miss the point? Do some distort the author's ideas? Have someone's comments forced you to rethink the selection? Keep a record of the discussion in your notebook. Then, when you begin to draft your paper, consider your essay as an extension of both your imaginary conversation with the author and the actual class discussion. If you've taken detailed notes of your own and the class's opinions about the selection, you should have more than enough information to get started.

What Are Opinions?

One of the primary aims of *America Now* is to help you learn through models and instructional material how to express your opinions in a persuasive, reasonable, civil, and productive fashion. But before we look at effective ways of expressing opinion, let's first consider opinions in general: What are they? Where do they come from?

When we say we have an opinion about something, we usually mean that we have come to a conclusion that something appears true or appears to be valid. But when we express an opinion about something, we are not claiming we are 100 percent certain that something is so. Opinion does not imply certainty and, in fact, is accompanied by some degree of doubt and skepticism. As a result, opinions are most likely to be found in those areas of thought and discussion where our judgments are uncertain. Since human beings know so few things for certain, much of what we believe, or discuss and debate, falls into various realms of probability or possibility. These we call opinions.

Journalists often make a distinction between fact and opinion. Facts can be confirmed and verified and therefore do not involve opinions. We ordinarily don't have opinions about facts, but we can and often do have opinions about the interpretation of facts. For example, it makes no sense to argue whether Washington, D.C., is the capital of the United States since it's an undisputed fact that it is. It's a matter of record and can be established with certainty. Thus, we don't say we have an opinion that Washington, D.C., is the nation's capital; we know for a fact it is. But it would be legitimate to form an opinion about whether that city is the best location for the U.S. capital and whether it should permanently remain the capital. In other words:

- *Washington, D.C., is the capital of the United States of America* is a statement of fact.
- *Washington, D.C., is too poorly located to be the capital of a vast nation* is a statement of opinion.

Further, simply not knowing whether something is a fact does not necessarily make it a matter of opinion. For example, if we don't know the capital of Brazil, that doesn't mean we are then free to form an opinion about which city it is. The capital of Brazil is a verifiable fact and can be identified with absolute certainty. There is no conflicting public opinion about which city is Brazil's capital. The answer is not up for grabs. These examples, however, present relatively simple, readily agreed-upon facts. In real-life disputes, a fact is not always so readily distinguished from an opinion; people argue all the time about whether something is a fact. It's therefore a good idea at the outset of any discussion or argument to try to arrive at a mutual agreement of the facts that are known or knowable and those that could be called into question. Debates over abortion, for example, often hinge on biological facts about embryonic development that are themselves disputed by medical experts.

An opinion almost always exists in the climate of other, conflicting opinions. In discourse, we refer to this overall context of competing opinions as public controversy. Every age has its controversies. At any given time, the public is divided on a great number of topics about which it holds a variety of different opinions. Often the controversy is reduced to two opposing positions; for example, we are asked whether we are pro-life or pro-choice; for or against capital punishment; in favor of or opposed to same-sex marriage, and so on. This book includes many such controversies and covers multiple opinions. One sure way of knowing that something is a matter of opinion is that the public is divided on the topic. We often experience these divisions firsthand as we mature and increasingly come into contact with those who disagree with our opinions.

Some opinions are deeply held, so deeply, in fact, that those who hold them refuse to see them as opinions. For some people on certain issues there can be no difference of opinion; they possess the Truth and all who differ hold erroneous opinions. This frequently happens in some controversies, where one side in a dispute is so confident of the truth of its position that it cannot see its own point of view as one of several possible points of view. For example, someone may feel so certain that marriage can exist only between a man and a woman that he or she cannot acknowledge the possibility of another position. If one side cannot recognize the existence of a different opinion, cannot entertain or tolerate it, argues not with the correctness of another's perspective but denies the possibility that there can legitimately be another perspective, then discussion and debate become all but impossible.

To be open and productive, public discussion depends on the capacity of all involved to view their own positions, no matter how cherished, as opinions that can be subjected to opposition. There is nothing wrong with possessing a strong conviction, nor with believing our position is the better one, nor with attempting to convince others of our point of view. What is argumentatively wrong and what prevents or restricts free and open discussion is twofold: (1) the failure to recognize our own belief or position as an opinion that could be mistaken; and (2) the refusal to acknowledge the possibility that another's opinion could be correct.

Is one person's opinion as good as another's? Of course not. Though we may believe that everyone has a right to an opinion, we certainly wouldn't ask our mail carrier to diagnose the cause of persistent heartburn or determine whether a swollen gland is serious. In such instances, we respect the opinion of a trained physician. And even when we consult a physician, in serious matters we often seek second and even third opinions just to be sure. An auto mechanic is in a better position to evaluate a used car than someone who's never repaired a car; a lawyer's opinion on whether a contract is valid is more reliable than that belonging to someone who doesn't understand the legal nature of contracts. If an airline manufacturer wants to test a new cockpit instrument design, it solicits opinions from experienced pilots, not passengers. This seems obvious, and yet people continually are persuaded by those who can claim little expert knowledge on a subject or issue: For example, how valuable or trustworthy is the opinion of a celebrity who is paid to endorse a product?

When expressing or evaluating an opinion, we need to consider the extent of our or another's knowledge about a particular subject. Will anyone take our opinion seriously? On what authority do we base our position? Why do we take someone else's opinion as valuable or trustworthy? What is the source of the opinion? How reliable is it? How biased? One of the first Americans to study the effects of public opinion, Walter Lippmann, wrote in 1925, "It is often very illuminating, therefore, to ask yourself how you get at the facts on which you base your opinion. Who actually saw, heard, felt, counted, named the thing, about which you have an opinion?" Is your opinion, he went on to ask, based on something you heard from someone who heard it from someone else, who in turn heard it from someone else?

How Do We Form Opinions?

How can we possibly have reasonable opinions on all the issues of the day? One of the strains of living in a democracy that encourages a diversity of perspectives is that every responsible citizen is expected to have informed opinions on practically every public question. What do you think about the death penalty? About dependency on foreign oil? About the way the media cover the news? About the extent of racial discrimination? Do you or don't you support gun control? Are you pro-choice or pro-life? What's your position on affirmative action? Must there be a wall separating church and state? Should the United States avoid foreign entanglements or participate in humanitarian intervention where necessary around the globe? Certainly no single individual is an expert on every public issue. Certainly no one person possesses inside information or access to reliable data on every topic that becomes part of public controversy. Still, many people, by the time they are able to vote, have formed numerous opinions. Where do these opinions come from?

Although social scientists and psychologists have been studying opinion formation for decades, the subject still retains a great deal of imprecision. The sources of opinion are multiple and constantly shifting, and individuals differ so widely in experience, cultural background, and temperament that efforts to identify and classify the various ways opinion is formed are bound to be tentative and incomplete. What follows is a brief, though realistic, attempt to list some of the practical ways that Americans come by the opinions they hold.

1. *Inherited opinions.* These are opinions we derive from earliest childhood—transmitted via family, culture, traditions, customs,

regions, social institutions, or religion. For example, young people may identify themselves as either Democrats or Republicans because of their family affiliations. Though these opinions may change as we mature, they are often ingrained. Many people retain inherited opinions into their early adulthood and even throughout their entire lives. The more traditional the culture or society, the more likely the opinions that grow out of early childhood will be retained and passed on to the next generation. One reason behind the countercultural movements of the late 1960s was the enormous increase in the number of American high school graduates who went on to college, which caused a rift between the educational levels of parents and children—a generational war of values that became the subject of countless movies and books at the time.

2. *Involuntary opinions.* These are opinions that we have not culturally and socially inherited nor consciously adopted but that come to us through direct or indirect forms of indoctrination. They could be the customs of a cult or the propaganda of an ideology. Brainwashing is an extreme example of how one acquires opinions involuntarily. A more familiar example is the constant reiteration of advertising messages: We come to possess a favorable opinion of a product not because we've ever used it or know anything about it but because we have been "bombarded" by marketing to think positively about it.

3. *Adaptive opinions.* Many opinions grow out of our willingness—or even eagerness—to adapt to the prevailing views of particular groups, subgroups, or institutions to which we belong or desire to belong. As many learn, it's easier to follow the path of least resistance than to run counter to it. Moreover, acting out of self-interest, people often adapt their opinions to conform to the views of bosses or authority figures ("follow the leader") or they prefer to succumb to peer pressure than to oppose it. An employee finds himself accepting or agreeing with an opinion because a job or career depends upon it; a student may adapt her opinions to suit those of a professor in the hope of receiving a better grade; a professor may tailor his opinions in conformity with the prevailing beliefs of colleagues; an athlete comes to agree with the dominant attitudes of her teammates. Adaptive opinions are often weakly held and readily changed, depending on circumstances. But over time they can become habitual and turn into convictions.

4. *Concealed opinions.* In some groups where certain opinions dominate, there may be individuals who don't share the prevailing attitudes but rather than adapt or "rock the boat" they keep their

opinions to themselves. They may do this merely to avoid conflict or out of much more serious concerns—such as a fear of ostracism, ridicule, retaliation, or job loss. A common example is seen in the person who by day quietly goes along with the opinions of a group of colleagues but at night freely exchanges "honest" opinions with a group of friends. Some individuals find diaries and journals to be an effective way to express concealed opinions, and many today find online chat rooms a space where they can anonymously "be themselves."

5. *Linked opinions.* Many opinions are closely linked to other opinions. Unlike adaptive opinions, which are usually stimulated by convenience and an incentive to conform, these are opinions we derive from an enthusiastic and dedicated affiliation with certain groups, institutions, or parties. For example, it's not uncommon for someone to agree with every position his or her political party endorses—this phenomenon is usually called "following a party line." Linked opinions may not be well thought out on every narrow issue: Someone may decide to be a Republican or Democrat or Green or Libertarian for a few specific reasons—a position on abortion, war, taxation, cultural values, environment, civil liberties, and so forth—and then go along with, even to the point of strenuously defending, all of the other positions the party espouses because they are all part of its political platform or system of beliefs. In other words, once we accept opinions A and B, we are more likely to accept C and D, and so on down the chain. As Ralph Waldo Emerson succinctly put it, "If I know your sect, I anticipate your argument."

6. *Considered opinions.* These are opinions we have formed as a result of firsthand experience, reading, discussion and debate, or independent thinking and reasoning. These opinions are formed from direct knowledge and often from exposure and consideration of other opinions. A person who has experienced poverty, discrimination, or disability will form attitudes about those conditions that in many respects will remain beyond dispute and will help endow her or his opinions on those and related topics with authority. Wide reading on a subject and exposure to diverse views help to ensure that our opinions are based on solid information and tested against competing opinions. One simple way to judge whether your opinion is carefully thought-out is to list your reasons for holding it. Some people who express opinions on a topic are not able to offer a single reason for why they have those opinions. Of course, reasons don't necessarily make an opinion correct, but people who can support their opinions with one or more reasons are more persuasive than those who cannot

provide any reasons for their beliefs. *America Now*'s twelve chapters, if the selections are read carefully and discussed and challenged in the context of the surrounding instructional material, are designed to help students learn the process of forming educated opinions that are backed up with reasons.

This list is not exhaustive, and readers are invited to think of other common sources and types of opinion. Nor are the sources and types above mutually exclusive; the opinions of any individual may derive from all six sources or represent a mixture of several. For example, someone may simply inherit an entrenched family opinion on some matter but, as time passes, come to test it so thoroughly in the context of competing opinions that it reaches the level of a considered opinion. A child growing up in a working-class home that, say, uncritically values trade unions may eventually, through a combination of experience, discussion, and a study of economics and labor history, become a highly knowledgeable advocate of trade unions. As students learn to express their opinions effectively, they will find it useful to question themselves about the origins and development of those opinions. By tracing the process that led to the formation of our present opinions, we can better understand ourselves—our convictions, our inconsistencies, our biases, our blind spots.

Participating in Class Discussion: Six Basic Rules

Discussion is a learned activity. It requires a variety of essential academic skills: speaking, listening, thinking, and preparing. The following six basic rules are vital to healthy and productive discussion.

1. *Take an active speaking role.* Good discussion demands that everyone participates, not (as so often happens) just a vocal few. Many students remain detached from discussion because they are afraid to speak in a group. This fear is quite common—so common that psychological surveys show that speaking in front of a group is generally one of our worst fears. A leading communication consultant suggests that people choke up because they are more worried about how others will respond than about what they themselves have to say. It helps to remember that most people will be more interested in *what* you say than in how you say it. Once you get over the initial fear of speaking in public, your speech skills will improve with practice.

2. *Listen attentively.* No one who doesn't listen attentively can participate in group discussion. This may sound obvious, but just

think of how many senseless arguments you've had because either you or the person with whom you were talking completely misunderstood what was said. A good listener not only hears what someone is saying but also understands *why* he or she is saying it. One of the most important things about listening is that it leads to one element that lively discussion depends on: good questions. When the interesting questions begin to emerge, you know good discussion has truly begun.

3. *Examine all sides of an issue.*   Good discussion requires that we be patient with complexity. Difficult problems rarely have obvious and simple solutions, nor can they be easily summarized in popular slogans. Complex issues demand to be turned over in our minds so that we can see them from a variety of angles. Group discussion broadens our perspective and deepens our insight into difficult issues and ideas.

4. *Suspend judgment.*   Class discussion is best conducted in an open-minded and tolerant spirit. To fully explore ideas and issues, you need to be receptive to the opinions of others even when they contradict your own. Remember, discussion is not the same as debate. Its primary purpose is communication, not competition. In discussion, you are not necessarily trying to win everyone over to your point of view. The goal of group discussion should be to open up a topic so that everyone in the group is exposed to a spectrum of attitudes. Suspending judgment does not mean you shouldn't hold a strong belief or opinion about an issue; it means that you should be willing to take into account rival beliefs or opinions. An opinion formed without an awareness of other points of view—one that has not been tested against contrary ideas—is not a strong opinion but merely a stubborn one.

5. *Avoid abusive or insulting language.*   Free and open discussion occurs only when we respect the beliefs and opinions of others. If we speak in ways that fail to show respect for differing viewpoints— if we resort to name-calling or use demeaning and malicious expressions, for example—we not only embarrass ourselves but we also close off the possibility for an intelligent and productive exchange of ideas. Contrary to what you might gather from some popular radio and television talk shows, shouting insults and engaging in hate-speech are signs of verbal and intellectual bankruptcy. They are usually the last resort of someone who has nothing to say.

6. *Come prepared.*   Discussion is not merely random conversation. It demands a certain degree of preparation and focus. To participate in class discussion, you must consider assigned topics before-

hand and read whatever is required. Develop the habit of reading with pen in hand, underlining key points and jotting down questions, impressions, and ideas in your notebook. The notes you bring to class will be an invaluable aid in group discussion.

From Discussion to Writing

As this book amply demonstrates, we live in a world of conflicting opinions. Each of us over time has inherited, adopted, and gradually formed many opinions on a variety of topics. Of course, there are also a good number of public issues or questions about which we have not formed opinions or have undecided attitudes. In many public debates, members have unequal shares at stake. Eighteen-year-olds, for example, are much more likely to become impassioned over the government reviving a military draft or a state raising the legal age for driving than they would over Medicaid cuts or Social Security issues. Some public questions personally affect us more than others.

Thus, not all the issues covered in this book will at first make an equal impact on everyone. But whether you take a particular interest in a given topic or not, this book invites you to share in the spirit of public controversy. Many students, once introduced to the opposing sides of a debate or the multiple positions taken toward a public issue, will begin to take a closer look at the merits of different opinions. Once we start evaluating these opinions, once we begin stepping into the shoes of others and learning what's at stake in certain positions, we often find ourselves becoming involved with the issue and may even come to see ourselves as participants. After all, we are all part of the public, and to a certain extent all questions affect us: Ask the eighteen-year-old if he or she will be equipped to deal with the medical and financial needs of elderly parents and an issue that appears to affect only those near retirement will seem much closer to home.

As mentioned earlier, *America Now* is designed to stimulate discussion and writing grounded in response to a variety of public issues. A key to using this book is to think about discussion and writing not as separate activities but as an interrelated process. In discussion, we hear other opinions and formulate our own; in writing, we express our opinions in the context of other opinions. Both discussion and writing require articulation and deliberation. Both require an aptitude for listening carefully to others. Discussion stimulates writing, and writing in turn stimulates more discussion.

Group discussion stimulates and enhances your writing in several important ways. First, it supplies you with ideas. Let's say that you are participating in a discussion about how we express identity (see Chapter 3). One of your classmates mentions some of the problems a mixed ethnic background can cause. But suppose you also come from a mixed background, and, when you think about it, you believe that your mixed heritage has given you more advantages than disadvantages. Hearing her viewpoint may inspire you to express your differing perspective on the issue. Your perspective could lead to an interesting personal essay.

Suppose you now start writing that essay. You don't need to start from scratch and stare at a blank piece of paper or computer screen for hours. Discussion has already given you a few good leads. First, you have your classmate's opinions and attitudes to quote or summarize. You can begin your paper by explaining that some people view a divided ethnic identity as a psychological burden. You might expand on your classmate's opinion by bringing in additional information from other student comments or from your reading to show how people often focus on only the negative side of mixed identities. You can then explain your own perspective on this topic. Of course, you will need to give several examples showing *why* a mixed background has been an advantage for you. The end result can be a first-rate essay, one that takes other opinions into account and demonstrates a clearly established point of view. It is personal, and yet it takes a position that goes beyond one individual's experiences.

Whatever the topic, your writing will benefit from reading and discussion, activities that will give your essays a clear purpose or goal. In that way, your papers will resemble the selections found in this book: They will be a *response* to the opinions, attitudes, experiences, issues, ideas, and proposals that inform current public discourse. This is why most writers write; this is what most newspapers and magazines publish; this is what most people read. *America Now* consists entirely of such writing. I hope you will read the selections with enjoyment, discuss the issues with an open mind, and write about the topics with purpose and enthusiasm.

The Practice of Writing

Suppose you wanted to learn to play the guitar. What would you do first? Would you run to the library and read a lot of books on music? Would you then read some instructional books on guitar playing? Might you try to memorize all the chord positions? Then would you get sheet music for songs you liked and memorize them? After all that, if someone handed you an electric guitar, would you immediately be able to play like Jimi Hendrix or Eric Clapton?

I don't think you would begin that way. You probably would start out by strumming the guitar, getting the feel of it, trying to pick out something familiar. You probably would want to take lessons from someone who knows how to play. And you would practice, practice, practice. Every now and then your instruction book would come in handy. It would give you basic information on frets, notes, and chord positions, for example. You might need to refer to that information constantly in the beginning. But knowing the chords is not the same as knowing how to manipulate your fingers correctly to produce the right sounds. You need to be able to *play* the chords, not just know them.

Learning to read and write well is not that much different. Though instructional books can give you a great deal of advice and information, the only way anyone really learns to read and write is through constant practice. The only problem, of course, is that nobody likes practice. If we did, we would all be good at just about everything. Most of us, however, want to acquire a skill quickly and easily. We don't want to take lesson after lesson. We want to pick up the instrument and sound like a professional in ten minutes.

Wouldn't it be a wonderful world if that could happen? Wouldn't it be great to be born with a gigantic vocabulary so we instantly knew the meaning of every word we saw or heard? We would never have to go through the slow process of consulting a dictionary whenever we stumbled across an unfamiliar word. But, unfortunately, life is not so easy. To succeed at anything worthwhile requires patience and dedication. Watch a young figure skater trying to perfect her skills and you will see patience and dedication at work; or watch an accident victim learning how to maneuver a wheelchair so he can begin again an independent existence; or observe a new American struggling to learn English. None of these skills is quickly and easily acquired. Like building a vocabulary, they all take time and effort. They all require practice. And they require something even more important: the willingness to make mistakes. Can someone learn to skate without taking a spill? Or learn a new language without mispronouncing a word?

What Is "Correct English"?

One part of the writing process may seem more difficult than others—correct English. Yes, nearly all of what you read will be written in relatively correct English. Or it's probably more accurate to say "corrected" English, since most published writing is revised or "corrected" several times before it appears in print. Even skilled professional writers make mistakes that require correction.

Most native speakers don't actually *talk* in "correct" English. There are numerous regional patterns and dialects. As the Chinese American novelist Amy Tan says, there are "many Englishes." What we usually consider correct English is a set of guidelines developed over time to help standardize written expression. This standardization—like any agreed-upon standards such as weights and measures—is a matter of use and convenience. Suppose you went to a vegetable stand and asked for a pound of peppers and the storekeeper gave you a half pound but charged you for a full one. When you complained, he said, "But that's what *I* call a pound." What if you next bought a new compact disc you'd been waiting for, and when you tried to play it you discovered it wouldn't fit your CD player. Life would be very frustrating if everyone had a different set of standards: Imagine what would happen if some states used a red light to signal "go" and a green one for "stop." Languages are not that different. In all cultures, languages—especially written languages—have gradually developed certain general rules and principles to make communication as clear and efficient as possible.

You probably already have a guidebook or handbook that systematically sets out certain rules of English grammar, punctuation, and spelling. Like our guitar instruction book, these handbooks serve a very practical purpose. Most writers—even experienced authors—need to consult them periodically. Beginning writers may need to rely on them far more regularly. But just as we don't learn how to play chords by merely memorizing finger positions, we don't learn how to write by memorizing the rules of grammar or punctuation.

Writing is an activity, a process. Learning how to do it—like learning to ride a bike or prepare a tasty stew—requires *doing* it. Correct English is not something that comes first. We don't need to know the rules perfectly before we can begin to write. As in any activity, corrections are part of the learning process. You fall off the bike and get on again, trying to "correct" your balance this time. You sample the stew and "correct" the seasoning. You draft a paper about the neighborhood you live in and as you (or a classmate or instructor) read it over, you notice that certain words and expressions could stand some improvement. And step by step, sentence by sentence, you begin to write better.

Writing as a Public Activity

Many people have the wrong idea about writing. They view writing as a very private act. They picture the writer sitting all alone and staring into space waiting for ideas to come. They think that ideas come from "deep" within and reach expression only after they have been fully articulated inside the writer's head.

These images are part of a myth about creative writing and, like most myths, are sometimes true. A few poets, novelists, and essayists do write in total isolation and search deep inside themselves for thoughts and stories. But most writers have far more contact with public life. This is especially true of people who write regularly for magazines, newspapers, and professional journals. These writers work within a lively social atmosphere in which issues and ideas are often intensely discussed and debated. Nearly all the selections in this book illustrate this type of writing.

As you work on your own papers, remember that writing is very much a public activity. It is rarely performed alone in an "ivory tower." Writers don't always have the time, the desire, the opportunity, or the luxury to be all alone. They may be writing in a newsroom with clacking keyboards and noise all around them; they may be writing at a kitchen table, trying to feed several children at the same time; they may be writing on subways or buses. The great English novelist D. H. Lawrence grew up in a small impoverished coal miner's cottage with no place for privacy. It proved to be an enabling experience. Throughout his life he could write wherever he happened to be; it didn't matter how many people or how much commotion surrounded him.

There are more important ways in which writing is a public activity. Writing is often a response to public events. Most of the articles you encounter every day in newspapers and magazines respond directly to timely or important issues and ideas, topics that people are currently talking about. Writers report on these topics, supply information about them, discuss and debate the differing viewpoints. The units in this book all represent topics now regularly discussed on college campuses and in the national media. In fact, all of the topics were chosen because they emerged so frequently in college newspapers.

When a columnist decides to write on a topic like same-sex marriage, she willingly enters an ongoing public discussion about the issue. She didn't just make up the topic. She knows that it is a serious issue, and she is aware that a wide variety of opinions have been expressed about it. She has not read everything on the subject but usually knows enough about the different arguments to state her own position or attitude persuasively. In fact, what helps make her writing persuasive is that she takes into account the opinions of others. Her own essay, then, becomes a part of the continuing debate and discussion, one that you in turn may want to join.

Such issues are not only matters for formal and impersonal debate. They also invite us to share our *personal* experiences. Many of the selections in this book show how writers participate in the discussion of issues by drawing on their experiences. For example, the essay by Lucia Perillo, "Definition of Terms," is based largely on the author's personal observations and experience, though the topic—disability—is one widely discussed and debated by countless Americans. You will find that nearly every unit of *America Now* contains a selection that illustrates how you can use your personal experiences to discuss and debate a public issue.

Writing is public in yet another way. Practically all published writing is reviewed, edited, and re-edited by different people before it goes to press. The author of a magazine article has most likely discussed the topic at length with colleagues and publishing professionals and may have asked friends or experts in the field to look it over. By the time you see the article in a magazine, it has gone through numerous readings and probably quite a few revisions. Though the article is credited to a particular author, it was no doubt read and worked on by others who helped with suggestions and improvements. As a beginning writer, it's important to remember that most of what you read in newspapers, magazines, and books has gone through a writing process that involves the collective efforts of several people besides the author. Students usually don't have that advantage and should not feel discouraged when their own writing doesn't measure up to the professionally edited materials they are reading for a course.

The Visual Expression of Opinion

Public opinions are expressed in a variety of ways, not only in familiar verbal forms such as persuasive essays, magazine articles, or newspaper columns. In newspapers and magazines, opinions are often expressed through photography, political cartoons, and paid opinion advertisements (or Op-Ads). Let's briefly look at these three main sources of visual opinion.

Photography

At first glance, a photograph may not seem to express an opinion. Photography is often considered an "objective" medium: Isn't the photographer simply taking a picture of what is actually there? But on reflection and careful examination, we can see that photographs can express subjective views or editorial opinions in many different ways.

1. A photograph can be deliberately set up or "staged" so that the picture supports a position, point of view, or cause. For example, though not exactly staged, the renowned World War II photograph of U.S. combat troops triumphantly raising the American flag at Iwo Jima on the morning of February 23, 1945, was in fact a reenactment. After a first flag-raising was photographed, the military command considered the flag too small to be symbolically effective (though other reasons are also cited), so it was replaced with a much larger one and the event reshot. The 2006 Clint Eastwood film *Flags of Our Fathers* depicts the reenactment and the photo's immediate effect on reviving a war-weary public's patriotism. The picture's meaning was also more symbolic than actual, as the fighting on the island went on for many days after the flag was raised. Three of the six Americans

"Flag Raising at Iwo Jima," taken by combat photographer Joe Rosenthal on February 23, 1945.

"Three Firefighters Raising the Flag," taken by Thomas E. Franklin, staff photographer for *The Record* (Bergen County, NJ), on September 11, 2001.

who helped raise the famed second flag were killed before the fighting ended. The photograph, which incidentally was also cropped, is considered the most reproduced image in photographic history.

2.   A photographer could deliberately echo or visually refer to a well-known image to produce a political or emotional effect. Observe how the now-famous photograph of firemen raising a tattered American flag in the wreckage of 9/11 instantly calls to mind the heroism of the Iwo Jima marines.

3.   A photographer can shoot a picture at such an angle or from a particular perspective in order to dramatize a situation, make someone look less or more important, or suggest an imminent danger. A memorable photograph of Cuban refugee Elian Gonzalez, for example, made it appear that the boy, who was actually in no danger whatsoever, was about to be shot (see p. 20).

4.   A photographer can catch a prominent figure in an unflattering position or embarrassing moment or can catch the same person in a flattering and lofty fashion. Newspaper or magazine editors can then decide based on their political or cultural attitudes whether to show a political figure in an awkward or commanding light.

5.   A photograph can be cropped, doctored, or digitally altered to show something that did not happen, For example, a photo of a young John Kerry was inserted into a 1972 Jane Fonda rally to show misleadingly Kerry's association with Fonda's anti-Vietnam activism. Dartmouth College has created a Web site that features a gallery of doctored news photos. (See cs.dartmouth.edu/farid/research/ digitaltampering/.)

6.   A photograph can be taken out of context or captioned in a way that is misleading.

These are only some of the ways the print media can use photographs for editorial purposes. Although most reputable news sources go to great lengths to verify the authenticity of photographs, especially those that come from outside sources, and enforce stiff penalties on photographers who manipulate their pictures, some experts in the field maintain that doctoring is far more common in the media than the public believes.

"We can no longer afford to accept news photography as factual data," claims Adrian E. Hanft III, a graphic designer, in an August 2006 photography blog. "If we are realistic," he continues, "we will come to the conclusion that much of the photography in the news is fake — or at least touched up to better tell the story. It is relatively simple to doctor a photo and everybody knows it. The fact that the term 'Photoshop it' is a part of the English vernacular shows just how accustomed to fake photography we have become. The interesting thing is that in the face of the massive amounts of doctored photos, most people still expect photos in the news to be unaltered. I think this has something to do with a human desire for photographs to be true. We know the cover photo of Teri Hatcher is touched-up but we don't question it because we *want* her to look like that. Likewise when we see news stories that confirm our beliefs we want them to be

true. As photo manipulation becomes easier and easier, there is an increase in the demand for photographs that confirm what people want to believe. The market responds by flooding the world with 'fake' photography. Today people can believe almost anything they want and point to photography that 'proves' their beliefs."

Political Cartoons

The art of American political cartoons goes back to the eighteenth century; it's claimed that Benjamin Franklin was responsible for one of the nation's earliest cartoons. Almost from the start, political cartoonists developed what would become their favored techniques and conventions. Because cartoonists hoped to achieve a sudden intellectual and emotional impact, usually with imagery and a brief written message, they soon realized that exaggeration worked better than subtlety and readily identified symbols were more quickly comprehended than nuanced or unusual imagery. The political cartoon is rarely ambiguous—it takes a decided position that frequently displays enemies negatively and friends positively. Rarely does a political cartoonist muddy the waters by introducing a mixed message or entertaining an opposing view. The cartoonist, unlike a columnist, cannot construct a full consecutive argument to support a position, so the strokes applied are often broad and obvious.

A political cartoon often combines a satirical perspective, using exaggerated humor and visual caricature, with an instantly recognized iconography. Given that they sometimes combine insulting satire and offensive imagery, cartoons can provoke more controversy than essays and columns. The world took note of this in 2006, after a Danish newspaper printed a number of cartoons depicting the prophet Muhammad that were considered outrageously profane in the Muslim world. Caricature and stereotypes can hit harder than words and cause deep offense more rapidly than other expressions of political opinion. Let's examine a few recent cartoons and see what makes them tick. Along the way we will look at the role of **iconography, exaggeration, irony, caricature, symbol,** and **context.**

First, a note about **context.** Chances are that if you don't know the political situation the cartoonist refers to, you won't "get" the cartoon's intended message. So it's important to remember that the cartoon's meaning depends on previously received information,

Facing page: "Elian Gonzalez," taken by Associated Press photographer Alan Diaz on April 22, 2000.

usually from standard news sources. In other words, most cartoonists expect their audience to know a little something about the news story the cartoon refers to. Unlike the essayist, the cartoonist works in a tightly compressed verbal and visual medium in which it is unusually difficult to summarize the political context or the background the audience requires for full comprehension. This is one reason that cartoonists often work with material from headline stories that readers are familiar with. For many cartoons, the audience needs to supply its own information to grasp the cartoons' full meaning.

Please note, too, that the following cartoons are included for illustrative purposes only. They were not selected for their political and social opinions or for their artistic skill but primarily because they conveniently demonstrate the major elements and techniques of the political cartoon. Many other recent cartoons could just as easily have been selected.

Let's examine a cartoon that appeared in *U.S. News & World Report* for September 25, 2006. The image is unambiguous: The United Nations building is rocketing upwards as a result of a nuclear explosion, torn away from its New York City site. Note the use of iconography. **Iconography** is the use of shorthand images that immediately suggest an incident, idea, era, institution, and so on. Such images are intended to reflect immediately and clearly what they stand for. For example, a teenager with a pack of cigarettes rolled up inside the sleeve of a t-shirt is iconographic of the 1950s; a cap and gown indicates an academic; a briefcase represents a businessperson or a public official; a devil is traditionally represented with horns and a pitchfork. In this cartoon the mushroom cloud represents a nuclear attack, and the building itself stands for the institution of the UN, which is labeled on the side in case someone doesn't recognize its familiar architecture. The cartoonist doesn't use a caption but instead includes the conventional dialogue balloon to indicate that someone is speaking. The speaker isn't pictured or identified but is clearly inside the building.

Who is speaking, and what's the point of the comment? The cartoonist expects his audience to know that a past UN secretary general, Kofi Annan, had been criticized for his soft handling of Iran's nuclear weapons program by continually issuing warnings without taking more concrete action. So the speaker is presumably the head of the UN, and the cartoon's message is that even after Iran uses its nuclear weaponry, the UN will *still* be issuing ultimatums. The cartoon thus satirizes the UN as powerless and ineffectual in the face of nuclear threat. Note how much political context the audience is

"When it's too late to warn Iran," by *U.S. News & World Report* cartoonist Doug Marlette, published on September 25, 2006.

asked to supply and how much information it needs to infer. Ask yourself: If you knew nothing of Iran's plans and the UN's involvement, would you be able to understand the cartoon at all? Also, imagine that you saw the cartoon without the secretary general's comment: How would you interpret the imagery?

Note, too, the cartoon's use of **exaggeration** and unrealistic depiction: Does anyone imagine that—outside of a comic strip—a nuclear blast would send an entire building skyward and totally intact, and that we could hear a single human voice? We are, of course, not expected to understand the events literally. Nor are we even to assume that Iran *will* attack the United States. The overall effect is to call attention to the weakness of the UN by showing its leader to be someone who is all talk and no action, who futilely issues a "last warning" even after the ultimate deed is done.

Let's turn to a somewhat more complicated cartoon that demonstrates the use of four features favored by political cartoonists: **caricature, symbol, irony,** and what might be called the **pictorialization of figurative idioms.** Mike Luckovich employs all of these in a cartoon that first appeared in the *Atlanta Journal-Constitution* on June 16, 2006, and was eventually picked up by several magazines. The cartoon relies on the traditional symbols for our two major political parties—the Democrats are represented by a donkey and the Republicans by an elephant. These symbols have been used by cartoonists since the nineteenth century and allow them to instantly identify party affiliation. The use of **caricature**—the artistic rendering of someone's physical features in an exaggerated manner for quick recognition—is seen in the depiction of Hillary Clinton, who is also given a badge so readers can be absolutely certain of her identity. Depending on their political perspective, cartoonists can use caricature for purposes of quick identification or as a way to demean, stereotype, or satirize someone.

Luckovich's cartoon also demonstrates another standard cartoon feature: the tendency to literalize a common idiom. For example, the cartoonist will take an ordinary expression that suggests an image and then literally render the image. Our language is full of such expressions: "a sly fox" suggests a devious person; "don't rock the boat" suggests we not disturb something; "know the score" suggests we are fully aware of information; "to jump the gun" suggests doing something without thinking about it carefully. A cartoonist will often use such expressions within the cartoon for two important reasons: (1) because it is idiomatic, the expression will be quickly understood;

"Monkey on Your Back," by *Atlantic Journal-Constitution* cartoonist Mike Luckovich, published on June 16, 2006. By permission of Mike Luckovich and Creators Syndicate, Inc.

and (2) because it contains an image, the expression will contribute to the cartoon's pictorial content. In this case, the cartoonist has Hillary Clinton refer to a "monkey on your back." The idiom was once a slang phrase for drug addicts burdened by their habits but has now shed its slang usage and become a common expression for being burdened or weighed down by something that is difficult to get rid of. Hillary means, of course, that the Republicans (the elephant) are encumbered by the war in Iraq (symbolized by the monkey). Thus, the cartoon appears to be pointing out the terrible burden the war in Iraq represents for the Republican Party.

But one reason Luckovich's cartoon received so much attention is that the cartoon seems to be saying much more. Without expressing it verbally, Luckovich's cartoon implies pictorially that Hillary may be the same uncomfortable burden or liability to the Democratic Party that Iraq is to the Republican. Note how the cartoonist establishes this visual analogy by suggesting through the size, position, and juxtaposition of the images that both Clinton and Iraq are equally burdensome to their respective parties. In other words, what the cartoon suggests is that a Clinton candidacy would be as hard on the Democrats as the Iraq war would be on the Republicans in the next presidential election.

It's important to see that Luckovich never says this directly. To "get" the cartoon's full meaning is to understand its clever use of **visual irony**. Although it's a large literary subject, irony can be understood simply as a contrast between what appears to be expressed and what is actually being expressed. The contrast is often humorous and could be sarcastic, as when someone says after you've done something especially dumb, "Nice work!" What appears to be expressed (verbally) in the cartoon is Hillary Clinton's critical observation that the war in Iraq is a burdensome liability for the Republicans in the next election; what is actually expressed (visually) is that she represents a similar liability for her own party. The audience is also supposed to understand that Hillary herself does not recognize her liability but— given her expression and finger-pointing gesture—only her political opponent's. Thus, the audience becomes aware of something the figure in the cartoon does not perceive. This resembles the kind of dramatic irony prevalent in novels and film. We frequently know something—for instance, that a character is being lied to or tricked—that the character does not. This sort of irony—the incongruity between a character's awareness and the audience's—is an essential element of storytelling and a key ingredient of dramatic tension and suspense (as we wait for the character to finally realize what we knew all along).

We need to know a number of things to understand and appreciate Luckovich's cartoon:

1. We need to know that donkeys and elephants stand for the Democratic and Republican parties, respectively.

2. We need to know that "Hillary" means Hillary Clinton, who is a leading Democrat and potential nominee for the presidency.

3. We need to know that the Republican Party (under George W. Bush) has been vigorously criticized for starting and continuing the war in Iraq.

4. We need to know what the expression "You've got a monkey on your back" means, literally and figuratively.

5. We need to be able to understand that the pictured monkey represents the war in Iraq (hence the label).

6. We need to perceive that the cartoonist has depicted both the donkey and the elephant weighed down by equivalent physical burdens (both Hillary and the monkey are noticeably larger than the two party symbols).

7. We need to see that visually the cartoon suggests that Hillary Clinton may be as much a burden on her party as the Iraq war is on the Republicans.

Now to a third cartoon, this one from the *New Yorker* (August 7–14, 2006), which demonstrates another common feature of the cartoonist's stock-in-trade: the succinct combination of topical issues. In this case, the cartoonist's humor covers two national debates—one the use of stem-cell research and the other the oil crisis. Like the anti-UN cartoon, this one also relies heavily on iconography—the instantly recognized Capitol building in Washington, D.C. The architecture, in fact, dominates the cartoon and dwarfs the unidentified male figures with briefcases, who might be members of Congress or lobbyists. The Capitol architecture lends the scene an aura of dignity and stateliness that is undercut by the cynical remark of the caption, which suggests that conservative pieties over the sacredness of stem cells would be easily set aside if the cells yielded crude oil. In other words, economic interests and profits would "of course," trump religious and ethical positions. The casually expressed remark suggests that the speaker would in no way protect stem cells from scientific use if they could help our oil supply.

Note that this cartoon depends almost entirely on its caption for its effect. There is nothing intrinsic to the overall drawing that necessarily links it to the caption. If there were no caption and you were invited to supply one, you might come up with any one of thousands of remarks on any number of topics or issues. The main function of the image is to set the remark in a political context. The remark can then be read as a satirical comment on how our current government works—on profits, not principles.

The relationship between the Capitol building and the caption does, however, suggest an ironic incongruity. The imposing image of the U.S. Capitol—like the UN in the cartoon on page 23, one of the world's most significant political buildings—would seem more in keeping with a principled rather than unprincipled comment. Thus, the overall image adds to the satire by making us aware of the separation between how a revered political institution should perform and how it actually does. For example, consider how the level of satire

"Of course it would be a different story entirely if we could extract crude oil from stem cells."

"Stem Cells," by *New Yorker* cartoonist Jack Ziegler, published on August 7–14, 2006.

would be reduced if the cartoonist used the same caption but instead portrayed two research scientists in a medical laboratory.

Opinion Ads

Most of the ads we see and hear daily try to persuade us to buy consumer goods like cars, cosmetics, and cereal. Yet advertising does more than promote consumer products. Every day we also encounter numerous ads that promote not things but opinions. These opinion advertisements (Op-Ads, for short) may take a variety of forms—political commercials, direct mail from advocacy groups seeking contributions, posters and billboards, or paid newspaper and magazine announcements. Sometimes the ads are released by political parties and affiliated organizations, sometimes by large corporations hoping to influence policy, and sometimes by public advocacy groups such as Amnesty International, the National Association for the Advancement of Colored People (NAACP), the National Rifle Association (NRA), or—as we see on page 30—the American Civil Liberties Union (ACLU).

This selection represents only one of hundreds of such opinion ads readers come across regularly in newspapers and magazines. To examine carefully its verbal and visual techniques—whether you agree with its message or not—will help you better understand the essentials of rhetorical persuasion.

At the center of the ad (which appeared in many magazines in 2000), we see two photographs. The man on the left nearly everyone will recognize as Martin Luther King Jr. The other photo will be familiar to many Americans, especially older ones, but may not be recognized by all—it is the convicted California mass murderer, Charles Manson. The ad's headline refers only to "the man on the left" and "the man on the right." According to the headline, then, King, one of the nation's most outstanding leaders, "is 75 times more likely to be stopped by the police while driving" than one of the nation's most horrific murderers. The headline and photos are intended to attract our attention. The image of King also powerfully suggests that the issue of civil rights is still alive. (The ad's creators expect us to set aside the facts that King has been dead for decades and Manson has never been released from prison. So there is no possibility that the particular man on the left "is" more likely to be subjected to a police search than the particular man on the right. Thus, the ad's central statement cannot be taken as literally true.)

Why doesn't the headline say "Martin Luther King is 75 times more likely to be stopped by the police while driving than Charles Manson"? Why does the ad deliberately not identify each photo? One reason may be that the ACLU is counting on King's iconographic status; he's an American icon who needs no identification. But what about Manson: Did you instantly recognize him? Why doesn't the ACLU balance the photos by portraying John F. Kennedy, another American icon, as the man on the right? The main point of the ad would not be at all affected if Kennedy were on the right

THE MAN ON THE LEFT
IS 75 TIMES MORE LIKELY TO BE STOPPED BY THE POLICE WHILE DRIVING THAN
THE MAN ON THE RIGHT.

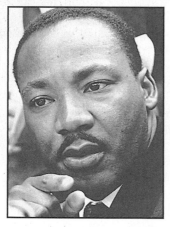

It happens every day on America's highways. Police stop drivers based on their skin color rather than for the way they are driving. For example, in Florida 80% of those stopped and searched were black and Hispanic, while they constituted only 5% of all drivers. These humiliating and illegal searches are violations of the Constitution and must be fought. Help us defend your rights. Support the ACLU. To learn more and to send your Members of Congress a free fax go to www.aclu.org/racialprofiling.

american civil liberties union
125 Broad Street, 18th Floor, NY, NY 10004 www.aclu.org

"The Man on the Left," an opinion advertisement that was part of the ACLU's 2000 campaign against racial profiling.

because the central issue is that African American drivers are more likely to be stopped than whites. Nor would the ad's message be affected if the photo on the right were simply of an anonymous, clean-shaven, white male. So, given the message, any white male could have been used instead of Manson. So why portray Manson?

Featuring Manson drives home the point that the system of stopping drivers based on their skin color is totally indiscriminate and doesn't take status, character, or virtue into account. The ACLU wants to surprise, even shock, its audience into realizing that the U.S. criminal justice system would stop and search one of America's most honored public figures while giving a free pass to one of the nation's most reviled convicts. Analyzing the ad in this way, however, raises an uncomfortable issue. If you don't recognize Manson (who was convicted in 1971 and has been rarely seen since his sentencing) and are still surprised or shocked by the headline, is it then because of the way *he* looks—the long hair, full beard, and glaring eyes? Does he look suspicious? If you think so, are you also engaging in a kind of "profiling," allowing yourself to think the man on the right ought to be stopped simply because he fits some kind of stereotype—a "hippie," a homeless person, a mentally ill individual? A good question to ask about a visual image presented in a way that assumes you know what or who it is: What are the unintended consequences if you don't know it? In this case, what happens to the ad's message if you don't recognize either figure from the 1960s?

Besides the visual argument outlined above, the ad also expresses in smaller print a verbal argument. In print advertising, this element usually contains the ad's central argument and is known as body copy, body text, or simply text to distinguish it from the headline, illustrations, and other visuals. The argument is essentially that "humiliating and illegal searches are violations of the Constitution and must be fought." The text does not state why or how racial profiling (a term not used in the ad) violates the Constitution. In other words, it assumes our assent and offers no reasons why we must be legally concerned about the issue. There is no mention of which part of the Constitution the police violate, nor is any relevant phrase of the Constitution quoted directly.

The argument depends wholly on statistical evidence that a disproportionate percentage of certain drivers are stopped by the police. Note that the headline and the body of the text appear to cite two different sets of statistics: The headline claims that someone like

King has a 75 percent greater chance of being stopped than a white person, while the text reads that "in Florida 80% of those stopped and searched were black and Hispanic, while they constituted only 5% of all drivers." These two statistics are offered with no attribution of sources (Who gathered them? Is the source reliable?) nor any dates (Are they recent?). We might also wonder why only Florida is mentioned. There is also an ambiguity introduced by mentioning the Florida statistic since we are then led to wonder what the statistic in the headline refers to. Is it only in Florida that the man on the left "is 75 times more likely to be stopped"? Or does that number represent a national figure? And is the number also meant to represent Hispanics, or does the "75" in the headline refer only to African Americans as represented by King? To question these numbers and their manner of presentation is not to dispute their accuracy or the seriousness of the issue, but only to demonstrate the necessity of responding to statistical evidence cautiously before giving our assent to an argument.

Nearly all opinion ads (and most ads in general) are action oriented. The purpose of persuasion is to produce a change in opinion or attitude that will produce social or political action. This ad, like most opinion ads, encourages a twofold action: (1) it asks the reader to assent to an opinion (in this case, that our Constitution is being violated); and (2) it asks directly for the reader's support, which could mean both to encourage the work of the ACLU and to assist it with donations. Note the text's final words: "Help us defend your rights. Support the ACLU." Because ads must work in such a compressed verbal format, some of the words we need to pay special attention to are pronouns. A reader may wonder why the final words didn't say, "Help us defend the rights of African Americans and Hispanics" (or "people of color"), since the ad never claimed that the rights of any other group were being violated. But "your rights" is intentionally all-inclusive: It stands for you, the reader, and everyone else. In a highly abbreviated way, the ad implies that whenever anyone's constitutional rights are violated, everyone's rights are violated.

The ad contains an extra visual feature that may take a while to notice or sink in. The ad isn't just a page in a magazine; it's designed to look like the sort of wanted poster the police and FBI display to help catch criminals or the kind often seen in pictures of the old West ("Wanted—Dead or Alive"). Note the discoloration from weather and the nails attaching it to what appears to be a wooden surface. Why did the designers do this? Why take the ad's image to another dimension? And how does imagining the ad as a wanted poster affect its overall argument and our response? The ACLU's intention, it seems, is to enforce the image of criminalization. One photo is of an actual psychopathic criminal, so the wanted poster image makes sense in its depiction of Manson (though he is already in prison). But why would King, one of the greatest Americans, appear on a wanted poster? The general effect appears to be that in the eyes of the highway police who are profiling black drivers, even someone as distinguished as King would be considered a criminal. The effect and implication of the wanted poster ramps up the visual rhetoric and contributes to the shock value of the advertisement.

Expressing Opinions: Two Annotated Student Essays

Below are two student essays that perfectly characterize the kind of writing that *America Now* features and examines. The essays provide you with effective models of how to express an opinion on a public issue in a concise and convincing manner. Both essays demonstrate the way writers respond to a public issue—in this case, acquaintance rape—and how in doing so they rely on the principles of productive discussion that have been outlined throughout this introduction. In fact, these two essays were especially selected because they perform a double service: The essays show writers clearly expressing opinions on a timely topic that matters to them and, at the same time, demonstrate how arguments can be shaped to advance the possibility of further discussion instead of ending it.

Each essay is annotated to help you focus on some of the most effective means of expressing an opinion. It's recommended that you first read both essays through and think about the points each writer is making. Then return to the essays and go over more slowly the key parts that are isolated for examination. This process is designed to help you see how writers construct arguments to support their opinions. It is an analytical process you should begin to put into practice on your own as you read and consider the many issues in this collection. A more detailed explanation of the highlighted passages and the numbered annotations that appear in the margins of these essays follows each selection.

How Should We Discuss Rape?

DARCY RICHIE

Calling for a New Dialogue on Rape

[THE DAILY PENNSYLVANIAN, THE UNIVERSITY OF PENNSYLVANIA]

1. Opinion essays can start dramatically with a story or specific incident.

2. Repetition can be an effective way to emphasize a point.

3. In opinion essays, readers should be clearly aware of the issues involved.

Last week, Claire Simon walked out of a club hand in hand with a man she met earlier in the week. Spring break had proven fruitful for bonding and meeting gorgeous men. Having lost her friends somewhere around her fifth drink, she proceeded to her hotel chaperoned only by this male companion. As payment for the trip, he showed her to her room. As payment for the trip, he made Claire and himself a drink. As payment for the trip, he ignored her almost inaudible cries of "don't."   1

Her cries weren't loud enough to make him stop. She only struggled through half of it and prayed during the rest because as her fear began to outweigh the alcohol, she succumbed to his strength and his ability to strangle her to death at any moment, if that was even "his thing." Even more, he seemed to get off on her struggling, feeling her cries erotic and her weakness powerful. Finally, they were both silent. He pranced off her body, zipped his pants and whispered, "How do you feel?" as if she simply had too much to drink and he had just put her to bed, as if he hadn't just changed her life forever.   2

Despite my anger over the issue of acquaintance rape, this essay will not be a statistical analysis of rape nor a story about Claire. It's a story about the man who took her home. In our society, we regularly demonize but rarely scrutinize. Acquaintance rape is still rape and it's still about power. Yet, despite efforts to inform women about the prevalence of acquaintance rape or to recognize its legitimacy, there is still a picture in too many female heads of a large, intimidating man jumping from dark corners when the protection of a crowd unexpectedly disappears. We rarely picture as rapists the helpful co-worker who has driven us home on many occasions or the gorgeous guy we try to talk to every other day after class, but the frequency of acquaintance rape   3 should tell us that these might be the very men to fear. This type of rape is not committed by some deviant, but rather by the people we are closest to, the people we trust, the people who know us best.

4. To be convincing, important claims should be backed up with evidence.

Psychologist Mary Koss and colleagues have documented research about the prevalence of acquaintance rape and rape in general, primarily on college campuses. In her study, the demographic profile of the 3,187 female and 2,972 male students was similar to the makeup of the overall enrollment in higher education within the United States. The findings indicate that one in four women surveyed had been raped, and 84 percent of those women knew their attackers. This is not just a number, but also a real image; think about it when you walk into a classroom dominated by women. More relevantly, one in 12 male students surveyed had committed acts that met the legal definition of rape or attempted rape, but 84 percent of those men who committed rape said that what they did was definitely not rape.   4

5. Use important points to develop coherently the essay's main contention.

Acquaintance rape makes a particular statement about men in this society. What if statistics are so high for acquaintance rape (in this circumstance, specifically for male-to-female rape) because there is something inherent in men that motivates them to need this power? Perhaps the inherent characteristic of men that motivates them to rape is a struggle to define what it actually means to be a man through messages of dominance, aggression, and an uncompromising demeanor. Perhaps as men struggle to express themselves, the idea that sex is a commodity is something tangible that they can hold on to. Perhaps in examining the male role in rape, we can begin to understand better why the media's sexualization of females translates, for so many men, into a justification to touch, fondle, and use force or coercion to lure their female acquaintances into unwanted sexual intercourse.   5

6. A chief purpose of effective opinion essays can be to stimulate further discussion.

The idea that so many men are painfully confused about their role in the sexual experiences they have, along with the prevalence of rape, suggests one truth: that we have overemphasized female fear in our message about rape, while neglecting the male's role. We teach women about safety and protection from the scary men in dark alleys. We teach women that acquaintance rape is still rape despite their sexual history and despite their relationship with their aggressor. We teach women that they deserve to be respected. But what are we teaching men? What messages are men   6 receiving through the media and through our words about how women are to be treated? We need to continue with young men this dialogue of respect for women.

Claire's experience dramatically illustrates our general message about rape: women beware. We usually use this kind of story to teach women to protect themselves. But these statistics won't change until we address the perspective of men and why they rape.

7

Comments:

The following comments correspond to the numbered annotations that appear in the margins of Darcy Richie's essay.

1. Richie opens her essay with a distressing story about a particular individual. In doing this, she puts a human face on the issue and makes her topic more concrete than if she had begun her essay by defining her subject in general terms. The kind of story she tells is commonly called a *cautionary* or *admonitory tale*—a warning to others that takes the form of a brief narrative (a fairy tale such as "Little Red Riding Hood" is a classic example of a fictional story told to children to warn them of the world's dangers). Many so-called urban legends began as admonitory tales. But true stories can also function this way. Professional journalists often use factual stories to illustrate how a general topic comes down to individual instances. Once they have introduced the specific example, they go on to make their general point. A writer's decision to open with a brief story or anecdote is a decision about *structure*.

2. Note how Richie begins three consecutive sentences the same way: "As payment for the trip . . ." This is an effective and common form of emphasis that dates back to the Greek and Latin classics. It is known technically as anaphora, though like nearly all rhetorical techniques, most writers use it without knowing its formal name. In this case, anaphora allows Richie to emphasize the increasing seriousness of the sequence of events. A writer's decision to repeat words or phrases for emphasis is a decision about *style*. You can easily rewrite her three sentences in other ways. For example, they could be combined into a single sentence: "As payment for the trip, he showed her to her room, made Claire and himself a drink, and then ignored her almost inaudible cries of 'don't.'" Read both versions aloud: Which

do you consider more effective? Why? Note, too, that Richie uses this type of emphasis again in her fourth paragraph. Can you spot it? Can you find other examples of this writing technique in the essay?

3. In her dramatic opening, Richie suggests but never states directly what issue she is addressing. She makes this clear at the start of her third paragraph when she clearly identifies the "issue" as "acquaintance rape." Richie is aware that a large part of the debate surrounding acquaintance rape is whether it constitutes a legitimate form of rape, not some gray area of sexual encounter where, due to circumstances, both male coercion and female consent are viewed as ambiguous. So before she proceeds further, she makes it clear to her readers that (a) her topic is acquaintance rape and (b) she regards it as a legitimate form of rape. That's why she goes on to compare both types of rape—by stereotypical strangers and by acquaintances—and indicates that women have as much to fear from one as from the other.

4. Richie wants to do more than argue that acquaintance rape is rape. That position is one that she presumes rather than attempts to demonstrate legally or philosophically. In a short essay, the writer obviously cannot cover every aspect of a complex issue. The definition of acquaintance rape is less important to Richie in this essay than its *frequency*. That such rape is "prevalent" is one of her key claims in the essay. But how do we know it's prevalent? Why should we take her word for it? How do we know her opening tale isn't a rare, isolated incident? To convince us that such rape is truly prevalent, therefore, and not just a matter of isolated instances here and there, she introduces statistical evidence. She cites a study that shows that one in four female students has been raped and that "84 percent of those women knew their attackers." Thus, for Richie, the statistical evidence proves that Claire Simon's experience was not uncommon and that the essay's opening story was not atypical. Since she is writing for a campus readership, Richie appropriately chooses statistical research based on evidence from college campuses.

5. Having maintained that acquaintance rape can be legitimately considered rape and having supplied evidence that it is prevalent, Richie then develops her main contention: "Acquaintance rape makes a particular statement about men in this society." In her third paragraph, Richie prepared readers for this point by stressing the importance of the male role: She tells us that her opening story wasn't about Claire Simon but "about the man who took her home." We can now see more fully the reason behind her use of the opening story. Her primary concern has been "examining the male role in

rape." In other words, her subject is not the particular unidentified male who accompanied Claire Simon to her hotel room but the male sex in general. Richie's fifth paragraph gives her essay coherence in that it closely links both the opening story and her two major points about acquaintance rape: it is rape, and it occurs frequently.

6. An essay's main contention or main point is not the same as its primary purpose. Richie's essay might have ended with the fifth paragraph in which she articulates her main point: that collective experience and statistical evidence suggest to her that males have an innate tendency toward dominance, aggression, and power, and that these "inherent characteristic[s]" can lead to rape. But her essay doesn't stop with that opinion. In her sixth paragraph, she reminds us of her title and suggests that her motive in writing the essay was to expand the dialogue on the topic and stimulate further discussion that would include the male perspective. Specifically, she hopes to reframe discussion of acquaintance rape so that less emphasis is given to "female fear" and more to the "male's role." Open discussion of an issue, however, is never advanced by a know-it-all and absolutist approach, or with what she terms "an uncompromising demeanor." Thus Richie was wise to preface all her earlier comments about innate male aggression in a hypothetical way ("What if . . . Perhaps . . . Perhaps . . . Perhaps"), suggesting that she doesn't have the answers but hopes to find them by "Calling for a New Dialogue on Rape."

KEVIN COLLINS

Acknowledging the Gray Area in Rape Dialogue

[THE DAILY PENNSYLVANIAN, THE UNIVERSITY OF PENNSYLVANIA]

1. Writing is often a response to the opinions of others.

If you're like me, and you have cells with Y chromosomes, these are the phrases that jumped out at you from Darcy Richie's recent column on rape: "There is something inherent in men that motivates them to need this power"; "the inherent characteristic of men that motivates them to rape"; "media sexualization of females translates, for so many men, into a justification [to] . . . use force or coercion"; "the statistics won't change until we address the perspective of men and why they rape"; "what are we teaching men?"   1

2. In setting up an opposing view, we often need to make some concessions.

Are these quotes taken out of context? Yes, to some degree. Do I concur with Richie's arguments on the prevalence of acquaintance rape and a need for dialogue? Yes, substantially, I do. But does this matter? Not very much, because while many of Richie's points are right and need to be made, the way she makes them alienates her male audience—and men are the readers she seems to be trying the hardest to reach.

2

3. Sharp contrasts of differing opinions can help frame an argument.

What is worse, this seems to be all too characteristic of the way the discussion on rape is generally conducted. Typically, rape is presented as a black and white issue, simple even. Rape is nonconsensual sex. What is consent? "No" means no; no "yes" means no; anything but "yes" means no; and an intoxicated "yes" doesn't mean yes either. Period. The problem with this approach is that it prematurely terminates a necessary discussion. Why? Because frankly, talking about rape in concrete rather than abstract terms reveals complexities with more questions than answers.

3

4. Illustrate general ideas with specific examples.

Drugging someone's drink to have sex with her is surely wrong, as is getting someone drunk for the same purpose. But what about one less drink than full intoxication? And what about one less than that, one less than that, and one less than that? Moreover, what if you, too, are drinking and are unable to judge her level of intoxication? And why, if two people are both equally drunk, is the man held legally responsible for both of their actions? Most importantly, if the issue is as simple as it is often portrayed, then why do my liberal, women's rights-supporting male friends raise these questions and others? They even talk (only half-jokingly) of a time in the not-so-distant future when written contracts certifying consent and sobriety will be necessary before sex, and if you've ever not had a condom when you needed one, try keeping track of a Breathalyzer and notary public.

4

5. Be alert to what could be an unwarranted or false generalization.

I offer an answer for only the last of these questions. The dominant discourse on rape does a disservice to its purpose in two profound ways. First, in preferring black and white clarity and refusing to openly and honestly explore the gray areas of consent, it ignores the aspects of the issue that most need clarification. Moreover, the images and stereotypes used when discussing rape deter men from constructively engaging with the issue. Our Y chromosomes are inherent, but a desire to rape certainly is not, and when we are broadly grouped with those that commit one of the most

5

heinous of crimes because of our sex, we feel alienated and even attacked.

The pedantic attitude—talking to men rather than talking with us—does not help either. Perhaps, then, it is not all so surprising that men are hesitant to talk about rape, for few people like to be simultaneously infantilized and demonized because of inborn characteristics. In preparing this column, I have discussed rape with a lot of people, and the most intelligent thing I've heard was that while we as a society need to discuss rape, the first and most important discussion must be in the bedroom. However, that is not enough. Culture change comes not from sermons or statistics, but rather from open dialogue and authentic encounters. And let's be honest: While certainly most men are not rapists, most rapists are men. Any successful, perspective-altering discourse must then include men as full participants. This is why men need to feel comfortable discussing rape, both amongst ourselves and with women and the broader society.   6

Many, if not most, men do not understand rape. In my all-male high school, we treated the subject casually and talked about being "raped" by tests and quizzes. I used to talk that way, too. I stopped when I went to Take Back the Night last year and heard women, much more courageous than most of us, speak out about being raped. This is the type of experience that may well change the way you think about rape, or perhaps get you thinking about it for the first time. This is not a discussion of rape in the abstract; instead, it is women speaking about rape as it really happens.   7

6. Personal testimony can be persuasive.

This is something that we all, men and women, need to hear. Join me at this year's Take Back the Night—this Wednesday at 7:30 p.m. on College Green—to support survivors of sexual assault, to begin the slow process of cultural change, and to show that men, too, stand up against these horrible crimes.   8

Comments:

The following comments correspond to the numbered annotations that appear in the margins of Kevin Collins' essay.

1. Collins makes it clear in his essay's opening that Richie's opinion column stimulated him to write a response. Although as we later discover, Collins had already formulated thoughts on the issue of ac-

quaintance rape, his essay is almost entirely based on his reaction to Richie's urgent call for a "new dialogue" on the issue. Note that he effectively jumps right into the dialogue by starting with several specific quotes from her essay. He doesn't summarize or paraphrase her remarks but wants his readers to encounter them again firsthand. This reminds those who had seen her essay of what she wrote, but there's another good reason to quote her directly—Collins can't assume all of his readers have read her essay. He also quotes selectively, his purpose being to pull together and highlight her remarks about males. In his opening words, he also clearly indicates that he is addressing primarily male readers.

2. In the discussion and debate of complex issues, it is unlikely that one person's opinion is 100 percent correct and the other's 100 percent wrong. In taking an opposing view, we often need to concede that our opponent may be right on some aspects of the issue. Collins does just this in his second paragraph where he admits that, to a certain extent, he has quoted "out of context," that he agrees with Richie's primary arguments, and that "many of her points are right." At first, this seems to be a fairly sizeable concession; after admitting all of this, what's left to debate? But Collins immediately explains that his complaint isn't with Richie's points but with the way she has presented them. In other words, his quarrel isn't with the substance of her argument but with its expression. We now see better why he used so many direct quotes from Richie's essay.

3. Collins disagrees with Richie primarily because of the way she has expressed her position, which he believes alienates male readers. He then proceeds to make his case by contrasting two approaches that one could take toward the issue: People either view acquaintance rape as simple or complex, abstract or concrete. In his opinion, the issue is typically discussed as "black and white," or simple. It's clear that he prefers to take a concrete, complex approach to the issue. Once he divides the issue into these two approaches, he can then try to persuade readers that his approach is preferable.

4. At the end of his third paragraph, Collins suggests that it is preferable to talk about rape "in concrete rather than abstract terms." In this way, we will perceive the issue as complex, and when we do that, he says, we will find that it leads to more questions than answers. But he doesn't simply tell us this; in the next paragraph, he specifically illustrates the kinds of questions a "concrete" discussion can lead to. Collins realizes that the word *concrete* itself is an abstract term and that he needs to supply readers with specific examples of

what it means in his case. He intends his subsequent questions to show how difficult it is to determine exactly when intoxication occurs and when a sexual encounter is consensual or nonconsensual.

5. Many opinion papers are supported by generalizations, and we need to be on the alert in responding to them: Some generalizations are bogus, hasty, biased, and so on, while others are based on adequate samples and evidence. Collins takes issue with Richie's suggestion that men may be inherently motivated to rape; he does not accept this as a general fact that applies to all males. Collins is aware, however, that some generalizations are appropriate. He later acknowledges, "While certainly most men are not rapists, most rapists are men." He thus views as false the generalization that all men are inherently rapists, but nevertheless accepts as true the generalization that most rapists are male. Collins not only opposes what he believes is Richie's unwarranted generalization about men, but he also strategically (and efficiently) uses it to advance his own argument that her demonization of men makes open dialogue on the issue of rape impossible.

6. Our personal experiences, especially if they have dramatically transformed our opinions, can be effectively introduced into an opinion essay. Note how Collins portrays himself—because of his attendance at a campus Take Back the Night event—as having gone from someone for whom rape meant little to someone who now understands how serious it is. This testimony helps create the impression that Collins's opinion on this issue is worth listening to. It makes him appear open-minded and trustworthy. One way to persuade people to change their minds is to show how you were persuaded to change yours.

Student Writers at Work

As undergraduates, both Darcy Richie and Kevin Collins were eager to express their opinions about a controversial campus issue. In doing so, they of course expected that not everyone would agree with their point of view. But this didn't deter them. They wanted to share their opinions with a large community and take a personal stand on an important public topic. They also wanted to encourage and stimulate more dialogue on the issue.

When informed their essays would be included in this book, each writer was also asked a few follow-up questions that focused on such matters as their motivation for writing, their methods of preparation, their sense of an audience, and their writing habits. Several other interviews with student writers are featured elsewhere in *America Now*.

Student Writer at Work: Darcy Richie
On Writing "Calling for a New Dialogue on Rape"

Q: What inspired you to write this piece for your column in the *Daily Pennsylvanian*?

A: I was inspired by conversations I had with many students around an issue that I have strong emotions toward. I think that the topic of rape is one that people can become complacent about because many feel that the issue doesn't affect them. I wanted to start conversations into the cause of rape . . . to suggest a change in the dialogue, and to draw more people into that dialogue.

Q: Who was your prime audience for the column?

A: Normally I've targeted my articles toward those I see as conservative. But in this article, I was trying to speak to everyone. I think we have all simply accepted rape as a problem, and accepted the solution—asking women to be careful—whether it has been successful or not.

Q: What response have you received to this piece?

A: The responses were at times aggressive because I think the topic put people on the defense and drew on emotions. However, I did receive a lot of supportive responses. No matter what the response to my writing, it affects my opinion—it might answer my questions, cause me to ask new ones, or call for me to defend my original answers.

Q: How did you prepare to write this piece?

A: I read many articles on rape prior to writing this article because I wanted to get a sense of the type of dialogue that already existed around the topic. I did not want to reinvent the wheel, and I wanted to see if there were any questions I felt had not been addressed, or any areas where I did not agree.

Q: Before you write, do you collaborate or bounce your ideas off others? Does discussion with others help you develop your points of view?

A: I always bounce my ideas off of other people. My friends tend to speak a lot about political issues, so not only do I bounce my ideas off of them, but I also get new ideas or new angles from our conversations.

Q: What topics most interest you as a writer?

A: To me the most interesting topics are ones that ask you to reach into your own emotion, or ones that draw on the public's emotion.

Q: What advice do you have for other writers?

A: I would say, take risks and do not be afraid to be vulnerable. As a student writer, as with anything else, opening yourself up to try new things, take chances, and stretch your thinking will have several benefits—helping others to open their minds and helping yourself to grow in your own thinking. Writing a column every week, for me, was like bungee jumping regularly. It got a lot easier to do something that scared me to death, but that has never lost its thrill.

Student Writer at Work: Kevin Collins
On Writing "We Need to Acknowledge the Gray Area in Rape Dialogue"

Q: What was your purpose in writing this piece for the *Daily Pennsylvanian*?

A: I was responding to another columnist, Darcy Richie, and her recent column on a need for a new rape dialogue. I agreed with most of the substance of her column, both on how disturbing the prevalence of rape—including the less often discussed date rape—is in general and especially on a college campus, and on the importance of a broader discussion. Specifically, what I was responding to was her tone. A new discussion is needed, but what also is needed is a discussion that includes men in the struggle against rape on campus—instead of a discussion that alienates the male population by portraying rape as fundamentally male instead of fundamentally wrong. Moreover, I felt a need to argue that a more constructive approach to combating the quite serious problem on campus is education and dialogue rather than villainization. Therefore, I wrote a column expressing both the importance of addressing rape and the importance of changing the tone of that discussion.

Q: What response have you received to this piece? Has the feedback you have received affected your views on the topic you wrote about?

A: The feedback was mainly positive and included responses from many who are actively involved in the women's movement on campus. There was some criticism from the left, saying that my tone was not serious enough, and there were others on the right who I would say did not understand the argument that I was attempting to articulate. There are several postings on the online version of the column that fairly express the range of reaction.

Q: Did you discuss the article with others before submitting it?

A: I will sometimes discuss columns in advance with others more knowledgeable in a particular field than I am. In this instance, I discussed the topic with some of the organizers of the Take Back the Night event I mention in my column. However, such discussion nearly always occurs, as it did in this instance, before I begin drafting my column, rather than as an editing process after I've written it. I'm looking for ideas to build upon rather than someone to rewrite my work.

Q: What topics most interest you as a writer? What interests you most as a reader?

A: Politics, but more specifically issues of relevance to my generation. In my own genre—political opinion columns—my favorite writers are E. J. Dionne of the *Washington Post* and Nicholas Kristoff, Maureen Dowd, and Paul Krugman of the *New York Times*. But more than reading, I listen to a lot of public radio. Especially programs like *This American Life* showcase new and interesting approaches to storytelling and writing that I don't see many other places.

Q: Did you revise your work? Work on multiple drafts? If so, how many drafts do you usually create? What are your goals as you revise?

A: My writing process works somewhat differently than the model of writing in which one starts with an outline and writes several drafts of revisions based on that outline. I tend to start by composing key phrases, and I build and rearrange these phrases into a more structured column. I usually revise that work once, but not usually more than once. However, I then go over the column with my editor, and that usually involves making several more changes to the column.

Q: What advice do you have for other student writers?

A: Read as much as you can, write as much as you can, and have people criticize your work as much as you can. These are the best ways to improve your writing. Also, I first applied for a position as a columnist on something of a whim, which just goes to show that if you try, you might have far more success that you ever expected.

Writing as Empowerment

Writing is one of the most powerful means of producing social and political change. Through their four widely disseminated gospels, the first-century evangelists helped propagate Christianity throughout the world; the writings of Adam Smith and Karl Marx determined the economic systems of many nations for well over a century; Thomas Jefferson's Declaration of Independence became a model for countless colonial liberationists; the carefully crafted speeches of Martin Luther King Jr. and the books and essays of numerous feminists altered twentieth-century consciousness. In the long run, many believe, "the pen is mightier than the sword."

Empowerment does not mean instant success. It does not mean that your opinion or point of view will suddenly prevail. It does mean, however, that you have made your voice heard, that you have given your opinions wider circulation, that you have made yourself and your position a little more visible. And sometimes you get results:

a newspaper prints your letter; a university committee adopts your suggestion; people visit your Web site. Throughout this collection, you will encounter writing specifically intended to inform and influence a wide community.

Such influence is not restricted to professional authors and political experts. This collection features a large number of student writers who are actively involved with the same current topics and issues that engage the attention of professionals—the environment, racial and ethnic identity, gender differences, media bias, and so on. The student selections, all of them previously published and written for a variety of reasons, are meant to be an integral part of each unit, to be read in conjunction with the professional essays, and to be criticized and analyzed on an equal footing.

America Now urges you to voice your ideas and opinions—in your notebooks, in your papers, in your classrooms, and, most important, on your campus and in your communities. Reading, discussing, and writing will force you to clarify your observations, attitudes, and values, and as you do, you will discover more about yourself and the world. These are exciting times. Don't sit on the sidelines of controversy. Don't retreat into invisibility and silence. Jump in and confront the ideas and issues currently shaping America.

1

Body Image: Is It a Serious Issue?

Are you content with the way you look? If so, you are in a minority, as opinion polls overwhelmingly demonstrate that most Americans are not happy with their physical appearance, and that women are generally less content with their looks than men. As individual self-esteem grows more and more dependent on physical attractiveness (some reports even show that attractive students may be more likely to obtain better grades and jobs), Americans now seem eager to go to extreme measures to alter or enhance their looks through drugs, radical diets, and, increasingly, cosmetic surgery. The mass appeal of such recent TV shows as *The Swan*, *Extreme Makeover*, or *I Want a Famous Face* further confirm this national obsession with physical appearance.

Does a woman's concern about her appearance all start with her mother? In "My Mother, My Hair," the noted linguist and bestselling author Deborah Tannen reports on how frequently mothers nag their daughters about their hair—even long after their daughters have been married with children of their own. Women, Tannen writes, have told her of mothers who criticize "almost every aspect of their lives" but "the topic I have heard about more than any other is hair." Could it be that authority figures such as mothers for girls— or fathers for boys—help give rise to what Annie Bradford Rispin calls in the next selection our "looks-obsessed culture"? In "Here's

Looking at You: Is Body Image Being Taken Too Seriously?" she examines some of the social and cultural forces behind our increasing preoccupation with physical appearance. Rispin, a University of Texas student, maintains that the pressures put on young people to conform to "our culture's increasingly unrealistic definition of beauty" is causing irreparable harm to many college students: "A poor body image," she concludes, "silences far too many in our generation—are we ready to talk back?"

In the following paired selections, two writers do talk back—to cosmetic surgeons about their practice. Although she believes that "cosmetic surgery is undoubtedly an unstoppable movement," the literary and cultural critic Camille Paglia invites plastic surgeons to take a broader view of human beauty. In "The Pitfalls of Plastic Surgery," she argues that "without a broader visual vocabulary, too many surgeons will continue to homogenize women, divesting them of authority and reducing them to a generic cookie-cutter sameness." It's not just women, however, who seek cosmetic surgery, Art Carey, a reporter for the *Philadelphia Inquirer*, reminds us. In "Men's Faces Go Under the Knife," Carey reports on how dismayed he was to see that the actor Robert Redford allowed "his weatherbeaten face and increasingly craggy looks" to be smoothed out by a plastic surgeon. Yet, despite his disapproval of such surgery, Carey is willing to entertain the arguments of a cosmetic surgeon who challenges Carey's preference for the "natural and authentic."

The chapter concludes with a popular 1947 advertisement (for Charles Atlas bodybuilding equipment), which suggests that the issue of body image may not be all that recent. "The Insult That Turned a 'Chump' into a Champ" reveals how the self-esteem of males has been linked for generations to muscular development and physical strength.

DEBORAH TANNEN

My Mother, My Hair

[LOS ANGELES TIMES / January 24, 2006]

Before You Read

How do you and your mother get along? Do you go shopping with your mother? Why or why not? According to Tannen, why do mothers and daughters fight about the daughters' appearances? Why do sons escape this scrutiny?

Words to Learn

déjà vu (para. 3): a feeling that you are experiencing something you have already experienced (n.)

beam (para. 3): to instantly transport (v.)

testily (para. 3): in an annoyed way (adv.)

lament (para. 4): to express grief verbally (v.)

contention (para. 5): controversy; argument (n.)

nondescript (para 7): lacking characteristics; plain (adj.)

fret (para. 8): to worry (v.)

relish (para. 13): to enjoy (v.)

"I love your hair when it's combed back," a woman says to her grown daughter. "It looks so beautiful that way."   1

That's a compliment, right? Well, it would be if she'd said it when her daughter's hair was combed back. But on this day, her daughter has let her hair fall forward, so the comment implies, "your   2

DEBORAH TANNEN, *a prolific writer and professor at Georgetown University, identifies herself as a linguist. "I study how people talk to each other, and how the ways we talk affect our relationships." Her most recent book,* You're Wearing That? Understanding Mothers and Daughters in Conversation, *explores mother-daughter communications. Throughout her research Tannen has discovered that "for girls and women, talk is the glue that holds a relationship together—and the explosive that can blow it apart."*

hair looks unattractive the way it is." When her daughter snaps, "Well I'm wearing it this way today!" her mother asks, "What's wrong with you? Why are you so sensitive?"

If a daughter has children of her own, it can be déjà vu all over 3
again. "She would look so much prettier if she just brushed her hair," a woman says of her granddaughter—and her daughter is beamed back to childhood, when her mother was always at her to brush her hair. "She's fine the way she is," the daughter responds testily. "Leave her alone." The grandmother wonders how a harmless remark got her in trouble.

"I never know what's going to set my 4
daughter off," one mother lamented to me. "Talking to her is like walking through a minefield."

> *"Talking to her is like walking through a minefield."*

Daughters and mothers agree on what 5
the hurtful conversations are. They disagree on who introduced the note of contention because they have different views of what the words imply. Where the daughter sees criticism, the mother sees caring. She was making a suggestion, trying to help, offering insight or advice. Isn't that a mother's job? Both are right, because caring and criticizing are bought with the same verbal currency. Any offer of help or advice—however well-intended, however much needed—implies you're doing something wrong.

Women have told me of their mothers—or their daughters— 6
criticizing almost every aspect of their lives: clothes, weight, home decoration, how they raise their kids—plus trivial things, such as how much salt they put in the soup. But the topic I have heard about more than any other is hair.

What is it about mothers and hair? Pondering this while riding a 7
bus, I scanned the women around me. Every one of them, I thought, would look better if her hair were different: longer or shorter, curlier or straighter, a more natural-looking color, a more stylish cut. Then I looked at the men. Every one of them had a nondescript hairstyle.

And I then realized: There isn't any hairstyle for women that's 8
nondescript. Every choice sends a message. Long, flowing hair that covers one eye: A woman who wants to look sexy. Short, sculpted hair: She's all business. Pulled back in a bun: Uptight! Repressed! As every hairstyle incurs a value judgment, no wonder mothers fret over their daughters' hair. And with so many styles to choose from, the chances are slim of picking one that others (including your mother) judge to be perfect.

Some of the resentment women feel about their mothers' atten- 9
tion to their hair (or clothes or weight) reflects their frustration that
women in our society are judged by appear-
ance, because mothers typically enforce society's expectations at home.

Mothers typically enforce society's expectations at home.

One woman tells me she said to her 10
mother: "I'm sorry, but my lifetime interest
in the topic of my hair has been exhausted."

One woman was annoyed when her mother commented that her 11
hairdo needed improvement—and ran to get a brush and conditioning mousse to fix it. Later in the visit, the daughter criticized her
mother's hair. She too applied mousse, then wound her mother's
thin, gray hair around cans. She felt a little guilty because her
mother's hair became stiff with dried mousse. But the next time they
talked, her mother said how pleased she was that they had done each
other's hair. She'd even told her best friend about it.

For the mother, how her hair looked wasn't the point. Attention 12
to hair reveals—and creates—intimacy. When a daughter is grown,
her mother may long to recapture the intense physical closeness she
had with her child, although her daughter may resist it.

On the other hand, the daughter may relish it. 13

"I'm 65," a woman told me, "and my mother still brushes my 14
hair out of my eyes." This can be maddening, but it can also be com-
forting because it's an intimate—and motherly—gesture.

One woman, while visiting her mother in the hospital, leaned 15
over the bedrail, full of worry. Her mother's first words were, "When
was the last time you did your roots?" The daughter immediately felt
not anger but relief. Through the tubes and the fever, her mother was
still there—still noticing, still caring.

 Read/Hear It Now: Listen to interviews and read more articles written by linguist Deborah Tannen, on her home page at Georgetown University, at
bedfordstmartins.com/americanow, Chapter 1.

Vocabulary/Using a Dictionary

1. What is a *compliment* (para. 2)? How is it different from *comple-
    ment?*

2. What is the relationship between *contention* (para. 5) and *tension?*

3. What is the difference between *implicit* (see *imply*, para. 5) and *explicit*? How is it related to *implicate*?

4. How is *ponder* (see *pondering*, para. 7) related to *ponderous*?

Responding to Words in Context

1. *Déjà vu* means to have a feeling of already having experienced something. What does it mean to have "déjà vu all over again" (para. 3)?

2. Figurative language is used to embellish an idea through imaginative language like metaphors, similes, personification, and hyperbole. What does it literally mean to walk through a minefield (para. 4)? What does the mother in Tannen's essay really mean? Why do you think she used this simile instead of more literal language?

3. In paragraph 9, Tannen uses the word *resentment* to describe the interactions between mothers and daughters. What is resentment? How is it different from anger?

Discussing Main Point and Meaning

1. What assumptions or stereotypes does Tannen say we have about women with different hair colors? Different hairstyles?

2. According to this essay, why is hair more important for women than for men?

3. Tannen states that "mothers typically enforce society's expectations at home" (para. 9). What does she mean? Do you agree with her? Why or why not?

4. In this essay, Tannen implies that daughters take their mothers' insights and advice as criticism rather than as helpful comments. What does it mean to criticize? To what extent is criticism based on how something is said or who says it rather than what is being said? How does the author relate criticism to caring?

Examining Sentences, Paragraphs, and Organization

1. Tannen begins her essay with a generic exchange between a mother and her grown daughter. How does this dramatization of a common exchange make you think about mothers and daugh-

ters? Did you think the mother's comment was a compliment? How did the context of the comment in the next paragraph make you rethink what the mother meant?

2. Why do you think Tannen uses so much dialogue in her essay? Whose dialogue—mothers' or daughters'—do you relate to more? Why?

3. Why do you think Tannen does not tell readers why mothers and daughters fight about hair so much until two-thirds of the way through her essay? Why does she let her readers discover her insights rather than stating them right away? How would her essay have been different if she had stated her thesis in the first paragraph rather than beginning with dialogue?

Thinking Critically

1. Miscommunications and arguments often escalate because of how we continue a conversation. In the second paragraph, when the daughter perceives that her mother is criticizing her and snaps back, her mother responds by asking her, "What's wrong with you? Why are you so sensitive?" How do you think the daughter is likely to respond to these questions? How could the mother have responded differently?

2. Tannen admits that while on the bus she found herself criticizing the hair of women she did not know. She did not, however, criticize the men's hairstyles. Do you think society seems to be more critical of women's appearances than of men's? Or do you think her statement is influenced by her gender—because she is female, she is more likely to criticize other females than males?

3. Do mothers and sons or fathers and sons have the same problems as mothers and daughters when it comes to communication? Why or why not?

In-Class Writing Activities

1. Tannen, who studies linguistics, uses dialogue in her essay to hook her readers and to personalize the issue. Through the use of dialogue, readers can understand how difficult it is to communicate with someone rather than take sides. Write an essay in which you explore a type of argument—perhaps you once argued with

your parents about a shirt you wanted to wear, or about your curfew, or even about how clean your room should be. Use dialogue to introduce readers to the argument and to present both sides of the argument without being biased.

2. While Tannen avoids making judgments about the mothers and daughters she writes about, she lets her particular word choice inform readers' opinions of her subjects. For instance, the daughter is "*beamed* back to childhood" and "responds *testily*" (para. 3). The mother *laments* (para. 4) rather than *complains* or *worries*. Tannen herself *ponders* (para. 7) the problem rather than *thinks* about it. Although many student writers use adjectives and adverbs to create more description, verbs are much more colorful words. Write an essay in which you describe or analyze a character, either a stranger on the bus or someone you know casually. Describe the person in a particular scene or taking a specific action. Then underline your verbs and see if you can replace them with more colorful or descriptive verbs. (Use the thesaurus for help.) Add adverbs. How does this change your writing style?

3. Write a character analysis of someone you know or are interested in, but not someone you know very well. Describe the person: what he or she looks like, how he or she acts and speaks, and other details that offer clues about the person. Come up with theories about the person's looks and actions. Then describe your judgments. Are you more likely to criticize certain types of people or look more favorably on others? Why or why not? What assumptions are you making about the person? What, if anything, does this reveal about you?

ANNIE BRADFORD RISPIN

Here's Looking at You: Is Body Image Being Taken Too Seriously?

[U. MAGAZINE, The University of Texas, Austin / Fall 2005]

Before You Read

Do you have a positive body image? Do you feel certain pressures from your classmates, the larger community, or even the media to look a certain way?

Words to Learn

waif (para. 2): a very thin, fragile-looking person; a homeless child or orphan (n.)

bulimia (para. 8): an eating disorder characterized by binge eating and then purging through vomiting and laxatives (n.)

anorexia nervosa (para. 8): an eating disorder characterized by a pathological fear of weight gain,

---

ANNIE BRADFORD RISPIN *graduated from the University of Texas, Austin, in 2000. Having earned an undergraduate degree in psychology, she is currently pursing her PhD in clinical psychology. She wrote this article in response to a magazine photo cover of Brooke Shields that she felt "obscured Brooke Shields the Person by displaying Brooke Shields the Body—as though beauty (at least for women) was a prerequisite for being interviewed about all of this other stuff that makes a person who she is!" She contacted the editors of U. Magazine to voice her opinion and was invited to write the following article. Her advice to other writers is this: "My opportunities to write have resulted mostly from me sticking my neck way out in some form or another, whether writing a letter to the editor or applying for a writing position 200 miles away and offering to telecommute. So my advice would be to go ahead and take the long shot when there's nothing to lose, and to keep trying. I would also advise student writers to take feedback in stride and to trust that even excellent writers need editing." For a "Student Writer at Work" interview with Rispin, see page 64.*

avoidance of food, and severe
weight loss (n.)
binge eating (para. 8): consumption
of large amounts of food in a
short time (n.)

phobia (para. 9): fear (n.)
impair (para. 9): to damage or
make worse (v.)
mannequin (para. 13): a lifesize
doll; a model (n.)

Body image problems often rear their ugly (no pun intended)   1
heads in college, although they are often masked, mistaken for vanity, shyness, cautiousness, or even normalcy. With widespread pressure among college students to look a certain

A negative body image may actually be the norm.

way, to have exact amounts of muscle or
body fat, or to achieve perfection, a negative
body image may actually be the norm. But
how can colleges and universities suffer from
a looks-obsessed culture when they are
training the future thinkers, doers, and leaders of the world?

The stress of college life can strike blows to anyone's self-esteem,   2
though there are other forces at work. A large part of the problem
comes from our culture. Just look at the trademark bodies of the
1990s — Kate Moss's black-and-white waif in the Calvin Klein Obsession ads; the tanned, washboard-bellied Diet Coke guy; the incred-
ible shrinking female cast of *Friends*. Youth and beauty seem to go
hand-in-hand in mainstream culture, and many college students strive
for the complete package: intelligence, looks, and status.

Unfortunately, many think those three traits are linked — an idea   3
reinforced by our media. Heroes are also smart and beautiful; often
villains are unattractive and unintelligent. We associate particular
physical characteristics with beauty, glamour, style, and sex appeal,
but no one ever explains why.

Linking external and internal qualities is such a powerful impulse   4
that it affects day-to-day behavior. "Everybody loves to stereotype
people," says Jessie Johnson-Tyas, a junior at the University of North
Carolina–Charlotte. "You look like this, so you must do this and you
must act like this. Having a certain type of body affects how people
interact with you."

Numerous studies indicate that people associate body type with   5
everything from personality traits to occupation. In a study conducted by Dr. Rick Gardner and colleagues at the University of Colorado in Denver, a group of undergraduate college students were exposed to pictures of the same male and female models, though the

images were distorted with a computer to vary in size. Students seeing larger versions of the models tended to assign them more undesirable personality traits compared with students who saw average- or thin-sized models. It has been shown that these perceptions are common in both genders, and that they tend to develop early in childhood—much like racial and gender stereotypes.

Although body image concerns have traditionally been considered a female concern, the problem affects many men as well. There are fewer culturally acceptable body types for men—one type championed by slick designers like Gucci or Versace, another by Abercrombie and Fitch or Ralph Lauren. More men are turning to diets, compulsive exercise, and even eating disorders to lose weight, change their body shape, and achieve the new ideal of male beauty. Although it's estimated that up to twenty percent of female college students suffer from an eating disorder, the American Anorexia Bulimia Association reports that men make up about ten percent of eating disorder sufferers. More recent data suggests that the percentage may be even higher, perhaps because of men's reluctance to seek help for a "woman's issue." 6

Matt Miller, a senior at Oklahoma City University, feels the heat. "Recently, you've started seeing a lot more health magazines for men. I've been influenced to exercise more to achieve a certain look." As a former dorm resident assistant, his exposure to body image problems and eating disorders helped him put things in perspective and focus more on goals than looks. Unfortunately, men suffering from an eating disorder may find it hard to find help. Many colleges house most of their body image resources in women's resource centers, a rather misleading practice. Perhaps as a result of this gender gap, men may be less likely to recognize that they have a problem, and may avoid seeking help. 7

These issues go far beyond asking your roommate if you look fat in your jeans. Extreme body image concerns often lead to eating disorders. Various factors contribute to bulimia, anorexia, and binge eating, although the psychology and medical communities suggest that the staggering increase in eating disorders over the past couple of decades is partly due to our culture's increasingly unrealistic definition of beauty. For example, the British Medical Association recently issued a report contending that extreme thinness among models and actresses contributes to the development of eating disorders in young women. 8

Ironically, athletes, typically thought to be in outstanding health, often suffer from eating disorders and exercise obsession. Much of 9 the pressure comes from a lingering fat phobia among coaches, trainers, and even doctors, says Dr. Mary Beth Diener, a psychologist at the University of Texas who treats students with body image concerns and eating disorders. "There is a perception out there—the less body fat, the better," she says. "Athletes get a lot of pressure from coaches and people who contribute to their training to be thinner and to have more muscle." Sadly, these ideas are a dangerous myth: not only can extreme thinness impair performance, but it can also cause long-lasting health problems, particularly in women.

David Holt, a sophomore at the University of Tennessee, realized   10
the severity of body image problems after watching several friends suffer from eating disorders. "I [realized] how big a problem it was, and I became more and more disgusted with the fact that . . . this could be elevated to being more important than intelligence, aptitude, [or] any of the things that actually matter." Since coming to college, his feelings have become more intense. "In high school, we were told that it . . . would go away," he says. "Then when you get to college, you see people who are twenty-five or twenty-six who still haven't gotten over it, and you wonder if it's ever going to happen."

Some progress is being made. University health centers and other   11
campus organizations give more attention to eating disorders, drug abuse, depression, and other consequences of poor body image. Outreach programs target groups at a high risk for body image problems and eating disorders, such as dormitories, athletic groups, and Greek organizations. And organizations like About-Face, a San Francisco–based group dedicated to exposing unrealistic depictions of women in the media, attack negative, demeaning, and stereotypical images of women head-on. Unfortunately, the campaign towards positive body image has yet to eliminate the problem.

Kirstin Ralston, a non-traditional, second-degree-seeking student   12
at the University of Texas at Austin, has noticed that even on her activist-friendly campus, no one steps forward to promote body acceptance and awareness of negative messages in the media. "I think that the biggest problem is that . . . you are dealing with people who have just come from home . . . they still believe in a very 'traditional' point of view. I think it isn't until they really start to develop their own [sense] of who they are that they start to realize just how bad the media . . . is. By that time, most of these traditional students have already left the campus." Other factors also influence students, says Ralson. "I am sure a number of these students struggle with body image issues every day and they think, 'If I stop this charade, no one

will like me, no one will want to be with me, and—good grief—who would want to marry me?'"

Many people suffering from a poor body image cite the media as   13
one source of concern. While the motives of advertisers aren't exactly complex (sell, sell, sell!), it's interesting to wonder why we have internalized their "ideal body image." Why does a non-existent—or barely existent—standard created on a runway or on Madison Avenue attract us? Maybe it's not just a matter of worshipping a human mannequin. Dr. Hue-Sun Ahn, a psychologist at the Princeton University Counseling Center, theorizes that "with the advancements in technology—whether it's the ability to create a computer-refined . . . unrealistic but 'perfect' image, or whether it's the increase of communication through electronic means—we [have fewer] opportunities to get to know people on a . . . personal level. [We don't see] the nonvisible qualities of a person, such as compassion, spiritedness, sense of humor, loyalty, along with all the human flaws, shortcomings, and imperfections." Could it be, in our culture of Instant Messages and cell phones, that we forget what people are really like, both internally and externally? More importantly, how many of us would like to remember?

Despite these obstacles, some people are optimistic. Holt and   14
Miller look to the future for change, both from the media tycoons who decide what we are exposed to, and from society finally shunning looks obsession—in the same way the civil rights movement, the women's movement, and other social movements changed the way we live together. Imagine living in a world where we revere human bodies for what they can do, rather than for an arbitrary set of physical features.

Fortunately, the medical profession has also been shifting its   15
views, recognizing that proper nutrition, regular exercise, and healthy lifestyles are far more significant indicators of overall health than weight or body size alone. Some ideas, though, have been painfully slow to develop. For example, few people recognize the influence of our fat-phobic culture on the growing rate of obesity in America. It's likely that many people taught to hate their bodies do not care for them as a result. Though our style-over-substance, form-over-function culture influences even highly trained professionals, more people are realizing that good health is not synonymous with the type of body idolized in fitness magazines.

Drawing attention to the problem is crucial. The thin, tanned,   16
sculpted celebrities promoting causes like animal rights or AIDS

awareness seem ill suited to hold benefit concerts or media events to promote body acceptance. Even among students, it's much more stylish to act on behalf of starving children in Africa than starving young middle-class women in America. However, unlike many of the causes that have been furthered by student activists, this is our battle. A poor body image silences far too many in our generation — are we ready to talk back?

For an annotated excerpt of this essay that highlights Rispin's writing strategies, see page 63.

 Read It Now: Check out more student opinions at *U Magazine: The National College Magazine* at **bedfordstmartins.com/americanow**, Chapter 1.

Vocabulary / Using a Dictionary

1. What is the difference between *intelligence* and *aptitude* (para. 10)?

2. *Synonymous* (para. 15) is an adjective. How does it relate to its noun, *synonym*? How is it related to the word *pseudonym*?

3. What does *charade* (para. 12) mean? How is it related to the game Charades?

Responding to Words in Context

1. In paragraph 2, Rispin urges her readers to "look at the trademark bodies of the 1990s." In this context, what does she mean by *trademark*?

2. In paragraph 6, Rispin says that men are reluctant to seek help for eating disorders because they are "a woman's issue." What does she mean by this phrase? Why does she use quotation marks around it?

3. In paragraph 9, Rispin begins her first sentence with the word *ironically*. What does *ironic* mean? How is her statement an example of irony?

Discussing Main Point and Meaning

1. Rispin claims in paragraphs 3 and 4 that we connect success with particular physical traits, like beauty and glamour, but no one ever explains why. How does she explain this linking of traits?

2. According to Rispin, to what extent are our ideals of beauty influenced by magazines, movies, television, and other media? Do you agree? Why or why not?

3. In paragraph 11, Rispin discusses the steps taken to combat negative body image and states that organizations "dedicated to exposing unrealistic depictions of women in the media, attack negative, demeaning, and stereotypical images of women head-on." How can images of beauty be demeaning and stereotypical?

Examining Sentences, Paragraphs, and Organization

1. Rispin assumes that technology is partly to blame for our looks-obsessed culture. Why does she blame technology? What kinds of technology does she mention? What kinds of technology, if any, influence how you look?

2. Rispin begins her introduction with her overview of body image problems and then asks a rhetorical question (a question to which the answer is already known). Is Rispin's use of rhetorical questions throughout her essay an effective strategy? Does she engage her audience? Explain your answer.

3. Rather than simply relying on her own research and opinions, Rispin includes quotes from students she has interviewed. She introduces each speaker and uses signal phrases and strong verb choices. How do the quotes work to support Rispin's thesis? How does she integrate them into her writing? What is the effect of all the quotes from students? Why does she not include quotes from others, such as medical professionals?

Thinking Critically

1. Students are taught in school that stereotyping is bad, but in paragraph 4 student Jessie Johnson-Tyas asserts that everyone loves to stereotype. What is enticing about stereotyping? Why do we stereotype? Is stereotyping based on looks different from stereotyping based on race or gender? Explain.

2. In paragraph 10, student David Holt describes friends who suffered from eating disorders because of the importance placed on looks in American culture. Is it true that Americans value looks above all else? What other factors might influence eating disorders?

3. Rispin argues that eating disorders and body image problems affect everyone—men and women, and people of different races and cultures. But how do you account for the societal assumption that body image problems affect only women? What differences are there between our ideas of the beautiful woman and the beautiful man? What similarities are there?

In-Class Writing Activities

1. Student Matt Miller says in paragraph 7 that his notion of the ideal male body came from reading men's fitness magazines. What magazines do you and your friends read? Flip through the photographs and advertisements and describe the bodies that you see. What traits do they have in common? How would you characterize these bodies? To what extent do the articles in the magazine reinforce the advertisements' ideas of beauty?

2. Interviewing is a particular skill that many writers must have. A writer must be able to formulate relevant questions that will lead to thoughtful answers, to find people to interview who are appropriate and representative of the general population, and to then choose good sound bites from the answers received. For this essay, write down your take on body image—is it an issue? What is the accepted body image in your community? Then compose five questions for your classmates relating to your stance. Write up your findings using your classmates' answers as support.

3. What kinds of technology do you use on a daily basis? How do these affect your interactions with people? Write an essay in which you discuss how your life has changed and how your interactions with people have changed based on your use of technology.

ANNOTATION Summarizing Professional Research and Opinion

In writing a short opinion paper, you will frequently find it necessary to summarize briefly a professional research study that supports your position. Why is this necessary? You need to do this because it demonstrates to readers that your position is not simply based on your own impressions or experiences but has been confirmed by those who are presumably experts. Observe how **Annie Bradford Rispin**, a University of Texas student, handles this process in **"Here's Looking at You: Is Body Image Being Taken Too Seriously?"** She wants to establish the point that people will make key snap judgments about others based merely on the way they look. She has found a research study that supports this point but, given the scope of her paper, can't cite it at length. Note that she clearly indicates the author and location of the study, thus showing its relevance to her argument, and very effectively offers a quick rundown of its central idea—that in a professionally conducted study, college students used a model's size to infer his or her personality traits.

Brief citation of study

Numerous studies indicate that people associate body type with everything from personality traits to occupation. In a study conducted by Dr. Rick Gardner and colleagues at the University of Colorado in Denver, a group of undergraduate college students were exposed to pictures of the same male and female models, though the images were distorted with a computer to vary in size.

Study results support Rispin's main argument

Students seeing larger versions of the models tended to assign them more undesirable personality traits compared with students who saw average- or thin-sized models. It has been shown that these perceptions are common in both sexes, and that they tend to develop early in childhood—much like racial and gender stereotypes.

—From "Here's Looking at You: Is Body Image Being Taken Too Seriously?" by Annie Bradford Rispin, page 55

Student Writer at Work: Annie Bradford Rispin
On Writing "Here's Looking at You: Is Body Image Being Taken Too Seriously?"

Q: What inspired you to write "Here's Looking at You"?

A: What started the process was an issue of the print edition of *U. Magazine* that featured an interview with Brooke Shields. The cover photo was a shot of Brooke Shields all stretched out in a swimsuit, lying in a bathtub for some reason. Now, Brooke Shields is a smart, talented, interesting woman, and it just struck me that this cover photo obscured Brooke Shields the Person by displaying Brooke Shields the Body—as though beauty (at least for women) was a prerequisite for being interviewed about all of this other stuff that makes a person who she is! I didn't think that was the right message to send to the college student population, which is at least 50% female. So I wrote the editor to complain about the cover photo, trying to explain my view. The editor wrote back and politely rebuffed my complaints, but also told me that I wrote well and invited me to write a piece on body image for the magazine. Naturally, I jumped at the chance.

Q: Who was your target audience for the piece?

A: I aimed for a broad college student population. Usually body image problems are associated with women, and there are good reasons for that, but I purposefully included a male voice as well to draw attention to the fact that this is not just a "female problem." I also included an interview with a nontraditional student for perspective from someone slightly older than the average college student—that demographic is really neglected in college publications.

Q: What response have you received to this piece?

A: Someone from a university counseling center e-mailed me about the piece and wanted my permission to use it as a handout for students. That was extremely satisfying. I was also happy to see the article featured in *U. Magazine*'s online "Top 25" articles in the history of the publication. That feedback reinforced my confidence that this was a topic that college students want and need to talk about.

PAIRED READINGS

Who's in Favor of Cosmetic Surgery?

CAMILLE PAGLIA

The Pitfalls of Plastic Surgery

[HARPER'S BAZAAR / May 1, 2005]

Before You Read

How do you feel about your looks? What do you think about people who get plastic surgery? Do they become more beautiful? More unique-looking? More or less natural looking?

Words to Learn

narcissism (para. 3): excessive self-love (n.)

endemic (para. 3): confined to a particular group or area (adj.)

coercive (para. 3): intending to persuade or pressure (adj.)

parochial (para. 6): insular; narrow in its view (adj.)

ingenue (para. 6): young female; an innocent young girl (n.)

ingratiating (para. 6): designed to win someone's favor (adj.)

dominatrix (para. 6): a female sexual aggressor (n.)

simpering (para. 7): silly; whiny (adj.)

nymphet (para. 7): a young, sexually attractive girl (n.)

esoteric (para. 7): confined to and understandable to a small group (adj.)

discrepancy (para. 8): divergence or disagreement (n.)

CAMILLE PAGLIA, *author, feminist, social critic, and agitator, is University Professor of Humanities and Media Studies at the University of the Arts in Philadelphia. Through her "militantly interdisciplinary" approach to writing, in which she incorporates theories from media, literature, history, and biology, Paglia hopes to renew creativity in the arts. She believes that "for committed writers in any genre (including nonfiction), writing is an approach to the world, a way of life."*

mogul (para. 8): a very rich or powerful person (n.)

émigré (para. 8): a person who leaves his or her country to live in another (n.)

femmes fatales (para. 8): dangerous, sexual women; dangerous seductresses (n.)

pantheon (para. 8): a group of the most admired people (n.)

snarky (para. 9): sarcastic; irreverent (adj.)

pneumatic (para. 9): inflated; as used in this essay, full-busted (adj.)

Amazonian (para. 9): having the characteristics of an Amazon, a mythical strong woman warrior (adj.)

anomalous (para. 9): different; abnormal (adj.)

nubile (para. 10): sexually mature (adj.)

subcutaneous (para. 11): below the skin (adj.)

repertoire (para. 12): a range of skills or special accomplishments (n.)

intuit (para. 12): to know instinctively (v.)

Plastic surgery is living sculpture: a triumph of modern medicine. 1
As a revision of nature, cosmetic surgery symbolizes the conquest of biology by human free will. With new faces and bodies, people have become their own works of art.

Once largely confined to the entertainment and fashion industries, plastic surgery has become routine in the corporate workplace 2
in the U.S., even for men. A refreshed, youthful look is now considered essential for job retention and advancement in high-profile careers. As cosmetic surgery has become more widespread and affordable, it has virtually become a civil right, an equal-opportunity privilege once enjoyed primarily by a moneyed elite who could fly to Brazil for a discreet nip and tuck.

The questions raised about plastic surgery often have a moralistic 3
hue. Is cosmetic surgery a wasteful frivolity, an exercise in narcissism? Does the pressure for alteration of face and body fall more heavily on women because of endemic sexism? And are coercive racist stereotypes at work in the trend among black women to thin their noses or among Asian women to "Westernize" their eyes?

Nothing will stop the drive toward the shimmering illusion of perfection.

All these ethical issues deserve serious 4
attention. But nothing, I submit, will stop the drive of the human species toward beauty and the shimmering illusion of perfection. It is one of our deepest and finest instincts. From prehistory on, tribal peoples flattened their skulls, pierced their noses,

elongated their necks, stretched their earlobes and scarred or tattooed their entire bodies to achieve the most admired look. Mutilation is in the eye of the beholder.

Though cosmetic surgery is undoubtedly an unstoppable move-   5
ment, we may still ask whether its current application can be improved. I have not had surgery and have no plans to do so, on the theory that women intellectuals, at least, should perhaps try to hold out. (On the other hand, one doesn't want to scare the horses!) Over the past 15 years, I have become increasingly uneasy about ruling styles of plastic surgery in the U.S. What norms are being imposed on adult or aging women?

I would suggest that the current models upon which many Amer-   6
ican surgeons are basing their reworking of the female face and body are far too parochial. The eye can be retrained over time, and so we have come to accept a diminished and even demeaning view of woman as ingenue, a perky figure of ingratiating girliness. Neither sex bomb nor dominatrix, she is a cutesy sex kitten without claws.

In the great era of the Hollywood studio system, from the 1920s   7
to the early '60s, pioneering makeup techniques achieved what plastic surgery does now to remold the appearance of both male and female stars. For example, the mature Lana Turner [see p. 68] of *Imitation of Life* or *Peyton Place* was made to look like a superglamorous and ravishingly sensual version of a woman of Turner's own age. The problem today is that Hollywood expects middle-aged female actors to look 20 or even 30 years younger than they are. The ideal has become the bouncy Barbie doll or simpering nymphet, not a sophisticated woman of the world. Women's faces are erased, blanked out as in a cartoon. In Europe, in contrast, older women are still considered sexy: Women are granted the dignity of accumulated experience. The European woman has a reserve or mystique because of her assumed mastery of the esoteric arts of love.

Why this cultural discrepancy? Many of the founders of Holly-   8
wood, from studio moguls to directors, screenwriters, makeup artists and composers, were European émigrés whose social background ranged from peasant to professional. European models of beauty are based on classical precedents: on luminous Greek sculpture, with its mathematical symmetry and proportion, or on Old Master oil paintings, with their magnificent portraiture of elegant aristocrats and hypnotic femmes fatales. As an upstart popular form with trashy roots in nickelodeons and penny arcades, Hollywood movies strove to elevate their prestige by invoking a noble past. The studios

Lana Turner and Lee Philips in the 1957 film *Peyton Place*.

presented their stable of stars as a Greek pantheon of resurrected divinities, sex symbols with an unattainable grandeur.

But Hollywood's grounding in great art has vanished. In this blockbuster era of computerized special effects and slam-bang action-adventure films, few producers and directors root their genre in the

9

ancestry of the fine arts. On the contrary, they are more likely to be inspired by snarky television sitcoms or holographic video games, with their fantasy cast of overmuscled heroes and pneumatic vixens. The profound influence of video games can be seen in the redefining of today's ultimate female body type, inspired by Amazonian super-heroines like Lara Croft: large breasts with a flat midriff and lean hips, a hormonally anomalous profile that few women can attain without surgical intervention and liposuction.

Maximizing one's attractiveness and desirability is a justifiable   10
aim in any society, except for the most puritanical. But it is worri-some that the American standard of female sexual allure may be re-gressing. In the post-1960s culture of easy divorce on demand, middle-aged women have found themselves competing with nubile women in their 20s, who are being scooped up as trophy second wives by ambitious men having a midlife crisis. Cosmetic surgery seems to level the playing field. But at what cost?

Good surgery discovers and reveals personality; bad surgery ob-   11
scures or distorts it. The facial mask should not be frozen or robotic. We still don't know what neurological risks there may be in long-term use of nonsurgical Botox, a toxin injected subcutaneously to paralyze facial muscles and smooth out furrows and wrinkles. What is clear, however, is that unskilled practitioners are sometimes admin-istering Botox in excessive amounts, so that even major celebrities in their late 30s and 40s can be seen at public events with frighteningly waxen, mummified foreheads. Actors who overuse Botox are forfeit-ing the mobile expressiveness necessary to portray character. We will probably never again see "great faces" among accomplished older women—the kind of severe, imperious, craggy look of formidable vi-sionaries like Diana Vreeland or Lillian Hellman.

The urgent problem is that today's cos-   12
metic surgeons are drawing from too limited a repertoire of images. Plastic surgery is an art form: Therefore, surgeons need training in art as well as medicine. Without a broader visual vocabulary, too many surgeons will continue to homogenize women, divesting them of authority and reducing them to a generic cookie-cutter sameness. And without a gift for psychology, surgeons cannot intuit and reinforce a woman's unique personality.

Without a broader visual vocabulary, too many surgeons will continue to homogenize women.

For cosmetic surgery to maintain or regain subtlety and nuance,   13
surgeons should meditate on great painting and sculpture. And
women themselves must draw the line against seeking and perpetuat-
ing an artificial juvenility that obliterates their own cultural value.

 Read It Now: Read additional articles by Camille Paglia published at
Salon.com at **bedfordstmartins.com/americanow**, Chapter 1.

Vocabulary/Using a Dictionary

1. What is the meaning of *Westernize* (para. 3)?
2. What is the meaning of *puritanical* (para. 10)? How is it related
   to the Puritans? To the word *pure*?
3. What is the definition of *juvenility* (para. 13)? How is it different
   from youthfulness?
4. What does *homogenize* mean (para. 12)? How is it related to ho-
   mogeneity? To heterogeneity?

Responding to Words in Context

1. In paragraph 2, Paglia states that plastic surgery "has virtually
   become a civil right." What is a civil right? How might surgery
   be considered a civil right?
2. Paglia makes the claim that women's faces are "erased" by our
   cultural ideals of beauty and plastic surgery (para. 7). What does
   she mean by *erased*?
3. What does Paglia mean by *facial mask* in paragraph 11? How is
   a facial mask different from a face?
4. In paragraph 6, Paglia uses the word *parochial*. Parochial, which
   means insular (from the Latin for island), or narrow, can also
   mean of or related to a local parish, as in a parochial school.
   Thus, the connotation of parochial is a narrow view based on
   fundamental, or religious, beliefs. Many of Paglia's words in this
   essay have religious connotations. Find other words in her essay
   that have religious connotations. Why do you think she uses so
   many words that refer to religion when writing about beauty?
5. Paglia often defines femininity by bounding it between two
   words that are antonyms, such as *ingenue* and *dominatrix*

(para. 6). How are these two words different? Why do you think she needs the comparison to define what women are?

Discussing Main Point and Meaning

1. What is a work of art? How do we determine what is art and what is not art? Can science or medicine be an art form?

2. What is Paglia's definition of the beautiful woman? How does her definition differ from the standard that she is speaking against?

3. Paglia states that plastic surgery is leveling the playing field (para. 10). What are the assumptions she is making about women who choose to have plastic surgery? What are her assumptions about women in general? How do her assumptions affect her argument?

Examining Sentences, Paragraphs, and Organization

1. How does the first paragraph of this essay set up expectations for Paglia's argument? How does it contrast with her title? How did you approach Paglia's argument after reading the title and then the first paragraph?

2. What does Paglia mean when she states in paragraph 6 that "the eye can be retrained over time, and so we have come to accept a diminished and even demeaning view of woman as ingenue, a perky figure of ingratiating girliness"? According to paragraph 6, how have cosmetic surgeons typically portrayed women?

Thinking Critically

1. In the first paragraph, Paglia insists that plastic surgery is "the conquest of biology by human free will." Later she states that the quest for perfection "is one of our deepest and finest instincts" (para. 4). Are people who undergo plastic surgery simply exercising free will? Are they giving in to the biological urge to be beautiful?

2. Paglia only considers the effect of plastic surgery on women and how middle-aged women are competing with women in their twenties for male attention. But how does plastic surgery affect men? Are women interested in changing themselves only to find a better mate? What about men?

3. Paglia says that her generation's idealized versions of beauty were based on European ideals of classical art and that current ideas of beauty are based on video game heroes like Lara Croft. She also claims that surgeons should look at examples of art to make better faces. Do art and video games influence our ideas of beauty, or do they reflect what society believes is beautiful?

In-Class Writing Activities

1. Paglia states that the technology of the movies of the 1920s to the early 1960s enhanced a star's appearance rather than changed her overall looks. Write an essay in which you characterize your own look or style, and examine a time when you changed your look for a specific purpose. How drastically did you change yourself? Why? Did it work? Did you find that your personality changed to fit your new look? Did people treat you differently? Would you do it again?

2. Paglia uses Lana Turner as her definition of beauty. Just a few years ago, Halle Berry was considered one of the most beautiful women in America because her facial features are almost mathematically symmetrical. Is beauty simply mathematics, or is it something more? Write an essay in which you determine what the definition of beauty is today and why.

3. Paglia calls for surgeons to return to art to rediscover beauty. Works of art can range from the classical sculptures and paintings to cubist work, to modern posters, movies, and even video games. Visit your local museum or museum Web site. In a short essay, describe your favorite work of art and include why it is your favorite. Consider if it is art and if it has staying power to become a classical representation of cultural values.

ART CAREY

Men's Faces Go Under the Knife

[THE PHILADELPHIA INQUIRER / February 19, 2006]

Before You Read

What type of man do you consider glamorous or authentic? What does it mean to grow old gracefully? What do you think about men who undergo plastic surgery? Do you still consider them masculine?

Words to Learn

salient (para. 1): standing out; significant (adj.)

narcissism (para. 1): excessive self-love (n.)

snipe (para. 2): to attack in speech or writing (v.)

injunction (para. 5): a formal command (n.)

dismay (para. 6): discouragement or alarm; unpleasant surprise (n.)

opine (para. 11): to speak an opinion strongly (v.)

sallow (para. 11): unhealthy looking; yellow-gray (adj.)

belle (para. 17): a beautiful woman (n.)

skittish (para. 19): unpredictably excitable (adj.)

stent (para. 22): a device placed in an artery to keep it open (n.)

Robert Redford used to be my hero. I admired him for many   1
reasons, not least because he seemed relatively immune to his profession's most salient occupational hazard—narcissism.

Art Carey, *a former wrestler and long-distance runner, writes the "This Way Up" column for the* Philadelphia Inquirer's *Image Section; previously he wrote a fitness column for thirteen years. Carey states, "In my writing, I try to do what Horace said good poetry should do—*dulce et utile, *to be sweet and useful, to delight and teach, to entertain and inform." He urges students to "write, write, write and then write some more" because writing "is, in many ways, a craft, a form of manual labor, like brick laying. The more you practice, the better you'll get."*

While others sniped about his weatherbeaten face and increas-   2
ingly craggy looks, I applauded. Here was a matinee idol willing to
grow old naturally, and to let it show.

In 2002, asked whether he'd consider cosmetic surgery, Redford   3
replied: "I'm not a face-lift person. I am
what I am. People should preserve their time

"They lose some of their   in history. I'm happy to make the best of
soul when they go under   what I've got.
the knife, and end up   "Everyone in Tinseltown is getting   4
looking body-snatched."   pinched, lifted and pulled. For many it's become a sick obsession. They lose some of their
soul when they go under the knife, and end up looking body-snatched."

When I read those words, I cheered. I'm a fanatic about being   5
natural, real, authentic. I'm opposed to cosmetic surgery because it's
artificial and phony. It makes a mockery of the injunction, "Be yourself." It feeds our obsession with appearance, our preoccupation with
the superficial, our terror of aging.

So you can imagine my dismay when it became obvious a couple   6
of years ago that Redford himself had submitted to the scalpel.

What's worse, the job was botched. In this humble layman's   7
opinion, Redford was better-looking—wrinkles and all—the way he
was, before his rugged features were stretched, smoothed and altered.

"Totally fake" is the verdict of Allan Wulc, who knows whereof   8
he speaks.

Wulc, 52, is a cosmetic surgeon who practices in Warrington,   9
Bucks County. He began his training as an ophthalmologist and
spent 10 years teaching and doing research at the University of Pennsylvania. He has written more than 40 papers, was a pioneering proponent of Botox for cosmetic purposes, and serves on the faculty of
Wills Eye Hospital, the Scheie Eye Institute, and Hahnemann University Hospital.

We were in Wulc's office looking at a photo of Redford on the   10
Web site Awful Plastic Surgery (www.awfulplasticsurgery.com).

Wulc's assessment: Redford had both upper and lower eyelids   11
done, a brow-lift, probably a face-lift because his jawline is so sharp.
His brow is now "effeminate," Wulc opined. His cheeks, sunken and
sallow, look "dead."

In short, Redford is no longer the Sundance Kid. He's been   12
carved into The Unnatural.

Failures occur more often—and are most noticeable—in those   13
who are cinematically handsome, "who look good in two dimen-

sions," Wulc said. Off the record, he listed several Hollywood leading men, and some Washington politicos, he was sure had undergone
cosmetic surgery. Many of these men have faces so ridiculously tight,
Wulc said, that they look hideous and scary.

I don't mean to pick on Redford. I feel sorry for him. Vanity has   14
disfigured his looks. In my book, he has slipped from masculine icon
to object lesson in the perils of cosmetic surgery.

The biggest peril is the temptation, on the part of both patient   15
and surgeon, to overreach, to try to make someone look too youthful, too pretty. Wulc, who studied piano, painting and sculpture in
Paris as an Amherst undergraduate, has an artistic bent. He knows
that a basic rule of aesthetics is that less is more. Accordingly, in
cosmetic surgery, his goal is not transformation, he says, but
"restoration."

His professional partner, Brenda Edmonson, who also trained in   16
ophthalmology before turning to cosmetic surgery, espouses the same
aim. About half her patients are men. She wants them to look like
who they are, but "refreshed."

"You have to be more conservative with men," says Edmonson,   17
33, an Alabama native who professes a Southern belle's knack for
catering to guys. "They want to look more youthful and still look
manly."

That makes men more challenging. They also have facial hair,   18
thicker skin, lower brows, more prominent foreheads, more pronounced jaws. Because many are balding, it's more difficult to hide
surgical scars.

But that's no reason for men to avoid cosmetic surgery, Edmon-   19
son says, embarrassing though it may be (some men are so skittish
they enter through the back door). Men who are fit could especially
benefit. "From the neck down, they look great," Edmonson says, "but
exercise gives the face a beating." Age finishes it off. "The face loses
volume and fullness," Edmonson says, "and everything goes south."

Edmonson listened politely as I expressed my objections to cos-   20
metic surgery.

"It's vain and shallow. It's a sign of decadence and the decline of   21
Western civilization," I lamented. "It's not natural and authentic."

"Is it natural and authentic to wear nice clothes?" Edmonson   22
parried. "To shave, and to wash and comb your hair? To run and lift
weights at the gym? You do those things to improve your appearance. Why is it any worse to take advantage of modern medical technology to rejuvenate your skin or repair damage caused by sun, time

and age? If you had cardiovascular disease, would you refuse a stent because it's not natural and authentic?"

Edmonson had a point. But I was still unconvinced. I want my   23
face to be a record of who I am, where I've been, what I've been through, a visual memoir of my life and times. Cosmetic surgery turns it into a work of fiction.

 Read It Now: Read more fitness columns by Art Carey, written for the *Philadelphia Inquirer*, at **bedfordstmartins.com/americanow**, Chapter 1.

Vocabulary / Using a Dictionary

1. What is an *ophthalmologist* (para. 9)? What is the difference between *ophthalmologist* and *ophthalmology*?
2. What does *espouse* (para. 16) mean?
3. Define *rejuvenate* (para. 22). How is it related to *juvenile*?

Responding to Words in Context

1. What does *body-snatched* mean in paragraph 4? What is Carey trying to imply with this statement about people's control over their looks?
2. You know that *object* means a thing. But what does *object* mean in paragraph 14 when Carey writes that Redford is an "object lesson in the perils of cosmetic surgery"?
3. What does it mean to look "manly" (para. 17), according to Carey? For that matter, what is a man? What is a woman? How, in terms of plastic surgery, do they look different?

Discussing Main Point and Meaning

1. Carey begins by stating that Robert Redford is his hero, but when Redford undergoes plastic surgery, Carey seems upset with his hero. When he states the faults he finds with Redford, one of the faults is that his craggy hero now has a brow that is "effeminate" (para. 11). What is the difference between masculine and effeminate? What do we think about men who have effeminate qualities? How does this make Redford, a man who refused plas-

tic surgery but plays the masculine lead in many of his movies, less of a hero?

2. In paragraph 15, Carey writes of the plastic surgeon Wulc, "in cosmetic surgery, his goal is not transformation . . . but 'restoration.'" What is the difference between transformation and restoration? How are they alike? Do you think there is a difference in terms of plastic surgery?

3. When Dr. Edmonson is defending plastic surgery in men, she asks Carey, "If you had cardiovascular disease, would you refuse a stent because it's not natural and authentic?" (para. 22). What is she saying about the natural body? What is she saying about plastic surgery and its benefits?

Examining Sentences, Paragraphs, and Organization

1. Redford states "I am what I am" in response to aging and refusing plastic surgery (para. 3.) This is a brief statement, and yet it echoes the philosopher Descartes's belief: "I think, therefore I am." What does it mean to "be" who you are? Why is this important for a movie star like Redford?

2. Although the essay begins with Robert Redford as a hero, paragraph 5 focuses on the author of the essay, Art Carey. In a total of five sentences, it uses *I* four times and the second-person address (*our*) a total of three times. How does this focus on the author affect your reading of the essay? Why do you think he has a paragraph that is strictly about his beliefs?

3. In paragraph 9, to show that he is right in saying that Redford is no longer a hero because he has submitted to the knife and has "overreached," Carey refers to plastic surgeon Wulc to back up and support his belief. In paragraph 9, Carey lists Wulc's credentials. Why do you think he introduces Wulc first in a short sentence and then creates a paragraph of his credentials? Is this enough to convince you that Redford has had plastic surgery?

Thinking Critically

1. Carey prefers Redford as an icon because he defies the Hollywood definition of handsome. Can you think of other older male stars? Are they still considered attractive? Can older men be attractive? Is it acceptable for men to undergo plastic surgery? Why or why not?

2. Carey isn't so much worried about Redford undergoing plastic surgery as he is worried about the difference between real and fake. Dr. Wulc seems to vindicate Carey when he says Redford's face looks "totally fake" (para. 8). What does *fake* really mean in Hollywood, the place — and industry — that is known for making and selling fictions? Can we expect people who are in the business of creating fictions to be real? What is real about a person's appearance?

3. Carey's complaint against plastic surgery is that it is "vain and shallow." He even goes so far as to say it is a sign of "the decline of Western civilization" (para. 21) based on the premise that plastic surgery is a fiction. Do you agree with him? Why or why not?

In-Class Writing Activities

1. Redford used to be Carey's hero because he defied the standards of Hollywood. Who is your hero? In an essay, define what a hero is, who you think embodies the qualities of being a hero, and why.

2. As a writer, you will be asked to do a great deal of research. Thanks to the Internet, much of your information can be found online, but as a good writer, you must be able to determine which Web sites are credible and which are not. In this article, Carey and Dr. Wulc looked up Robert Redford on the Web site Awful Plastic Surgery (www.awfulplasticsurgery.com). Look up the site yourself. In an essay, analyze this site. How would you characterize this Web site? Do you think it is a credible source? Who created it, and who sponsors it? What do you think is its purpose? Do you think it makes a good argument for or against plastic surgery? Can you find a better Web site that argues against plastic surgery? Compare and contrast the two Web sites.

3. One of the biggest complaints against plastic surgery, as Carey states, is that it is not natural, that is not authentic (para. 21). What does it mean to be natural or authentic in the case of plastic surgery? Write a definition essay in which you define the word *authentic*, making use of comparing and contrasting, descriptive details, specific examples, classification, process, cause and effect, analysis, and any other methods.

CHARLES ATLAS

The Insult That Turned a "Chump" into a Champ

Body building is a relatively recent phenomenon. For centuries, workers developed muscles while on the job—farming, lifting, hauling, and so on. The blacksmith, for example, was often the strongest person in American villages. It was only after the rapid expansion of clerical and sales jobs in the twentieth century that people stopped developing their muscles through their work and instead began developing them through working out. In other words, muscles became symbolically important when they were no longer physically required. One of the first people to profit from this modern cultural trend was Charles Atlas (1892–1972), who not only invented one of the earliest types of isometric workouts but—more significantly—designed a marketing strategy that has ensured his place in American culture. Ads for Charles Atlas's "Dynamic Tension" method began appearing in the 1920s and continue to appear in print and online. One of the most famous of these ads appeared in 1947: "The Insult That Turned a 'Chump' into a Champ."

Web **Read/See It Now:** Learn more about Charles Atlas and his body building and fitness methods at **bedfordstmartins.com/americanow**, Chapter 1.

Discussing the Unit

Suggested Topic for Discussion

To what extent can we and should we control how others perceive us based on appearance? Is stereotyping about appearance a useful tool for understanding certain groups of people based on certain chosen traits, or is it harmful?

Preparing for Class Discussion

1. The "America Then" section of this chapter (p. 79) points out that "it was only after the rapid expansion of clerical and sales jobs in the twentieth century that people stopped developing their muscles through their work and instead began developing them through working out. In other words, muscles became symbolically important when they were no longer physically required." Arguably, the symbolic importance of muscles was always there, but it reversed itself: Having muscles once meant you were poor and had to work for a living; then, when most jobs stopped involving them, muscles meant you were rich enough to have the leisure of exercising. Has the meaning or symbolic importance of obesity undergone a change? What is the relationship between a culture's changing beauty ideals and its socioeconomic reality?

2. The Charles Atlas ad (p. 80) represents a body that has been modified through intense exercise, nutritional supplements, and the like. The modified body in the ad is meant to represent empowerment. Similarly, despite her critique of it, Paglia sees plastic surgery as a type of empowerment that levels the playing field. Tannen shows how control over hair is exercised by mothers and daughters. In some cultures, people compare not only how many surgeries they have undergone, but also how much money they have spent on plastic surgeries, just as they brag about how many piercings or tattoos they have. There are even online communities where young girls compare and compete to be the better anorexic or bulimic. Yet Carey, the only male voice in this chapter, believes that plastic surgery, at least for men, does not represent empowerment but instead is the result of societal brainwashing. Does modifying the body (however subtly or drastically) represent empowerment? Explain.

From Discussion to Writing

1. Paglia and Carey take very different stances on plastic surgery. Paglia believes that it is empowerment when it comes to women, but Carey believes that plastic surgery, at least when it comes to his hero, Robert Redford, is vain and shallow. To what extent are our ideas of plastic surgery influenced by the gender of the person undergoing the surgery?

2. Is an obsession with appearance detrimental to a culture? Rispin believes that it causes a great deal of harm among students, and Carey believes that it is a sign of the downfall of Western civilization, although the Charles Atlas advertisement would have you believe that it is the sign of the acceptance of civilization.

3. How do we talk about a person's appearance? Go back through the essays and underline how the various authors describe people or themselves. What is important to the viewer? How do you think these descriptions match up with the people's own concept of their appearance?

Topics for Cross-Cultural Discussion

1. Paglia uses some adjectives that are derived from the names for certain cultures, such as *Amazonian, puritanical,* and *Westernized.* How does culture and community dictate what is beautiful? What defines beauty in subcultures within the United States? Of cultures outside of the United States?

2. Many ideals of beauty are based on tradition — either artistic tradition, as Paglia insists; religious tradition, such as tribal scarring or the Hindu bindi; familial traditions; or even economic traditions. Are your ideas of beauty informed by artistic, religious, familial, or economic traditions? Or something else?

2

Social Networking: How Is Facebook Changing Student Life?

Over the past few years we have witnessed the stupendous rise of what is being called "Me Media": social networking Web sites such as MySpace, Friendster, Facebook, Tribe.Net, and YouTube. This chapter focuses on one of the most popular among college students, Facebook, a site started by Harvard undergraduates and put into operation on that campus in February 2004. The site now attracts students from nearly every college in the country. As of May 2006, the site had nearly 8 million registered members. You are very likely one of them.

Does Facebook serve any useful function, or is it just another distraction to keep students from their tasks? And why is it so addictive? The selections that follow offer two different perspectives: one from a college professor, the other from a college student. In "Facing the Facebook," Michael Bugeja points out that professors are less likely to be aware of Facebook than are their students, and most have little awareness of the site's enormous impact. Bugeja worries that Facebook is just another misuse of technology: "Information technology in the classroom," he writes, "was supposed to bridge digital divides and enhance student research. Increasingly, however, our networks are being used to entertain members of 'the Facebook Generation' who text-message during class, talk on their cellphones during labs, and listen to iPods rather than guest speakers in the wireless lecture hall." As a communications professor, he also worries about the true nature of the community building that Facebook enthusiasts claim.

In "The Facebook Addiction Spreads," Angela Adair Fowler, a student at Mississippi State University, agrees with Bugeja that Facebook is both addictive and distracting, an "entertaining timewaster." But Adair is encouraged by the opportunities Facebook offers for social networking and the expansion of public discourse: "Facebook is a place for unlimited communication—where anyone can talk to anyone without barrier. And we can do it all on our own time, without leaving our own comfort zone."

MICHAEL BUGEJA

Facing the Facebook

[THE CHRONICLE OF HIGHER EDUCATION / February 27, 2006]

Before You Read

Do you use Facebook, MySpace, or other social networking sites? Can you think of ways that such sites are productive? Can they be harmful in a college environment?

Words to Learn

evidenced (para. 4): clearly shown or proven (v.)
provosts (para. 5): high-ranking university administrators (n.)
judiciary (para. 5): a system of courts of law (n.)
assessing (para. 5): estimating the value or worth of something (v.)
ubiquitous (para. 6): seeming to be everywhere at the same time (adj.)
Janus (para. 8): a Roman god, shown with two faces on opposite sides of his head (n.)

distinguishable (para. 11): capable of being shown as being different (adj.)
troll (para. 12): to patrol an area in search of something (slang, v.)
syllabi (para. 24): plural of *syllabus*; an outline of the main points of a course (n.)
discern (para. 24): to be able to recognize or to see as being different (v.)

MICHAEL BUGEJA, *professor and director of the Greenlee School of Journalism and Communication at the University of Iowa, has worked as a reporter, correspondent, and editor. He has written over twenty books, most recently* Interpersonal Divide: The Search for Community in a Technological Age *(2005), and is a contributor to the* Chronicle of Higher Education *and other publications. His research focuses on ethics, technology, and the media, mainly how technology is changing how we communicate. Bugeja says of his writing, "I am a good writer precisely because I also love community, learning about people and their stories, listening to how they speak, and observing how they interact."*

Information technology in the classroom was supposed to bridge   1
digital divides and enhance student research. Increasingly, however,
our networks are being used to entertain members of "the Facebook
Generation" who text-message during class, talk on their cellphones
during labs, and listen to iPods rather than guest speakers in the wireless lecture hall.

That is true at my institution, Iowa State University. With a total   2
enrollment of 25,741, Iowa State logs 20,247 registered users on
Facebook (see http://www.facebook.com), which bills itself as "an
online directory that connects people through social networks at
schools."

While I'd venture to say that most of the students on any campus   3
are regular visitors to Facebook, many professors and administrators
have yet to hear about Facebook, let alone evaluate its impact.

On many levels, Facebook is fascinating—an interactive, image-   4
laden directory featuring groups that share lifestyles or attitudes.
Many students find it addictive, as evidenced by discussion groups
with names like "Addicted to the Facebook," which boasts 330 members at Iowa State. Nationwide, Facebook tallies 250 million hits
every day and ranks ninth in overall traffic on the Internet.

That kind of social networking affects all levels of academe: 5

- Institutions seeking to build enrollment learn that "technology"
  rates higher than "rigor" or "reputation" in high-school focus
  groups. That may pressure provosts to continue investing in technology rather than in tenure-track positions.

- Professors and librarians encounter improper use of technology
  by students, and some of those cases go to judiciary officials who
  enforce the student code.

- Career and academic advisers must deal with employers and parents who have screened Facebook and discovered what users
  have been up to in residence halls.

- Academics assessing learning outcomes often discover that technology is as much a distraction in the classroom as a tool.

To be sure, classroom distractions have plagued teachers in less   6
technological times. In my era, there was the ubiquitous comic book
hidden in a boring text. A comic book cannot compare with a computer, of course. Neither did it require university money at the ex-
pense of faculty jobs.

John W. Curtis, research director at the American Association of   7
University Professors, believes that investment in technology is one of

several factors responsible for the well-documented loss of tenure-track positions in the past decade.

Facebook is not the sole source of those woes. However, it is a   8
Janus-faced symbol of the online habits of students and the traditional objectives of higher education, one of which is to inspire critical thinking in learners rather than multitasking. The situation will only get worse as freshmen enter our institutions weaned on high-school versions of Facebook and equipped with gaming devices, iPods, and other portable technologies.

Michael Tracey, a journalism professor at the University of Col-   9
orado, recounts a class discussion during which he asked how many people had seen the previous night's *NewsHour* on PBS or read that day's *New York Times*. "A couple of hands went up out of about 140 students who were present," he recalls. "One student chirped: 'Ask them how many use Facebook.' I did. Every hand in the room went up. She then said: 'Ask them how many used it today.' I did. Every hand in the room went up. I was amazed."

Christine Rosen, a fellow at the Ethics and Public Policy Center,   10
in Washington, D.C., believes experiences like that are an example of what she calls "egocasting, the thoroughly personalized and extremely narrow pursuit of one's personal taste." Facebook "encourages egocasting even though it claims to further 'social networking' and build communities," she says. Unlike real communities, however, most interactions in online groups do not take place face-to-face. It's no surprise, she says, that "people who use networks like Facebook have a tendency to describe themselves like products."

To test that, I registered on the Iowa State Facebook and noticed   11
that the discussion groups looked a lot like direct mailing lists. Some, in fact, were the same or barely distinguishable from mailing lists compiled in *The Lifestyle Market Analyst*, a reference book that looks at potential audiences for advertisers. For instance, "Baseball Addicts" and "Kick Ass Conservatives" are Facebook groups, while "Baseball Fanatics" and "Iowa Conservatives" are the names of commercial mailing lists. You can find "PC Gamers," "Outdoor Enthusiasts," and advocates for and against gun control on both Facebook and in marketing directories. "It is ironic," Rosen says, "that the technologies we embrace and praise for the degree of control they give us individually also give marketers and advertisers the most direct window into our psyche and buying habits they've ever had."

Online networks like Facebook allow high levels of surveillance,   12
she adds, and not just for marketers. "College administrators are

"College administrators troll profiles for evidence of illegal behavior."

known to troll the profiles on Facebook for evidence of illegal behavior by students," she says. "Students might think they are merely crafting and surfing a vast network of peers, but because their Facebook profile is, in essence, a public diary, there is nothing to stop any one else—from marketers, to parents, to college officials—from reading it."

Her comments bear out. For instance, a panel at the University of   13
Missouri at Columbia has been formed to educate students about Facebook content that may violate student-conduct policies or local laws. A Duquesne University student was asked to write a paper because the Facebook group he created was deemed homophobic. Students at Northern Kentucky University were charged with code violations when a keg was seen in a dorm-room picture online.

My concerns are mostly ethical. In my field, I know of students   14
who showcase inappropriate pictures of partners or use stereotypes to describe themselves and others on Facebook. What does that mean in terms of taste, sensitivity, and bias? I know of disclosures about substance abuse that have come back to haunt students under investigation for related offenses. I know of fictitious Facebook personae that masquerade as administrators, including college presidents.

Facebook forbids such fabrications. According to Chris Hughes,   15
a spokesman, misrepresentation is against the directory's "Terms of Service."

"In other words," he says, "you can't create a profile for Tom   16
Cruise using your account. When users report a profile, we take a look and decide if the content seems authentic. If not, we'll remove the user from the network."

Shortly after interviewing Hughes, I heard from Michael Tracey,   17
the Colorado journalism professor, who learned that an account had been opened in his name on MySpace (see http://www.myspace.com), another networking site, "with photos and all kinds of weird details." He suspects a student from the course he spoke with me about is behind the ruse.

Unless we reassess our high-tech priorities, issues associated with   18
insensitivity, indiscretion, bias, and fabrication will consume us in higher education.

Christine Rosen believes that college administrators "have embraced technology as a means of furthering education, but they have failed to realize that the younger generation views technology largely   19

The younger generation views technology largely as a means of delivering entertainment.

as a means of delivering entertainment—be it music, video games, Internet access, or television—and secondarily, as a means of communicating."

What can we do in the short term about the misuse of technology, especially in wireless locales?   20

The Facebook's spokesman, Hughes, is not overly concerned. He notes that students who use computers in classrooms and labs routinely perform "a host of activities online while listening to lectures," like checking e-mail, sending instant messages, or reading the news.   21

"Usage of Facebook during class," he says, "doesn't strike me as being that different than usage of those other tools."   22

"If professors don't want their students to have access to the Internet during class," Hughes adds, "they can remove wireless installations or ask their students not to bring computers to class."   23

Some less-drastic measures include clauses in syllabi warning against using Facebook or other nonassigned Internet sites during class. Some professors punish students who violate such rules and reward those who visit the library. Others have stopped using technology in the classroom. A few institutions are assessing how to respond to Facebook and similar digital distractions. Last fall the University of New Mexico blocked access to Facebook because of security concerns. My preference is not to block content but to instill in students what I call "interpersonal intelligence," or the ability to discern when and where technology may be appropriate or inappropriate.   24

That, alas, requires critical thinking and suggests that we have reached a point where we must make hard decisions about our investment in technology and our tradition of high standards. Because the students already have.   25

Web **Read It Now:** Read more opinions on academic issues published by *The Chronicle of Higher Education* at **bedfordstmartins.com/americanow**, Chapter 2.

Vocabulary / Using a Dictionary

1. The word *troll* (para. 12) is used in this essay as slang. Where did the term originate, and how does that relate to the meaning as used here?

2. Christine Rosen, who is quoted in this essay, uses the term *ego-casting* (para. 10). What does *ego* mean? What other words use that as a root?

Responding to Words in Context

1. Bugeja points out in paragraph 14 that his concerns about Facebook are "mostly ethical." What does this imply about how he views Facebook?

2. Bugeja uses the word *surveillance* (para. 12) to describe how college administrators and marketers can use Facebook profiles. What are the implications of this word? What other words have the same meaning but imply different things?

Discussing Main Points and Meaning

1. What does the author mean by *social networking* (para. 5)? How does Facebook help or hinder social networking?

2. How does the author raise the points of sensitivity, bias, and stereotypes in the essay? Do they contribute to the topic? Why or why not?

Examining Sentences, Paragraphs, and Organization

1. Why do you think the author chooses to use a bulleted list early in the essay? Does the list help the readability of the essay? Hinder it? Why?

2. Besides Facebook, what other types of technology does the author refer to? Do these references flow naturally? Find an example and explain.

3. Review the essay and locate examples of direct quotations. Why does the author use so many quotations? How do they tie the various topics together?

Thinking Critically

1. What is the author's tone in this piece? What kind of bias, if any, does it show?

2. What is the author specifically critiquing? Is it the students themselves, Facebook, a combination, or something else entirely?

3. Bugeja writes that "unlike real communities, however, most interactions in online groups do not take place face-to-face" (para. 10). What does this say about his view of what constitutes a community? Do you agree with his assessment? Why or why not?

4. How does the author support his arguments and opinions about Facebook and the use of technology on campus? What do these choices tell you about this issue and his stance on it?

In-Class Writing Activities

1. Aside from Facebook, think about what other technologies could be disruptive to the classroom environment. Write a few paragraphs about some of these possible disruptions.

2. The author suggests some ways to deal with what he considers to be the misuse of technology on campus. Can you propose any other ideas?

3. According to Bugeja, technology—like Facebook—can disrupt the classroom. But can you come up with ways in which similar technology has actually helped the classroom environment? Remember to use supporting arguments and evidence.

ANGELA ADAIR FOWLER

The Facebook Addiction Spreads

[THE REFLECTOR, Mississippi State University / January 14, 2005]

Before You Read

Can spending time at a Web site be addictive? What other activities can be thought of as addictive? What, if anything, is positive about spending time at social networking sites?

Words to Learn

pestilence (para. 1): a usually fatal disease; an evil influence (n.)

unremitting (para. 1): persistent (adj.)

virulence (para. 1): the quality of being poisonous or infectious (n.)

epidemic (para. 3): a disease spreading rapidly by infection (n.)

deprivation (para. 3): the absence or loss of something needed (n.)

discourse (para. 4): conversation or exchange on a topic (n.)

encompass (para. 9): to include (v.)

A new pestilence is sweeping across the land with unremitting   1
virulence. You may have thought you were safe from it. You may
have even thought you would be able to control the disease and remain immune from it. No such luck. It has spread to this campus. It
has spread to your homes and offices. It has even spread to your
home computer. The name of the disease: Facebook.

Don't act like you don't know what I'm talking about. Don't act   2
like you haven't already spent hours adding friends and joining random groups, including the group entitled "I'm addicted to Joining
Random Facebook Groups."

ANGELA ADAIR FOWLER, *who was a senior English major when she wrote
this article for her school newspaper,* The Reflector, *is now a graduate student in English at Mississippi State University.*

If you actually haven't encountered this epidemic, whose side ef-   3
fects may cause grade reduction and sleep deprivation, I will explain.
Facebook is possibly the greatest and most entertaining timewaster
disguising itself as a unifying college community since study groups.
Registration is simple; you must have a university e-mail address to
join.

You can then create your profile, much like a typical forum Inter-   4
net site, and start viewing profiles along common interests, joining
groups and adding friends. After that, you can begin to indulge in the
witty and highly intellectual discourse about cartoons and living in a
van down by the river.

You can convince yourself that you're doing something produc-   5
tive and noteworthy, especially when you join or form an organization group, or even meet new people from the many other colleges
hosted on Facebook. But let's face it: Facebook is entertaining and
addictive, pure and simple. Most of the groups center about various
movies, TV shows and hobbies. Even more include what we would
call Mississippi State University (MSU) in-jokes, hooking people with
Waffle House, the wave guy, hatred of online homework, and various fan clubs for random unknown individuals. The anti-University
of Mississippi groups are among the most popular on the site.

You do get more than entertainment from Facebook, though. As   6
I was browsing Facebook last night, presumably doing research for
this article, a certain sense of satisfaction crept up on me. I was seeing
people online that I had noticed throughout campus, some had even
been classmates. I saw how people I knew were connected to other
people, and even other people I knew. I suddenly understood just
how interconnected this university is. Eventually, with possibly three
degrees of separation—much like the famous Kevin Bacon game—
everyone knows everyone.

Not only does everyone know everyone, I began to realize that   7
people were actually talking and finding
common interests outside of their own
group of friends. How often does that really
happen walking across campus? We see
people every day, and we talk to people on
the cell phone between classes, but where
can we find the free discourse of Facebook
anywhere else outside of organizations?
Facebook is a place for unlimited communi-

*Facebook is a place
for unlimited
communication—
where anyone can talk
to anyone without a
barrier.*

cation—where anyone can talk to anyone without barrier. And we can do it all on our own time, without leaving our own comfort zone.

And where can you find a place that you only talk about one   8
common interest. People do not have a sign on their foreheads proclaiming they're interested in '80s movies and skeeball. Neither can you simply ask, "Hey, I was looking for someone who likes Bob Marley and, hey, you look like just the type . . ." That's where Facebook comes in. Not only can you join the Bob Marley group, you can also click the link to Bob Marley in your "interests." The site will perform an instant search through profiles to find all the people who groove to Marley.

And I've only been talking about people from MSU. On this site,   9
we can have similar conversations with college students all over America. Our relatively small MSU community can expand to encompass like-minded "scholars" from far and wide. We can discuss sushi with a guy from Maine!

As with any form of entertainment, especially on the Internet, we   10
must use moderation so we will not end up joining the group "Facebook Made Me Fail My Exams!" We must remember that with a great forum site, comes great responsibility. Your Bush group can wait until after physics homework. Just keep repeating that to yourself, and you may believe it.

For an annotated excerpt of this essay that highlights Fowler's writing strategies, see page 98.

Yes, we're in for a rough semester. And   11
the epidemic may not depart without casualties. But not to worry: Someone will probably create a twelve-step program to break the habit of Facebook . . . with its own Facebook group.

 Read It Now: Read more student editorials at *The Reflector*, the student paper at Mississippi State University, at **bedfordstmartins.com/americanow**, Chapter 2.

Vocabulary / Using a Dictionary

1. What is the root of the word *virulence* (para. 1)? How does this relate to the meaning of the word?

2. What is the definition of *profile* (para. 4)? How is it used in this essay?

3. What does the word *indulge* (para. 4) mean? Why is it used in this essay?

Responding to Words in Context

1. What does it mean to be addicted to something? What other words could the author have used that would have the same meaning?

2. What are *side effects* (para. 3)? Why would the author use this term as she did?

3. What does the author mean by the phrase *free discourse* (para. 7)? Why does she use this as opposed to *conversation* or *discussion*?

Discussing Main Points and Meaning

1. How personal a reaction does the author seem to have to Facebook? How would this essay be different if the writer had taken a more distant tone?

2. Describe the author's reaction after she creates an account and browses Facebook. How does this relate to the idea of addiction?

3. Overall, what is the author's opinion of Facebook? Do you agree with her? Why or why not?

Examining Sentences, Paragraphs, and Organization

1. How does the author move from discussing the addictive nature of Facebook to discussing the benefits of it?

2. Examine the author's use of short paragraphs. How does this choice affect the feel of the essay?

3. Notice the use of the semicolon in paragraph 3. What is the purpose of the semicolon, and why is it used there?

Thinking Critically

1. What are "loaded words"? Locate some in this essay and explain how and why they are used. What do they tell you about the author's perspective? How do they affect your reaction to her perspective?

2. What kind of relationship does the author assume with her readers? How does she convey this in her writing? To what effect?

3. How do you think the author intends the phrase, "witty and highly intellectual discourse about cartoons and living in a van down by the river" (para. 4) to be taken? Why would she use it in this way?

In-Class Writing Activities

1. Can you think of any productive uses for Facebook? How does Facebook contribute to the concept of community?

2. Consider how writers sometimes use sarcasm and irony to convey their messages. Write a paragraph in which you try to convince someone of something while using these tools.

3. The author relies heavily on imagery of disease in her essay. What other metaphors would you apply to the topic of Facebook? Why? What do your choices suggest about your opinion of Facebook?

ANNOTATION Finding Analogies

An effective way to clarify an idea and make it vivid for a reader is through the use of analogy. An analogy is essentially an extended comparison in which we use one thing to explain another. For example, we explain the way the heart works by comparing it to a pump. Analogies are used, especially in science, to make something abstract or complex simpler to visualize and understand. We can also use analogies in our opinion essays to illuminate large issues or observable trends (such as the latest methods of social networking). These analogies can be informal (not fully elaborated as in some scientific analogies) and deliberately exaggerated for emphasis (as when we describe politicians we don't like as "Nazis" or call a set of social programs a "war on poverty"). In "The Facebook Addiction Spreads," Angela Adair Fowler, a Mississippi State University student, opens her essay with an effective analogy: She invites us to consider the popular online program Facebook as if it were a rapidly spreading disease. Note how she carefully selects her vocabulary to support the comparison, choosing words that are typically associated with an epidemic. In doing this, she immediately establishes the contagious aspects of Facebook, which she later develops in her essay, and suggests as well a humorous sense of alarm.

Fowler's word choices reflect her analogy of Facebook as a disease.

A new pestilence is sweeping across the land with unremitting virulence. You may have thought you were safe from it. You may have even thought you would be able to control the disease and remain immune from it. No such luck. It has spread to this campus. It has spread to your homes and offices. It has even spread to your home computer. The name of the disease: Facebook.

—From "The Facebook Addiction Spreads" by Angela Adair Fowler, page 93

Discussing the Unit

Suggested Topic for Discussion

The authors in this chapter discuss Facebook as a social networking tool, an addictive activity, an interference with class time, a new way to post personal ads, and more. How do you view Facebook? As an addictive waste of time? A valuable discussion tool? A good or bad influence in the classroom or school environment? Does it help people make friends, or does it encourage people to form social connections using only their computer screens? Is it any, all, some, or none of these to you?

Preparing for Class Discussion

1. Fowler argues that Facebook and other social networking sites are addictive, but she also points out many productive and genuinely entertaining things that can come out of it. Is her view balanced? Can something be both addictive and productive? Why is Facebook so popular? Why might someone find it addictive? How do these factors relate to the potential usefulness of Facebook and to cultural attitudes surrounding it?

2. Bugeja is concerned about the negative effects of technology in the classroom. Is he overreacting? Could he be ignoring potential positive uses for the same technology he decries, or do you think that his points are legitimate?

From Discussion to Writing

1. Do you think that you could become addicted to something in the ways the essays in this chapter describe? Think about your various activities. Why are some more likely to be considered addictive than others?

2. The essays in this chapter describe how unrestrained and almost exhibitionist many users of Facebook become online. Do you think that they act this way in person? What could cause a person to act so different online as opposed to offline?

Topics for Cross-Cultural Discussion

1. Can a social networking site like Facebook help or hinder cross-cultural discussion and understanding? Does the anonymous nature of an online discussion environment help some users get past their first impressions, or are first impressions not bypassed so easily?

2. Do students in other countries use social networking sites such as Facebook? Do you know of any such sites? How are they like or unlike Facebook? What cultural differences or similarities do you observe?

3

Cultural Identities: Can We Live Dual Lives?

Many people in America today struggle with divided identities. They come from a mixed racial, ethnic, or religious heritage, belong to multiple nationalities, or have lost touch with their roots and backgrounds. When asked *who* they are, *where* they come from, or *what* group they belong to, many Americans have no simple answer. As the well-known Indian American author Jhumpa Lahiri writes in "My Two Lives," she grew up feeling "neither Indian nor American." Unlike friends who came from earlier immigrant groups and called themselves Irish Americans or Italian Americans, her roots were different: Her friends "were several generations removed from the frequently humiliating process of immigration, so that the ethnic roots they claimed had descended underground whereas mine were still tangled and green."

Much of the pressure of a divided identity comes from the belief that an individual is forced to choose one culture over the other. In "'FOBs' vs. 'Twinkies': The New Discrimination Is Intraracial," Grace Hsiang, a freshman at the University of California, Irvine, approaches an issue that may be unfamiliar to many Americans—the contentious ways that Asian Americans discriminate against each other, with FOBs (Fresh Off the Boat) clinging to their ethnic heritage and "Twinkies" ("yellow on the outside, white on the inside") assimilating wholeheartedly to American customs. A similar conflict is depicted in a recent advertising campaign for the American Indian College Fund, as ads like "If I Stay on the Rez" show individual students who prefer to stay on the reservation for their education as a means to preserve Native American language and culture.

"I don't feel at home when I'm told to be more Pakistani, and I certainly don't feel at home when I'm told to be more American," claims a Muslim student from the University of Chicago, Isra Javed Bhatty. In "Reppin' Islam," she considers not only the problems of living a bicultural existence but also the way her identity is additionally complicated by her religion. Continually frustrated by the way Americans—both liberal and conservative—mistake Islam for its specific political or cultural manifestations, she has "turned to Islam as a refuge from the maddening pressure to fit into a cultural category."

JHUMPA LAHIRI

My Two Lives

[NEWSWEEK / MSNBC.COM / March 6, 2006]

Before You Read

How do you define your cultural heritage? Do you think of your heritage as different from "American"? If so, why? How much of your cultural heritage is influenced by your family?

Words to Learn

shuttle (para. 1): to go back and forth frequently (v.)

dal (para. 2): a dried legume (such as lentils or peas); an Indian dish made of spiced legumes (n.)

cusp (para. 4): edge, verge (n.)

ineffectually (para. 4): not producing the proper or intended effect; futile (adv.)

spar (para. 5): to fight (v.)

steadfast (para. 6): constant; firm in belief (adj.)

ascendancy (para. 7): domination (n.)

I have lived in the United States for almost 37 years and anticipate growing old in this country. Therefore, with the exception of my first two years in London, "Indian-American" has been a constant way to describe me. Less constant is my relationship to the term. When I was growing up in Rhode Island in the 1970s I felt neither

1

JHUMPA LAHIRI was born in 1967 in London and raised in Rhode Island. Her first book, Interpreter of Maladies *(1999), a collection of stories, won the 2000 Pulitzer Prize for Fiction, the PEN/Hemingway Award, and the American Academy of Arts & Letters Addison M. Metcalf Award, among other accolades. Lahiri, who has an MA in creative writing, an MA in comparative literature, and a PhD from Boston University, finds writing to be a personal challenge: "I've never written for anyone other than myself," she says. "No matter what people say or expect, at the end of the day, they're not the one in the room with me, writing."*

Indian nor American. Like many immigrant offspring I felt intense pressure to be two things, loyal to the old world and fluent in the new, approved of on either side of the hyphen. Looking back, I see that this was generally the case. But my perception as a young girl was that I fell short at both ends, shuttling between two dimensions that had nothing to do with one another.

> *I felt intense pressure to be two things, loyal to the old world and fluent in the new.*

At home I followed the customs of my parents, speaking Bengali   2
and eating rice and dal with my fingers. These ordinary facts seemed part of a secret, utterly alien way of life, and I took pains to hide them from my American friends. For my parents, home was not our house in Rhode Island but Calcutta, where they were raised. I was aware that the things they lived for—the Nazrul songs they listened to on the reel-to-reel, the family they missed, the clothes my mother wore that were not available in any store in any mall—were at once as precious and as worthless as an outmoded currency.

I also entered a world my parents had little knowledge or control   3
of: school, books, music, television, things that seeped in and became a fundamental aspect of who I am. I spoke English without an accent, comprehending the language in a way my parents still do not. And yet there was evidence that I was not entirely American. In addition to my distinguishing name and looks, I did not attend

> *According to my parents I was not American, nor would I ever be.*

Sunday school, did not know how to ice-skate, and disappeared to India for months at a time. Many of my friends proudly called themselves Irish-American or Italian-American. But they were several generations removed from the frequently humiliating process of immigration, so that the ethnic roots they claimed had descended underground whereas mine were still tangled and green. According to my parents I was not American, nor would I ever be no matter how hard I tried. I felt doomed by their pronouncement, misunderstood and gradually defiant. In spite of the first lessons of arithmetic, one plus one did not equal two but zero, my conflicting selves always canceling each other out.

When I first started writing I was not conscious that my subject   4
was the Indian-American experience. What drew me to my craft was the desire to force the two worlds I occupied to mingle on the page as I was not brave enough, or mature enough, to allow in life. My first

book was published in 1999, and around then, on the cusp of a new century, the term "Indian-American" has become part of this country's vocabulary. I've heard it so often that these days, if asked about my background, I use the term myself, pleasantly surprised that I do not have to explain further. What a difference from my early life, when there was no such way to describe me, when the most I could do was to clumsily and ineffectually explain.

As I approach middle age, one plus one equals two, both in my   5
work and in my daily existence. The traditions on either side of the hyphen dwell in me like siblings, still occasionally sparring, one outshining the other depending on the day. But like siblings they are intimately familiar with one another, forgiving and intertwined. When my husband and I were married five years ago in Calcutta we invited friends who had never been to India, and they came full of enthusiasm for a place I avoided talking about in my childhood, fearful of what people might say. Around non-Indian friends, I no longer feel compelled to hide the fact that I speak another language. I speak Bengali to my children, even though I lack the proficiency to teach them to read or write the language. As a child I sought perfection and so denied myself the claim to any identity. As an adult I accept that a bicultural upbringing is a rich but imperfect thing.

While I am American by virtue of the fact that I was raised in this   6
country, I am Indian thanks to the efforts of two individuals. I feel Indian not because of the time I've spent in India or because of my genetic composition but rather because of my parents' steadfast presence in my life. They live three hours from my home; I speak to them daily and see them about once a month. Everything will change once they die. They will take certain things with them—conversations in another tongue, and perceptions about the difficulties of being foreign. Without them, the back-and-forth life my family leads, both literally and figuratively, will at last approach stillness. An anchor will drop, and a line of connection will be severed.

I have always believed that I lack the authority my parents bring   7
to being Indian. But as long as they live they protect me from feeling like an impostor. Their passing will mark not only the loss of the people who created me but the loss of a singular way of life, a singular struggle. The immigrant's journey, no matter how ultimately rewarding, is founded on departure and deprivation, but it secures for the subsequent generation a sense of arrival and advantage. I can see a day coming when my American side, lacking the counterpoint India has until now maintained, begins to gain ascendancy and weight. It is

in fiction that I will continue to interpret the term "Indian-American," calculating that shifting equation, whatever answers it may yield.

Web **Read It Now:** Read additional *Newsweek* editorials at **bedfordstmartins.com/ americanow**, Chapter 3.

Vocabulary / Using a Dictionary

1. What does *fundamental* (para. 3) mean? How is it related to *fundamentalist*?
2. What does the term *singular* mean in paragraph 7?
3. What does *deprivation* mean in paragraph 7? What are some of its antonyms?
4. How is *subsequent* in paragraph 7 related to *sequential*? To *sequel*?

Responding to Words in Context

1. In paragraph 2, Lahiri states that she felt like her parent's culture was an "alien way of life." What does she mean by *alien*? Why does she feel that her family's way of life is alien?
2. In paragraph 5, Lahiri confesses, "I no longer feel compelled to hide the fact that I speak another language." What does *compelled* mean? How can someone be compelled to hide their language or identity?
3. Why does Lahiri believe that her parents keep her from feeling "like an imposter" (para. 7)? What does it mean to be an imposter? What kind of imposter does she think she is?

Discussing Main Point and Meaning

1. More than once Lahiri speaks about the hyphen as central to her identity. What significance does the hyphen have for her? How does the hyphen represent her experiences?
2. Part of Lahiri's problems with her cultural identity have to do with fitting in and with feeling—or not feeling—like an authority. What does it mean to have a culture? What does it mean to be

an authority on one's culture? In what ways does Lahiri feel that she is not an authority on her culture? How is she an authority?

3. Why did perfection keep Lahiri from claiming her identity? How has her view changed since she has matured and started her own family?

Examining Sentences, Paragraphs, and Organization

1. In paragraph 3, Lahiri uses a metaphor to describe her own feelings of being an immigrant among Irish Americans and Italian Americans: "But they were several generations removed from the frequently humiliating process of immigration, so that the ethnic roots they claimed had descended underground whereas mine were still tangled and green." What does this sentence mean? Do you think it is effective to use a metaphor? Why do you think she chooses this metaphor?

2. While Lahiri struggles with her cultural identity in the first half of her essay and her life, she defines the two sides of identity in the second-to-last paragraph. How does this paragraph define what culture is for Lahiri? What do you think is the purpose of placing this definition of her culture in this paragraph rather than in the first or last paragraph?

3. In paragraph 5, Lahiri picks up a statement from paragraph 3 — "one plus one did not equal two but zero, my conflicting selves always canceling each other out" — and returns to it, stating, "As I approach middle age, one plus one equals two, both in my work and in my daily existence." What are the differences between the two paragraphs that lead to the different mathematical expressions? What happens in the paragraph between that causes the change in Lahiri's perception of her cultural identity?

Thinking Critically

1. Culture is a very tricky concept in our country. Lahiri states that she is American because she was raised in the United States, but she is Indian because of her parents. Is being born in a certain place enough to imbue someone with the culture of that place, or are there more dimensions to culture than just location? What is culture exactly?

2. Lahiri's article on her cultural identity focuses on family. Her traditions on either side of the hyphen dwell in her "like siblings," she attributes her Indianness to her parents, and her comfort with her identity seems to be connected to her wedding and her own nascent family, where she is allowed to define culture differently than her parents did. To what extent do you think family informed Lahiri? How does your family inform you? How does family interact with or compete with outside forces such as school, television, books, and so on?

In-Class Writing Activities

1. Lahiri explores her cultural identity through fiction writing. Her first book, *Interpreter of Maladies,* which won a Pulitzer Prize, is a collection of short stories about Indian Americans dealing with various cultural forces such as tradition, love, and family. Describe your own cultural identity. What traditions, rules, and forces create that identity? How do you rebel against them? Write a short story or an autobiographical piece in which a person who shares your cultural history deals with all these forces.

2. Culture does not always have to do with where one was born or raised. It can have to do with how your family acts and how its traditions and beliefs inform you; it can have to do with the traditions of your friends and others in your community. Write your own cultural biography in which you discuss the influencing factors on your life that have made you who you are.

3. We tell different stories about ourselves based on who our audience is. When Lahiri communicated with her friends, she left out pertinent information about her Indian heritage. When she was communicating with her parents, she most likely left out information about her schooling and about her classmates. Write a short essay in which you describe yourself to your close friends. Then, rewrite the essay as if you were applying for school or a job. What is different about the language? How does it reflect the boundaries of the group you are attempting to fit in with? Did you leave out certain information about yourself to fit in with one group or another? Why or why not?

GRACE HSIANG

"FOBs" vs. "Twinkies": The New Discrimination Is Intraracial

[PACIFIC NEWS SERVICE, University of California, Irvine / April 15, 2005]

Before You Read

Do you identify yourself as belonging to a particular community? Do you think there are different groups within that community? How do they treat each other? Is there mutual respect, or is there mutual discrimination?

Words to Learn

harassment (para. 1): unwelcome verbal or physical conduct (n.)

marginalize (para. 1): to relegate to a marginal or unimportant position in a group (v.)

slurs (para. 2): insulting remarks (n.)

Today in my sociology class, the teacher asked the students to   1
volunteer our own experiences with racism or ethnic harassment. I imagined the responses would once again feature the ongoing battle between white vs. minority. Instead, to my surprise, most of the

---

GRACE HSIANG *attends the University of California, Irvine, as a double major in international studies and literary journalism. She writes that her essay "is a look at how racism and discrimination operates within a community. We are too often examining the scrutiny of those who are different from us and criticizing the 'other' for the continuation of discrimination. However, discrimination often exists within ourselves and until we fix the problems within, we cannot begin to attack those outside."*

students told of being discriminated against and marginalized by members of their own ethnic group.

In the Asian community, the slurs heard most often are not terms such as "Chink" or "Jap," but rather "FOB" ("Fresh Off the Boat") or "white-washed" (too assimilated). When Asian Americans hit puberty, they seem to divide into two camps, each highly critical of the other. Members of the first cling to their ethnic heritage. They tend to be exclusive in their friendships, often accepting only "true Asians." They believe relationships should remain within the community, and may even opt to speak their parents' native language over English in public.

> To my surprise, most students told of being discriminated against by members of their own ethnic group.

Members of the second group reject as many aspects of Asian culture as possible and concentrate on being seen as American. They go out of their way to refuse to date within the community, embrace friends outside their ethnic circle, and even boast to others about how un-Asian they are. "My coworker is Vietnamese," 19-year-old Carol Lieu remarked, "but she will yell at you if you speak it to her and pretend that she doesn't understand."

Second-generation Asian Americans often face pressure from their parents, who believe that the privileges we are allowed in this country make us spoiled and ungrateful. Many of us very much want to belong to our parents' community, but we cannot completely embody one culture when we are living in another. The pressures we face force many of us to feel we must choose one culture over another. We can either cling to our parents' ideology, or rebel against it and try to be "American."

The problems start when those who have made one choice discriminate against those who have made the other. I've heard ethnocentric Asians speak with disgust about Asians who wear Abercrombie and Fitch (which is viewed as the ultimate "white" brand), or make fun of those who don't know their parents' language. "People act disappointed that I can't speak Japanese fluently," a student of Mexican and Japanese ancestry in my sociology class complained this morning. "I don't see anyone giving me credit for speaking fluent Gaelic." This ethnocentric perspective even made it into the recent hit movie *Harold and Kumar Go to White Castle*. John Cho's character complains about a girl who is pursuing him despite his lack of interest: She "rambles on about her East Asian Students Club or whatever. Then I have to actually pretend that I give a s - - t or she calls me a Twinkie . . . yellow on the outside, white on the inside."

On the other side, second-generation kids who refuse to assimi-   6
late are called FOBs. The cars they drive are derided as "Rice Rock-
ets," and their pastimes and ways of dressing are stereotyped as ex-
clusively Asian. "We live in America," one freshman political science
major recalls more assimilated friends telling her. "Don't bring your
culture here."

Not all young Asian Americans buy into the dichotomy between   7
"FOBs" and "Twinkies." Many, like me, understand the term "Asian
American" in all its complexity, and embrace all sides of our identity.
Rather than identifying with one culture or another, my friends and I
accept both. You should identify with your heritage "because that's
who you are," Ricky Kim, founder of the online journal *Evil Monito*,
has said. "But don't be ignorant of the culture you grew up in—
that's being ungrateful."

Asian Americans grow up experiencing enough difficulties living   8
_____ in a predominately white country with the
For an annotated excerpt of   face of a foreigner. The gap between races is
this essay that highlights   wide enough without drawing lines within
Hsiang's writing strategies,   ethnicities and communities. We can avoid
see page 115.   this internal discrimination simply by recog-
_____   nizing that we are of two cultures—and that
in itself creates a new culture that should be fully celebrated.

 Read It Now: Read more editorials and news articles at the *Pacific News Service* and *New American Media* site at **bedfordstmartins.com/americanow**,
Chapter 3.

Vocabulary/Using a Dictionary

1. The subtitle of this article is "The New Discrimination is Intraracial." What does *intraracial* mean?
2. How is being *marginalized* different from *harassment* (para. 1)?
3. What does the term *ideology* mean (para. 4)? How it is related to
   an *ideologue*?

Responding to Words in Context

1. Hsiang uses the word *community* quite often in her essay. What
   does *community* mean literally according to the dictionary? How

does Hsiang use it throughout her essay? What does this tell you about how Hsiang defines *community*?

2. What does it mean to embody one culture while living in another (para. 6)? How does one embody a culture? How do we often force people to embody a culture?

3. In paragraph 5, Hsiang looks at the problem of discrimination and states that it happens when one group perceives another group as choosing a particular ethnic identity. In this case, discrimination happens between those who want to be "true" Asian Americans and those who choose to be "white." What does it mean to be "true"? What does it mean to be "white"? Why is Abercrombie and Fitch a "white brand"?

Discussing Main Point and Meaning

1. Hsiang refers to racial slurs throughout her article. In fact, her article is titled " 'FOBs' vs. 'Twinkies.' " What do racial slurs mean when one racial or ethnic group uses them against another?

2. More than once Hsiang uses the term *ungrateful*. She describes Asian American parents who believe that their children are "spoiled and ungrateful" (para. 4) because they do not fully embrace their parents' culture. And Ricky Kim is quoted in the article as saying, "But don't be ignorant of the culture you grew up in—that's being ungrateful" (para. 7). What does it mean to be ungrateful? Why do you think that is a particular argument for and against assimilation in the Asian American community, as described by Hsiang?

3. Hsiang's article focuses on a dichotomy, or a division into two opposed things or ideas. In this case, the dichotomy is between FOBs and Twinkies, or "true" (unassimilated) Asians and "white" (assimilated) Asians. Dichotomies, however, may embody the logical fallacy of either-or. An example of this logical fallacy is "you are either with us or against us," which ignores a third option, that of negotiation or compromise. How does Hsiang show the complexity of culture? Does she fall into the same trap of defining culture through a dichotomy?

Examining Sentences, Paragraphs, and Organization

1. In what ways does Hsiang's opening paragraph introduce her central issue? What is that issue—can you state it in other terms?

Why is Hsiang surprised by the class's response? How does her surprise clarify her central issue? How does it help the reader to accept the issue as one that is worth paying attention to? In other words, how does it make it harder for a reader to say, "So what?"

2. In paragraph 4, Hsiang begins to get to the heart of intraracial marginalization. She writes, "The pressures we face force many of us to feel we must choose one culture over another" and then begins to look at the choices offered to Asian Americans. Can someone choose his or her culture?

3. While Hsiang talks about dichotomies within her community, her essay has a tendency to emphasize those dichotomies by using one paragraph to describe one group and another paragraph to describe the other group. She goes back and forth between the two groups in her writing. Why do you think she organizes her essay in this way? How does it reflect on the author's ethos — her credibility to discuss this particular issue?

Thinking Critically

1. In paragraph 2, Hsiang discusses the rift that happens in the Asian American community. She describes it as happening around puberty, with some members becoming insular in their approach, while others opt to assimilate. Why do you think people, especially teenagers, have a tendency to choose groups to belong to? Have you ever witnessed this happening in your community, family, or school?

2. Hate crimes are defined as violence or hostility perpetrated against a person because of his or her race, gender, religion, sexual orientation, ethnicity, or disability. In short, it is when a person commits an act against another person because of perceived differences. Based on what you have read in Hsiang's essay, can a crime or discrimination against a person by another person who belongs to the same group be considered a hate crime? Explain your answer.

3. How do you define culture? Is it possible for members of a community to have multiple cultures?

In-Class Writing Activities

1. Hsiang identifies the problem of discrimination as beginning around puberty, and some of the traits that she describes have to

do with age—for example, shopping at Abercrombie and Fitch. Write an essay in which you describe and detail teenage culture as opposed to adult culture. What traits are shared among teenagers? What is expected of a normal teenager? What teenagers are seen as different? Describe any discrimination that happens within the group.

2. Hsiang mentions that the movie *Harold and Kumar Go to White Castle* exposes issues of conforming to one's culture or one's perceived cultural group by one's peers. In a short essay, write about a movie that you have seen that also exposes intraracial discrimination. Describe the movie and analyze how it shows this discrimination. Does it offer any solutions? Does it shed new light on the issue of intraracial discrimination?

ANNOTATION Developing Ideas through Comparison

One of the most common ways to develop an essay's central idea is by setting up two contrasting positions. A historian, for example, examines the battle of Gettysburg by contrasting the different military strategies of Union versus Confederate generals. Or a sportswriter contrasts the different tennis tactics of Venus Williams versus her sister Serena. Depending on the writer's goal, such contrasts can be briefly stated or comprise practically the entire body of the essay. Observe how **Grace Hsiang** of the University of California, Irvine, constructs the bulk of **"'FOBs' vs. 'Twinkies': The New Discrimination Is Intraracial"** around two opposing views as she explains and develops the main point of her essay: that discrimination can take place between members of the same minority group. In this case, she looks at second-generation Asian Americans and finds two contrasting camps that she clearly identifies: those who cling to their ethnic heritage and those who want to fully assimilate into American culture. Note that these two contrasting positions help her establish the body of her argument.

Hsiang compares two groups to support her argument on intrarracial discrimination.

    In the Asian community, the slurs heard most often are not terms such as "Chink" or "Jap," but rather "FOB" ("Fresh Off the Boat") or "white-washed" (too assimilated). When Asian Americans hit puberty, they seem to divide into two camps, each highly critical of the other. Members of the first cling to their ethnic heritage. They tend to be exclusive in their friendships, often accepting only "true Asians." They believe relationships should remain within the community, and may even opt to speak their parents' native language over English in public.

    Members of the second group reject as many aspects of Asian culture as possible and concentrate on being seen as American. They go out of their way to refuse to date within the community, embrace friends outside their ethnic circle, and even boast to others about how un-Asian they are. "My coworker is Vietnamese," 19-year-old Carol Lieu remarked, "but she will yell at you if you speak it to her and pretend that she doesn't understand."

    —From "'FOBs' vs 'Twinkies': The New Discrimination Is Intraracial," by Grace Hsiang, page 109

AMERICAN INDIAN COLLEGE FUND

If I Stay on the Rez

[THE NEW YORK TIMES MAGAZINE / June 25, 2006]

Before You View

How do we recognize people of different racial and ethnic identities? How does dress affect what we may think of someone?

The AMERICAN INDIAN COLLEGE FUND, *founded in 1989, is a Denver-based nonprofit organization that distributes scholarships to Native American students and supports tribal colleges across the country. Richard Williams, the organization's executive director, describes the "If I Stay on the Rez" advertising campaign: "[The ads] have all been so striking and have really shattered people's misconceptions about Indian people . . . I think that's why they are so memorable." (For more information, visit the group's Web site at www.collegefund.org.)*

Discussing Main Point and Meaning

1. One of the goals of the American Indian College Fund (AICF), the group who sponsors the ad, is to help American Indian students stay on or near their reservations. What does it mean to belong to a place or a group? What is home? How is home a cultural institution?

Home | Shop Our Store | Contact Us

ABOUT US   SCHOLARSHIPS & STUDENTS   TRIBAL COLLEGES   YOUR SUPPORT   NEWSROOM

AMERICAN
INDIAN
COLLEGE
FUND

ABOUT US

Donate NOW

Tell A Friend

Newsletter

Overview
History & Mission
President's Message
Board of Trustees
Our Supporters
Did You Know?
Inside the Fund

History & Mission

In the wake of the civil rights and American Indian self-determination movements of the 1960s, tribal leaders realized they would have to take control of the direction of education in order to reverse centuries of misguided and failed federal education policies.

Salish Kootenai College in Pablo, MT

In 1968, the Navajo Nation created a first-of-its-kind educational institution - a college controlled by the tribe, located on the reservation and established specifically to provide higher education to tribal members. With that monumental event, the tribal college movement was born. Since then, the number of tribal colleges and universities has grown to 32, located in 11 states and serving more than 250 American Indian Nations from every geographic region in the United States.

Tribal colleges are beacons of hope for social and economic change in the communities they serve. These institutions are vital to Native America and beneficial to the country as a whole because they help Native communities in the fight against poverty. At the same time, tribal colleges preserve language and culture by integrating these important elements into their curriculum.

When the American Indian College Fund was launched, providing scholarship support to the tribal colleges was its primary mission.

Tribal colleges receive little or no local or state tax support, so corporate, foundation and private donations are crucial. As the success of the tribal colleges grows, so does the need for private-sector support.

Tribal college presidents recognized the need to establish an organization to raise private-sector funds for the colleges and to compliment the efforts of its sister organization, the American Indian Higher Education Consortium. As a result, the American Indian College Fund was established in 1989. Originally located in New York City, the Fund's consolidated its headquarters to one Denver, Colorado office in 2002.

The American Indian College Fund's Mission

The American Indian College Fund's mission is to raise scholarship funds for American Indian students at qualified tribal colleges and universities and to generate broad awareness of those institutions and the Fund itself. The organization also raises money and resources for other needs at the schools, including capital projects, operations, endowments or program initiatives, and it will conduct fundraising and related activities for Board-directed initiatives.

Today, the Fund also supports cultural preservation projects, capital construction and other programs at the tribal colleges.

TCUs (tribal colleges and universities) serve large proportions of older students, women, those with dependent family members, first-generation college students, and many others who previously had little access to post-secondary education in their communities.

Institute for Higher Education Policy research findings

2. A *poster child* is a person who is seen as being representative of a particular group. The AICF ad is meant to appeal to a particular group of people—American Indians—without alienating them or being derogatory. How is Ricky Desjarlais, the Indian shown in the AICF ad, a poster child for American Indian college students? How is he a poster child for American students?

3. The AICF ad supports Indian identity and development and stresses the importance of learning in one's native language. How are language and culture related?

Examining Details, Imagery, and Design

1. Though printed here in black and white, the original colors of this advertisement are very vivid; Desjarlais is dressed in a bright red shirt and dark jeans, and wears a large belt buckle, while the background is blurred and has muted tones. What is the effect of having a crisp foreground image and a blurred background image? Why do you think the background is blurred?

2. The advertisement uses two different typefaces. How are they different? What textual information do they convey? What are the different connotations of the two typefaces?

3. What is the focal point or the first thing you notice in this advertisement? What did you initially think it was trying to sell or argue? What are its underlying aims?

Thinking Critically

1. As a student, what do you think is most important when looking for a college? Do you belong to any cultural groups? Do you think maintaining your cultural identity and heritage is an important part of your college education?

2. Historically, education has been used to assimilate American Indians into white industrialized society. From 1879 to 1918, the Carlisle Indian Industrial School in Carlisle, Pennsylvania, took American Indian children from their reservations and taught them industrial skills while also working to assimilate them by cutting their hair, which was taboo to many tribes, teaching them in English, forbidding their native language, and changing their names. In what ways is the "If I Stay on the Rez" advertising

campaign having a conversation with this particular type of history? How can education be used to change or preserve culture?

3. What do you think are the benefits of maintaining a separate cultural identity? Are there any drawbacks? If one group or culture decides to separate itself from other groups or cultures to preserve its heritage, is that considered simply a strategy for cultural survival? Or is it discrimination?

In-Class Writing Activities

1. This advertisement is meant to persuade students to choose a particular college based on their unique identity. In a short essay, explain why, beyond the academic programs available, you chose the college you now attend. What about the community attracted you? How does your particular school support your identity? Has it caused you to change your identity in any way to fit in or conform?

2. How would you "sell" your school to prospective students? Sketch out or describe an advertisement you would create to convince students to come to your school. Picture your audience—who are its members? What will appeal most to them? What would you emphasize in the advertising copy? What visuals would you include, and why?

3. Language is an important part of the American education system. High school and college graduates are required to learn at least one language. In a short essay, describe your language experience. Did your study of language help you to understand a new culture? How did you feel having to communicate in a language in which you were not fluent?

ISRA JAVED BHATTY

Reppin' Islam

[DISKORD / CAMPUS PROGRESS, University of Chicago / May 2005]

Before You Read

Does the way you dress affect how people see you? What do your clothes say about who you are?

Words to Learn

prevailing (para. 1): continuing to be fashionable or common (adj.)

hijaab (para. 1): the practice of dressing modestly; a head covering worn by Islamic women (n.)

inherent (para. 2): essential; belonging by nature or habit (adj.)

misconstrued (para. 3): judged wrongly; misinterpreted (adj.)

conflate (para. 3): to combine two things as one (v.)

agitation (para. 4): violent excitement (n.)

monolithic (para. 4): from a single piece; a huge, rigid, and undifferentiated whole (adj.)

Venn diagram (para. 4): a graph that uses circles to show overlapping and different traits (n.)

manifestations (para. 5): public showings or demonstrations (n.)

mandates (para. 5): orders; authoritative commands (n.)

I suppose I look a bit threatening to the conservative eye, which more often than not considers the uncommon as a threat to the pre-

ISRA JAVED BHATTY *is a recent graduate of the University of Chicago with degrees in economics and Near Eastern languages and civilizations. She wrote "Reppin' Islam" after a fellow attendee at a women's history conference asked her to write about her response to misconceptions about Islam. For Bhatty, this was "a great way to combat ignorance concerning the treatment of women in Islam." She writes, "I wanted to offer a voice—my voice—to the often objectified and pitied notion of the Muslim woman. The contemporary popular press has largely crafted the identity of Muslims; I have always shaped my own identity, and I sought to do the same thing with this article."* For a "Student Writer at Work" interview with Bhatty, see page 127.

vailing social order. In my oversize football jerseys, eight-year-old cargo pants, and tie-dyed hijaab, I look pretty original—like a misplaced Pakistani girl whose ordinarily white shawl got lost somewhere in the sixties, whose body got stuck in the wardrobe of an impressionable white suburban teen, and whose identity is neither Pakistani nor American, but, instead, a mix of black, white, and brown. I am just some as-of-yet unidentified type of Muslim. But a Muslim, and a rather obvious one, nonetheless.

My parents immigrated to America in 1983, the year of my birth.   2
Although I wasn't born here, this is the only country I've called my home. That is not to say that I've always felt at home here, though, because I haven't. I don't feel at home when I'm told to be more Pakistani, and I certainly don't feel at home when I'm told to be more American. I remember the kids who decided to call my house the day after 9/11 to cuss out my mother and tell us to go back "home." I suppose they were implying that we're not American enough for their nation. Perhaps they thought, as many do, that there is an inherent conflict in being both Muslim and American. I haven't yet found one. I don't really know how to prove "Americanness." But I think a lot of Muslims tried to prove just that during the post-9/11 "backlash" by plastering American flags all over their property. My dad made sure to stick a flag in our yard, one on each door, and two on the car. Just in case.

In my opinion, trying to prove a cultural identity is nearly impos-   3
sible, especially to people who already think that they know what a Muslim is supposed to look like, or dress like, or talk like. I have never tried to prove that I am American. I just assume that my American social surroundings have been responsible for forming parts of me, the parts that are seen as foreign or "Amrikan" to my fellow immigrants such as my taste for hip-hop and oversize jerseys. That's not very Pakistani, and to some, it's not very Muslim either. But as I see it, anyone who believes as such fails to realize that it is impossible to be raised as an un-American, or non-American, in America. I am annoyed when cultural behaviors are confused with an already misconstrued and misunderstood religion, and I've made some feeble attempts on various occasions to clarify the tenuous connection. By now, I'm accustomed to conservatives making statements that constantly conflate religion and culture. I've almost given up trying to argue with them; it is an exercise in frustration. As I've said, the uncommon is threatening.

The uncommon is threatening.

Well-meaning liberals are the ones that really get to me, however,   4
probably because I've set my expectations too high for them. At a
women's history conference a month ago, a speaker referred to
Islam's oppression of women. My initial reaction was one of embar-
rassment, but that quickly turned into agitation, and I made it a point
to announce publicly the fact that she was confusing cultural and political representations of "Islam" for the religion itself. I think I also
gave a word of caution about treating religion as a monolithic force,
but I limited myself. I know I could've gone on ranting, maybe making allusions to the likes of Samuel Huntington and Edward Said and
Lévi-Strauss[1] so that my educated audience wouldn't think I was
some oppressed little Muslim village girl talking out of the side of her
neck. At the time, I wish I had had a Venn diagram with me to make
it easier for them to distinguish what is the religion of Islam and what
is the cultural or political influences of a particular region. The oh-so-
oppressive face-veil: not religion. A lack of women's rights: not religion. Economic stagnation: not religion. Political corruption: not
religion. Terrorism: not religion. Sigh.

Of course, there are certain manifestations of "Islam" that are   5
genuinely religious. My tie-dyed hijaab is religious. I have had many
a liberal try to convince me of the oppressiveness of my hijaab. The
way I see it, wearing the hijaab is liberating.

> *I want people to look at me and see a woman who doesn't conform.*

I want people to look at me and see a
woman who doesn't conform to popular
culture, who'd much rather be judged on her
voice and her mind than on her body, and
who prefers an outward expression of the
religious legacy and commitment to justice that she holds at the
center of her life. Many of those who assert the hijaab-is-oppressive
argument fail to recognize that Islamic guidelines for dress are not
just for women, and often confuse cultural or political "limitations"
experienced by Muslim women living under certain regimes' Islamic
mandates. In the end, I place dress as secondary to more important

---

[1]*Samuel P. Huntington* (b. 1927): professor of political science at Harvard and author
of such controversial studies as *The Clash of Civilizations* (1993) and *Who Are We:
The Challenges to America's National Identity* (2004). *Edward Said* (1935–2003):
well-known American-Palestinian literary theorist, outspoken professor at Columbia
University, and pro-Palestinian activist. *Claude Lévi-Strauss* (b. 1908): celebrated
French anthropologist whose 1962 study *The Savage Mind* helped initiate the struc-
turalist movement.

manifestations of the freedom of expression. And hijaab has never held me back from pursuing goals that I feel are truly important.

Then there's that issue of gender segregation in the mosque, also religious. I'll be blunt: When I'm praying, I really don't want to be distracted, and frankly, men can be distracting. Of course, it's important to recognize that general prayer is not limited to a mosque setting, or even confined to a specific format. In that sense, gender segregation in prayer is not as pervasive as many assert. Furthermore, selecting a very limited illustration of a religion and then asserting that this one is representative of the whole is also playing into the cultural/religious stereotyping. Just like hijaabs differ across cultures and regions, so do the specific languages and manners of prayer. And respecting differences, cultural and otherwise, is a foremost tenet of Islam. My own cultural mutt-ness has been with me for many years now. In a way, I've turned to Islam as a refuge from the maddening pressure to fit into a cultural category. I'm satisfied with my singular identity as a Muslim, and I don't care to submit to any culture. Regardless of whose name I rep on the back of my sports jersey, or the brand etched into the pocket of my pants, I guess my tie-dyed hijaab says it best: I only really rep Islam.

Web **Read It Now:** Read more student opinion published by the University of Chicago's journal, *Diskord,* and by *Campus Progress,* a national network of progressive campus publications, at **bedfordstmartins.com/americanow,** Chapter 3.

Vocabulary / Using a Dictionary

1. What is a *social order* (para. 1)?
2. What does *tenuous* (para. 3) mean? What are its roots?
3. How are *allusion* (para. 4*)* and *illusion* different?
4. How are *refuge* (para. 6) and *refugee* related?

Responding to Words in Context

1. What does *conservative* (para. 1) mean? How does Bhatty use the term in her essay? How is it used politically? What are its antonyms?

2. Bhatty states in paragraph 1 that her identity is "neither Pakistani nor American, but, instead, a mix of black, white, and brown." What do the terms *black*, *white*, and *brown* mean? Does this series of colors remind you of any others? What is the total effect of the sentence in defining who Bhatty is?

3. In paragraph 4, Bhatty warns against "treating religion as a monolithic force." What does she mean by *monolithic force*? Why does she give this warning?

4. What does Bhatty mean when she writes "I only really rep Islam" (para. 6)?

Discussing Main Point and Meaning

1. According to Bhatty, what is Islam about? How does this differ from the stereotypes she describes in her essay?

2. Bhatty is annoyed with people who, she says, "conflate religion and culture" (para. 3). What is the difference between the two? How are they similar? How do conservatives conflate religion and culture? How do the liberals that Bhatty encounters at her conference?

3. Bhatty sees herself as subversive. In her first paragraph, she describes herself as a nonconformist in her clothes and her tie-dyed hijaab. How are the individual elements of her clothing considered subversive to the various cultures? How are they subversive when worn collectively?

Examining Sentences, Paragraphs, and Organization

1. The final sentence of Bhatty's essay, which her title refers to, is "Regardless of whose name I rep on the back of my sports jersey, or the brand etched into the pocket of my pants, I guess my tie-dyed hijaab says it best: I only really rep Islam." How does this sentence encapsulate Bhatty's multiplicity of identity?

2. In paragraph 4, Bhatty describes her annoyance at a women's history conference. She wants to make particular points to convince her audience that religion and politics are different, but she is very much aware of her own credibility with her audience. How does she attempt to strengthen this for the conference

speaker? How does she strengthen it for an audience of college students throughout the essay?

3. Bhatty's essay is organized in a very particular way. How does she make the transition from her own appearance to current events? How does she use these paragraphs to define herself in light of all the various influences in her life?

Thinking Critically

1. Bhatty writes about Americanness, especially in a post-9/11 world. After 9/11, she tells us, many Muslims attempted to be seen as more American by putting up American flags. How do you assert your American identity? What does it mean to be an American? Has our definition of *American* changed since 9/11?

2. How can the uncommon be threatening (para. 3)? Who defines what is common and what is uncommon? Who is likely to be threatened by the uncommon?

3. Bhatty states that she wears the hijaab not because she is oppressed but because she finds it liberating. How can wearing a piece of clothing or a tradition that is associated with a culture or religion be liberating? When is it not liberating? How does Bhatty define the difference in her essay?

In-Class Writing Activities

1. Bhatty describes how she had to defend her culture against a group of people who made particular assumptions about it. Pretend that you have to go to a conference and defend your culture. First, list all the assumptions the audience might make about your culture. Then, try to combat those assumptions and define who or what you believe you are.

2. In her essay, Bhatty looks at all the various factors that create who she is. In a short essay, describe yourself, how you identify yourself, and the influencing factors in your life that have made you the unique individual that you are.

3. Bhatty's essay is especially relevant given the discrimination that has taken place in the wake of 9/11 against people who look or dress outside of the mainstream. Part of the problem is that Americanness is difficult to define. In your words, and using

specific evidence and examples from Bhatty's essay and from your own experiences, define what it means to be American. Is this a good thing or a bad thing, given that Americans are not viewed favorably in many other countries? What has influenced your understanding of Americanness?

Student Writer at Work: Isra Javed Bhatty
On Writing "Reppin' Islam"

Q: Why did you write "Reppin' Islam"?

A: I had gone to a women's history conference the month before the article was published. After hearing a speaker refer to Islam's alleged oppression of women, I cautioned the audience against confusing culture with religion. A fellow attendee was an editor for *Diskord* magazine and asked me to write an article about my response, as an American Muslim, to today's common misconceptions about Islam.

Q: Were you writing for a primarily student audience?

A: *Diskord* caters to a progressive audience. However, my audience was the mainstream American public. Misconceptions about Islam are not confined to any one political or ideological group; they pervade many segments of American society.

Q: What feedback have you received on the piece?

A: I have received overwhelmingly positive feedback and was pleasantly surprised to have the article picked up by other publications. The response has given me more confidence in being myself and speaking out for truth.

Q: Have you read or seen other work on women and Islam that has sparked your interest?

A: Islam, for better or for worse, has captured nationwide attention and I have seen a handful of articles in newspapers showcasing various members of the American Muslim community. For example, the *Chicago Tribune* profiled the executive director of the Inner-city Muslim Action Network, a group I work with focused on improving the conditions of urban life in America. (See "Muslim Confronts Needs of City," *Chicago Tribune*, May 3, 2006.)

Q: What advice would you give to an aspiring student writer?

A: Don't be over-concerned with the perceptions of your audience. Always remain true to yourself in your writing.

Discussing the Unit

Suggested Topic for Discussion

Despite the varied cultural identities of the writers in this chapter, each of them communicates in English. Language is a very powerful tool and cultural identifier. Lahiri uses written language to discover her own identity and speaks to her children in Bengali. Hsiang shows us how language becomes a test of how Asian or American a person is. In the AICF advertisement, language is the reason to stay on the reservation. How is language used to define a culture? Based on your education, which requires a foreign language, how would you describe American language? What kind of language do you use when you are with your friends? Is it different from the language you use when you are in school or at home with your parents? How do we use language to show we belong to a particular group?

Preparing for Class Discussion

1. Naming is important to an individual's identity. While we may not be able to choose how we look or what family we come from, sometimes even feeling like an imposter in our family as Lahiri did, we can choose what cultural traditions we keep as well as how we name ourselves. How do the various writers in this chapter name themselves? What do they consider to be identifying features or characteristics that help define who they are?

2. Each of the writers struggles not just with a cultural heritage but with being American. What does it mean to be American? This issue is especially important given the post-9/11 world in which we live and in which immigration reform is an important political theme. America has long been characterized as a cultural "melting pot"—that is, each group that comes to the United States is melted into an American. Do the writers reflect this melting-pot characterization, or do they resist it?

From Discussion to Writing

1. Given the importance of language, do you believe that there should be a national language for the United States? If so, what should it be? Write a persuasive essay in which you argue for

your position, paying attention to exigence and ethos, as well as evidence you use to support your claim.

2. What communities are you a part of? Which are most important to you and why? How do you identify yourself within each? How does this change, depending on what group you are interacting with? What author in this chapter do you most identify with and why?

Topics for Cross-Cultural Discussion

1. As the readings in this chapter convey, culture is defined in many ways by the expression of individuals—whether that expression comes in the form of wearing a tie-dyed hijaab to represent a peaceful religion or practicing other traditions. What cultural traditions do you, your family, and your extended community practice? Do they revolve around holidays, food, dress, ceremonies (such as weddings, births, and deaths)? How have you incorporated or refused to incorporate them into who you are?

2. In Hsiang's essay, some Asian American students accuse others of being white. Because the majority of Americans belong to this racial category, it is often seen as representative of *American*. But is "white" a culture? Explain your answer.

4

Can Genetics Explain
Who We Are?

Did human life originate in Africa? That theory was proposed decades ago by numerous archeologists and anthropologists who had based their conclusions on the scientific dating of bones and artifacts. But recently the theory has been proven even more scientifically persuasive as a result of current research into DNA. Using evidence from the human genetic code, scientists have been able to identify different races and calculate their migrations to various parts of the earth. In "The Greatest Journey," the *National Geographic* reporter James Shreeve tells the story—now "hidden in our genes"—of our original ancestors' journey out of Africa, a tale that begins with one woman: "Scientists now calculate," Shreeve reports, "that all living humans are related to a single woman who lived roughly 150,000 years ago in Africa."

Yet our ancestral story is also the story of each of us alive today. After watching as a young man the enormously popular TV series *Roots* in 1977, the prominent African American writer and scholar Henry Louis Gates Jr. experienced a *Roots* envy that has lasted to the present day. He recently decided to team up with a group of geneticists and genealogists to trace his roots (and those of a few other distinguished African Americans) once and for all. "The stories that we found," Gates claims in "My Yiddishe Mama," "are not the sort found in textbooks.... We were able to find stirring stories of heretofore anonymous individuals who made heroic contributions against seemingly insurmountable odds."

130

When two Pennsylvania State University professors launched a project to test the DNA of college students to determine their genetic makeups, they discovered, as Penn State student Megan Rundle reports, how racially "mixed" many students truly are. In "Unearthing Family Roots," she cites some surprising results and depicts a range of student responses from excitement to disappointment. Reporting on the same genetic tests, the *New York Times* in an editorial summarized the results and applauded the aims of the project: "to shake students out of rigid and received notions about the biological basis of identity."

JAMES SHREEVE

The Greatest Journey

[NATIONAL GEOGRAPHIC / March 2006]

Before You Read

What significance does the phrase *human family* hold for you? Despite the complex differences among individuals, what common bonds connect us all?

Words to Learn

mutations (para. 7): random changes in chromosomes or genes resulting in new traits or characteristics that can be inherited (n.)

chromosome (para. 7): a rod-shaped structure within a cell nucleus carrying the genes that determine sex and inherited characteristics (n.)

JAMES SHREEVE*'s science writing has appeared in such publications as the* Atlantic Monthly, Discover, National Geographic, Science, *and* Smithsonian. *He is the author of* The Genome War: How Craig Venter Tried to Capture the Code of Life and Save the World *(2004) and* The Neandertal Enigma: Solving the Mystery of Modern Human Origin *(1995) and coauthor of* Lucy's Child: The Discovery of a Human Ancestor *(1989).*

analogous (para. 9): similar in some respects, so that an analogy might be drawn (adj.)

repertoire (para. 10): the range of techniques, abilities, or skills that someone possesses (n.)

imperceptible (para. 15): something so slight that it can barely be perceived (adj.)

millennia (para. 16): periods of one thousand years, especially periods that begin or end in a year that is a multiple of 1000 (n.)

indigenous (para. 17): originating in and typical of a region or country (adj.)

parvenu (para. 19): someone who has recently become wealthy or risen to a high position (n.)

ubiquitous (para. 20): present everywhere at once, or seeming to be (adj.)

contentious (para. 22): causing or likely to cause disagreement or disputes between people with differing views (adj.)

Everybody loves a good story, and when it's finished, this will be the greatest one ever told. It begins in Africa with a group of hunter-gatherers, perhaps just a few hundred strong. It ends some 200,000 years later with their six and a half billion descendants spread across the Earth, living in peace or at war, believing in a thousand different deities or none at all, their faces aglow in the light of campfires and computer screens.   1

In between is a sprawling saga of survival, movement, isolation, and conquest, most of it unfolding in the silence of prehistory. Who were those first modern people in Africa? What compelled a band of their descendants to leave their home continent as little as 50,000 years ago and expand into Eurasia? What routes did they take? Did they interbreed with earlier members of the human family along the way? When and how did humans first reach the Americas?   2

In sum: Where do we all come from? How did we get to where we are today?   3

For decades the only clues were the sparsely scattered bones and artifacts our ancestors left behind on their journeys. In the past 20 years, however, scientists have found a record of ancient human migrations in the DNA of living people. "Every drop of human blood contains a history book written in the language of our genes," says population geneticist Spencer Wells, a National Geographic explorer-in-residence.   4

The human genetic code, or genome, is 99.9 percent identical throughout the world. What's left is the DNA responsible for our individual differences—in eye color or disease risk, for example—as well as some that serves no apparent function at all. Once in an evolutionary blue moon, a random, harmless mutation can occur in one   5 of these functionless stretches, which is then passed down to all of that person's descendants. Generations later, finding that same mutation, or marker, in two people's DNA indicates that they share the same ancestor. By comparing markers in many different populations, scientists can trace their ancestral connections.

In most of the genome, these minute changes are obscured by the genetic reshuffling that takes place each time a mother and father's DNA combine to make a child. Luckily a couple of regions preserve the telltale variations. One, called mitochondrial DNA (mtDNA), is passed down intact from mother to child. Similarly, most of the Y chromosome, which determines maleness, travels intact from father to son.   6

The accumulated mutations in your mtDNA and (for males) your Y chromosome are only two threads in a vast tapestry of people who have contributed to your genome. But by comparing the mtDNA and Y chromosomes of people from various populations, geneticists can get a rough idea of where and when those groups parted ways in the great migrations around the planet.   7

In the mid-1980s the late Allan Wilson and colleagues at the University of California, Berkeley, used mtDNA to pinpoint humanity's ancestral home. They compared mtDNA from women around the world and found that women of African descent showed twice as much diversity as their sisters. Since the telltale mutations seem to occur at a steady rate, modern humans must have lived in Africa twice as long as anywhere else. Scientists now calculate that all living humans are related to a single woman who lived roughly 150,000 years ago in Africa, a "mitochondrial Eve." She was not the only woman alive at the time, but if geneticists are right, all of humanity is linked to Eve through an unbroken chain of mothers.   8

All living humans are related to a single woman who lived roughly 150,000 years ago in Africa.

Mitochondrial Eve was soon joined by "Y chromosome Adam," an analogous father of us all, also from Africa. Increasingly refined DNA studies have confirmed this opening chapter of our story over and over: All the variously shaped and shaded people of Earth trace their ancestry to African hunter-gatherers.   9

Looking more closely at DNA markers in Africa, scientists may have found traces of those founders. Ancestral DNA markers turn up most often among the San people of southern Africa and the Biaka Pygmies of central Africa, as well as in some East African tribes. The   10

① **African Cradle**
Most paleoanthropologists and geneticists agree that modern humans arose some 200,000 years ago in Africa. The earliest modern human fossils were found in Omo Kibish, Ethiopia. Sites in Israel hold the earliest evidence of modern humans outside Africa, but that group went no farther, dying out about 90,000 years ago.

② **Out of Africa**
Genetic data show that a small group of modern humans left Africa for good 70,000 to 50,000 years ago and eventually replaced all earlier types of humans, such as Neandertals. All non-Africans are the descendants of these travelers, who may have migrated around the top of the Red Sea or across its narrow southern opening.

③ **The First Australians**
Discoveries at two ancient sites—artifacts from Malakunanja and fossils from Lake Mungo—indicate that modern humans followed a coastal route along southern Asia and reached Australia nearly 50,000 years ago. Their descendants, Australian Aborigines, remained genetically isolated on that island continent until recently.

④ **Early Europeans**
Paleoanthropologists long thought that the peopling of Europe followed a route from North Africa through the Levant. But genetic data show that the DNA of today's western Eurasians resembles that of people in India. It's possible that an inland migration from Asia seeded Europe between 40,000 and 30,000 years ago.

⑤ **Populating Asia**
Around 40,000 years ago, humans pushed into Central Asia and arrived on the grassy steppes north of the Himalaya. At the same time, they traveled through Southeast Asia and China, eventually reaching Japan and Siberia. Genetic clues indicate that humans in northern Asia eventually migrated to the Americas.

⑥ **Into the New World**
Exactly when the first people arrived in the Americas is still hotly debated. Genetic evidence suggests it was between 20,000 and 15,000 years ago, when sea levels were low and land connected Siberia to Alaska. Ice sheets would have covered the interior of North America, forcing the new arrivals to travel down the west coast.

Human Migration Map. Based on the "Human Migration" map from pages 64–65 of the March 2006 issue of *National Geographic*, with permission of *National Geographic Maps*. Sources for the information presented here are Susan Antón, New York University; Alison Brooks, George Washington University; Peter Forster, University of Cambridge; James F. O'Connell, University of Utah; Stephen Oppenheimer, Oxford University; Spencer Wells, National Geographic Society; and Ofer Bar-Yosef, Harvard University.

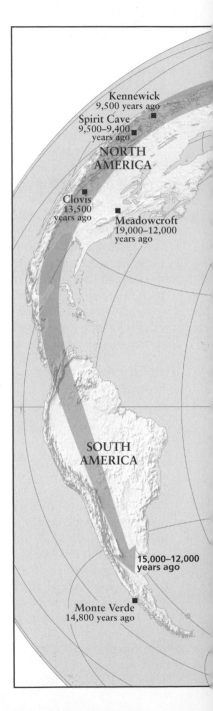

Kennewick
9,500 years ago

Spirit Cave
9,500–9,400
years ago

NORTH
AMERICA

Clovis
13,500
years ago

Meadowcroft
19,000–12,000
years ago

SOUTH
AMERICA

15,000–12,000
years ago

Monte Verde
14,800 years ago

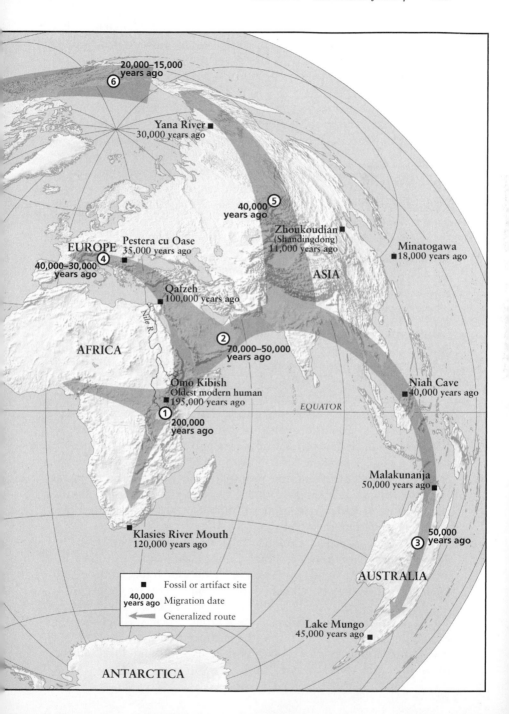

20,000–15,000
years ago
⑥

Yana River ■
30,000 years ago

40,000 ⑤
years ago

Zhoukoudian ■
(Shandingdong)
11,000 years ago

Pestera cu Oase
EUROPE 35,000 years ago

Minatogawa
■ 18,000 years ago

40,000–30,000
years ago ④

ASIA

Qafzeh
100,000 years ago

②
70,000–50,000
years ago

AFRICA

Niah Cave
■ 40,000 years ago

Omo Kibish
Oldest modern human
■ 195,000 years ago

EQUATOR

① 200,000
years ago

Malakunanja
50,000 years ago ■

Klasies River Mouth
120,000 years ago

50,000
③ years ago

AUSTRALIA

■ Fossil or artifact site

40,000
years ago Migration date

◄─── Generalized route

Lake Mungo
45,000 years ago

ANTARCTICA

San and two of the East African tribes also speak languages that feature a repertoire of unique sounds, including clicks. Perhaps these far-flung people pay witness to an expansion of our earliest ancestors within Africa, like the fading ripples from a pebble dropped in a pond.

What seems virtually certain now is that at a remarkably recent   11
date—probably between 50,000 and 70,000 years ago—one small wavelet from Africa lapped up onto the shores of western Asia. All non-Africans share markers carried by those first emigrants, who may have numbered just a thousand people.

Probably between 50,000 and 70,000 years ago one small wavelet [of emigrants] from Africa lapped up onto the shores of western Asia.

Some archaeologists think the migration   12
out of Africa marked a revolution in behavior that also included more sophisticated tools, wider social networks, and the first art and body ornaments. Perhaps some kind of neurological mutation had led to spoken language and made our ancestors fully modern, setting a small band of them on course to colonize the world. But other scientists see finely wrought tools and other traces of modern behavior scattered around Africa long before those first steps outside the continent. "It's not a 'revolution' if it took 200,000 years," says Alison Brooks of George Washington University.

Whatever tools and cognitive skills the emigrants packed with   13
them, two paths lay open into Asia. One led up the Nile Valley, across the Sinai Peninsula, and north into the Levant. But another also beckoned. Seventy thousand years ago the Earth was entering the last ice age, and sea levels were sinking as water was locked up in glaciers. At its narrowest, the mouth of the Red Sea between the Horn of Africa and Arabia would have been only a few miles wide. Using primitive watercraft, modern humans could have crossed over while barely getting their feet wet.

Once in Asia, genetic evidence suggests, the population split. One   14
group stalled temporarily in the Middle East, while the other followed the coast around the Arabian Peninsula, India, and beyond. Each generation may have pushed just a couple of miles farther.

"The movement was probably imperceptible," says Spencer   15
Wells, who heads the National Geographic Society's Genographic Project, a global effort to refine the picture of early migrations. "It was less of a journey and probably more like walking a little farther down the beach to get away from the crowd."

Over the millennia, a few steps a year and a few hops by boat 16
added up. The wanderers had reached southeastern Australia by
45,000 years ago, when a man was buried at a site called Lake
Mungo. Artifact-bearing soil layers beneath the burial could be as old
as 50,000 years—the earliest evidence of modern humans far from
Africa.

No physical trace of these people has been found along the 8,000 17
miles from Africa to Australia—all may have vanished as the sea rose
after the Ice Age. But a genetic trace endures. A few indigenous
groups on the Andaman Islands near Myanmar, in Malaysia, and in
Papua New Guinea—as well as almost all Australian Aborigines—
carry signs of an ancient mitochondrial lineage, a trail of genetic
bread crumbs dropped by the early migrants.

People in the rest of Asia and Europe share different but equally 18
ancient mtDNA and Y-chromosome lineages, marking them as descendants of the other, stalled branch of the African exodus. At first,
rough terrain and the Ice Age climate blocked further progress. Europe, moreover, was a stronghold of the Neandertals, descendants of
a much earlier migration of pre-modern humans out of Africa.

Finally, perhaps 40,000 years ago, modern humans advanced 19
into the Neandertals' territory. Overlapping layers of Neandertal and
early modern human artifacts at a cave in France suggest that the two
kinds of humans could have met. How these two peoples—the des-
tined parvenu and the doomed caretaker of a continent—would have
interacted is a potent mystery. Did they eye each other with wonder
or in fear? Did they fight, socialize, or dismiss each other as alien
beings?

All we know is that as modern humans and distinctly more so- 20
phisticated toolmaking spread into Europe, the once ubiquitous
Neandertals were squeezed into ever shrinking pockets of habitation
that eventually petered out completely. On current evidence, the two
groups interbred rarely, if at all. Neither mtDNA from Neandertal
fossils nor modern human DNA bears any trace of an ancient
mingling of the bloodlines.

About the same time as modern humans pushed into Europe, 21
some of the same group that had paused in the Middle East spread
east into Central Asia. Following herds of game, skirting mountain
ranges and deserts, they reached southern Siberia as early as 40,000
years ago. As populations diverged and became isolated, their genetic
lineages likewise branched and rebranched. But the isolation was

rarely if ever complete. "People have always met other people, found them attractive, and had children," says molecular anthropologist Theodore Schurr of the University of Pennsylvania.

Schurr's specialty is the peopling of the Americas—one of the   22
last and most contentious chapters in the human story. The subject seems to attract fantastic theories (Native Americans are the descendants of the ancient Israelites or the lost civilization of Atlantis) as well as ones tinged with a political agenda. The "Caucasoid" features of a 9,500-year-old skull from Washington State called Kennewick Man, for instance, have been hailed as proof that the first Americans came from northern Europe.

In fact most scientists agree that today's Native Americans de-   23
scend from ancient Asians who crossed from Siberia to Alaska in the last ice age, when low sea level would have exposed a land bridge between the continents. But there's plenty of debate about when they came and where they originated in Asia.

For decades the first Americans were thought to have arrived   24
around 13,000 years ago as the Ice Age eased, opening a path through the ice covering Canada. But a few archaeologists claimed to have evidence for an earlier arrival, and two early sites withstood repeated criticism: the Meadowcroft Shelter in Pennsylvania, now believed to be about 16,000 years old, and Monte Verde in southern Chile, more than 14,000 years old.

The DNA of living Native Americans can help settle some of the   25
disputes. Most carry markers that link them unequivocally to Asia. The same markers cluster in people who today inhabit the Altay region of southern Siberia, suggesting it was the starting point for a journey across the land bridge. So far, the genetic evidence doesn't show whether North and South America were populated in a single, early migration or two or three distinct waves, and it suggests only a rough range of dates, between 20,000 and 15,000 years ago.

Even the youngest of those dates is older than the opening of an   26
inland route through the Canadian ice. So how did the first Americans get here? They probably traveled along the coast: perhaps a few hundred people hopping from one pocket of land and sustenance to the next, between a frigid ocean and a looming wall of ice. "A coastal route would have been the easiest way in," says Wells. "But it still would have been a hell of a trip."

Beyond the glaciers lay immense herds of bison, mammoths, and   27
other animals on a continent innocent of other intelligent predators. Pushed by population growth or pulled by the lure of game, people spread to the tip of South America in as little as a thousand years.

The genes of today's Native Americans are helping to bring their ancestors' saga to life. But much of the story can only be imagined, says Jody Hey, a population geneticist at Rutgers University. "You can't tell it with the richness of what must have happened." 28

With the settling of the Americas, modern humans had conquered most of the planet. When European explorers set sail 700 years ago, the lands they "discovered" were already full of people. The encounters were often wary or violent, but they were the reunions of a close-knit family. 29

Perhaps the most wonderful of the stories hidden in our genes is that, when unraveled, the tangled knot of our global genetic diversity today leads us all back to a recent yesterday, together in Africa. 30

 Read It Now: Read current and past issues of *National Geographic* online at bedfordstmartins.com/americanow, Chapter 4.

Vocabulary / Using a Dictionary

1. What are the root words and origin of *artifact* (para. 4)?
2. What is the relationship between the words *genetic* (para. 5) and *genesis*?
3. What is the root word and origin of *archaeologists* (para. 12)?
4. How does the root word of *neurological* (para. 12) help to explain the meaning of the word?

Responding to Words in Context

1. Shreeve uses the term *genetic reshuffling* in relation to the combination of male and female DNA (para. 6). What is the meaning of the phrase *genetic reshuffling*?
2. In paragraph 8, Shreeve uses the term *humanity's ancestral home*. What is the meaning of *home* in this phrase?
3. Shreeve makes several references to *DNA markers* (paras. 5, 10) to help to explain key points. What is the meaning of the term *DNA marker*?

Discussing Main Point and Meaning

1. According to the geneticists cited by Shreeve (para. 8), what continent represents the common home of all human beings? Also,

recent discoveries by scientists suggest that "all living humans" share a common mother who lived 150,000 years ago. What name do scientists use to refer to this woman? Why?

2. In paragraph 4, Shreeve cites geneticist Spencer Wells, who asserts that, "every drop of human blood contains a history book written in the language of our genes." Explain the meaning of Wells's statement.

3. In paragraph 12, Shreeve states that the migration out of Africa involved an evolutionary "revolution." According to the author, what were the elements of this revolution?

4. On some levels, Shreeve's essay contains the elements of a scientific detective story because it uses "clues" to explain the migration of human beings out of Africa. In paragraph 17, for example, he asserts that indigenous groups, including those in Malaysia and Papua New Guinea, may also have come from Africa. In the absence of "physical traces," how does he account for this theory?

Examining Sentences, Paragraphs, and Organization

1. Describe the nature of Shreeve's introduction and explain whether you believe it's effective.

2. In paragraph 3, Shreeve pauses to ask, "Where do we all come from? How did we get to where we are today?" How does the writer answer these questions? In terms of the essay's organization, what purpose do these questions serve?

3. What is the meaning of the term *human genetic code*, or *genome*, used in paragraph 5? According to paragraph 5, what discoveries and insights regarding humankind resulted from scientific analysis of the genetic code or genome?

4. Shreeve states that the "peopling of the Americas" was one of the "last and most contentious chapters in the human story" (para. 22). In what way is the story contentious?

Thinking Critically

1. In many ways, Shreeve's essay rests on evidence related to DNA to explain early human migration. Specifically, what does the writer tell us about the significance of DNA found in "living Native Americans" (para. 25)? What clues does the DNA provide?

2. In paragraphs 16 and 17, Shreeve acknowledges that no "physical trace" has been discovered that links Australians, as well as indigenous groups on the Andaman Islands and in Papua New Guinea. In the absence of obvious physical connections, how can scientists link this group to the original African population? Explain your answer.

3. Review the map of human migration. How does this illustration help us to answer the question "Where do we all come from?" (para. 3).

In-Class Writing Activities

1. The Neandertals are described in paragraphs 18, 19, and 20 as "descendants of a much earlier migration of pre-modern humans out of Africa" (para. 18). For reasons that scientists don't entirely understand, this group—approximately 40,000 years ago—essentially "stalled," and their culture faded out. Scientists, unable to explain the Neandertals' situation, refer to it as a "potent mystery" (para. 19). Using your imagination and the few details provided in the text, develop a theory that explains why this once dominant culture faded into oblivion. Then, write a letter, in the persona of a Neandertal, that explains to the contemporary world the reasons why your civilization declined.

2. Shreeve's essay presents powerful evidence that links all human beings to a common mother and a common place of origin. How does this information affect the manner in which you perceive other racial and ethnic groups? In a freewrite, explain how Shreeve's essay affects your perception of "other" groups. How does this scientific information impact your way of seeing and relating to others whom you may once have viewed as different?

HENRY LOUIS GATES JR.

My Yiddishe Mama

[THE WALL STREET JOURNAL / February 1, 2006]

Before You Read

How far back can your trace your family heritage? How important to you is your knowledge of your own genetic past?

Words to Learn

methodology (para. 1): the methods or organizing principles underlying a particular area of study (n.)

abyss (para. 4): a chasm or gorge so vast that its extent is not visible (n.)

archival (para. 5): relating to the storage of records in an archive (adj.)

affinities (para. 7): natural likings or inclinations toward somebody or something (n.)

insurmountable (para. 9): impossible to overcome or deal with successfully (adj.)

panoply (para. 14): an impressive and magnificent display or array (n.)

putative (para. 14): generally regarded as such; supposed (adj.)

HENRY LOUIS GATES JR. *is a preeminent scholar of African American literature, author, and groundbreaker. Gates is currently the W. E. B. Du Bois Professor of the Humanities, the chair of the Department of African and African American Studies, and the director of the W. E. B. Du Bois Institute for African and African American Research at Harvard University. He got his start writing when, as a junior at Yale, he wrote essays about living in the Tanzanian bush for his school newspaper. Writing did not always come easily for Gates. The first African American to attend the University of Cambridge had difficulty in school. He remembers, "When I wrote my first essay, my supervisor said it was the worst essay she had ever read, because I didn't know how to explicate a text. I went to her and I said, 'Surely there must be books to teach me this method?' She said, 'No, no, you're born with it.' " Not taking no for an answer, Gates went to a bookstore, bought all the books on literary theory, studied them, and did very well in school. He later went on to help shape the nascent field of African American studies.*

Since 1977, when I sat riveted every night for a week in front of   1
my TV, I have had *Roots* envy. Even if scholars remain deeply skeptical about his methodology. Alex Haley went to his grave believing
that he had found the ethnic group from which his African ancestors
originated before surviving the dreaded Middle Passage.[1]

Two years before, I proudly told a fellow student at Cambridge,   2
an Anglo-Ghanaian, that I could trace my slave ancestors back to
1819, the birth date of Jane Gates, my paternal great-great-
grandmother. I wondered if he could do better?

He invited me to accompany him to the University Library,   3
where, buried deep in the stacks, he found a copy of Burke's Peerage,
then walked me through his mother's English ancestry with certainty
back to one Richard Crispe who died in 1575, and who, the book
said "probably" descended from William Crispe, who had died in
1207. His father's side, members of the Asante people in Ghana, he
could trace to the 17th century. The roots of my *Roots* envy?

After years of frustration, I determined to do something about it.   4
So I decided to invite eight prominent African Americans to allow
their DNA to be tested and their family histories to be researched for
a documentary film. When the paper trail would end, inevitably, in
the abyss of slavery, we would then try to find their African roots
through science.

Having been involved in after-school programs, I was hoping to   5
get inner-city school kids engaged by the wonders of both genetics
and archival research.

But I had ulterior motives, too. I wanted to find my white patri-   6
arch, the father of Jane Gates's children. Maybe genetics could verify
the family legend that the father of Jane's children was an Irish man
from Cresaptown, Md., a slave-holder named Samuel Brady. Perhaps
I could give Jane her Thomas Jefferson-Sally Hemings[2] moment!

I also had hopes for my African origins. Throughout my adult life,   7
I've always been drawn to Nigeria's Yoruba culture—to its cuisine, its
legends, its rhythms and its songs. As a Fela Ransome-Kuti album
played in my head, I wondered whether geneticists could determine
that I had physical, not only spiritual, affinities to the Yoruba.

---

[1]*Middle Passage:* The especially dangerous journey made by slave ships traveling
across the Atlantic from Africa to the Americas.
[2]*Sally Hemings:* An African American servant who lived with Thomas Jefferson in his
home at Monticello. Despite widespread assumptions that Jefferson was the father of
Hemings's children, no definitive DNA evidence confirms this.

Our genealogists as well as our geneticists were given a tough as-   8
signment. Five generations ago, each of us has 32 ancestors, or two to
the fifth power. If we go back 10 generations, or 300 years, each of
us has 1,024 theoretical ancestors, or two to the 10th power. Even
with genetics, we can only trace two of our family lines. The first
African slaves arrived in Virginia in 1619; the slaves were freed in
1865, and appeared with two legal names for the first time in the
1870 census. Penetrating the name barrier of 1870 required detailed
and imaginative sleuthing through the records of slave-holders, praying that they somehow mentioned one of their slaves by first name, in
wills, tax records or estate division papers.

The stories that we found are not the sort found in textbooks,   9
which tend either to recreate Black History through the narratives of
great women and men, or else through broad social movements. We
were able to find stirring stories of heretofore anonymous individuals
who made heroic contributions against seemingly insurmountable
odds. If the promise of America was the right to own land, very few
blacks were able to do so before the middle of the 20th century. But
some did.

Oprah Winfrey's great-great-grandfather, Constantine Winfrey, a   10
farm worker in Mississippi, had the audacity to approach a white
man, John Watson, in 1876, and make a wager: If he picked 10 bales
of cotton in one year, Watson would give Winfrey 80 acres of his
land in return. (In 1870, a bale of cotton weighed 500 pounds.) On
June 21, 1881, a property deed recorded the land exchange between
the two. Constantine is listed in the 1870 census as illiterate; 10 years
later, he had learned to read and write. And when, in 1906, the local
"colored school" was slated for destruction, Constantine arranged to
save it by having it moved to this property.

Chris Tucker's great-great-grandfather, Theodore Arthur Bryant   11
Sr., sold off parcels of his land to his black neighbors for below-
market prices so that they would not join the Great Migration to the
North, thereby saving the black community of Flat Rock, Ga.

Whoopi Goldberg's great-great-grandparents, William and Elsa   12
Washington, in 1878 received 104.5 acres in Alachua County, Fla.,
under the Southern Homestead Act of 1866.[3] Less than 10% of black
petitioners in Florida received land. "My country 'tis of thee,"
Whoopi exclaimed, when she received this news. "My country."

---

[3]*Southern Homestead Act of 1866:* A law passed by Congress that promised to make
plots of land available to blacks or whites willing to live on and cultivate the land.

In the case of the astronaut Mae Jemison, we were able, incred-   13
ibly, to trace three of her family lines deep into slavery, including dis-
covering both a fourth great-grandmother and a fourth or fifth great-
grandfather. Four of our subjects are descended from people who
owned property in the 1800s, two well before the Civil War, and two
more by 1881. The latter two, freed in 1865, in effect got their 40
acres, if not the mule.[4]

Our genetic research also yielded a rich panoply of results, and a   14
few surprises. My subjects share common ancestry with, among
others, members of the Mbundu of Angola,
the Kpelle of Liberia, the Tikar of Cameroon,
the Igbo of Nigeria, the Mandinka and the
Pepel of Guinea-Bissau, the Makua of Mo-
zambique, and the Bamileke of Cameroon. I
had expected the revelation of their African
roots to form the dramatic climax of our re-
search. But our subjects' reactions to their putative genetic identities
remained somewhat abstract.

> *Genealogy trumped genetics. It was as if Africa was "so long, so far away."*

What really stirred them was the light shed on their American   15
heritage, their known world, as Edward Jones put it. It was a world
they could touch and imagine, through the branches of their family
trees. Genealogy trumped genetics. It was as if Africa, as the poet
Langston Hughes wrote, was "so long, so far away." Roots, like
charity, start at home.

Contrary to conventional wisdom, and contrary to those who   16
worry about "the geneticization of identity," our sense of identity—
in this case at least—seems to be more
deeply rooted in the histories of family members we can name than in anonymous ancestors emerging out of the dense shadows of
an African past, unveiled through a process
admittedly still in its infancy. For my subjects, genealogy seems to have been a way of
staking a claim on a richer American identity, an identity established through indi-
vidual triumphs like the attainment of literacy and the purchasing
of land.

> *Genealogy seems to have been a way of staking a claim on a richer American identity.*

---

[4] *40 acres and a mule:* A colloquial phrase for the compensation to be awarded to freed
slaves after the Civil War.

What of my own case of "Roots" envy? We advertised for, and   17
found, two male descendants of Samuel Brady, and compared their
Y-DNA with mine. My haplotype, common in Western Ireland and
the Netherlands, has as much in common genetically with Samuel
Brady as it does, I suppose, with half of the males in Galway and Am-
sterdam. So much for that bit of family lore.

On the other hand, our genealogical research uncovered, to my   18
astonishment, one of my fifth great-grandfathers and two fourth
great-grandfathers, two born in the middle of the 18th century. I
learned that one, John Redman, a Free Negro, even fought in the
American Revolution. Despite the fact that we didn't find Jane
Gates's children's father, we believe that we have found her mother, a
slave, born circa 1799.

As for my mitochondrial DNA, my mother's mother's mother's   19
lineage? Would it be Yoruba, as I fervently hoped? My Fela
Ransome-Kuti fantasy was not exactly borne out. A number of exact
matches turned up, leading straight back to that African Kingdom
called Northern Europe, to the genes of (among others) a female
Ashkenazi Jew. Maybe it was time to start listening to "My Yiddishe
Mama."

Web **Read It Now:** Read more Henry Louis Gates essays and interviews archived by
Stanford University at **bedfordstmartins.com/americanow**, Chapter 4.

AMERICA THEN . . .1977

ALEX HALEY

Roots

A major landmark in television history was reached in 1977, when ABC broadcast the miniseries Roots for eight consecutive evenings, capturing the attention of Americans as no other TV program ever had. Its success was phenomenal: The miniseries, which took two years to film, was seen by 130 million viewers, and its final episode remains one of the most watched television shows of all time. Roots stimulated a keen interest in genealogy and oral history, inspiring numerous African Americans (such as the scholar Henry Louis Gates Jr., who alludes to it in his essay above) to search for their family histories.

The television dramatization was based on Alex Haley's bestselling and Pulitzer Prize–winning book, Roots: The Saga of an American Family. A combination of fact and fiction, the book was first published in a condensed format by Reader's Digest in 1974 and

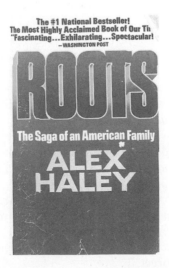

LeVar Burton as Kunta Kinte in the 1977 miniseries *Roots*.

then appeared in its entirety in 1976, America's bicentennial year. At the center of the 688-page book is Haley's Gambia-born ancestor, Kunta Kinte, who was taken to America as a slave in 1767 at the age of seventeen. Haley worked on the book for twelve years, beginning with recollections of conversations with relatives on his front porch in Henning, Tennessee, moving to a journey up the Gambia River in Africa, and finally doing painstaking research at the British Parliament, various historical societies, and the Library of Congress.

As the miniseries begins, we see Kunta Kinte (played by LeVar Burton) in the Gambian village of Juffure, where he is being initiated into manhood. The story then moves to his sudden capture and humiliation and continues with the ordeal of the Atlantic crossing, his auction in Annapolis, his escape and recapture, and the birth of his daughter, Kizzy, who is sold into slavery at sixteen. In the second half of the saga, we follow Kizzy's family through the Civil War, a hard-won freedom, and a new home in Tennessee. The miniseries won nine Emmy Awards, including a Best Lead Actor award for Louis Gossett Jr., a Television Critics Circle Award, a Golden Globe Award, and a George Foster Peabody Award "for dramatically exposing us to an aspect of our history that many of us never knew but all of us will never forget."

Vocabulary/Using a Dictionary

1. How does the word *document* help provide a meaning for *documentary* (para. 4)?
2. How does *genealogy* differ from *genetics* (para. 15)?
3. How does the root word for *anonymous* (para. 9) suggest its meaning?

Responding to Words in Context

1. What does Gates mean when he uses the term *imaginative sleuthing* in paragraph 8?
2. Why does Gates use the word *audacity* to describe the behavior of Oprah Winfrey's great-great-grandfather (para. 10)? What is the meaning of the word?
3. What does Gates mean when he refers to the *known world* (para. 15) of his subjects?
4. What is the meaning and significance of Gates's assertion that "Roots, like charity, start at home" (para. 15)?

Discussing Main Point and Meaning

1. According to Gates, what influences motivate him to learn more about his ancestors?
2. What reasons does Gates cite as the basis for his affinity with Nigeria's Yoruba culture (para. 7)?
3. What does the writer mean when he states that "genealogy trumped genetics" (para. 15)?

Examining Sentences, Paragraphs, and Organization

1. What reason does Gates cite in paragraph 6 as the "ulterior motives" for his genetic search?
2. In explaining the historical conditions that make his search more challenging, Gates explains that it was not until 1870, years after the slaves were freed in 1865, that African Americans appeared on the census with two legal names (para. 8). What does this fact imply about the treatment of slaves before 1870?

3. What is the meaning of the writer's assertion (para. 16) that for his subjects "genealogy seems to have been a way of staking a claim on a richer American identity"?

4. How does the concluding paragraph serve to explain the article's title?

Thinking Critically

1. Gates initiates his search with the belief that his "white patriarch" is Samuel Brady, a former slaveholder (para. 6). What does Gates learn about his possible relationship to Brady? Why is this significant?

2. What does Gates mean when he refers to the "somewhat abstract" response of subjects when they learn the results of the genetic research (para. 14)?

3. In paragraph 16, Gates refers to concerns regarding "the geneticization of identity." What does he mean by this phrase? Does his research contribute to or lessen concerns about this process?

4. In explaining the accomplishments of his genealogical search, Gates refers to discoveries regarding "heretofore anonymous individuals" (para. 9). What stories does he cite? Why are they significant?

In-Class Writing Activities

1. Gates's essay unfolds as a kind of detective story in which he uses genetic science to explore a family legend. Consider some of the family legends within your family. These might consist of stories or anecdotes that have been passed down from previous generations, which may or may not be true. Select one of these family legends—the most interesting one or the one that you know most about—and compose a narrative that tells this story and attempts to expand on it.

2. Gates's narrative involves the conflict between something that he assumed to be true and a reality that was different. Within your own life, have you experienced similar conflicts between some aspect of family life that you once believed to be true but later discovered was false? Write a brief essay in which you explain your initial beliefs, your process and discoveries, and your conclusions.

3. Today there are many ways (aside from genetics) to trace one's genealogy or family history. Attempt to conduct a genealogy that traces your family tree. You might begin by talking to your relatives and examining family artifacts, but you should also consider other means such as libraries, local historical societies, and the Internet.

MEGAN RUNDLE

Unearthing Family Roots

[THE DIGITAL COLLEGIAN, Pennsylvania State University / December 5, 2005]

Before You Read

How much do your assumptions about race and, specifically, about your own racial background, affect your sense of identity?

Words to Learn

typology (para. 3): study, analysis, or classification based on types or categories (n.)

Old English (para. 4): the earliest form of the English language,

used until approximately AD 1150. (n.)

resonate (para. 10): to have an effect or impact beyond that which is immediately apparent (v.)

A. J. Dobbins knew that despite the dark color of his skin, the   1
roots of his family tree extend across many different countries. "My
family comes in all different shades," Dobbins said. "Some of us are
darker, and some of us are so light we can pass for white. I've always
been taught that there's more to race than color." But Dobbins then
noted that even he didn't imagine the results he would get from one
of Penn State's latest technological advancements.

MEGAN RUNDLE *is a junior majoring in English and journalism at Penn
State. She has been on the staff of the* Digital Collegian *for two years, covering the diversity news beat, contributing as a book reviewer, and currently
serving as arts editor. Rundle describes what inspired her to write "Unearthing Family Roots. "My editor, Erin James, came to me and said she had
an idea for a story that could end up being a really interesting feature about a
professor on campus who was conducting DNA testing to teach his students
about their backgrounds. I went to one of the meetings where students found
out their results and then had a discussion session about what they learned. It
was one of the most interesting discussions I've ever heard." For a "Student
Writer at Work" interview with Rundle, see page 159.*

THE NEW YORK TIMES EDITORIAL BOARD

Debunking the Concept of "Race"

[THE NEW YORK TIMES / July 30, 2005]

Black Americans who explore their family histories typically hit a dead end in the early 19th century, when black Americans who were slaves were not listed in the census by name. Now some black Americans are trying to fill in the gap with genetic screening tests that purport to tell descendants exactly where in Africa their ancestors came from. But, like most people, those who think of themselves as African-American will need to search well beyond Africa to find all of their origins.

This point came through with resounding clarity recently at Pennsylvania State University, where about 90 students took complex genetic screening tests that compared their samples with those of four regional groups. Many of these students thought of themselves as "100 percent" white or black or something else, but only a tiny fraction of them, as it turned out, actually fell into that category. Most learned instead that they shared genetic markers with people of different skin colors.

Ostensibly "black" subjects, for example, found that as much as half of their genetic material came from Europe, with some coming from Asia as well. One "white" student learned that 14 percent of his DNA came from Africa—and 6 percent from East Asia. The student told *The Daily Collegian,* the student newspaper, earlier this year: "When I got my results I was like, there's no way they were mine. I thought it was just an example of what the test was supposed to look like. Then I was like, Oh my God, that's me."

Prof. Samuel Richards, who teaches a course in race and ethnic relations at Penn State, uses the test results to shake students out of rigid and received notions about the biological basis of identity. By showing students that they aren't what they think they are, he shows them that race and ethnicity are more fluid and complex than most of us think. The goal is to make students less prejudiced and more open to a deeper discussion of humanity. If the genetic testing fad pushes things in this direction, it will have served an important purpose in a world that too often thinks of racial labels as absolute—and the last word when it comes to human identity.

Thanks to cooperation between Sam Richards, senior lecturer in sociology, and Mark Shriver, associate professor of anthropology and genetics, Dobbins (senior, sociology) took a DNA test that showed his genetic racial breakdown. The test was offered to students in Sociology 119 (Race and Ethnic Relations) last spring and again to those taking the class this fall.

2

Richards explained that the test is a complex process taken   3
through a tissue sample from a cheek swab. Researchers then break
down the sample to find a person's genetic makeup by comparing it
to "parent" samples taken in different countries. Shriver has worked
on the project for five years with Tony Frudakis, a researcher from an
innovative genetic research company called DNAPrint. "This test,"
he observed, "says we're really all mixes . . . and the idea that people
can fit into specific categories is one of the fallacies of race typology."

About six weeks after taking his test, Dobbins was a little sur-   4
prised to learn that he was more than a
quarter of something other than African.

"This test says we're
really all mixes"

Dobbins, whose results showed he was 28
percent Caucasian, 70 percent sub-Saharan
African and 2 percent Native American,
claimed that while he wasn't expecting that combination of numbers,
he's always known his family had at least some Caucasian blood in it.
"I come from a slave family, but I have an Old English last name," he
said. "If you put my dad next to his brothers, you wouldn't even
know they were related."

A student facilitator for Penn State's Race Relations Project   5
(RRP), Dobbins is one of Richard's former students and a former
teaching assistant for the class. "When I found out I was almost a
third white and told my friends their initial reaction was 'Shut up, no
you're not,' and I had to get out the results and actually show them."

Dobbins' grandmother, Mae Dobbins of Maryland, knew her   6
family was more than just African but was a little surprised at the
numbers the results showed: "Before my mother died, she told me
that a white man had fathered some of her siblings, and my husband
had some Caucasian on his side as well." "If you go back," she said,
"you'll find that most people have a mixture of races at their roots."
Dobbins' father, Aaron Dobbins Sr., agreed, saying that he would
love to have the opportunity to take the test. "We know we have a
lot of diversity in our blood," Dobbins Sr. added. "I'm almost surprised they didn't find more diversity."

Another RRP facilitator, Brianna Ford, decided to take the test   7
because she had been reading journals from people who had already
been tested. "I never really knew what I was," Ford (junior-crime,
law and justice) noted. "A lot of people who took it and wrote their
journals didn't seem to care, and I knew I would care." When Ford
got her results back, she was completely shocked to learn that she
was 8 percent East Asian, 8 percent Sub-Saharan African, 19 percent

Native American and 65 percent European. Ford admitted to being disappointed and frustrated by her parents' reactions because they automatically assumed the test was wrong. "My parents started arguing over whose side of the family I got the Asian and African from," she said. "I wondered if I was better off not knowing, but now I know I can use it to push further and learn more."

According to Laurie Mulvey, codirector of the Race Relations 8
Project, people react in different ways after learning their results. Mulvey organizes discussion groups where people meet to share their experiences and feelings about their test results and race relations at Penn State. She trains student facilitators to conduct progressive discussions about race issues. "For some people, knowing the results doesn't change anything because they feel they're still the same person they've always been," Mulvey reported. "Some people are really excited by their results, and sometimes people get disappointed as well."

> "We're really all a lot more closely related than we think."

Lauren Wenner (senior-public relations and sociology), for ex- 9
ample, was disappointed to learn she was 96 percent European and 4 percent Native American. "When I told my friends about my disappointment, they were like, 'Well, Lauren, you're white,'" she said. "But now after I've had time to think about it, I think it's a good thing to know that I can be this open-minded about diversity and not really have any physical reason to be."

Shriver said the next phase of the project involves traveling back 10
to Europe next semester for several months to work on getting more samples. The test uses parent samples from Northwest Europe, but Shriver hopes to break this down further. Dobbins acknowledged that the most important thing he's learned from this experience is that he really can't assume anything about people anymore. "Science doesn't lie," he remarked. "We all make assumptions, and people can tell you their experiences and how it's changed them, but until you have a personal experience and it resonates in you, I guess you really can't describe it. This test just shows that we're really all a lot more closely related than we think."

For an annotated excerpt of this essay that highlights Rundle's writing strategies, see page 158.

Web **Read It Now:** Read more student editorials at *The Digital Collegian,* Penn State's online campus newspaper, at **bedfordstmartins.com/americanow.**

Vocabulary / Using a Dictionary

1. What is the root word and origin of *technological* (para. 1)? What other words can be constructed from this common root?
2. How is the word *anthropology* (para. 2) related to *sociology* (para. 2)? What are the root words of each?
3. How does the root word of *facilitator* (para. 5) help to suggest its definition?

Responding to Words in Context

1. What does A. J. Dobbins mean when he says that "there's more to race than color" (para. 1)?
2. How is the phrase *genetic racial breakdown* (para. 2) related to *genetic makeup* in paragraph 3?
3. What meaning does the word *typology* assume in paragraph 3?

Discussing Main Point and Meaning

1. What assumption underlies Dobbins's classmates' statement, "Shut up, no you're not" (para. 5)? What beliefs prompted his friends to make this statement?
2. According to Mark Shriver's comment in paragraph 3, what was one of the most informative results of the test? What implied assumption does Shriver challenge?
3. What does Shriver mean in paragraph 3 when he refers to "one of the fallacies of race typology"? What is the significance of this information?
4. According to Rundle, what range of feelings are displayed by students after they learn more about their racial composition (para. 8)?
5. How does Shriver, a professor of anthropology and genetics, explain his motivation for the use of genetics testing in a sociology course (para. 3)?

Examining Sentences, Paragraphs, and Organization

1. What essential questions does Rundle raise in her opening paragraph? Is it an effective introduction to her essay? Explain.

2. Consider the effect of introducing and concluding the essay with references to Dobbins. What impact does this framing device have on the essay? How would the essay be different without these references?

3. Brianna Ford initially questioned whether she was "better off not knowing" her racial composition (para. 7). How does her thinking change in this regard? How is this developed in paragraph 7? What reasons does she give for her opinions?

Thinking Critically

1. In summarizing his experience, how does Dobbins explain the value of the genetic testing process (para. 10)? How does he appear to have changed as a result of his exposure to this genetic information?

2. What are the implications or meaning of Dobbins's statement in paragraph 10 that "science doesn't lie"? What is the larger meaning of the statement?

3. In paragraph 8, Laurie Mulvey is identified as a codirector of the Race Relations Project. How would you describe her role? Why is it important?

4. Would you participate in the genetic testing process? Why or why not?

In-Class Writing Activities

1. Many of the students in Rundle's essay identify themselves as members of a single racial group rather than of several. How widespread is this phenomenon? To find out, take a survey and ask a group of peers or classmates how they identify themselves. You might also ask what racial, cultural, or ethnic designations they use. Then, write an essay that describes and reflects on your findings. Consider what the results mean.

2. Reflect on the varied responses of the students who volunteered to take the genetic identification test for their sociology class. Consider, too, the impact of the test on students, including Dobbins, who asserts that "we're really all a lot more closely related than we think" (para. 10). Given the nature of this test, should it made available—voluntarily—to any student who requests it? After considering the various consequences of testing, write a

short essay that argues for or against making such a test available to those who wish to volunteer. Make certain to provide adequate support for your position.

ANNOTATION Beginning with an Individual Case

An effective way to open an essay is with an individual instance, with the concrete experiences of a single person. This writing strategy is quite common in everyday journalism: A reporter may begin coverage of a disastrous hurricane by first describing the experiences of a particular survivor and then follow with an account of the overall damages. An item on increasing fuel costs might open with comments from a single consumer at the gasoline pump. This is the way **Megan Rundle**, a Penn State student, decides to begin a report of a fascinating and important study her college undertook to determine participants' ethnic backgrounds through DNA testing. The opening paragraph of "**Unearthing Family Roots**" is especially effective since she also uses it to establish suspense: The reader doesn't know right away what "results" her subject is referring to. As a result, she makes her subject's surprise also the reader's. Note that she doesn't provide a context for the opening until the second paragraph and waits until the fourth to provide A. J. Dobbins's test results.

Rundle begins with the experience of A. J. Dobbins.

She creates suspense by referring to "results."

Rundle explains DNA test, providing context for Dobbins and experiences of other students.

1   A. J. Dobbins knew that despite the dark color of his skin, the roots of his family tree extend across many different countries. "My family comes in all different shades," Dobbins said. "Some of us are darker, and some of us are so light we can pass for white. I've always been taught that there's more to race than color." But Dobbins then noted that even he didn't imagine the results he would get from one of Penn State's latest technological advancements.

2   Thanks to cooperation between Sam Richards, senior lecturer in sociology, and Mark Shriver, associate professor of anthropology and genetics, Dobbins (senior, sociology) took a DNA test that showed his genetic racial breakdown. The test was offered to students in Sociology 119 (Race and Ethnic Relations) last spring and again to those taking the class this fall.

— From "Unearthing Family Roots" by Megan Rundle, page 152

Student Writer at Work: Megan Rundle
On Writing "Unearthing Family Roots"

Q: What response have you received to "Unearthing Family Roots" from other students at Penn State?

A: Because the topic [of genetic testing] itself was so interesting, I received a lot of e-mails from people who were curious about getting tested to find out their own history. I'm definitely interested in taking part in the process.

Q: How are the topics of race and genetic testing viewed on your campus? And how do your views compare?

A: As a journalist, it's important for me to keep my stories objective. Like any college campus, Penn State has its own issues with diversity and racism, and I really thought this professor [Mark Shriver, professor of sociology] did a great job trying to eliminate boundaries caused by those things; but instead of flat out saying that in my story, I painted the picture of different students to let the readers decide for themselves.

Q: Do you collaborate or bounce your ideas off others at the *Daily Collegian?*

A: Working in a newsroom means there are tons of other qualified writers to help with ideas, editing, and writer's block. That's definitely helped improve my writing.

Q: How long did it take you to write and revise "Unearthing Family Roots"?

A: The original piece was actually much longer. Unfortunately the day it was going to run we just didn't have the text space and we had to cut some of the story. It was hard to go through and decide what was "important" enough to keep, but it also allowed me to test my editing skills and learn a lesson about the craft.

Q: Will your future career be centered on writing?

A: I don't think there is a career out there right now where it's not important to be a good writer or know how to use visuals as a way to express ideas.

Discussing the Unit

Suggested Topic for Discussion

How important is the concept of race in the formation of our identities? Each of the authors, in his or her own way, subverts and reverses traditional ideas about race and skin color as determinants of identity. As these new genetic realities are disseminated throughout our society, how will individuals alter their ways of identifying themselves and others? How will genetics alter our ideas regarding race—and the systems of classification that depend on race? Will individuals and institutions, including governments, employers, and educational systems, develop new means of classifying and identifying human beings?

Preparing for Class Discussion

1. How does each writer in this chapter challenge your sense of "individual" identity? How do they use genetics to question commonplace and accepted systems of identification and classification?

2. What does each essay imply about the role of genetics in the process of determining individual identity? What surprised you most about the discoveries and arguments put forth in the readings in this chapter?

3. What similarities and differences does each essay express in terms of their ideas? What about their structure and organization? Which essay do you most identify with, and why?

From Discussion to Writing

1. Think about the immediate and practical effects, including possibly negative consequences, that might result from what Gates terms the "geneticization of identity." For example, consider how the new use of DNA testing (as illustrated in Rundle's essay) might impact school diversity programs and admissions policies, congressional districting, social programs, and the like.

2. The *New York Times* editorial sidebar that accompanies Rundle's article offers the newspaper's response to the genetic

testing at Penn State. The *Times* refers to genetic testing as a "fad," though one that might accomplish an important purpose. Given what you know about this testing, write an essay that argues whether genetic testing will remain a "fad"—meaning a temporary phenomenon—or will become and remain a standard feature of contemporary life. In composing your essay, be sure to include adequate support for your position.

Topics for Cross-Cultural Discussion

1. If you participated in genetic testing and learned—like many of the students at Penn State—that your background was composed of many variations, how would this impact the manner in which you identity yourself? Would you formally acknowledge your multicultural roots?

2. Do you think that people in countries outside of the United States are as interested in race and racial identity as Americans are? How do you account for this?

5

Gender Differences:
How Real Are They?

It is commonly observed that males and females display different types of behavior from early childhood on. As early as preschool, children recognize certain sex-role identities—they know who's a boy and who's a girl, for example. At play, little boys tend to be more aggressive and competitive, while girls' behavior is generally more social and accommodating. What social scientists are deeply interested in finding out, however, is whether these differences are mainly biological and genetic (that is, boys and girls are "wired" differently) or the result of cultural conditioning (that is, boys and girls are brought up differently). If our society expects boys to be more aggressive or better at math and science, will they automatically fulfill that expectation? As a consequence of social expectations, will girls be more inclined to avoid the hard sciences and enter the "caring" professions? In this chapter, several selections address the issue of gender differences as they manifest themselves in social skills, education, interests, and innate academic dispositions. To start discussion with a quick dramatic contrast, the chapter opens with a Jerry Scott and Jim Borgman cartoon that comically depicts what happens "When Guys Hang Out" and "When Girls Hang Out."

When the president of Harvard University, Lawrence H. Summers, presented some remarks in January 2005 on diversifying the science and engineering workforce, he unleashed a thunderstorm of public controversy by suggesting that the continuing low percentage

The Top 10 Toys for Girls	The Top 10 Toys for Boys
1. Barbie	1. Video games
2. Bratz	2. "Star Wars" merchandise
3. Dora the Explorer	3. Legos
4. Disney Princess	4. Hot Wheels
5. Video games	5. Spider-Man toys
6. iPod / MP3 players	6. Xbox
7. My Little Pony	7. Thomas the Tank Engine
8. LeapFrog	8. Batman merchandise
9. Elmo	9. Bicycle
10. American Girl	10. PlayStation 2

Source: National Retail Federation, 2005
From the *Boston Globe*, November 18, 2005.

of women in math and science might be explored with respect to innate differences. (For the full transcript, see www.president.harvard.edu/speeches/2005/nber.html.) Summers's remarks were picked up by the major media and provoked heated discussion on the airwaves and in numerous journals and periodicals. Though it started in academia, the controversy quickly spread throughout the popular media, including the nation's most widely read magazine, *Parade*. Popular columnist Marilyn vos Savant, who is listed in the *Guinness Book of World Records* as possessing the highest IQ ever recorded, confronted the issue. In "Are Men Smarter Than Women?" she poses the core question and attempts to offer in a brief space an objective opinion: "Does the gender disparity in science give credence to the idea that men are more intelligent than women? My answer is 'no.'" The reasons she gives may surprise you.

The issue was also covered by a prominent Harvard scientist who felt responsible for supplying Summers with key findings that help support the role of innate differences. In "Sex Ed: The Science of Difference," the well-known and best-selling author and psychologist, Steven Pinker, refers to his own study, *The Blank Slate*, in which he notes a number of statistical differences in the mental and biological makeup of males and females. But these differences don't interest Pinker as much as does a broader question arising from the Summers controversy: "What are we to make of the breakdown of standards of intellectual discourse in this affair," he asks, and then wonders if certain topics—such as gender disparity—are simply "taboo" by definition and therefore cannot be openly discussed, a situation he believes is lethal to the academic spirit of free inquiry.

If, for whatever reason, males appear to perform better in some academic skill areas than females, why do boys do so much worse in school than girls? Why is the college graduation rate considerably higher today for young women than for young men? These are questions that have been closely studied by University of Alaska psychology professor Judith Kleinfeld, who notes, "In the late 1970s, more females than males began to enroll in college. Since then a gender gap in college attendance and graduation arose in favor of females and has widened. No reversal of this trend is in sight." Does this disparity in academic performance suggest that females are generally smarter than males? Consider the issue in reverse: If studies now showed that males were outperforming females academically, would the conclusion be that males were more intelligent?

If the brains of girls and boys "learn differently," as recent scientific studies suggest, should our educational system take that into account? In "My Brain Has a Sex?" a Tufts student, Daphne LaBua, poses some key questions that surround the problems of adequately educating our nation's children and cautiously suggests that "single-sex classrooms provide an alternative."

From the *Cincinnati Enquirer,* January 1, 2006.

JERRY SCOTT *and* JIM BORGMAN *are cartoonists who work together on the comic strip* Zits *for the* Cincinnati Enquirer. *Borgman, who has worked at the* Enquirer *for thirty years, says the hardest part of his job is "facing that blank piece of paper." When describing his collaborative work with Jerry Scott, his best friend, Borgman says, "to be able to take a story and boil it down like he does to a few words that are nuanced and have a great sense of timing and character, well, it's an underrated talent. He teaches me every day." In 2001 they won the National Cartoonist Society's Ruben award for* Zits.

MARILYN VOS SAVANT

Are Men Smarter Than Women?

[PARADE MAGAZINE / July 17, 2005]

Before You Read

Does whether you're a man or woman determine your ability to do well in the sciences? Does proficiency in science indicate greater intelligence?

Words to Learn

inherent (para. 1): existing as an essential characteristic or part of (adj.)

analytical (para. 7): able to separate things into their essential elements; connected or involved with analysis (adj.)

formulate (para. 7): to draw up something carefully and in detail (v.)

Dear Marilyn,   1

How do you view the idea that the gender disparity in the sciences might be due to differences in the inherent aptitudes of women? I'm curious to hear a thoughtful and objective opinion on this controversial subject.

> *Melissa Hardison*
> *Tallahassee, Fla.*

A gender gap exists in many occupations, but the disparity in the   2
sciences hits close to one of the scariest marks of all, which is the reason a controversy erupted: Are men smarter than women?

MARILYN VOS SAVANT *is a columnist, author, executive, and* Guinness Book of World Records *holder for highest IQ for five years in both the child and adult categories. The publicity over her high IQ led to her long-running question-and-answer column in* Parade *in which she answers questions concerning mathematics, philosophy, and many other subjects. She has been quoted as saying, "To acquire knowledge, one must study; but to acquire wisdom, one must observe."*

Who's Smarter?

When asked that question, PARADE columnist Marilyn vos Savant and her husband, Dr. Robert Jarvik, instinctively point to each other. Marilyn, of course, was in the *Guinness Book* for having the highest IQ ever recorded. But Dr. Jarvik—inventor of the Jarvik-7 and Jarvik-2000 artificial hearts, used to support patients with congestive heart failure—is no intellectual lightweight either. What do they talk about over dinner? "Medicine and world affairs are the main topics of discussion," says Marilyn. "For entertainment, we love music, dance and going to movies." Both are avid runners but don't enjoy sports and never play games. Marilyn adds, "Rob is more competitive than I am—but, then again, everybody is!"

The concern unfolds in two questions: (1) Are women handi-   3
capped by their upbringing, social pressures, discrimination from
men, and more—not just in science but also in other areas? (2) Or
are women less bright than men?

Some Answers

The answer to the first question is too obvious for argument: 4
Yes, and in my opinion, upbringing is the No. 1 cause—not discrimination, conscious or not, from men. Just as significant is the fact (not
the problem) that many women are far more interested in their families than outside work, and society clearly approves. Top positions do
require time, energy and dedication to goals that may even be selfish.
The second question is the hot spot. The average IQ of females is
equal to the average IQ of males. But averages can be misleading. In
the case of intelligence tests, many more males score at the top and
the bottom of the intelligence scale. This could account for the
greater number of men in the sciences and—on the other end—in
the prison population. So: Does the gender disparity in science give
credence to the idea that men are more intelligent than women? My
answer is "no," and these are my reasons:

• **No evidence indicates that the sciences attract the brightest people.** The unspoken assumption that science attracts the smartest people is the foundation upon which we have built the conclusion: "If the sciences are filled with men, men must be smarter, unless women have a good excuse for being absent." I believe that science—like chess—attracts bright people, but only the ones with certain personality characteristics. Those traits might be more common in men. In the case of chess, the game was developed by males for intellectual sparring with other males. Maybe females simply don't find the game as fascinating. And note that dictators—who aren't any stronger than other men—are never women. Maybe females just don't have whatever it takes to bulldoze their way to this dubious sort of "success." No one thinks the paucity of women in the field of ruthless domination is because they aren't smart enough! So why should anyone be shocked to find that most bright people—including women—would flee from the sight of a microscope?!

To me, it is clear that the brightest people are spread over all sorts of other occupations. Motherhood is likely among them, and why not? I was a stay-at-home mom while my children were small, and I loved it.

• **Even professionally administered IQ tests are primitive measures of intelligence.** Intelligence tests are fine for practical purposes, but not for analytical ones. Too much unavoidable bias (not prejudice) is present: Any test-maker (not just IQ test creators) must first develop standards upon which the test-takers will be judged. In other words, to test intelligence, the designer must formulate a definition of intelligence. Now, who could possibly do this?

Can Intelligence Be Defined?

In my opinion, defining intelligence is much like defining beauty, and I don't mean that it's in the eye of the beholder. To illustrate, let's say that you are the only beholder, and your word is final. Would you be able to choose the 1000 most beautiful women in the country? And if that sounds impossible, consider this: Say you're now looking at your picks. Could you compare them to each other and say which one is more beautiful? For example, who is more beautiful—Katie Holmes or Angelina Jolie? How about Angelina Jolie or Catherine Zeta-Jones? I think intelligence is like this. So many factors are involved that attempts to measure it are useless. Not that IQ tests are

Attempts to measure intelligence are useless.

useless. Far from it. Good tests work: They measure a variety of mental abilities, and the best tests do it well. But they don't measure intelligence itself. Perhaps most convincing of all are these facts from other outposts in the animal kingdom:

- **Female chimpanzees** learn complex tasks as easily as males.
- **Female gorillas** can be taught sign language as well as males.
- **Female guide dogs** are as capable at their work as males.
- **Female dolphins** perform practical jokes as often as males.
- **Female parrots** are able to mime and talk as well as males.
- **Female rats and mice** run mazes just as efficiently as males.

Would you prefer to adopt a male puppy because you thought   9
you could teach him more tricks? No, you know better. (And we
don't find more female moths in our light fixtures!) Why should anyone think that human females are an exception?!

 Read It Now: Check out Marilyn vos Savant's Web site where you can read more of her essays, ask her questions, and participate in online discussion at **bedfordstmartins.com/americanow**, Chapter 5.

Vocabulary / Using a Dictionary

1. What is the meaning of the prefix *dis* in *disparity* (paras. 1, 2, 4)? What does the root word mean? Name three other words that use the same prefix.

2. What is the root word and origin of *credence* (para. 4)? What meaning does it suggest for the word *credibility*?

3. What is the root of the common word *intelligence*? Of what Latin words is it made up? What do the words mean?

Responding to Words in Context

1. Consider the usage of the word *hot* in the sentence "The second question is the hot spot" (para. 4). How does the literal meaning of *hot* differ from its connotative (implied nonliteral) meaning? How do you interpret the meaning of the sentence?

2. What is the meaning of *unspoken assumption* in paragraph 5? Can you provide an example of an unspoken assumption from outside the essay?

3. What does the phrase "paucity of women" (para. 5) mean? What is another way to express that idea?
4. What is the meaning of the figurative expression *eye of the beholder* (para. 8)?
5. In referring to problems with IQ tests, the writer cites "unavoidable bias (not prejudice")" (para. 7). How does *bias* differ from *prejudice*?

Discussing Main Point and Meaning

1. According to vos Savant (paras. 3 and 4), what are some reasons that account for the fact that there are fewer women than men involved in science? What cause does the writer believe is the most significant? Do you agree? Why or why not?
2. What does vos Savant mean when she asserts that "intelligence tests are fine for practical purposes, but not for analytical ones" (para. 7)? How do practical and analytical purposes differ?
3. Why does the writer believe that intelligence is so difficult to measure?

Examining Sentences, Paragraphs, and Organization

1. The essay begins with a letter to *Parade* magazine in which the writer introduces the topic and requests an answer. How effective is this device as an introduction? Does vos Savant answer the question asked?
2. How does the writer's use of headings and bullet points contribute to the clarity of the essay and to the argument she is making?
3. Why does vos Savant include quotation marks around the word "success" in paragraph 5?

Thinking Critically

1. In attempting to explain the difficulties inherent in defining intelligence, vos Savant develops a comparison between measuring beauty and intelligence. What is the basis of this comparison? Is it valid? Why or why not?
2. The writer, in implying an analogy between intelligence in humans and that of animals, provides several specific examples

(para. 8). Is the analogy, or comparison, a valid one? Explain your answer.

3. For vos Savant, what is the connection between women in science, the game of chess, and the facts that dictators are not female (para. 5)? How do these references serve to support her argument?

In-Class Writing Activities

1. Vos Savant responds to a letter inquiring about the "gender disparity" in science and possible differences in the "inherent aptitudes" of women. Review the question and the writer's main points and then decide whether vos Savant makes an effective case answering this important question and explaining the "gender gap" in science. Then, write an essay that argues your position.

2. The writer does not dispute that currently there are fewer female scientists than male. Consider the nature of the problem and write several paragraphs that propose strategies for influencing women to seek careers in science.

3. Printed with vos Savant's essay in *Parade* is an opinion poll that asks the following questions: "Are men smarter than women? Are women smarter than men? Or, do you agree with Marilyn?" Respond to these questions in a brief essay, supporting your argument with evidence.

STEVEN PINKER

Sex Ed: The Science of Difference

[THE NEW REPUBLIC / February 14, 2005]

Before You Read

Are some ideas simply too controversial to consider, even for the sake of determining whether they are wrong? Should we examine taboo questions in the name of scholarship and free inquiry? Should we ask whether men or women are smarter?

Words to Learn

blithe (para. 1): casual; heedless (adj.)

heinous (para. 1): hatefully or shockingly evil (adj.)

disparities (para. 3): differences; incongruities (n.)

unexceptionable (para. 4): not lending itself to dispute (adj.)

fatwa (para. 4): a legal opinion or decree declared by an Islamic religious leader (n.)

hullabaloo (para. 6): uproar (n.)

cogitation (para. 7): the act of thinking or reflecting (n.)

solicitous (para. 7): concerned; meticulously careful; eager (adj.)

milieu (para. 8): the setting in which something occurs; environment (n.)

specious (para. 8): deceptive; false; not genuine (adj.).

STEVEN PINKER *is a professor of psychology at Harvard University and a science writer and popular author. His research areas are visual cognition and language development in children, although for the past fifteen years he has focused on the distinction between irregular verbs and regular verbs "because the two kinds of verbs neatly embody the two processes that make language possible: looking up words in memory, and combining words (or parts of words) according to rules." One piece of invaluable advice from an editor when Pinker was working on a book for a general audience was that he "should write for an old college roommate—someone as smart as I was but who didn't happen to go into my field." He explains, "Respecting the intelligence of readers and acknowledging their lack of specialized knowledge are the two prerequisites for good science writing."*

innumeracy (para. 10): unfamiliarity with mathematical concepts and methods (n.)

tenured (para. 10): having been granted a permanent position (e.g., as a professor at a university) (adj.)

apostasy (para. 13): defection; abandonment of a previous loyalty or faith (n.)

laudable (para. 14): worthy of praise; commendable (adj.)

When I was an undergraduate in the early 1970s, I was assigned   1
a classic paper published in *Scientific American* that began: "There is an experiment in psychology that you can perform easily in your home.... Buy two presents for your wife, choosing things ... she will find equally attractive." Just ten years after those words were written, the author's blithe assumption that his readers were male struck me as comically archaic. By the early '70s, women in science were no longer an oddity or a joke but a given. Today, in my own field, the study of language development in children, a majority of the scientists are women. Even in scientific fields with a higher proportion of men, the contributions of women are so indispensable that any talk of turning back the clock would be morally heinous and scientifically ruinous.

Yet to hear the reaction to Harvard President Lawrence   2
Summers's remarks at a conference on gender imbalances in science, in which he raised the possibility of innate sex differences, one might guess that he had proposed exactly that. Nancy Hopkins, the eminent MIT biologist and advocate for women in science, stormed out of the room to avoid, she said, passing out from shock. An engineering dean called his remarks "an intellectual tsunami," and, with equal tastelessness, a *Boston Globe* columnist compared him to people who utter racial epithets or wear swastikas. Alumnae threatened to withhold donations, and the National Organization of Women called for his resignation. Summers was raked in a letter signed by more than 100 Harvard faculty members and shamed into issuing serial apologies.

Summers did not, of course, say that women are "natively infe-   3
rior," that "they just can't cut it," that they suffer "an inherent cognitive deficit in the sciences," or that men have "a monopoly on basic math ability," as many academics and journalists assumed. Only a madman could believe such things. Summers's analysis of why there might be fewer women in mathematics and science is commonplace among economists who study gender disparities in employment,

though it is rarely mentioned in the press or in academia when it comes to discussions of the gender gap in science and engineering. The fact that women make up only 20 percent of the workforce in science, engineering, and technology development has at least three possible (and not mutually exclusive) explanations. One is the persistence of discrimination, discouragement, and other barriers. In popular discussions of gender imbalances in the workforce, this is the explanation most mentioned. Although no one can deny that women in science still face these injustices, there are reasons to doubt they are the only explanation. A second possibility is that gender disparities can arise in the absence of discrimination as long as men and women differ, on average, in their mixture of talents, temperaments, and interests—whether this difference is the result of biology, socialization, or an interaction of the two. A third explanation is that child-rearing, still disproportionately shouldered by women, does not easily coexist with professions that demand Herculean commitments of time. These considerations speak against the reflex of attributing every gender disparity to gender discrimination and call for research aimed at evaluating the explanations.

Summers did not, of course, say that women are "natively inferior."

The analysis should have been unexceptionable. Anyone who has fled a cluster of men at a party debating the fine points of flat-screen televisions can appreciate that fewer women than men might choose engineering, even in the absence of arbitrary barriers. (As one female social scientist noted in *Science Magazine*, "Reinventing the curriculum will not make me more interested in learning how my dishwasher works.") To what degree these and other differences originate in biology must be determined by research, not fatwa. History tells us that how much we want to believe a proposition is not a reliable guide as to whether it is true.   4

Nor is a better understanding of the causes of gender disparities inconsequential. Overestimating the extent of sex discrimination is not without costs. Unprejudiced people of both sexes who are responsible for hiring and promotion decisions may be falsely charged with sexism. Young women may be pressured into choosing lines of work they don't enjoy. Some proposed cures may do more harm than good; for example, gender quotas for grants could put deserving grantees under a cloud of suspicion, and forcing women onto all university committees would drag them from their labs into endless meetings. An exclusive focus on overt discrimination also diverts   5 attention from policies that penalize women inadvertently because of the fact that, as the legal theorist Susan Estrich has put it, "Waiting for the connection between gender and parenting to be broken is waiting for Godot."[1] A tenure clock that conflicts with women's biological clocks, and family-unfriendly demands like evening seminars and weekend retreats, are obvious examples. The regrettably low proportion of women who have received tenured job offers from Harvard during Summers's presidency may be an unintended consequence of his policy of granting tenure to scholars early in their careers, when women are more likely to be bearing the full burdens of parenthood.

Conservative columnists have had a field day pointing to the Harvard hullabaloo as a sign of runaway political correctness at elite universities. Indeed, the quality of discussion among the nation's leading scholars and pundits is not a pretty sight. Summers's critics have repeatedly mangled his suggestion that innate differences might be one cause of gender disparities (a suggestion that he drew partly from a literature review in my book, *The Blank Slate*) into the claim that they must be the only cause. And they have converted his suggestion that the statistical distributions of men's and women's abilities are not identical to the claim that all men are talented and all women are not—as if someone heard that women typically live longer than men and concluded that every woman lives longer than every man. Just as depressing is an apparent unfamiliarity with the rationale behind political equality, as when Hopkins sarcastically remarked that, if Summers were right, Harvard should amend its admissions policy, presumably to accept fewer women. This is a classic confusion between the factual claim that men and women are not indistinguishable and the moral claim that we ought to judge people by their individual merits rather than the statistics of their group.

6

> Summers's critics have mangled his suggestion that innate differences might be one cause of gender disparities.

Many of Summers's critics believe that talk of innate gender differences is a relic of Victorian pseudoscience, such as the old theory that cogitation harms women by diverting blood from their ovaries to their brains. In fact, much of the scientific literature has reported numerous statistical differences between men and women. As I noted in

7

----

[1] *waiting for Godot:* A reference to Samuel Beckett's play *Waiting for Godot,* used here to imply a sense of endless or fruitless waiting.

The Blank Slate, for instance, men are, on average, better at mental rotation and mathematical word problems; women are better at remembering locations and at mathematical calculation. Women match shapes more quickly, are better at reading faces, are better spellers, retrieve words more fluently, and have a better memory for verbal material. Men take greater risks and place a higher premium on status; women are more solicitous to their children.

Of course, just because men and women are different does not   8
mean that the differences are triggered by genes. People develop their talents and personalities in response to their social milieu, which can change rapidly. So some of today's sex differences in cognition could be as culturally determined as sex differences in hair and clothing. But the belief, still popular among some academics (particularly outside the biological sciences), that children are born unisex and are molded into male and female roles by their parents and society is becoming less credible. Many sex differences are universal across cultures (the twentieth-century belief in sex-reversed tribes is as specious as the nineteenth-century belief in blood-deprived ovaries), and some are found in other primates. Men's and women's brains vary in numerous ways, including the receptors for sex hormones. Variations in these hormones, especially before birth, can exaggerate or minimize the typical male and female patterns in cognition and personality. Boys with defective genitals who are surgically feminized and raised as girls have been known to report feeling like they are trapped in the wrong body and to show characteristically male attitudes and interests. And a meta-analysis of 172 studies by psychologists Hugh Lytton and David Romney in 1991 found virtually no consistent difference in the way contemporary Americans socialize their sons and daughters. Regardless of whether it explains the gender disparity in science, the idea that some sex differences have biological roots cannot be dismissed as Neanderthal ignorance.

> Just because men and women are different does not mean that the difference is triggered by genes.

Since most sex differences are small and many favor women, they   9
don't necessarily give an advantage to men in school or on the job. But Summers invoked yet another difference that may be more consequential. In many traits, men show greater variance than women, and are disproportionately found at both the low and high ends of the distribution. Boys are more likely to be learning disabled or retarded but also more likely to reach the top percentiles in assessments of

mathematical ability, even though boys and girls are similar in the bulk of the bell curve. The pattern is readily explained by evolutionary biology. Since a male can have more offspring than a female—but also has a greater chance of being childless (the victims of other males who impregnate the available females)—natural selection[2] favors a slightly more conservative and reliable baby-building process for females and a slightly more ambitious and error-prone process for males. That is because the advantage of an exceptional daughter (who still can have only as many children as a female can bear and nurse in a lifetime) would be canceled

> The idea that some sex differences have biological roots cannot be dismissed as Neanderthal ignorance.

out by her unexceptional sisters, whereas an exceptional son who might sire several dozen grandchildren can more than make up for his dull childless brothers. One doesn't have to accept the evolutionary explanation to appreciate how greater male variability could explain, in part, why more men end up with extreme levels of achievement.

What are we to make of the breakdown of standards of intellectual discourse in this affair—the statistical innumeracy, the confusion of fairness with sameness, the refusal to glance at the scientific literature? It is not a disease of tenured radicals; comparable lapses can be found among the political right (just look at its treatment of evolution). Instead, we may be seeing the operation of a fascinating bit of human psychology.   10

The psychologist Philip Tetlock has argued that the mentality of taboo—the belief that certain ideas are so dangerous that it is sinful even to think them—is not a quirk of Polynesian culture or religious superstition but is ingrained into our moral sense. In 2000, he reported asking university students their opinions of unpopular but defensible proposals, such as allowing people to buy and sell organs or auctioning adoption licenses to the highest-bidding parents. He found that most of his respondents did not even try to refute the proposals but expressed shock and outrage at having been asked to entertain them. They refused to consider positive arguments for the proposals and sought to cleanse themselves by volunteering for campaigns to oppose them. Sound familiar?   11

[2] *natural selection*: A biological term associated with evolution and the concept that stronger species survive and flourish while weaker species fade out.

The psychology of taboo is not completely irrational. In main-   12
taining our most precious relationships, it is not enough to say and
do the right thing. We have to show that our heart is in the right
place and that we don't weigh the costs and benefits of selling out
those who trust us. If someone offers to buy your child or your
spouse or your vote, the appropriate response is not to think it over
or to ask how much. The appropriate response is to refuse even to
consider the possibility. Anything less emphatic would betray the
awful truth that you don't understand what it means to be a genuine
parent or spouse or citizen. (The logic of taboo underlies the horrific
fascination of plots whose protagonists are agonized by unthinkable
thoughts, such as *Indecent Proposal* and *Sophie's Choice*.[3])

Sacred and tabooed beliefs also work as membership badges in   13
coalitions. To believe something with a perfect faith, to be incapable of apostasy, is a sign of fidelity to the group and loyalty to the cause. Unfortunately, the psychology of taboo is incompatible with the ideal of scholarship, which is that any idea is worth thinking about, if only to determine whether it is wrong.

> *The belief that men and women are psychologically indistinguishable became sacred.*

At some point in the history of the mod-   14
ern women's movement, the belief that men and women are psycho
logically indistinguishable became sacred. The reasons are understandable: Women really had been held back by bogus claims of
essential differences. Now anyone who so much as raises the question
of innate sex differences is seen as "not getting it" when it comes to
equality between the sexes. The tragedy is that this mentality of
taboo needlessly puts a laudable cause on a collision course with the
findings of science and the spirit of free inquiry.

Web Read It Now: Read *The New Republic* online and check out more Steven
Pinker essays at his home page at Harvard's Department of Psychology at
bedfordstmartins.com/americanow, Chapter 5.

---

[3]*Indecent Proposal . . . Sophie's Choice*: A reference to two films in which the main
characters are confronted with difficult moral choices.

Vocabulary / Using a Dictionary

1. Both *discrimination* and *explanation* (para. 3) are nouns formed by adding the suffix *-ation* to a verb. What does "ation" mean? What is the difference between discrimination and explanation?

2. Pinker uses several words in this reading that are constructed by adding a prefix and a suffix to a common root word. An example is *disproportionately* (para. 3) What is the meaning of the root word? What are the meanings of prefixes and suffixes? Together, how do they suggest the meaning of this word?

3. *Incapable* and *incompatible* (para. 13) both contain the prefix *in*. What does it mean? How does it contribute to the meaning of the root words?

4. What is the root word and origin of *laudable* (para. 14)?

Responding to Words in Context

1. If the word *tsunami* refers to a destructive ocean wave (para. 2), what is the meaning of the phrase *intellectual tsunami*? What image does the phrase produce?

2. Consider the phrase *mutually exclusive* in relation to the other words in the sentence in paragraph 3. Given the context, what is the meaning? What are "mutually exclusive" explanations?

3. What does Pinker mean when he states that an explanation must be determined by research, not fatwa? Why use this particular word and not a more common term?

4. *Tenure clock* and *biological clock* (para. 5) are both figurative references to time. What does each expression mean?

5. What is the meaning of the phrase *Victorian pseudoscience* in paragraph 7?

Discussing Main Point and Meaning

1. In paragraph 3, Pinker attempts to clarify Harvard President Lawrence Summers's remarks when he states that Summers did not say that women are "natively inferior." What does Pinker mean by the phrase *natively inferior*? How does this statement relate to the writer's larger meaning?

2. In paragraph 3, the writer attempts to explain why women make up only 20 percent of the workforce in science, engineering, and technology. What three reasons does he offer?

3. In paragraph 6, Pinker states that critics condemned Summers for remarks that were taken from Pinker's book, *The Blank Slate*. According to Pinker, how have Summers's critics misconstrued his comments?

4. In asserting that the response to Summers's comments "should have been unexceptionable," Pinker refers to the behavior of men at a party (para. 4). How does this example serve the writer's purpose?

5. In analyzing the debate around Summers's comments, Pinker introduces his own ideas of what he believes are legitimate differences between men and women. What gender differences does the writer assert to be true on a "statistical" basis?

6. Pinker, in responding to charges against Summers, cites a number of negative consequences that result when individuals overestimate "the extent of sex discrimination" (para. 5). According to the writer, what are these costs?

Examining Sentences, Paragraphs, and Organization

1. In paragraph 1, the writer begins with a description of a 1970s psychology experiment. Why do you think Pinker begins with this anecdote? Is it an effective introduction? Explain your answer.

2. In paragraph 2, Pinker describes the negative responses to Summers's comments at a conference dealing with the topic of gender imbalances. Why does he restate the responses to Summers's remarks? What purposes do they serve within his essay?

3. In paragraph 10, the writer refers to the controversy surrounding Summers's remarks as a "breakdown of standards of intellectual discourse." According to Pinker, what are the elements of this breakdown? Why reiterate them at this point in the essay?

4. In the final paragraphs of his essay, Pinker discusses what he terms the "mentality of taboo" within our culture (paras. 11, 12, 13). How does he use this concept to support the conclusion he advances in the final paragraph? How effective is it? Explain your position.

Thinking Critically

1. What does Pinker think, ultimately, of Summers's comments? What does he think of Summers's critics? Why does he consider the controversy important enough to comment on it—and what is his main take on the controversy? Support your answer with examples from the essay.

2. Do you agree with Pinker's ideas on the differences between men and women? Why or why not?

3. Are men and women "psychologically indistinguishable" (para. 14)? How has the women's movement contributed to contemporary ideas about men and women? Are today's ideas about men and women helpful to the overall status of women?

In-Class Writing Activities

1. Based on the information that Pinker provides regarding the controversial incident at Harvard, which contributed to the resignation of President Summers, what do you believe? Should Summers have resigned? Or is Pinker essentially correct in making a case that Summers was misinterpreted and the reaction too extreme? Given what you know about this incident, write a brief essay that describes your position. Focus specifically on the response to Summers's remarks.

2. In commenting on the topic of male and female differences, Pinker offers some examples. Can you think of some additional differences? Write an essay in which you describe examples of those differences. Or, make the opposite case, that men and women are essentially alike.

JUDITH KLEINFELD

What's Going On . . . and What's Going Wrong . . . with Our Boys?

[OPEN SPACES / Volume 8, Issue 2, 2006]

Before You Read

In today's world, who has the best opportunity to achieve success, men or women? Are "good men" getting harder to find?

Words to Learn

refrain (para. 2): a phrase or verse heard at intervals throughout a song (n.)

dearth (para. 4): a scarcity or lack of something (n.)

tentacles (para. 9): long flexible organs around the mouth or on the head of some animals, often used in holding, grasping, or moving (n.)

stagnating (para. 10): becoming stale or impure through not moving (adj.)

toxemia (para. 13): a condition produced by the presence of bacterial toxins or poisons in the blood (n.)

ambivalence (para. 30): the presence of two opposing ideas or attitudes (adj.)

malaise (para. 43): a feeling of illness or general discontent (n.)

advocacy (para. 44): active verbal support for a cause or position (n.)

JUDITH KLEINFELD is the director of the Northern Studies Program and professor of psychology at the University of Alaska, Fairbanks. She has written numerous articles and books on gender and cross-cultural issues in relation to education and student performance. She has also published a book, Go for It: Finding Your Own Frontier *(2003), about how living on the frontier shaped her life, ultimately leading her to study the learning styles of the overlooked populations of Eskimo, Indian, and Aleut children in Alaska. In her preface she writes, "On a frontier, you can make the most of yourself and contribute the most to others while, at the same time, have a whale of a good time. You don't have to go to Alaska to find a frontier. You can find your own Alaska anywhere."*

Call her Susan. Sinking into a caramel leather couch with her at   1
a Christmas party, I was trying to see, delicately, if she wanted to talk
about it. The morning newspaper had carried a story about the guy
she was going with. He had been arrested for driving while intoxicated . . . and driving with a suspended license.

Why was Susan going with such a man? With her athletic figure   2
and pixie blonde hair, she reminded me of the verse "All things bright
and beautiful." Susan was not only beautiful, she was smart and
kind. In her early thirties, she wanted to marry. Her family never
stopped asking her, "Are you meeting people (meaning a good
man)?" And she knew she would hear this refrain many times when
she went home for the holidays.

Yes, she wanted to talk about it. Thoughtful as always, she sent   3
me a card the next day to thank me for the conversation, for putting
her particular problem in the context of the larger question: What's
going on . . . and what's going wrong with guys? She was not going
with this guy because she wanted "to save" him, she assured me. She
did not have "rescue fantasies." The problem was that she could not
find a good man. She felt she had to "settle" for a man like him.

"A good man is hard to find," the old saying goes. A good man is   4
getting harder and harder to find. Why? Why are attractive and educated young women like Susan facing a dearth of suitable mates?

"A fine young man"—we used to see so many of them. Ambi-   5
tious and conscientious, willing to shoulder the responsibility of supporting and protecting a family, wanting to "be a man," these men,
so many of them, seem gone with the wind of another era.

What Has Happened?

The gender gap in college graduation rates now means that one   6
out of four college educated women will not have a college educated
man to marry. In his 2005 book, *The Minds of Boys: Saving Our
Sons from Falling Behind in School and in Life,* Michael Gurian summarizes the dismal statistics:

- Boys get the majority of the D's and F's in most schools.
- Boys make up 90 percent of our discipline problems.
- Of children diagnosed with learning disabilities, 70 percent are
  boys.
- Of children diagnosed with behavioral disorders, 80 percent are
  boys.

- Of high school dropouts, 80 percent are young males.
- According to the U.S. Department of Education, our sons are on average a year to a year and a half behind girls in reading and writing skills.
- Over 80 percent of schoolchildren on Ritalin or similar drugs are boys.
- Young men now make up less than 44 percent of our college population.

After decades of worrying about the problems of girls, we are finally waking up to the problems of boys. Yes, girls used to fall behind boys in high school mathematics and science. This particular gender gap has just about closed. 7

The problems of boys are far more serious than the problems of girls ever were. But we have yet to give these problems serious attention. The issue not only affects the success and well-being of men. They also affect the success and well-being of women. Like Susan. 8

For the last few years, I have been studying the problems of boys. I have been interviewing college students, asking them why so many more young women compared to young men are choosing to go on to college. Together with a team of other researchers and graduate students, I have interviewed high school seniors, males and females, on their plans after high school and the reasons for their choices. I have held focus groups of high school girls and boys and reviewed the research literature, books and articles with titles like "Hopeful Girls/Troubled Boys." The "boy problem" is like an octopus with tentacles stretching out in different directions. You can grab hold of different tentacles—low school achievement, high suicide rates, the gender gap in college attendance—and follow any one to the core. 9

I chose to cut into this problem by focusing on this question: Why are young women surging into college while young men are stagnating? In the late 1970s, more females than males began to enroll in college. Since then a gender gap in college attendance and graduation arose in favor of females and has widened. No reversal of this trend is in sight. According to a report released in 2003 by the U.S. Department of Education's National Center 10

Why are young women surging into college while young men are stagnating?

for Education Statistics, the college gender gap is expected to increase. Even in white upper income homes (incomes above $70,000), according to a 2003 study by the American Council of Education, young women aged 24 years or younger outnumber young men in college enrollment.

The growing gender gap in college attendance and graduation   11
has serious consequences. The economy has changed. The global economy requires more and more people with highly developed verbal and symbolic skills, the ability to cooperate with others of different background, and the ability to multitask. These are areas in which women tend to excel and in which young men tend to lag behind. Less educated young men tend to earn less, to be unemployed for longer times, and to pay less in taxes. But the issue goes beyond economic concerns. Less educated young men are also more apt to be involved with the criminal justice system and less likely to vote and participate in civic affairs.

Reasons for the College Gender Gap

"Sheena" and her two brothers, "Tom" and "Dave," offer a mi-   12
crocosm of the problem. Their own parents are puzzled: All three children grew up in the same family. All went to the same schools and had the same opportunities. Why did Sheena go to college while her two brothers did not?

The reason one of her brothers, Dave, did not go to college is not   13
difficult to explain. Throughout school, Dave had learning disabilities. Males are far more apt to have neurological and other developmental problems than females, a biological phenomenon that leads to about twice as many males in special education classes. The problems are apparent even before birth. Complications of pregnancy such as toxemia, abruptio, spontaneous abortion, and birth trauma are almost twice as common when the fetus is male.

Sheena had the academic ability to go to college. She had always   14
gotten good grades in school. She went to work right after high school as a sales clerk in order to save money for college. When she unexpectedly won a scholarship to the University of Alaska, she quit her job, and her mother proudly drove her up the hill to register for classes. Practical and self-assured, Sheena knows what she wants: a college education that will lead to a good job where she can do satisfying work, a good income, and a comfortable lifestyle.

Tom is the puzzle. He had the academic ability to do well in col-   15
lege, although he never bothered to get good grades in school. After

high school graduation, Tom just drifted. He kept his old high school job as a pizza deliveryman. He wanted to work at night, he said, and hang out with his friends.

My interviews with high school and college students suggest the   16
following reasons for the college gender gap, for the difference between young women like Sheena and young men like Tom:

1. Women of all backgrounds see a college degree as a vital edu-   17
cational investment while many men do not. The reason young women are pouring into college in the students' views, is no mystery. Women now are expected to support themselves. They can not expect a husband to take care of them and their children:

> The issue is the divorce rate. I interviewed my girlfriend who is a college student. She explained that women are dominating college classes because they want to be able to support themselves and not depend on a man. "They always let women down," she laughs.

The young women are all too aware that almost 50 percent of   18
marriages will end in divorce. Many of their parents (and some women in college) have already experienced a divorce. Their parents, especially their mothers, urge them to go to college so that they will not be stuck in a bad marriage. Furthermore, as many young women emphasized and the young men agreed, their boy friends expect young women nowadays not to be a financial burden to their husbands.

A college degree is their ticket to a desirable job. If they do not go   19
to college, what are their alternatives? A low-paying job as a sales clerk?

Young men, in contrast, see themselves as having a variety of at-   20
tractive options, and college is not necessarily the most attractive. They can join the military. They can get a high-paying construction job. With their physical strength and vigor, they can earn good money fast. Why should they pay to go to college when they can be paid for working?

The problem is that many of these young men get caught in what   21
one career guidance counselor labeled "The Trap." Sure, they can make good money while they are young and strong. But as their backs give out, as they want more regular hours and a home life, many want another kind of life. Now they are moving toward middle age, they have bills to pay, their school skills are awfully rusty, and they are left with few options.

2. Some young men have distorted beliefs about the labor market   22
and the incomes they can earn without a college education. A number

of young men believe their economic opportunities are greater without college. While some are undoubtedly correct, given their particular abilities and skills, I was amazed at the amount of misinformation high school senior boys had about the labor market.

> Like a few guys I know can get low level jobs working construction and work their way up. They can easily make more than $20,000 a year, which is more than many teachers.

The fact is that wages for young men with only a high school education have declined by twenty percent over the last twenty years. In 1979, inflation-adjusted hourly wages for less-educated men averaged $10.47 an hour, while in 1999, hourly wages averaged only $8.68, according to a 2003 study by the Center for Law and Social Policy, "Boom Times a Bust: Declining Employment Among Less-Educated Young Men." Many young men did not see things this way: 23

"An education is something that is no longer necessary to make it in our society."

> I know of several people not too much older than myself who have managed to cut out a relatively good life for themselves with very good salaries, and more than half dropped out of high school. It just seems that an education is something that is no longer necessary to make it in our society, and therefore it is not worth wasting one's time or money on.

For some young men, the skilled crafts may indeed offer as much or more pay and as satisfying work as employment requiring a college education. But most of the young men we interviewed did not have clear goals in mind. They were drifting. Indeed, some were in college because they did not know what else to do.   25

3. Some young men felt intimidated by smart, persistent young women and chose economic arenas where they did not have to compete with them. While in school, the men had to compete with determined young women who garnered the lion's share of the awards: 26

"I do not want to go to college because I feel I am inferior to women in this aspect."

> From personal experience, I do not want to go to college because I feel I am inferior to women in this aspect. Take for example my senior class in high school, there were only six full rides given to males and twenty given to the females. There were twice as many guys in my graduating class of over four hundred.

24

Some of the young men had a fragile sense of their own   27
competence:

> Men feel that the determined women are overpowering them. So the
> men think that since so many females are outperforming them, suc-
> cess will be hard to come by.

This young man recommended self-pep talks to deal with "intim-   28
idation by persistent women":

> If you are a male, don't let the successful women burst your bubble.
> Everyone can be successful, regardless of his or her gender.

4. In some cases, families were more apt to help their daughters   29
with college tuition than their sons. Paying for college was a big
problem for many young men and women. Some students pointed
out that their parents were more likely to finance their sisters' education. It was fine for Sheena's brother to deliver pizza at night, for example, but Sheena's parents would not have allowed their young
daughter to go to strange apartments at night. Parents expected more
independence and self-sufficiency from their boys:

> All the friends I have that are young women have parents that are fi-
> nancing their college education. Young women are also more likely
> to get sympathy from their parents in financial matters than the sons.
> I know this from personal experience.

While mothers were eager for their daughters to get an education   30
and have more independence and a better life than they had, several
boys mentioned that fathers expressed more ambivalence:

> My nephew is graduating from high school this year and he isn't
> going to college. His father never went to college and does not en-
> courage him or his brother. His father is worried that if his sons get a
> degree they will think that they are smarter than he is and their rela-
> tionship may break down. My father was the same way. In fact, my
> father spent my college money on a Porsche during his midlife crisis.

5. Young men and young women both wanted independence but   31
were apt to define it differently. While young men were apt to define
independence as getting out of the house and getting a job, young
women were apt to define independence as going to college. As one
young man put it:

> I noticed that a majority of my friends who were staying home were
> guys. Since they all had the chance to go to college, I always wonder
> why they didn't. When I asked a few of the guys, all their answers

generally stated that they wanted to make money and buy their own place so they could get away from their parents and hang out. I got the feeling that they thought this was some cool and manly thing to do, to get out on your own, make your own money and your own rules. They soon found out that their ideal life of freedom was much harder to pull off than they thought. Most of them are now living at home with their parents.

6. Young women were more apt to enjoy the activity of schooling   32
and had less trouble doing assignments that required reading and writing skills. Both the young women and young men pointed out that many young men did not particularly enjoy school activities or see any value to them.

> Men are more focused on the physical achievements rather than mental achievements. Men tend to start a job like construction or fixing cars that doesn't require much of an education and yet pays well. I see that school teaches things that most men do not think they will ever use in the jobs that they see themselves in. These jobs are things like mechanics, construction workers, or, in some cases, professional wrestler.

One young military couple provided an apt illustration of these   33
sex differences. The wife, bright and ambitious, appeared in class with her husband (usually) in reluctant tow. He did not want to go to college, he explained, because he "would rather work with his hands and not be stuck behind a desk doing the dirty work." His wife got him to go to college when he didn't want to go by telling him, "You know that you can have a college education and still work with your hands."

7. Young women saw themselves as encouraged by the women's   34
movement and their teachers to make something of themselves. Many young men felt that they were receiving little encouragement to go to college. The young women emphasized that they were getting a clear and consistent, even an insistent message: Women now had opportunities that they never had before. The world was now open to them as women. They could and should achieve:

> All throughout elementary school we're taught that in the "old days," women didn't go to school and that women hardly held any important positions in any historical events. I think this prompts many young women to go to college and attempt "to make a difference" and become someone who may someday be read about in future history books.

Many of the young men felt ignored or even put down in school: 35

> Achievements women make scholastically or athletically are praised
> as a great step for women whereas male achievements unless particu-
> larly spectacular are generally glossed over. Males are made to feel
> ashamed for the actions of their ancestors, and as a result get far less
> encouragement to excel.

8. Some young men were frustrated by what they saw as discrim-   36
ination against them in scholarships. Young men did not resent the
opportunities that had opened for women. They applauded women's
success, recognized the energy and determination of their girl friends,
and were more than a little relieved that they were no longer expected
to be the sole support of a family. They also supported the ideal of
gender equality. Where the feminist movement brought protests of
injustice was sex discrimination in scholarships. They too needed
money for college, badly, and many scholarships were not open to
them:

> I checked websites and found that I am eligible for less than 30% of
> the scholarships offered. I am a victim of reverse-discrimination. I
> haven't done anything wrong; my only crime is being a middle class
> white male. My parents make just enough money to not receive fed-
> eral grant money. I am now at a predetermined disadvantage based
> on my gender and color of my skin.

Sports scholarships are becoming more widely available to young   37
women because of Title IX regulations regarding gender equity. The
other side of the coin is that fewer sports scholarships are available to
young men, and some of the young men only went to college because
of a sports scholarship:

> For me, I wouldn't be here today if it weren't for basketball. I have
> never been a big fan of school. Talking to my girl friend, she is here
> also because of basketball. But basketball isn't the reason she is
> in college. She is using basketball as an opportunity to get a free
> education.

9. Some young men seem to have given up. If the battle for   38
school success will be lost anyway, why bother to play the game?
Many of the girls we interviewed, as well as boys, labeled boys as
"lazy."

> Things are most certainly changing and guys don't really seem to care
> anymore.

Stubbornly refusing to go to college could be in itself a message   39
of protest:

> There is a lot more discontent among young males than among
> young females. This discontent urges many young men to "buck the
> system" and avoid advanced schooling: a college education can be
> seen as conformist and counterproductive.

Many women, in contrast, radiated satisfaction with the way the   40
world was moving:

> Personally I think it is awesome that there are so many women en-
> rolling in college. It's not that I am happy that more guys are skip-
> ping college, but as a woman it is a nice thing to see, we keep moving
> up in the world.

To interview so many bright, focused, and determined young   41
women was indeed a delight. The young women not only had plans.
Many of them had backup plans. They knew what they wanted and
they saw college was the way to get where they wanted to go. They
were being "pushed," they said, while so many boys were not being
pushed.

To interview many of the boys, on the other hand, was disturb-   42
ing. Many were indeed "fine young men," ambitious, conscientious,
wanting to find satisfying work and have a family. But many others
were drifting. When asked what they wanted to do after high school,
the boys could usually come up with an answer. But further probing
revealed that they had happened to come across this idea when
searching the web or listening to the radio a few days ago. So many
boys seemed to be internalizing a concept of themselves as "lazy" and
"not as smart as girls." They were accepting what others said about
them.

The Need for a Boys' Project and Advocacy for Boys

The gender gap in college attendance is a symptom of a deeper   43
malaise that is affecting many young men. For more than thirty years,
society has been encouraging girls to be ambitious, to move into
fields formerly dominated by men. In a single generation, the
women's movement has created profound cultural change. That such
change can be created in one generation demonstrates the power of a
social movement that enlists the support of the schools, the media,
the family, the foundations, the agencies of government. Now it is the
boys who are being left behind. We need to give boys the same encouragement and opportunities we are giving to girls.

This will not be easy. The stereotype that men are still the patri-   44
archy, holding the positions of power, weakens advocacy for boys. In
addition, many men and boys do not like
the image of themselves as in need of special
help, as weak and whining. The most effective advocacy group for boys may well be
women, who worry not only about their
sons but also about their daughters, so
bright and beautiful, who nonetheless may find themselves in the
predicament of women like Susan.

> "The most effective
> advocacy group for boys
> may well be women."

 Read It Now: Read select articles in the online edition of *Open Spaces* magazine and additional writings by Judith Kleinfeld at **bedfordstmartins.com/
americanow**, Chapter 5.

Vocabulary / Using a Dictionary

1. What is the origin of the word *conscientious* (para. 5)?
2. What is the origin of the word *microcosm* (para. 12)? How does
   the root word suggest its meaning?
3. What is the origin and root word of *alternatives* (para. 19)?
4. What is the prefix and origin of *patriarchy* (para. 44)?

Responding to Words in Context

1. Kleinfeld writes that her female subject, Susan, does not have
   "rescue fantasies" (para. 3). Explain this reference. Can you provide a more accurate description of Susan's problem?
2. The writer asserts that the global economy requires "verbal and
   symbolic skills" (para. 11). What does she mean by *symbolic
   skills*?
3. What is the meaning of Kleinfeld's reference to "inflation-
   adjusted hourly wages" in paragraph 23? What is an "inflation-
   adjusted" wage? How does this impact men?
4. In paragraph 26, what does the writer mean by saying that
   women "garnered the lion's share" of awards?
5. In paragraph 42, Kleinfeld writes that "boys seemed to be internalizing a concept of themselves"? In this sense, what does *internalizing* mean?

Discussing Main Point and Meaning

1. What point does Kleinfeld make early on (para. 6) about male and female graduation rates?
2. What is the basis of the writer's information regarding male and female behavior (para. 9)?
3. According to Kleinfeld (para. 17), why are women "pouring into college"?
4. In what manner are the young men referred to in paragraph 22 "misinformed" regarding their earning power?
5. In paragraph 29, Kleinfeld explains that some families are more willing to help daughters to attend college. Why?
6. In attempting to explain the changes in male and female performance over a generation, the writer refers in her conclusion to the impact of the women's movement. According to Kleinfeld, what effects has the movement had on the current gender disparity?

Examining Sentences, Paragraphs, and Organization

1. Kleinfeld begins her essay with an anecdote. How do Susan's problems help to highlight the problems that become the focus of the essay? Why does the author frame the essay—which is about the status of men—through a perspective aimed at women readers?
2. To explain what the author describes as a new gender gap in college attendance, she refers to the example of Sheena and her brothers. How does their situation illustrate the larger problem with which the writer is concerned? Is the writer's use of examples and quotations persuasive? Why or why not?

Thinking Critically

1. Consider the essay's title. Overall, what, according to Kleinfeld, is "going wrong" with boys? What do you think would help improve the lives and potential of boys today?
2. Respond to Kleinfeld's use of statistics to support her claim that boys are falling behind in certain ways. Do the statistics surprise you? Does she make a convincing argument?
3. Kleinfeld explains what she sees as some of the challenges facing young men. Which of these (nonphysical) problems seem the most serious?

4. In paragraph 22, the writer cites "typical" misinformation that young men possess regarding the current labor market. What does she provide as an example of this misinformation? Why is the misinformation so serious?

5. What does the writer mean when she asserts (para. 44) that "the most effective advocacy group for boys may well be women"? How does this relate to the anecdote that Kleinfeld employs to begin the essay?

In-Class Writing Activities

1. According to the research cited by the writer in paragraph 6, boys are responsible for 90 percent of the discipline problems in schools across the country. To what extent was this statistic true in your high school? Write a brief essay that responds to this statistic, either by arguing that it is or is not true. Like Kleinfeld, use specific examples that help to support your position.

2. In paragraph 9, the writer describes "the 'boy problem'" as being like an "octopus" in that it has so many "tentacles" or parts. Consider the nature of this simile (the use of the word *like* or *as* to compare one object or experience to another). What other similes could be used to describe the same problem? Write several similes that describe this issue.

3. Kleinfeld's essay poses a problem that may be familiar in that it deals with young adults. She states, specifically, that boys "are being left behind" (para. 43), but she does not advocate or advance specific ways of dealing with the problem that she describes in so much detail. After reflecting on this problem, and the idea that "we need to give boys the same encouragement and opportunities we are giving to girls" (para. 43), brainstorm some methods of accomplishing a solution. Use your ideas as the basis of an essay titled "What *Should* Go On with Our Boys?"

DAPHNE LABUA

My Brain Has a Sex?

[THE TUFTS DAILY, Tufts University / October 26, 2005]

Before You Read

Do men and women learn in different manners? Should male and female students be separated? Do single-sex classrooms offer more effective places for learning?

Words to Learn

predecessors (para. 1): people or things previously in existence that have been replaced or succeeded by someone or something else (n.)

implemented (para. 2): to have put something into action (v.)

fluctuating (para. 6): changing often between high levels and low levels (adj.)

icons (para. 8): people or things widely admired; symbols of a movement, society, and so on (n.)

albeit (para. 9): a term to add information that is different from what you have already said (conj.)

DAPHNE LABUA, *a 2006 graduate of Tufts University, was a senior majoring in political science and French when she wrote "My Brain Has a Sex?" LaBua comments: "The subject of the article first sparked my interest in a class that I was enrolled in, 'Media, Politics, and the Law.' We discussed the idea of same-sex education in public schools, and how more and more studies are proving that men and women process information differently. Could this knowledge help the struggling institution of public education in our country? After reading a BBC news article on the issue, I decided to write my own article." Her advice: "Never avoid writing about a subject that makes you uncomfortable. We learn more about who we are by forcing ourselves outside of our comfort zones. Some of the best articles I have ever read have fundamentally challenged my personal beliefs."*

Men and women are equal, and therefore, women should have   1
all of the same rights as men. Because of this, no distinction should be
made between boys and girls when it comes to education and other
forms of socialization. Isn't that what women have been fighting for
since winning the right to vote in 1920? It's been a long struggle, and
we are achieving our goals. Women are going places their predecessors never thought they could.

So how is someone like myself, who wholeheartedly supports   2
women's rights, supposed to react to ideas like, let's say, separating
students in the public school system by sex?

What of the evidence
that suggests that boys'
and girls' brains learn
differently?

My first reaction was "No way!" But what
of the evidence that suggests that boys' and
girls' brains learn differently? Scientific studies illustrate the varying conditions under
which boys and girls effectively absorb
knowledge, and schools that have imple-
mented a curriculum that caters towards the different needs of each
gender show signs of academic improvement.

Allow me to digress for a moment. I am currently enrolled in a   3
political science class called "Media, Politics and the Law," taught by
Professor Michael Goldman. During the first class, we were handed a
Culture Quiz, which asked us to agree or disagree with 50 statements
produced by the public clash of private values that have fueled the
American culture wars. One of the first statements was: Men are
more jealous over sexual infidelity, while women care more about
emotional betrayal.

Yes, the stereotypes suggest that women require more emotional   4
support in a relationship while men, fearing inadequacy in the bedroom, are more jealous of their partner's infidelity because they do
not want their women to know that something "better" exists. This
is why a woman's level of experience with the opposite sex is such a
big deal to some men. But to what extent are these stereotypes results
of differences in the biology of the male and female brains?

Let me assert here that I believe that women and men should be   5
unquestionably equal in the eyes of the law (and in the eyes of one
another, but I cannot affect free will). But should men and women
necessarily be viewed as being the same?

Recently, I came across a BBC article entitled "Your Brain's Sex   6
Can Make You Ill," in which a doctor claims that "we should be
looking at diseases as male and female." The article argues that doctors and scientists now have proof that being male or female makes

one more susceptible to different diseases, and that because men's and women's brains are different, we should change the way we study and diagnose disease. These conclusions, scientists claim, should affect the way in which treatment drugs are prescribed, especially since most of the drugs available today have only been tested on men and may not work as effectively on women, as it has been demonstrated that women's brains change throughout their lives as a result of fluctuating hormone levels.

Some ardent feminists might argue that these ideas can be manip-   7
ulated against women to prove that they are somehow unequal to men, and that the ideology of "separate but equal" would be brought back to suppress women's civil rights. Personally, I do not believe that this will happen. Once the differences between the sexes (or ethnicity, race, or religion) can be embraced as enriching components of our collective culture, they can be used to foster a greater understanding of human behavior and humanity in general.

Granted, it must first be universally and unconditionally recog-   8
nized that "different" does not mean "less capable." History has proven repeatedly that this is very difficult to do, but today, women have established themselves as strong forces. There will always be those who argue that the place of the woman is at home and at her husband's side. But with many powerful female icons like Princess Diana and Hillary Clinton, and popular television shows like *Sex in the City* and *Desperate Housewives*, women will continue to break through the glass ceiling.

If science has proven that gender affects the brain, and if the brain   9
determines how we interact with one another and learn, then perhaps the conditions under which we effectively absorb knowledge are also determined by our gender. Like the BBC article suggests for drug treatments, quality of education would be optimized in a personalized situation, or one-on-one tutoring. But the costs of such an operation at the public level would be prohibitive. Single-sex classrooms provide an alternative. This doesn't necessarily mean that boys and girls would not get a chance to interact in the hallways and at lunchtime, unless entire schools were designated as either male or female, which I do not think would be legal in the public school system. The gender socialization that takes place in most public schools today would still exist, albeit to a lesser degree. If a district can afford to have more teachers, particularly those who are trained and sensitive to gender-specific issues which might affect students' learning methods, then programs which separate children into single-sex classrooms should

merit attention. What would your response be if I were to suggest that such separation-by-sex should occur only in elementary and middle schools, when children begin to establish but do not cement the way in which they learn information and approach education?

My brain does have a sex, which in turn affects the way in which   10
I perceive and interact with the world around me. But to what extent should we allow biological factors to deter-

To what extent should we allow biological factors to determine how we choose to educate ourselves?

mine how we choose to educate ourselves? And what are the risks involved in doing so?

Here is a fact which cannot be denied: 11
The education system in the U.S. is faltering. Still deeply and shamefully segregated despite *Brown v. Board of Education,* our school system needs our attention. The very foundations of our future are being forsaken for a formless threat thousands of miles away that is less likely to kill the average American than is a bee sting. One possible solution

For an annotated excerpt of this essay that highlights LaBua's writing strategies, see page 200.

which might improve the situation in our public schools is the separation of children into moderately personalized educational environments geared towards optimizing their learning experiences.

 Read It Now: Read more opinions by Tufts University students in the *Tufts Daily* at **bedfordstmartins.com/americanow**, Chapter 5.

Vocabulary / Using a Dictionary

1. What is the root word and origin of *curriculum* (para. 2)? How does the root word shape the meaning of *curriculum*?

2. What is the meaning of *fidelity* in the word *infidelity* (paras. 3, 4)? How does the prefix alter the word's meaning?

3. What is the noun form of the verb *optimize*? (para. 9) What is its meaning and origin?

Responding to Words in Context

1. How do the phrases *let's say* and *no way* (para. 2) establish a tone? How does the tone of these phrases affect the writer's message?

2. How do you interpret the meaning of the phrase *culture wars* in paragraph 3? Who are the opponents in this battle?

3. What does LaBua mean by the term *feminists* in paragraph 7? Who are *ardent feminists*, as implied by the writer?

4. According to the writer, what is the relationship between television programs like *Sex in the City* and *Desperate Housewives* and the "glass ceiling" (para. 8)? What connotations does the phrase *glass ceiling* have?

5. What are *gender-specific issues* (para. 9)?

Discussing Main Point and Meaning

1. What does LaBua mean by the phrase *separate but equal* in paragraph 7? What is the origin of the phrase? Why does she perceive this ideology as dangerous?

2. What does the writer cite as an example of a stereotype in paragraph 4? To what degree is this stereotype valid, according to the writer?

3. What does the writer mean in paragraph 6 when she refers to male and female diseases? What does she perceive in paragraph 7 as the danger of this classification of disease by gender?

4. What is the meaning of the writer's reference to "gender socialization" in paragraph 9? What is the purpose of gender socialization in the educational system?

5. As a supporter of equality for women, how does LaBua feel about the prospects for single-sex education?

Examining Sentences, Paragraphs, and Organization

1. LaBua opens her essay with references to women's long struggle for equal rights as well as a statement of her own beliefs. How does this introduction relate to her second paragraph and the suggestion of separating students by gender?

2. In paragraph 3, the writer digresses in a way that allows her to discuss her political science class. How does this digression affect her essay? Does this add to or weaken her overall point?

3. Evaluate the overall organization of the essay. Does the organization contribute to the writer's persuasiveness? What, if anything,

would you have done differently in organizing and presenting this argument? Explain.

Thinking Critically

1. What is LaBua's main argument? How persuasive is she? Do you agree with what she proposes? Why or why not?

2. What is the meaning of the reference in paragraph 11 to *Brown v. Board of Education*? How is its ruling, in which the Supreme Court overturned the doctrine of "separate but equal," relevant to LaBua's thesis?

3. The writer cites Princess Diana and Hillary Clinton as icons of female power. What purpose are these references intended to serve? Can you identify other women who represent more powerful icons?

4. In the final paragraph, the author refers to a "formless threat thousands of miles away." What is the meaning of this allusion? How does it relate to the overall meaning of the essay?

In-Class Writing Activities

1. In digressing to her political science class, the writer is able to tie her own discussion of gender issues to the "culture wars" in the larger society. This provides context and allows her to discuss information regarding gender stereotypes as they were presented in her political science course. Evaluate the effectiveness of this device in a short editorial response to the writer.

2. LaBua's essay builds gradually to a long paragraph that outlines an argument for single-sex education, based on what she believes regarding male and female differences. Consider her suggestion and list what you believe might be the possible benefits and disadvantages of single-sex education.

3. Near the conclusion, the writer emphasizes the idea that her brain "does have a sex" that impacts or influences her perception of the world. To what extent does gender affect the way you see the world? Explain and provide examples.

ANNOTATION The Art of Argument: Anticipating Resistance

One effective strategy when taking a position you think may be unpopular or controversial is to indicate that you too were once inclined to find the position untenable. In that way you not only show you identify with your audience but you also help persuade your audience to identify with your transformed view. In other words, if you once believed what they did, then it's possible they in turn could be encouraged to accept what you believe now. We are offered an effective illustration of this argumentative strategy in a column by a Tufts University student, **Daphne LaBua**. In the opening paragraphs of "**My Brain Has a Sex?**" the writer first asserts that "no distinction should be made between boys and girls when it comes to education." She makes it clear that this is a statement that she and all other feminists would endorse. But in the next paragraph, after indicating that her "first reaction" to "separating students in the public school system by sex" was "No way!" she introduces the "scientific studies" on gender differences that have transformed her position on the issue. By framing her argument in this way, she retains her feminist identity and makes her position appear far more credible.

LaBua begins by establishing her feminist perspective.

Men and women are equal, and therefore, women should have all of the same rights as men. Because of this, no distinction should be made between boys and girls when it comes to education and other forms of socialization. Isn't that what women have been fighting for since winning the right to vote in 1920? It's been a long struggle, and we are achieving our goals. Women are going places their predecessors never thought they could.

1

She then introduces an idea that would seem counter to feminism.

LaBua identifies with her readers' likely reaction, then supports her position with scientific evidence.

So how is someone like myself, who wholeheartedly supports women's rights, supposed to react to ideas like, let's say, separating students in the public school system by sex? My first reaction was "No way!" But what of the evidence that suggests that boys' and girls' brains learn differently? Scientific studies illustrate the varying conditions under which boys and girls effectively absorb knowledge, and schools that have implemented a curriculum that caters towards the different needs of each gender show signs of academic improvement.

2

— From "My Brain Has a Sex?" by Daphne LaBua, page 194

Discussing the Unit

Suggested Topic for Discussion

What explains the disparities between men and women in such areas as education and employment? Are men or women smarter? Should we even ask this question? Does the mere suggestion of gender differences indicate a bias? Are boys falling behind? Are women discriminated against in the sciences? What can be done to equalize status of men and women in our society?

Preparing for Class Discussion

1. How does each writer approach the concept of gender and possible gender differences? How do the writers differ or agree regarding issues of gender? Which essay did you find most controversial and why?

2. What problems does each writer identify? What solutions or remedies do they advocate? Which do you agree most with?

3. Do you see disparities between men and women in terms of success in your family, community, and college environment? If so, what are these disparities? Why do you think they exist? Are there different expectations for males and females in your life? What might be done to improve success levels (for men and/or women)?

From Discussion to Writing

1. What are the central issues and problems regarding gender at the beginning of the twenty-first century? What gender stereotypes still exist? Are these stereotypes harmful? In what manner? What new stereotypes have emerged, and what do you attribute them to?

2. Who are the genuine "victims" of our beliefs and policies regarding gender? Kleinfeld makes a strong case that men have been victimized by changes ostensibly associated with the women's movement. How real are the problems of young men? What should be done to solve these challenges?

3. Kleinfeld asserts that young men have been disadvantaged by the progress of women, while LaBua perceives a "glass ceiling" that still confronts women. Which writer's view of the world is more accurate?

4. If some gender differences are valid, as several writers assert, should men and women be educated in different classrooms? Would the single-sex classrooms that LaBua proposes resolve the problems of the glass ceiling or the issues that Kleinfeld identifies? What would such a classroom look like? How effective would it be?

5. Finally, why is it so difficult to discuss issues relating to gender? What does this difficulty or discomfort tell us about ourselves? How might this sensitivity, which creates so many impediments to discussion and learning, be alleviated?

Topics for Cross-Cultural Discussion

1. The essays in this chapter deal specifically with men and women in the United States, where, according to law, discrimination on the basis of gender is illegal. The government has created legal and other remedies to resolve problems arising from gender discrimination. How do other nations and societies deal with questions of gender and gender inequity? What specific lessons can we learn from other cultures regarding our attitudes about gender? What does it mean to be a man? To be a woman? How do the answers differ elsewhere in the world? Do you think all cultures would understand the *Zits* cartoon that opened the chapter?

2. Consider that some women who emigrate to the United States come from countries where they have not had the rights and protections that exist today in America. How might they experience social and political life here? How might these women, who perhaps are still assimilating into U.S. culture or who perhaps lack language skills, be vulnerable in ways that American women are not? How can this country, its citizens and government, and specifically its academic institutions assist this specific population to prevent abuse and victimization? Or, consider that some women emigrate from countries where women have significant social and political power—perhaps countries where women have been elected president. How might they experience social and political life in the United States?

Do Words Matter?

Do the words we use matter—personally, socially, and politically? Does it, or should it, make any difference if we call a college student a *girl* instead of a *woman*? Or if we say *colored people* instead of *people of color*? How easy is it to give serious offense by simply making a wrong or an inappropriate word choice? How and why do words take on such power? Must we carefully monitor everything we say and how we say it? In this chapter, we look at various ways that specific words can alter our perspectives and shape our attitudes.

We begin with the impact of particular words on large political issues. In "Changing Warming," the well-known political columnist and word-watcher William Safire takes a close look at what he calls "terminological politics"—that is, the way political opponents employ different words and expressions to their advantage. By attributing recent weather disturbances to *climate change* instead of the older term, *global warming*, Safire wonders, are certain parties misrepresenting and misleading the public as to the seriousness of this environmental issue? As Safire succinctly puts it, "who names an issue usually carries the day."

One common tool of "terminological politics" is euphemism—the use of a term that is less direct than an ordinary word and considered potentially less offensive. For example, the job that was known years ago as *garbage man* is now referred to as *sanitation worker*. People prefer to say an animal has been *put to sleep* instead of *put to death*. Euphemism can be used to disguise a real event or shed a positive light on something that is actually negative. For example, in "Awash in Euphemisms," John Leo, a popular columnist for *U.S. News & World Report*, reports on how airlines prefer to call a *plane crash* a *hull loss* and how educators are favoring the expression *deferred success* over the plain old *failed*. For many, the term *illegal alien* seems overly harsh, and a number of replacement labels have been vying for acceptance, as cartoonist Tamara Shopsin depicts in her version of how the Statue of Liberty's message might read today.

Certain members of groups would just as soon return to the words the euphemisms were intended to replace. In "Queering the Campus, Loud and Clear," Emory University student Jaclyn Barbarow isn't cautious about using the Q-word or identifying herself as *queer*. To help attain more visibility on campus and to foster awareness of the wide range of sexual orientations, she provides a brief dictionary of terms relating to sex and gender. Only by knowing the meaning of these terms, Barbarow suggests, can other students understand the "issues faced by those of us who identify as queer, gay, lesbian, bisexual, transgender or intersex." In the next selection, essayist Lucia Perillo looks at herself along similar lines, preferring to call herself *crippled* rather than use the "overly sanitized" word *disabled*.

The chapter concludes with a view of language few people ever consider: the many words our language doesn't have. Languages throughout the world, Adam Jacot de Boinod reminds us, make use of words and idioms for which English has no equivalent. For example, he writes in "Global Wording" that one of the Australian aborigine languages has a verb that means "to walk along in the water searching for something with your feet." English has borrowed many words "from other cultures for centuries," he maintains, yet laments that "there are so many we've missed."

WILLIAM SAFIRE

Changing Warming

[THE NEW YORK TIMES MAGAZINE/August 14, 2005]

Before You Read

Have you ever been confused by a word or phrase that has more than one possible meaning? Have you ever misinterpreted a word or phrase? What was the result?

Words to Learn

temperate (para. 1): mild and restrained in behavior or attitude (adj.)

phenomenon (para. 2): a thing or occurrence that is apparent to the senses; something unusual or extraordinary (n.)

benign (para. 4): mild; harmless (adj.)

lexicographers (para. 7): people who study the individual word meanings that make up the vocabulary of a language; people who write dictionaries (n.)

parlance (para. 7): the style of speech or writing used by people in a particular context or profession (n.)

The contentious phrase *global warming*, first used by United Press International in 1969, seems to be undergoing a certain cooling; contrariwise, the more temperate phrase *climate change* is getting hot.   1

Many think the terms are synonymous. "I think *climate change*   2 and *global warming* are used interchangeably," says Jay Gulledge of the Pew Center on Global Climate Change (a name that, in squeezing

---

Pulitzer Prize–winner WILLIAM SAFIRE, *who writes a regular column for the* New York Times *on language and etymology called "On Language," is a former presidential speech writer. Safire, who describes himself as libertarian conservative, often explores the use of language in the political arena. His rules for writing include, "If you reread your work, you can find on rereading a great deal of repetition can be avoided by rereading and editing."*

the two terms together, notably drops *warming*). "When people talk about the general phenomenon of climate change, they assume the process of global warming." But he knows that scientists draw a distinction: "Since global warming has been well established, scientists have begun to focus more and more on other aspects of climate, necessitating the use of the more inclusive phrase *climate change*."

Over at the Brookings Institution, its environmental boss detects   3
a whiff of terminological politics. "Polling data suggest that much of the public considers the term *climate change* less threatening than *global warming*," says David Sandalow. "As a result, politicians eager to downplay risks tend to use the term *climate change*."

At Greenpeace, an active environmentalist lobby, they don't like   4
the change to *climate change*. "*Change* sounds mellow and gentle," notes Kert Davies, its research director.

> *The term* climate change *was too benign . . . it didn't evoke any urgency.*

"Communications specialists during the Clinton administration determined that the term *climate change* was too benign, that it didn't evoke any urgency. Vice President Gore used *global warming* in his book *Earth in the Balance*. But now that the 90s label switch has switched back, Davies of Greenpeace argues that the verb change is not only weak but also misleading: "It's really 'disruption,' and it isn't benign at all."

The opposing view is heard from James Mahoney, the Bush ad-   5
ministration's director of the—you guessed it—Climate Change Science Program. "*Climate change* is a more encompassing and technically accurate term to describe the changes in earth systems," Mahoney says, adding that "*global warming* is an oversimplification, and by definition does not allow for the occurrence of warming in one region and simultaneous cooling or stability in others."

NASA's glossary tries valiantly to be apolitical, defining G.W. as   6
"warming predicted to occur as a result of increased emissions of greenhouse gases," partly man-made, while C.C. is used by scientists "in a wider sense to also include natural changes in climate." United Nations usage differs, treating C.C. as change attributable directly or indirectly to human activity.

In the nomenclature struggle, who names an issue usually carries   7
the day. Lexicographers and usagists take no sides, but in common parlance as reflected by the search engines, the neutral climate change has put a chill into the scarier global warming.

Web **Read It Now:** For more Safire articles on language, go to bedfordstmartins.com/americanow, Chapter 6.

Vocabulary / Using a Dictionary

1. What does *contentious* mean in paragraph 1? In what sense can a phrase be "contentious"? What are the roots of the word?

2. What is a *glossary* (para. 6)? Where does the word come from? Does a glossary differ from a dictionary?

3. What does *apolitical* mean in paragraph 6? How does it differ from *political*? How does the first syllable *a* change the word's meaning? Can you think of other words that are formed the same way?

Responding to Words in Context

1. What is meant by *more inclusive* in paragraph 2? Why exactly is climate change "more inclusive" than global warming? Is that good or bad? Why does one side in the debate prefer the more "inclusive" or "encompassing" (para. 5) term?

2. Why don't some environmental activist organizations like the word *change*? What is wrong with the word? What term do they prefer and why?

3. Safire says in paragraph 6 that "NASA's glossary tries valiantly to be apolitical." Why does Safire call this attempt "valiant"? What does that word usually mean? What does its use in this context suggest about Safire's opinion?

Discussing Main Point and Meaning

1. Safire deals with the phenomenon of global warming in his essay. What does the writer mean when he states that *global warming* is "cooling," while the phrase *climate change* "is getting hot" (para. 1)?

2. According to Safire, why does Kert Davies of Greenpeace object to the phrase *climate change* (para. 4)? Why does Davies believe that *climate change* is "not only weak but also misleading" (para. 4)?

3. Why do you think Safire refers to climate change as "neutral" in paragraph 7? Do you consider it be a neutral expression? Has Safire cited any organizations that do not see the term as neutral?

4. Safire claims that "Lexicologists and usagists take no sides." In your opinion, is Safire taking no sides in this issue?

Examining Sentences, Paragraphs, and Organization

1. How does Jay Gulledge of the Pew Center explain the shift in usage from *global warming* to *climate change* (para. 2)?

2. Safire explains (para. 4) that members of the Clinton administration rejected the term *climate change*. For what reason? By contrast, why do members of the Bush administration reject the term *global warming* and prefer the phrase *climate change* (para. 5)?

3. Safire states that "in the nomenclature struggle, who names an issue usually carries the day" (para. 7). What does he mean, and what does this statement imply about the power of words?

Thinking Critically

1. Safire describes the "terminological politics" of global warming. Why is the terminology significant? Since both terms refer to the same phenomenon, how important are the words used to name this condition?

2. Safire states that lexicographers "take no sides," but, in his closing words, states "the neutral climate change has put a chill into the scarier global warming" (para. 7). What is his point?

3. The phenomenon of global warming, or climate change, has assumed political connotations, as shown by the distinct differences in the manner that Democratic and Republican presidents refer to this process. What can we determine about the political differences of Presidents Clinton and Bush from the words that they use when commenting on this particular phenomenon?

In-Class Writing Activities

1. Safire describes in detail the confusion that results from differing interpretations of political terms. Differences in the interpretation of a word or phrase are relatively common in everyday life. What does it mean, for example, to receive a "good" grade for aca-

demic work? How is it different from an "average" grade? Begin
by identifying several words from your own life—not necessarily
your academic life—that have resulted in confusion or dissent.
Consider the context or situation in which the confusion occurred as well as the result. Review the most interesting, personally significant words and make a short list. Select one example
and use it as the basis for a short essay. Make sure that you describe the setting in which the example occurred as well as the result. In writing your conclusion, think about what the experience
taught you regarding the nature of words.

2. Which of the meanings associated with the terms *climate change*
and *global warming* appears more accurate? Why? After considering the question, briefly review the article and annotate or
shade references that support your position. Write several paragraphs that state your opinion and offer evidence from the text as
support.

JOHN LEO

Awash in Euphemisms

[TOWNHALL.COM/February 27, 2006]

Before You Read

Have you ever chosen a word to lessen the impact of a negative message? How did your language choice affect your listener's response?

Words to Learn

pluralistic (para. 2): accepting or affirming diversity (of beliefs, people, etc.) (adj.)

semantic (para. 2): of or relating to meaning, especially in language (adj.)

gratuity (para. 4): a favor or gift, especially in the form of money (n.)

intimidating (para. 7): coercive or threatening (adj.)

manipulation (para. 8) managing or unfairly controlling someone or something for one's own gain (n.)

compliant (para. 9): willing to submit (adj.)

deferred (para. 10): postponed or delayed (adj.)

mandatory (para. 11): required (adj.)

migrated (para. 13): traveled or moved (v.)

colonialism (para. 14): a reference to control by one power over a dependent power, or colony (n.)

JOHN LEO *is a columnist and contributing editor at* U.S. News & World Report, *a weekly magazine that covers political and current events, and a contributing columnist to* Townhall.com, *described as "a one-stop mall of ideas in which people congregate to exchange, discuss, and disseminate the latest news and information from the conservative movement." Leo wrote this piece for* Townhall *to show how different groups create euphemisms— new language that is meant to make an unpleasant idea or term less offensive. Leo shows how the current trend toward euphemism is often used to advance a political cause, to malign the opposition, or to make very difficult situations or conflicts seem benign.*

"Hull loss," a term used by the airlines, means a plane crash in ordinary English.

"A pluralistic plan" is a hiring quota and "semantic violence" usually means criticism or yelling. Mercenaries are now "security contractors." "Sheltering in place" is a happy-talk reference to quarantine, according to an NPR report. New Orleans police rejected the term "looting" after Katrina, but they conceded "the possibility of appropriation of non-essential items from businesses."

William Lutz, author of *Doublespeak*, reports that if a doctor in Britain removes the wrong kidney, this is written down as an "error of laterality." Also in Britain, the Church of England suggests that the words "living in sin" should be banished and replaced by a "covenanted relationship."

In Santa Barbara, patrons in an "adult" club cannot hand a tip to the "exotic dancers" but they are urged to put money into "a non-human gratuity receptacle."

In the insult war on the Web, irate liberal bloggers call their opponents "wingnuts," whereas angry conservative bloggers prefer to call liberal antagonists "moonbats."

The word "liberal" continues to fade, those on the left prefer "progressive," and the term "liberal Republican" is now obsolete. The media use "moderate Republican," which has the added polemical advantage of implying that conservative Republicans are immoderate. "Advocacy" is the generic Washington word for lobbying. "Out of the mainstream" means "not on our side." Individual congressmen are enriching the language. Senator Charles Schumer contributed "deeply held beliefs," a reference to his fear that a Catholic on the Supreme Court might vote to overturn *Roe v. Wade.* Rep. John Murtha gave us the euphemism "redeployment," which is smoother than simply saying, "let's quit Iraq now."

Leaking closely held government or corporate information is a terrible offense, a gross violation of duty and maybe even treason. Unless, of course, you agree with the leaker. In that case, he is a "whistleblower." If demonstrators and agitators take their case to the streets, even in a muscular and intimidating way, we needn't worry. They are simply engaging in "direct action" which sounds much better than "Brownshirt behavior."

"Enhanced interrogation" (torture) has been used so much that it seems to be settling in as a normal term.

Torture and torture-light are discussed in calming language—"environmental

1

2

3

4

5

6

7

8

manipulation," "stress positions," "sensory manipulation." "Enhanced interrogation" (torture) has been used so much that it seems to be settling in as a normal term, even though such enhancement can be fatal. The same sort of semi-acceptance may explain why "extraordinary rendition" (outsourced torture) is mostly dropping its "extraordinary" and entering the common language as just plain "rendition."

The Palestinians made a language breakthrough after a few, um, activists who were trying to shoot a missile into Israel, managed to blow themselves up instead. The Palestinians referred to this as "a work accident." "Targeted killings," which will need to be replaced with a true euphemism, is a preferred new term of choice for "assassination." "Soft compliant

GIVE ME
YOUR
UNDOCUMENTED
IMMIGRANTS
ILLEGAL ALIENS
~YOUR~
PERMANENT
TEMPORARY
RESIDENTS
GUEST WORKERS
AND
ANCHOR BABIES

Paul Vitello of the *New York Times* writes, "Murky self-described patriot groups call them 'terrorists.' On combative talk radio shows the term is 'illegal aliens.' Advocates for immigrants prefer the Emma Lazarus–evoking 'economic refugees.' The most common label attached to the estimated 12 million foreign-born people living in the United States without visas may be 'illegal immigrants,' even though some grammarians argue that the adjective can modify actions and things (like left turns and hallucinogenic drugs) but not people. President Bush, a proponent of offering citizenship to at least some of them, has used the more optimistic and implicitly promising term 'undocumented immigrants.'"   From "The Uncitizens," *New York Times*, March 26, 2006. Drawing by Tamara Shopsin.

entry" is militarese for a raid on an Iraq dwelling that doesn't force
allied troops to kick down the door.

Educationese continues to favor words that cloak failure; so as   10
not to impair self-esteem "negative gain" sometimes appears as a description of falling test scores. A number of schools have eliminated
"F" as a mark, and "suboptimal outcome" means failure. In Britain
members of the Professional Association of Teachers suggested that
schools drop the word "fail." The teachers wanted to use "deferred
success," as in, "Good news, Mom! I've been successful on my math
test, in a positive, deferred way. Aren't you proud?"

Other additions to educationese include "mandatory discontin-   11
ued attendance" (suspension) and "post instructional behavioral ad-
justment period" (detention).

In UN-speak, the term "unsafe abortions" means illegal abor-   12
tions. It is used by those who wish to correct the lack of safety by
making abortion a legal right worldwide. "Anti-Zionism" at any UN
gathering translates easily as "anti-Semitism."

"Cruelty-free" was a term used by animal rights activists to   13
lament testing of drugs and consumer products on animals. Now the
term has migrated to "cruelty-free cream" made of soy and "cruelty-
free chocolate" made with no milk, though the old-fashioned cruel
chocolate probably tastes better. A "flexitarian" is one who eats
vegetarian dishes at home, but will eat meat, fish, or fowl at times,
usually when dining out.

"Economic colonialism" is a leftist term for trade. On our mad-   14
cap campuses, PC folk keep inventing terms that make speech sound
like action, so if they want to punish someone, they can do so while
strongly (and hypocritically) defending free speech. "Expressive behavior," "verbal conduct" and "verbal action" all mean "speech."
"Non-contact sexual harassment" includes jokes, rumor, or any comment that a woman might consider inappropriate.

The language game requires players to insert a strong negative word   15
for what your opponent wants (e.g., the death tax) and eliminate similar
hot-button words used on your side. Just as "abortion" has virtually disappeared from the names and language of abortion-rights groups, the
word "embryo" is fading from the vocabulary of those who favor "embryonic stem cell research." Since polls show that the public reacts negatively to the news that minute human embryos are created and destroyed
in the research, the media now speak of "early stem cells." The troubling
word "cloning" is fading too; "therapeutic cloning" is replaced by its
technical term, "somatic cell nuclear transfer."

Massive layoffs in the auto industry have given us "volume-related production schedule adjustments."

Massive layoffs in the auto industry 16 have given us "volume-related production schedule adjustments" (GM usage) and "career alternative enhancement program" (Chrysler usage). And when the boss says, "We have to leverage our resources," he means, "You will be working weekends." If you don't, you risk being "deinstalled" (fired).

 Read It Now: Read another Leo article on language and peruse an archive of his editorials at **bedfordstmartins.com/americanow**, Chapter 6.

Vocabulary / Using a Dictionary

1. Consider the literal meaning of *doublespeak* (para. 3), a term formed through the combination of two relatively common words. What new meanings are expressed as a result of combining the two base words? What is another word for *doublespeak*?

2. Investigate the origin of the term *Brownshirt*. How does it help to explain the phrase *Brownshirt behavior* (para. 7)?

Responding to Words in Context

1. Examine paragraph 2 for references to post-Katrina violence that occurred in New Orleans. Why might the police reject the word *looting*, but admit to "the possibility of appropriation of non-essential items"? Why is *appropriation* preferable to *looting*? How does it change the meaning of the event in question?

2. Paragraphs 10 and 11 both contain euphemisms relating to education. Given the context, what is the connotation of such euphemistic phrases as *negative gain* and *deferred success*? How do these euphemisms help to give meaning to the term *educationese*?

Discussing Main Point and Meaning

1. In paragraph 8, Leo cites several euphemisms relating to torture. Examine these terms and determine how they alter the meaning of the activity to which they refer.

2. In paragraph 14, the writer refers to "PC folk" on "madcap campuses." What attitudes toward campus life do these terms convey?
3. Several paragraphs contain words that end with the suffix *-ese* (paras. 9, 10, 11). These words include *militarese* and *educationese*. How does this suffix alter the meaning of these words? What terms, in plain language, do these euphemisms refer to?

Examining Sentences, Paragraphs, and Organization

1. Explain how the first paragraph, written as a single sentence, contributes to the meaning of the essay as a whole. What image does the phrase *hull loss* bring to mind? What specific word pictures can you envision?
2. Notice that paragraph 6 concludes with the phrase, "let's quit Iraq now." Why does the author choose this politically charged phrase? Why is the euphemism *redeployment* easier to accept than the more direct phrase referring to the same action?
3. Writers sometimes organize essays so that their subject matter develops from minor points to more important and memorable points. How does Leo organize his writing? What is the effect of concluding the essay with images of firings and layoffs among American car manufacturers?

Thinking Critically

1. Consider the overall impact of the euphemisms that Leo discusses in this essay. After carefully examining several specific terms, describe how these euphemisms are intended to affect the reader. Based on the examples given in the text, are the effects primarily negative? Positive? Something else? Explain your answer.
2. The widespread use of euphemisms reflects the values and ethics of contemporary society. What do the euphemisms discussed in this essay imply about the world we live in?
3. What is Leo's main point about euphemisms and the evolving nature of language?

In-Class Writing Activities

1. Assume the role of an anthropologist (one who studies human beings, their cultures, and developments) who lives in a future

society, say one hundred years from now. Your assignment is to examine the language habits of Americans in the early twenty-first century, focusing specifically on the use of euphemistic speech. By examining the use of euphemism, what can you determine about the nature of these early residents and the society in which they lived? After listing as many examples of euphemism as you can, compose a short essay in which you reveal some vital facts and characteristics of early twenty-first-century life.

2. Leo dedicates a significant portion of his essay to describing the use of euphemism as it relates to our system of education. He writes: *Educationese* "favor[s] words that cloak failure" to avoid damaging self-esteem (para. 10). As a student, consider first the positive value of euphemisms that attempt to preserve or enhance self-esteem while minimizing attention to failure. Then, analyze the negative impact of these euphemisms on student growth and progress. Write an essay in which you adopt the perspective of an elementary school–aged student and analyze the impact of the euphemisms cited in paragraph 10. When you have finished, shift roles and assume the persona of a parent. Write a second response in which you examine the impact of these euphemisms from a parental point of view.

3. Working in groups, brainstorm examples of several euphemisms not contained in Leo's essay. Make use of the suffix *-ese* to describe the often euphemistic language associated with groups and organizations. For example, healthcare providers might use *medicalese*. What other groups and organizations might be prone to use euphemisms? Then, work with your group to compose a letter or memo that relies heavily on euphemisms.

JACLYN BARBAROW

Queering the Campus, Loud and Clear

[THE EMORY WHEEL, Emory University/October 14, 2005]

Before You Read

In what context did you first hear the word *queer*? What meanings does the word hold for you? Are they primarily negative or positive?

Words to Learn

audible (para. 1): loud or clear enough to be heard (adj.)

incomprehensible (para. 1): impossible or very difficult to understand (adj.)

respective (para. 2): varying according to each of the people or things concerned (adj.)

orientation (para. 6): the positioning of something in relation to other things; the direction in which someone's thoughts, interests, or tendencies lie (n.)

collective (para. 6): made or shared by everyone in a group (adj.)

ambiguous (para. 13): having two or more possible meanings; not clear; indefinite (adj.)

JACLYN BARBAROW *is a recent graduate of Emory University with a degree in religion. She was a member of the editorial board of the* Emory Wheel *for three years and was the opinion editor her senior year at Tufts University. She believes that "editorials are an important component of public opinion, both in understanding it and in shaping it. Because I plan to be involved in social justice activism, writing editorials will always be an important aspect of my life." Barbarow wrote "Queering the Campus" to generate publicity for LBGT awareness and to "open up dialogue about the ways we define ourselves, and increase understanding of the labels people take on or are given." According to Barbarow, "If you exist in the world, then you have an opinion. If you have an opinion, then you should share it. Nothing good can come from staying quiet about the issues that matter to you."*

I've never had a problem being visible. Or audible. My whole   1
family is made up of the type of people who take up a lot of space,
and we don't deal well with being ignored. So when I found myself
part of a community plagued by invisibility and silence, I had to be a
wallflower for a little while, standing back and really listening to the
voices around me. Some were meek yet assured; some were overbearing and incomprehensible.

Awareness is a tricky thing to request. Is belligerent awareness   2
better than passive blindness? I don't intend to choose. At Emory, I
don't usually have to. Most people are confused at worst, pleasant at
best, but passive on average. When I hold hands with my girlfriend
on campus, the first group glances at our clasped hands, glances at
our respective faces, then chests, then wonders if we're actually both
women. The second group smiles and says hello, even if they don't
know us. But the vast majority of people at Emory don't notice. Unfortunately, any kind of passivity, though tacit acceptance, means an
ignorance of issues faced by those of us who identify as queer, gay,
lesbian, bisexual, transgender, or intersex. These issues include being
denied the right to marry and form families, the lack of safety in public places (e.g., for masculine-looking or cross-dressing women in a
women's bathroom), and the impossibility of fitting into a checkbox
on application forms. So, here. I'll do my part in educating you.

Sex refers to a person's biological "femaleness" or "maleness"   3
and is usually assigned at birth, but sometimes after puberty or as the
result of voluntary surgery.

Gender refers to a social role, generally understood in terms of   4
masculine and feminine traits; it is often related to how a person is
raised and is generally assumed to corre-
spond to the person's physical sex at birth.

> Gender *refers to a social role, generally understood in terms of masculine and feminine traits.*

Sexuality refers to a person's attractions,   5
generally sexual, but also romantic or emotional.

Sexual orientation is a self-identification,   6
dependent on a person's gender and collective attractions.

Gay men and women are attracted to people of their own gender.   7
Lesbian is the more appropriate term for a gay woman.   8
Bisexuals are men or women attracted to people of "both" gen-   9
ders. (I put "both" in quotation marks for a reason I will explain
later.) This refers to attraction, not action—bisexuality does not
imply promiscuity.

Transgender people live as a different gender than their sex or   10
upbringing would imply.

Genderqueer, a term often understood to mean transgender,   11
refers to people who do not fit neatly into a gender category. (Some
people may choose to use "gender neutral" pronouns, such as "ze"
instead of "he" or "she" and "hir" instead of "him," "her," "his," or
"hers.")

Transsexuals are people who have had, or plan to have, biologi-   12
cal steps taken to change to the sex that corresponds with the gender
with which they identify.

Intersex people are those who are born with (or develop at pu-   13
berty) ambiguous sexual characteristics or a mix of characteristics
that do not allow for an either/or definition. (This is why I put
"both" in quotation marks. There are not only two sexes.)

Queer people can be gay, lesbian, bisexual, transgendered, gen-   14
derqueer, transsexual, intersex, or more than one of the above. Coin-
cidentally, queer people can also be none of the above, choosing instead to identify themselves under a broad
term that means, at its most basic level, "not
like everyone else."

Silence will not protect us.

So, now you're wondering why I felt the   15
need to define all that, and why on earth
anyone would dedicate a week to becoming aware of the above identities. My simple answer is because silence will not protect us, to use
the words of Audre Lorde. Because if it was just about sex, we
wouldn't have to stand up for our rights to
go to the bathroom, get married, or change
our names. Because queer kids recognize
their sexualities around the same time
straight kids recognize theirs. And because
the right to exist should never be a fight.

For an annotated excerpt of
this essay that highlights
Barbarow's writing strategies, see page 222.

Web **Read It Now:** Check out more student opinion published by the *Emory Wheel*
at bedfordstmartins.com/americanow, Chapter 6.

Vocabulary / Using a Dictionary

1. What is the archaic meaning of the word *incomprehensible*
   (para. 1)? How does it differ from the contemporary meaning?
2. What is the root word of *belligerent* (para. 2)? What is its origin?

3. What is the meaning of the *trans-* in *transgender* (para. 2)? What is another word that can be formed from this prefix?

Responding to Words in Context

1. What does Barbarow mean when she refers to herself as a *wall-flower* (para. 1)? How does this definition differ from the identity that she presents in the body of the essay?

2. What does the writer mean when she explains that the college community is "plagued by invisibility and silence" (para. 1)?

3. What is implied by the phrase *tacit acceptance* (para. 2)? Why does Barbarow reject this form of acceptance?

4. According to Barbarow, what meanings are associated with the term *queer* or *queer people* (para. 14)?

5. How does the writer distinguish *sexuality* from *sexual orientation* (paras. 5, 6)? What is the primary difference between the two terms?

6. According to Barbarow, how does *sex* differ from *gender*, as explained in paragraphs 3 and 4? What is the importance of this distinction?

Discussing Main Point and Meaning

1. How do you interpret the title of Barbarow's essay? How does it seek to generate interest or attention?

2. How does Barbarow describe the Emory community? According to the writer, what are the three reactions of her classmates when they see her walking with her girlfriend?

3. What does the writer mean by "Awareness is a tricky thing to request" (para. 2)? What is her main argument? That is, what does she want to persuade her readers to think or do?

4. According to Barbarow, what is at stake when others remain ignorant of the questions that she confronts (para. 2)?

Examining Sentences, Paragraphs, and Organization

1. How does Barbarow's opening sentence establish the tone of her essay and prepare her readers for her message?

2. Barbarow explains that she intends to educate her audience, the readership of her campus newspaper. In what sense? How does

her description of the community she wishes to "educate" compare to the larger community that you are a part of?

3. In one sense, Barbarow's essay is a kind of "primer" that can be used to teach or enlighten. Why does she choose to define what she considers key terms? What lessons is she trying to convey?

4. Describe the form of Barbarow's essay. How does this specific organizational structure support her message? Is it effective? Would you have organized the essay differently? Why or why not?

Thinking Critically

1. How important is it—in terms of becoming aware of queer identities and the issues that gay communities face—to understand the terms that Barbarow defines in her essay? For example, the difference between transgender people and transsexuals? Are there other groups on your campus, besides the gay community, who might wish to "educate" others by explaining identifying terms or by raising issues regarding basic rights?

2. In her closing paragraph, Barbarow asserts that she has not written the piece simply to educate the reader "about sex." What exactly do you think she means? What is her essay really about?

3. On one level, Barbarow asserts that the "queer people" she represents seek the same rights that straight people possess. In the same essay, she attempts to define them as distinct and different. Are those two goals compatible? Explain your answer.

In-Class Writing Activities

1. Barbarow writes that she seeks to break the "silence" on campus around issues of sexual orientation. Her essay provides a description of sexual terms that are seldom discussed so directly in a campus newspaper. In expressing her ideals, Barbarow employs the rhetorical style of the manifesto, the public declaration of principles or intentions. (The root word for *manifesto* is "to manifest: to show plainly.") Consider what your own key principles, in relationship to your identity and community, are and attempt to express them in a manner that parallels Barbarow's.

2. In composing her essay, Barbarow refers to an audience of college students she addresses simply as "you." Assume that you are a member of the audience that she seeks to educate. Compose a

personal letter to Barbarow in which you respond to her key points.

3. Now, respond to Barbarow's key assertions in the form of an editorial letter addressed to the *Emory Wheel*, the college newspaper in which the writer's essay originally appeared. How would your response differ in writing to another, less personal audience?

ANNOTATION Varying Sentences

When you read essays that sound choppy or monotonous or both, it is usually because the writer has constructed the same type of sentence over and over. Here's an example: "This summer I went on a trip to Spain. Our group visited three cities, Madrid, Barcelona, and Seville. Madrid was very hot and crowded. We saw a bullfight there at Las Ventas bullring. I was disgusted by the way the bulls are treated. Bullfighting is inhumane and should be outlawed." Note that the sentences essentially sound alike. The writer makes no attempt to combine thoughts or information, and the overall effect is a dull and repetitive "da-dum, da-dum, da-dum." That's why good writers make a conscious attempt to vary their sentences. Observe how Emory University student **Jaclyn Barbarow** uses different sentence structures, lengths, and openings in the first paragraph of "**Queering the Campus, Loud and Clear.**"

Barbarow varies the length, structure, and rhythm of sentences to keep readers' interest.

I've never had a problem being visible. Or audible. My whole family is made up of the type of people who take up a lot of space, and we don't deal well with being ignored. So when I found myself part of a community plagued by invisibility and silence, I had to be a wallflower for a little while, standing back and really listening to the voices around me. Some were meek yet assured; some were overbearing and incomprehensible.

— From "Queering the Campus, Loud and Clear" by Jaclyn Barbarow, page 217

LUCIA PERILLO

Definition of Terms

[PMS, #5/2005]

Before You Read

What meanings do you associate with the word *cripple*? Would you use this term in everyday speech?

Words to Learn

etymologically (para. 1): referring to the origin and historical development of a word or its derivations (adv.)

pathos (para. 2): a quality that arouses feelings of pity, sympathy, tenderness, or sorrow (n.)

epithets (para. 3): terms, often abusive in nature, used to characterize a person or thing (n.)

recapitulation (para. 3): the activity of repeating or summarizing (n.)

exhilarated (para. 4): feeling elated or cheerful (adj.)

derivation (para. 5): the origin or source of something: for example, a word or name (n.)

stymied (para. 8): blocked or thwarted (adj.)

propriety (para. 11): the state of being proper (n.)

eccentric (para. 13): deviating from an accepted or established pattern (adj.)

Lucia Perillo, *who writes creative nonfiction and short stories, is most known for her poetry, which has won her prizes including the Kingsley Tufts Poetry Award for her latest book,* Luck Is Luck *(2005). Originally her dream was to work with wildlife, but a period of unemployment and her development of multiple sclerosis led her to pursue writing as a career, in part because, according to Perillo, it seemed glamorous. Four books later, Perillo believes that writing poetry "still* seems *glamorous, when it's working properly—but it's usually not working. It gets harder as you go along because your standards and aspirations are much higher. It gets more laborious and takes a lot longer. What I want to accomplish now is more ambitious."*

gnomic (para. 16): having the qualities of a gnome, the fabled race of dwarflike creatures who live underground (adj.)

archetypal (para. 17): a model after which similar things are patterned (adj.)

Sometimes I call myself *cripple*, a word derived from the Old English *creopan*, meaning, "to go bent down." So, etymologically, cripples are creepy. Our bodies house the worst sort of luck, and I would bet that most people are afraid to see themselves in the bent form's mirror. As if bad bodyluck were contagious, and traveled via the eye's beam—a belief that seems somehow intuitively logical. Even though my animal fortune has packed its bags and headed south, I'm not immune to a hitch in my swallow whenever I cross the paths with the likes of me.

As a member of the population to which the word applies, I am given some latitude in my use of *cripple* as an aggressive form of self-description. In doing so I may intend to suggest that I have become hardened to its connotations, or that I am a realist about my body's state, or that I am using the word to announce my affinity with a subculture that aspires to outlaw status. Each of these meanings enshrines some sort of little fib. As in the obvious fact that my outlaw status is belied by my helplessness, which causes any swaggering to possess a tinge of pathos.

Because *cripple* is one of those somewhat archaic words that describes a population conventionally seen as oppressed, it now comes off as a slur when spoken in the company of upright citizens. We all know such words, slurs that are mainly racial and which take on a showboat quality when they come from the mouths of their intended targets. Even the word *nigger*, which has been called "the nuclear bomb of racial epithets," had some air added to the pronunciation of its final syllable and was turned into a badge of honor by black comics and rappers of the late-twentieth century. Now when it crops up in the news, in some recapitulation of its deliverance, its gets coded as *the N-word*, as a way of clarifying intention, of saying *I am not a racist* even though the expression *the N-word* is cloying, pathetic.

> Cripple *comes off as a slur when spoken in the company of upright citizens.*

Perhaps it is the weak who are most exhilarated by damning themselves. When I was a cowering child I fell in love with the words *wop*, *dago*, and *guinea*, because Italians were the gladiators of my

town, where we were not an insignificant minority—the vowels in
our last names clanked like armor. I was not tough but thought some
metal might flake off the words and land on me. And so I rehearsed
them with abandon.

Dago from the Spanish for James, *Diego*—somehow the nation-   5
alities got swapped around. The derivation of *wop* is more murky; it
could mean *dandy*, or could mean *sour wine*. *Guinea* from *Guinea
Negro*, a linkage between Africans and people from southern Italy,
forged by the dark skin that I don't have. This was the name we
loved best, the one that alluded to the coveted brown tint—the
darker the skin, the more status attached. *Guinea!* we yelled as we
pushed each other off the floating dock and into the toxic river. In
which we Italians were not afraid to swim, though now I sometimes
wonder what those poisoned waters did to me.

To me it seems illogical that a word should be permitted to some   6
people and not to others. The problem is intention, I suppose, the assumption being that a member of a community can use an old (cor-
roded by time, and now become appalling) label in a manner that expresses brotherhood, while at the same time armoring the community
against those who would besiege it. The intentions of outsiders, on
the other hand, can't be so easily trusted. This assumes that the distinction between insider and outsider is easy to make: we need to
know skin tone or the number of vowels in a name. The urban accent
or the wheelchair. To get permission to say *cripple* I have to let
people see me.

It also has an antique feel, like a butter churn or apple press, or   7
like some remnant of the vocabulary of grandparents from the Old
World who never really got the hang of English. To make the label
more aggressive, and maybe chummier, the brotherhood of those
foiled by bad bodyluck sometimes shortens it to *crip*, as in: *the crip
community*. Never having been much of a club-joiner, however, I
find myself too aloof for the bonhomie of *crip*.

My friend whose family calls her *gimp* says that this name did   8
sting at first, though she assumes they use it to assure her she's not
being pitied. When she asked what I am called, I realized that my
family doesn't call me anything. They do not refer to *my condition* as
a matter of their not wishing to appear ill bred. Earlier in my disease
they were probably as stunned and stymied as I was—and in those
days it seemed possible to evade the body if we simply did not speak
of it. This was a proven tactic, which had served us well in regards
to sex.

Now, when backed into a corner, my family calls me *disabled*,   9
the static electricity clumping into quotation marks around the word.

Disabled isn't cloying exactly, though it does strike me as overly sanitized in its depiction

---
Disabled *isn't cloying*
exactly, though it does
strike me as overly
sanitized.

---

of a state that is so oftentimes a mess. I have been appointed to the pedestrian committee as a representative of the *disabled community* in the small city where I live, despite my protest that bad bodyluck is a condition so variable that no one person, certainly no one as self-absorbed as me, could have a command of the various blows it deals.

My dislike for *disabled* comes from its being cobbled together   10
from negation: not able, like *in*-valid. I like to think I could do anything with the right technology, which only the economies of scale have worked against—it seems by now there ought to be some kind of robotic superstructure to stand me up and walk me. Or a lightweight jetpack (because as early as the mid-1960s, Bell Aerosystems had invented barrels and chairs that flew, all this technology prior to the electronic age that shrunk the phone booth into something smaller than a cigarette pack). One can only assume that the fear of litigation halted the development of jetpacks. That the fear of zombies halted the development of electric bones that would let the *cripples* march.

There it is again, the word I could not resist. *In your face* we say of   11
people who like to invade social boundaries. All my life I have had trouble with being able to correctly gauge the boundary's circumference. A mild form of dyslexia. It seemed as though my choice was either making an unwelcome assault on propriety, or saying nothing; I could never come up with the witty harmless quip. And my inarticulateness has waltzed me through a life of blunders. *Describe me*, I often ask my friends. Skipping over all the bag lady paraphernalia I've acquired of late, they say: *You'll say anything that pops into your head.*

Partly this is due, I think, to my being such a blank slate, the sub-   12
urban girl with no history and no hobbies, no striking characteristics at all except for an oddly shaped nose and a tendency to laugh at odd moments. A good student but not exceptional. Pretty, but not too. Not bad enough to be interesting in a James Dean sort of way, just a likeable whiner, a slacker before the coinage of the word. Thoughtful but slow-witted. On the high school track team, I often stopped to walk.

And now at last I do have a unique identity, though it is not at all   13
what I envisioned — still better than nothing, I sometimes think. Now
I am: *bag lady on a cart jury-rigged with lights and crutches.* Know
me slightly, and I am disarmed sufficiently to qualify as a *kook.*
Know me well, and I become merely an *eccentric.*

The name I find most accurate to my current state is a word our   14
society has circled half a rotation past: *handicapped.* Derived from
the eighteenth-century manner of wagering by placing money in a
cap. Perhaps America abandoned the word because of the folksiness
of its constituents, the words *handy* and *cap*, which seem too slight
for the body's grueling sage. But my affection for the word comes
from one of my primal reading experiences, a story by Kurt Vonnegut called "Harrison Bergeron" that was first published in 1961,
when I was three. I must have read it in junior high and now, looking
at it for the first time in over thirty years, I see that though its version
of Big-Brother futurism is hammered out with a heavy mallet, the
central image still appeals to me.

In the story, a couple is watching a ballet on TV, the dancers   15
weighted with "sash-weights and bags of birdshot, and their faces
were masked, so that no one, seeing a free and graceful gesture or a
pretty face, would feel like something the cat drug in." Those who
are smart (like the husband watching) must wear earphones through
which the government broadcasts raucous noises to disturb their
thoughts. This image — of the body weighted with a canvas sack full
of pellets — turns out to be a not-bad approximation of what my disease actually *feels* like. It spooks me to think about why in junior
high school I would have so deliberately filed the story in my brain's
otherwise jumbled cabinet.

There is also a genteel quaintness associated with *handicapped,*   16
versus the technological *disabled. Crippled,* on the other hand,
comes out of the gnomic European setting of fairy tales, which is
the basis of its appeal. Both the crippled troll and the hag have
power, though we know the plot will end up righting the topsy-
turvyness created by the story's mandatory magic spell. The troll
will get his come-uppance or the hag will be transformed into a
beautiful queen.

The small city where I live shares some qualities with the arche-   17
typal setting of fairy tales, in that its streets are clogged with young
people at night, the primary colors of their hair massaged into
phantasmagoric shapes. Sometimes I'll be rolling along the streets
and a shout will ring from the dampness and the dark — *Cripple*!

I realize how visible I am, how I have lost forever and utterly, the ability to blend in.

This will unhinge me not because the word is offensive but because I realize how visible I am, how I have lost, forever and utterly, the ability to blend in. Like the protagonist of the fairy tale, I have finally gotten what was once my fervent wish.

 Read It Now: To read more works by Lucia Perillo, go to **bedfordstmartins .com/americanow**, Chapter 6.

Vocabulary / Using a Dictionary

1. What does *archaic* (para. 3) mean? What are some of its antonyms?
2. What is the meaning and origin of the word *bonhomie* (para. 7)? How does the word derive from its roots?
3. How does the addition of a prefix in *disabled* (para. 9) and *in-valid* (para. 10) alter the meaning of the root words? How does the addition of a hyphen in the word *invalid* affect its meaning?

Responding to Words in Context

1. Perillo asserts that her "outlaw status is belied by [her] helpless-ness, which causes any swaggering to possess a tinge of pathos" (para 2). What does Perillo seem to imply about her own "out-law status"?
2. In recalling her Italian childhood, Perillo reveals that she "fell in love with the words *wop*, *dago*, and *guinea*" (para. 4). For the writer, what was the appeal of these terms, usually considered ethnic slurs? What does she mean when she adds that "the vowels in our last names clanked like armor" (para. 4)?
3. What does Perillo mean when she refers to herself as a "blank slate" (para. 12)? What does this image contribute to your under-standing of the writer?

Discussing Main Point and Meaning

1. Consider Perillo's title. Why might the writer have used such a generic phrase to name her essay? What, if any, are the advan-tages of using this title?

2. In defining herself, why does Perillo prefer the word *cripple* (para. 1) or *handicapped* (para. 14) to the more polite or euphemistic expressions? Discuss the Old English meaning of the term *creopan* (para. 1). What does it contribute to the writer's self-definition?

3. According to Perillo, what is the appeal of the story "Harrison Bergeron" by Kurt Vonnegut (para. 14)? What specific image does the story provide to assist in describing Perillo's current condition? Why is it important to the writer?

Examining Sentences, Paragraphs, and Organization

1. In paragraph 4, Perillo writes that "it is the weak who are most exhilarated by damning themselves." What exactly does she mean by this? What examples does she provide to support this point?

2. In paragraph 11, Perillo describes her use of the term *cripple* as "in your face," an invasion of "social boundaries." Explain the meaning of these two references.

3. How do Perillo's language choices reflect her identity and values? How do these choices serve to characterize her? Overall, how does the writer's assessment of herself affect your vision of her?

4. Perillo, in the conclusion of her essay (para. 17), admits that she feels "unhinged" when someone shouts the word *cripple* at her. Why does this word, which she uses herself, evoke such a response? What does this final paragraph contribute to our understanding of the entire essay?

Thinking Critically

1. Though Perillo's essay deals with her life story, it also focuses on what might be termed *identity politics*. As a reader, do you consider her work to be a memoir? Something else? Explain your response.

2. In some ways, Perillo's preference for the word *cripple* seems a movement away from the euphemistic, politically correct speech often employed when referring to the handicapped. What do you think are the writer's motives for identifying herself as a cripple?

3. Describe the writing style that Perillo employs for this essay. How does her style affect you as a reader? Cite passages from the essay to support your conclusions.

In-Class Writing Activities

1. Perillo lists some words that she "fell in love with" as a child (para. 4). What specific words (negative, positive, or otherwise) do you recall from your childhood? Terms that you applied to yourself or others? What was the significance of these words to you as a child? What do you think of them now?

2. Perillo identifies several terms that relate to her life and to how her body is viewed by others (i.e., cripple). With Perillo's essay as a model, write two to three paragraphs that include terms that relate to your "visibility" in the world. What words, when applied to yourself, have "unhinged" you? "Exhilarated" you?

ADAM JACOT DE BOINOD

Global Wording

[SMITHSONIAN/March 2006]

Before You Read

The English language is rich with words from other cultures and countries. What words can you think of that were derived from other languages and became part of English? How have these words changed our vocabulary?

Words to Learn

obsession (para. 2): an idea or a feeling that completely occupies the mind (n.)

embassies (para. 2): residences of ambassadors (n.)

voracious (para. 3): unusually eager or enthusiastic about an activity (adj.)

articulating (para. 6): the activity of expressing thoughts, ideas, and feelings coherently or clearly (v.)

One day while I was working as a researcher for the BBC quiz   1
program *QI,* I picked up a weighty Albanian dictionary and discovered that the Albanians have no fewer than 27 words for eyebrows

---

His work on a British quiz show called QI *sparked* ADAM JACOT DE BOINOD's *fascination with words and a book idea—*The Meaning of Tingo and Other Extraordinary Words from Around the World *(2006)—from which "Global Wording" was adapted. In the course of his research for the book, de Boinod read approximately 220 dictionaries, 150 Web sites, and many other books on language. According to Jacot de Boinod, although we rely on words to describe our world, "Words don't necessarily keep the same meaning. Simple descriptive words such as* rain *or* water *are clear and necessary enough to be unlikely to change," while more complex words are likely to morph and evolve.*

and the same number for mustache, ranging from *mustaqe madh*, or brushy, to *mustaqe posht*, or drooping at both ends. Soon I was unable to go near a secondhand bookshop or library without seeking out the shelves where the foreign-language dictionaries were kept. I would scour books in friends' houses with a similar need to pan for gold.

My curiosity became a passion, even an obsession. In time I combed through more than two million words in hundreds of dictionaries. I trawled the Internet, phoned embassies and tracked down foreign-language speakers who could confirm my findings. Who knew, for example, that Persian has a word for "a camel that won't give milk until her nostrils have been tickled" (*nakhur*)? Or that the Inuits have a verb for "to exchange wives for a few days only" (*areodjarekput*)? Why does Pascuense, spoken on Easter Island, offer *tingo*, which means "to borrow things from a friend's house, one by one, until there's nothing left"? [2]

> *The English language has a tendency to naturalize foreign words. . . . But there are so many we've missed.*

The English language has a long-established and voracious tendency to naturalize foreign words: *ad hoc, feng shui, croissant, kindergarten*. We've been borrowing them from other cultures for centuries. But there are so many we've missed. [3]

Our body-conscious culture might have some use for the Hawaiian *awawa*, for the gap between each finger or toe; the Afrikaans *waal*, for the area behind the knee, or the Ulwa (Nicaragua) *alang*, for the fold of skin under the chin. Surely we could use the Tulu (India) *karelu*, for the mark left on the skin by wearing anything tight. And how could we have passed up the German *Kummerspeck*, for the excess weight one gains from emotion-related overeating? (It translates literally as "grief bacon.") [4]

Gras bilong fes, from the Papua New Guinea Tok Pisin, is more poetic than "beard"; it means "grass belonging to the face." And how about the German *Backpfeifengesicht*, or "face that cries out for a fist in it"? [5]

> *How about the German Backpfeifengesicht, or "face that cries out for a fist in it"?*

In Wagiman (Australia), there's an infinitive—*murr-ma*—for "to walk along in the water searching for something with your feet." The Dutch have *uitwaaien*, for "to walk in windy weather for fun," but then Central American Spanish speakers may win a prize for articulating [6] forms of motion with *achaplinarse*—"to hesitate and then run away in the manner of Charlie Chaplin."

In Russian, they don't speak of crying over spilled milk; they say   7
kusat sebe lokti, which means "to bite one's elbows." That may be better than breaking your heart in Japanese, because *harawata o tatsu* translates literally as "to sever one's intestines." To be hopelessly in love in Colombian Spanish is to be "swallowed like a postman's sock" (*tragado como media de cartero*). That happy state may lead to dancing closely, which in Central American Spanish is *pulir hebillas* ("to polish belt buckles").

Malaysians recognize *kontal-kontil,* or "the swinging of long earrings or the swishing of a dress as one walks." Fuegian, in Chile, has   8
a word for "that shared look of longing where both parties know the score yet neither is willing to make the first move" (*mamihlapinatapei*). But Italian has *biodegradabile,* for one "who falls in love easily and often."

Persian has *mahj,* for "looking beautiful after a disease"—   9
which, deftly used, might well flatter (*vaseliner* in French, for "to apply Vaseline") some recovered patients. But you'd have to lay it on pretty thick for a *nedovtipa,* who in Czech is "someone who finds it difficult to take a hint."

On Easter Island, it may take two to tingo, *but it takes only one to* hakamaru.

On Easter Island, it may take two to   10
tingo, but it takes only one to *hakamaru,* which means "to keep borrowed objects until the owner has to ask for them back." Of course, words once borrowed are seldom returned. But nobody is going *harawata o tatsu* over that.

Web **Read It Now:** To hear more from Jacot de Boinod on interesting words he discovered during his research, go to **bedfordstmartins.com/americanow**, Chapter 6.

Vocabulary / Using a Dictionary

1. What are meanings of the active verbs *scour, combed,* and *trawled* (paras. 1, 2)? How are they related?

2. *Ad hoc* is composed of a Latin prefix and root (para. 3) What is the literal meaning of the root words? How do they differ from the generally accepted meaning of the phrase?

3. What is the meaning of *feng shui* (para. 3)? Where does this phrase originate?

4. The phrase "two to *tingo*" (para. 10) is a variation on a colloquial English expression. What is the original English phrase? What does it mean?

Responding to Words in Context

1. Jacot de Boinod states that English tends "to naturalize" words from other languages (para. 3). What is the meaning of *naturalize*?

2. The Inuits are an aboriginal tribe who inhabit remote areas of Greenland and the Canadian Arctic. What does their usage of the verb *areodjarekput* (para. 2) imply about their culture?

3. What is the meaning of "crying over spilled milk" (para. 7)? How is it related to the Russian expression that means "to bite one's elbows" (para. 7)?

4. Why does the writer believe that the phrase *gras bilong fes* (para. 5) might be preferable to *beard*?

Discussing Main Point and Meaning

1. Jacot de Boinod explains that his interest in word meanings evolved from *curiosity* to *passion* and finally to *obsession* (para. 2). How do these three terms differ? What do the words suggest about the writer's changing attitudes regarding definitions?

2. How does the writer justify his developing fascination with unusual word meanings?

3. Consider the meaning of the verb *tingo* (para. 2), a term used by the Pascuense. How does this usage of this word expand or alter the American conception of friendship?

4. In Colombian Spanish, the condition of being hopelessly in love is defined as feeling "'swallowed like a postman's sock'" (para. 7). What attitude toward love does this simile imply?

Examining Sentences, Paragraphs, and Organization

1. At the end of paragraph 1, Jacot de Boinod explains that while visiting friends' houses he would "scour" books to search for new or unusual word meanings as if panning for "gold." What does this introductory language imply about the nature of the

writer's quest? According to Jacot de Boinod, what initial discovery prompted this search?

2. In paragraph 4, the writer provides several words that might be relevant to Americans' "body-conscious culture." Identify the first four examples that he cites. This paragraph ends with a reference to the German word *Kummerspeck*. How is this word related to the other examples in the same paragraph?

3. According to Jacot de Boinod, what is the central idea that logically connects the three colorful examples provided in paragraph 6?

4. What strategy does the writer employ to conclude his essay? How does the word *hakamaru* expand our understanding of Easter Island culture? How does this definition relate to the larger meaning of the essay?

Thinking Critically

1. Jacot de Boinod appears to appreciate the unique, humorous, and often figurative (nonliteral) meanings of some of the words that he describes. For example, in referring to the Colombian Spanish and Central American Spanish attitudes toward love, he employs a richly imagistic expression. Specifically, he explains that love "may lead to dancing closely," a state that in Central America may be referred to as *pulir hebillas* (para. 7). How does the writer define this phrase? What figurative associations are evoked by this definition?

2. Several words cited by Jacot de Boinod expand our perception of life and human nature. Consider, for example, the meanings of the Wagiman (Australia) infinitive *murr-ma* and the Dutch term *uitwaaien* (para. 6). What definitions does the essay provide for these terms? In what manner do the meanings enhance our perception of human behavior?

3. Many of the words defined by Jacot de Boinod imply something unique regarding the specific culture in which the terms originate. What do the terms *tingo* (para. 2) and *hakamuru* (para. 10) suggest about the cultural practices of Easter Island?

4. Some of the words selected by Jacot de Boinod are highly evocative; that is, they prompt vivid images that help to enhance our understanding. Consider the specific examples from Malaysia, Chile, and Italy cited in paragraph 8. Does the Malaysian word *kontal-kontil* have an equivalent word in English? What sensory image

comes to mind when you reflect on the definition? What about the word *mamihlapinatapei* (from Chile) and *biodegradabile* (from Italian)? What concrete images do these words suggest? What do these words contribute to our understanding of human nature?

In-Class Writing Activities

1. Early in Jacot de Boinod's essay, he asserts that English has a long history of assimilating foreign words. In support, he refers to several relatively common "naturalized" words, including *feng shui, croissant,* and *kindergarten.* His fundamental assertion seems to be that we have "missed" many other potentially valuable and descriptive words. Make a list of the foreign words that he defines and then determine which five of those words should become an official part of the English language. Write a brief essay that explains exactly why these five words should become part of common English usage. For each of the five words, provide an example that justifies its inclusion into our language.

2. Almost all of the foreign words defined by the writer relate to everyday activities and practices. Write a paragraph that incorporates as many of these foreign words as possible. (Make sure to provide footnotes or a glossary so that someone who has not read "Global Wording" can determine exactly what you are saying!) Follow by writing a paragraph that uses common English words in place of the foreign terms. Which of the two versions do you believe is more effective? Which is more interesting? Explain your reasoning in the concluding paragraph of the second version.

3. Jacot de Boinod (para. 3) lists four foreign words that have been naturalized into common English usage. List four additional such words that in the recent past have been naturalized into English. Then write a couple of paragraphs that evaluate the impact these words exert on our language and on our perception of the world around us.

Discussing the Unit

Suggested Topic for Discussion

While the writers in this unit express different themes relating to the use of words, each conveys a highly distinct identity that emerges from his or her individual use of language. In reflecting on the readings, consider the relationship between words and identity as expressed in each writer's essay. How do words serve to communicate and express a sense of self? Also, how do words serve other essential functions and purposes? Can you name several? Finally, think about how each essay makes use of differing qualities, including tone, purpose, and structure, to express an important point.

Preparing for Class Discussion

1. Each of the five writers—Safire, Leo, Barbarow, Perillo, and Jacot de Boinod—address a different word-related topic. In reviewing their essays, identify the topic at the center; for example, Leo informs the reader regarding several new euphemisms that are coming into use. Perillo's focal point involves the language that she employs to describe her condition and the words that others use. How do the other three writers spotlight a specific point or purpose?

2. In addressing individual interests, each writer employs words in differing ways. Consider the varied rhetorical styles used by these five writers. Barbarow's assertive essay mixes qualities associated with a primer, an elementary textbook, as well as a manifesto, a direct statement of policy or ideology. Like Barbarow, Perillo uses an aggressive tone and approaches her topic, which is also personal, in a direct manner. What are the defining qualities of style that each of the other three writers uses to express his or her ideas?

3. In each of the five essays, the writers employ structure to assist in conveying meaning. Leo structures his essay by beginning with a one-sentence paragraph containing a single striking example. Barbarow and, to some extent, Jacot de Boinod use introductions that attempt to "hook" the reader through the careful, first-person use of personal experience. Their introductions invite the reader to continue, to learn more about the individual who is introduced in the first paragraph. How do the other three writers use structure to serve or enhance the goals of their writing?

From Discussion to Writing

1. Write an essay that compares and contrasts two of the writers on the basis of their writing styles. Make certain that you provide an

adequate introduction and a thesis that clearly states what you will compare. In the body of the essay, make specific references to each writer's style to explain your thesis and assist the reader in understanding your point. In your conclusion, indicate which writer uses style more effectively and why.

2. To what extent does an essay's structure or form determine its overall effectiveness? Consider the impact of structure in at least two of the essays in the unit. Compose an essay in which you analyze the contribution of structure as it relates to the writer's meaning or main point. In your opinion, which two essays make the strongest use of structure? How do the structures of the essays affect your attitude toward the writers' topics?

Topics for Cross-Cultural Discussion

1. Most good dictionaries indicate what language a specific word comes from. Examine an unabridged dictionary and make a list of the languages that have contributed words to English. What languages have made the most significant contributions? What does this imply about the nature of those languages, the societies in which they originated, and our own multicultural nation?

2. Like Jacot de Boinod, review several foreign-language dictionaries, either online or, better, in a bookstore. Then, write a brief essay in which you locate at least six interesting and useful words along with their definitions. Using these words, write an essay that makes a personal point about what you have learned about words.

7

The American Language Today: How Is It Changing?

"Our inventions are wont to be pretty toys," wrote Henry David Thoreau in *Walden* (1854), "which distract our attention from serious things.... We are in great haste to construct a magnetic telegraph from Maine to Texas; but Maine and Texas, it may be, have nothing important to communicate." In "The Pleasures of the Text," Charles McGrath echoes Thoreau's sentiment, asking in the conclusion of his entertaining essay on text-messaging whether this brand new communications technology is truly groundbreaking. "The most depressing thing about the communications revolution," McGrath reports, "is that when at last we have succeeded in making it possible for anyone to reach anyone else anywhere and at any time, it turns out that we really don't have much we want to say."

How did Americans communicate quickly before the technological advances of the twentieth century? Frequently, they relied on the telegraph, as we see in an "America Then" feature. Since the telegraph companies charged by the word, users were tempted to be overly succinct, a practice that led to many amusing examples of writing.

Even if, as McGrath suggests, we don't have much to say, *how* we say it can be important, as Michigan State University student Elissa Englund contends in "Good Grammar Gets the Girl." Speaking from her personal experience with an online dating service,

Englund has observed firsthand that too many guys flunk elementary grammar. Since an increasing number of first encounters happen today in writing, she argues, the first impression you make will be "based solely on how you express yourself through the English language." She generously offers a few simple rules that will improve anyone's first verbal impression.

But is it possible to be too concerned over "correct" usage? Should our usage simply be suitable to our audience and the occasion? When speaking with friends on the street do we need to worry about following strict grammatical rules? The next selection takes a serious look at this issue as it applies to inner-city schoolchildren trying to move from the language of home and neighborhood to the Standard English of school and society. In "'My Goldfish Name Is Scaley': There's Nothing to Correct," Rebecca Wheeler, an educational researcher and consultant, argues that the traditional system of grammatical "correction" long practiced by writing teachers is inefficient and counterproductive: "Students using vernacular language," she claims, citing studies, "are not making errors in Standard English, but instead, are writing correctly in the language patterns of the home dialect." Once students can see this, they can then "code-switch" from one language to the other.

CHARLES McGRATH

The Pleasures of the Text

[THE NEW YORK TIMES MAGAZINE/January 22, 2006]

Before You Read

Why do you text-message? How is it different from e-mailing or talking on the phone? What are its advantages and disadvantages, and how does texting affect your daily life?

Words to Learn

stenography (para. 1): the art of writing in shorthand (n.)

shorthand (para. 1): a rapid form of writing in which characters, abbreviations, or symbols are substituted for letters, words and sounds (n.)

contractions (para. 2): shortened words (n.)

homophones (para. 2): words that sound similar (n.)

ubiquitous (para. 2): having the quality of being everywhere (adj.)

vogue (para. 2): fashion; style (n.)

versatile (para. 2): easily able to change; having many uses (adj.)

concision (para. 2): the state or quality of being concise or short (n.)

hieroglyphics (para. 3): a system of picture writing used by ancient Egyptians (n.)

rebus (para. 4): a picture that represents words or syllables (n.)

laggards (para. 6): people who perpetually fall behind (n.)

avid (para. 6): enthusiastic (adj.)

There used to be an ad on subway cars, next to the ones for bail bondsmen and hemorrhoid creams, that said: "if u cn rd ths u cn gt a gd job & mo pa." The ad was promoting a kind of stenography   1

CHARLES McGRATH *is the former editor of the* New York Times Book Review *and the* New Yorker *and a frequent contributor to the* New York Times Magazine *and other publications. In "The Pleasures of the Text" and other essays on writing and language, McGrath tries to place literature and language in a larger context.*

training that is now extinct, presumably. Who uses stenographers anymore? But the notion that there might be value in easily understood shorthand has proved to be prescient. If u cn rd these days,

You can conduct your entire emotional life by transmitting and receiving messages on your cellphone.

and, just as important, if your thumbs are nimble enough so that u cn als snd, you can conduct your entire emotional life just by transmitting and receiving messages on the screen of your cellphone. You can flirt there, arrange a date, break up, and—in Malaysia at least—even get a divorce.

Shorthand contractions, along with letter-number homophones ("gr8" and "2moro," for example), emoticons (like the tiresome colon-and-parenthesis smiley face) and acronyms (like the ubiquitous "lol," for "laughing out loud"), constitute the language of text-messaging—or txt msg, to use the term that txt msgrs prefer. Text-messaging is a refinement of computer instant-messaging, which came into vogue five or six years ago. But because the typical cell-phone screen can accommodate no more than 160 characters, and because the phone touchpad is far less versatile than the computer keyboard, text-messaging puts an even greater premium on concision. Here, for example, is a text-message version of *Paradise Lost* disseminated by some scholars in England: "Devl kikd outa hevn coz jelus of jesus&strts war. pd'off wiv god so corupts man (md by god) wiv apel. devl stays serpnt 4hole life&man ruind. Woe un2mnkind."

As such messages go, that one is fairly straightforward and unadorned. There is also an entire code book of acronyms and abbreviations, ranging from CWOT (complete waste of time) to DLTBBB (don't let the bedbugs bite). And emoticonography has progressed way beyond the smiley-face stage, and now includes hieroglyphics to indicate drooling, for example (:-) . . .), as well as secrecy (:X), Hitler (/.#( ) and the rose (@{rcub};--). Keep these in mind; we'll need them later.

As with any language, efficiency isn't everything. There's also the issue of style. Among inventive users, and younger ones especially, text-messaging has taken on many of the characteristics of hip-hop, with so much of which it conveniently overlaps—in the substitution of "z" for "s," for example, "a," for "er" and "d" for "th." Like hip-hop, text-messaging is what the scholars call "performative"; it's writing that aspires to the condition of speech. And sometimes when it makes abundant use of emoticons, it strives not for clarity so much as a kind of rebus-like cleverness, in which showing off is part of the point. A text-message version of *Paradise Lost*—or of the prologue, anyway—that tries for a little more shnizzle might go like this: "Sing hvnly mewz dat on d :X mtntp inspyrd dat shephrd hu 1st tot d chozn seed in d begnin hw d hvn n erth @{rcub};-- outa chaos."

Not that there is much call for Miltonic messaging these days. To use the scholarly jargon again, text-messaging is "lateral" rather than "penetrative," and the medium encourages blandness and even mindlessness. On the Internet there are several Web sites that function as virtual Hallmark stores and offer ready-made text messages of breathtaking banality. There are even ready-made Dear John letters, enabling you to dump someone without actually speaking to him or her. Far from being considered rude, in Britain this has proved to be a particularly popular way of ending a relationship—a little more thoughtful than leaving an e-mail message but not nearly as messy as breaking up in person—and it's also catching on over here.

Compared with the rest of the world, Americans are actually laggards when it comes to text-messaging. This is partly for technical reasons. Because we don't have a single, national phone company, there are several competing and incompatible wireless technologies in use, and at the same time actual voice calls are far cheaper here than in most places, so there is less incentive for texting. But in many developing countries, mobile-phone technology has so far outstripped land-line availability that cellphones are the preferred, and sometimes the only, means of communication, and text messages are cheaper than voice ones. The most avid text-messagers are clustered in Southeast Asia, particularly in Singapore and the Philippines.

There are also cultural reasons for the spread of text-messaging elsewhere. The Chinese language is particularly well-suited to the telephone keypad, because in Mandarin the names of the numbers are also close to the sounds of certain words; to say "I love you," for example, all you have to do is press 520. (For "drop dead," it's 748.) In China, moreover, many people believe that to leave voice mail is rude, and it's a loss of face to make a call to someone important and have it answered by an underling. Text messages preserve everyone's dignity by eliminating the human voice.

Text-messaging preserves the feeling of communication—without the burden of actual intimacy or substance.

This may be the universal attraction of text-messaging, in fact: 8
it's a kind of avoidance mechanism that preserves the feeling of
communication—the immediacy—without, for the most part, the
burden of actual intimacy or substance. The great majority of text
messages are of the "Hey, how are you, whassup?" variety, and
they're sent sometimes when messenger and recipient are within
speaking distance of each other—across classrooms, say, or from one
row of a stadium to another. They're little electronic waves and nods
that, just like real waves and nods, aren't meant to do much more
than establish a connection—or disconnection, as the case may be—
without getting into specifics.

"We're all wired together" is the collective message, and we'll   9
signal again in a couple of minutes, not to say anything, probably,
but just to make sure the lines are still working. The most depressing
thing about the communications revolution is that when at last we
have succeeded in making it possible for anyone to reach anyone else
anywhere and at any time, it turns out that we really don't have
much we want to say.

Web **Read It Now:** Read *Wikipedia*'s take on the history and social impact of the
text message at **bedfordstmartins.com/americanow**, Chapter 7.

Vocabulary / Using a Dictionary

1. What does *prescient* (para. 1) mean? How is it related to *con-science*?

2. What is an *acronym* (para. 2)? How is it related to the word *pseudonym*?

3. What does *banality* mean (para. 5)? What form is it? What is its adjective form?

Responding to Words in Context

1. What does McGrath mean when he states that "text-messaging is 'lateral' rather than 'penetrative'" (para. 5)?

2. In paragraph 7, McGrath states that text-messaging is a favored means of communication in China because "text messages preserve everyone's dignity by eliminating the human voice." What

is *dignity*, and how can the deletion of verbal communication preserve it?

3. McGrath closes his essay by stating, "when at last we have succeeded in making it possible for anyone to reach anyone else anywhere and at any time, it turns out that we really don't have much we want to say" (para. 9). What, according to McGrath, are people saying to one another? What should we be saying? Why, according to McGrath, aren't we saying it?

Discussing Main Point and Meaning

1. McGrath complains that text-messaging does little more than to update people about the writer's whereabouts or state of mind — "Hey, how are you, whassup?" (para. 8). These messages are a way of communicating one's state of being or of reaching out to people to let them know they exist. Do you think this qualifies as communication? What is the purpose of communication?

2. McGrath states that text-messaging is an "avoidance mechanism" (para. 8), that it eliminates the human voice and all the indignities and intimacies and the substance that can go along with speaking with another person. How can communicating with people be a way of avoiding them? Have you ever used communication or speech in such a way that you avoided speaking to a person?

3. Relationships are now breaking up by way of text-messages. McGrath believes this to be a sign that text-messaging is robbing people of intimacy by reducing language to its most basic components of sounds and pictures. Do you agree? How would you feel if you received a break-up text-message? Would it hurt less? Would it hurt more? What kind of emotion is apparent in the written language that is not apparent in speaking?

4. The rise of text-messaging has spawned its own type of communication according to McGrath. What are the types of communication that he lists in paragraph 5? How do these types of communication prove that text-messaging has created only "breathtaking banality" rather than substantive and intimate communication? Do you agree with McGrath, or do you think he has overlooked pertinent information?

Examining Sentences, Paragraphs, and Organization

1. Describe the overall tone of McGrath's essay. What specific passages stand out in terms of tone? How effective is his tone in terms of the argument he makes?

2. In paragraph 2, McGrath states that "shorthand contractions, along with letter-number homophones ('gr8' and '2moro,' for example), emoticons (like the tiresome colon-and-parenthesis smiley face) and acronyms (like the ubiquitous 'lol,' for 'laughing out loud'), constitute the language of text-messaging—or txt msg, to use the term that txt msgrs prefer." What is the effect of including these examples of shorthand in the essay? Does McGrath think text-messaging is an actual language? Explain your answer.

3. McGrath introduces his article on text-messaging with an ad on subway cars for stenography, a type of shorthand that has gone out of style with the advent of technology. How does McGrath compare shorthand with text-messaging? What does the comparison imply about the future of text-messaging, especially in light of McGrath's final paragraph?

Thinking Critically

1. René Descartes is a famous philosopher who is known for the phrase, "I think, therefore I am." In this way, language, however simple, is essential to being and fits in with what McGrath accuses text-messaging of saying: "I am here." But according to McGrath, communication should have substance, style, and intimacy. Is text-messaging communication? Does text-messaging have all of those things? Why or why not? Do you think text-messaging is a language?

2. How is text-messaging different from writing? How do the differences point to differences in communication needs? Do you think text-messaging shows how communication is evolving or how it is regressing? Explain your answer.

3. The rendition of the Miltonic verse into text-messaging is a type of translation. McGrath's first example is a summary of the epic poem that chronicles the fall of man (para. 2). His second is a translation of a few lines of text (para. 4). Compare the original and the translation below:

Sing Heav'nly Muse, that on the secret top / Of Oreb, or of Sinai, didst inspire / That Shepherd, who first taught the chosen Seed, / In the Beginning how the Heav'ns and Earth / Rose out of Chaos.

Sing hvnly mewz dat on d :X mtntp inspyrd dat shephrd hu 1st tot d chozn seed in d begnin hw d hvn n erth @{rcub};-- outa chaos.

How are they different? How are they similar? How does this translation affect the voice and meaning of the poem?

In-Class Writing Activities

1. In McGrath's essay, we get to see two different translations of Milton's epic poem, *Paradise Lost*, in text-messaging. Those who are familiar with the poem may feel that something is missing in the text-message translation. Take your favorite song lyrics and translate them into text-message language. Then, write a short essay in which you compare the two versions. Is there any difference in the meaning? Is there any difference in how you react emotionally to the song? How do your answers change if you place the text-message next to the full lyrics?

2. For one day, record your phone conversations by jotting notes down in a journal, record the e-mails you send to your friends, and keep a log of your text-messages. Then, characterize and compare the three types of electronic communications. Does the substance of communication change based on the medium of transmission? Why or why not?

3. One of the attractions of text-messaging is its brevity or shortness. You can type only so much because of the limitations of the cellphone. In some ways, text-messaging requires a person to be more creative with his or her language; it can even be poetic. Try it out for yourself: Using text-messaging language, write a poem. What did you learn about words and images when you were writing the poem? What did you learn about the plot of the poem in its relation to its length?

AMERICA THEN . . . 1844–2006

The Telegram

Radio relay towers, about 50 miles apart, will gradually replace thousands of miles of telegraph poles and wires.

Now, telegrams "leapfrog" storms
through RCA Radio Relay

With the radio relay system, developed by RCA, Western Union will be able to send telegraph messages without poles and wires between principal cities.

"Wires down due to storm" will no longer disrupt communications. For this new system can transmit telegrams and radiophotos by invisible electric microwaves. These beams span distances up to fifty miles between towers and are completely unaffected by even the angriest storms. Moreover, the radio relay system is less costly to build and maintain.

This revolutionary stride in communications was made possible by research in RCA Laboratories—the same "make it better" research that goes into all RCA products.

And when you buy an RCA Victor radio or television set or Victrola* radio-phonograph, or even a radio tube replacement, you enjoy a unique pride of ownership. For you know, if it's an RCA it is one of the finest instruments of its kind that science has achieved.

Radio Corporation of America, RCA Building, Radio City, New York 20, N.Y... Listen to The RCA Victor Show, Sundays, 4:30 P.M., Eastern Time, over NBC Network.

Research in microwaves and electron tubes at RCA Laboratories led to the development by the RCA Victor Division of this automatic radio relay system. Here you see a close-up view of a microwave reflector. This system also holds great promise of linking television stations into networks.

 RADIO CORPORATION of AMERICA

Victrola, T. M. Reg. U. S. Pat. Off.

An ad (c. 1940) promoting the technology of the telegram.

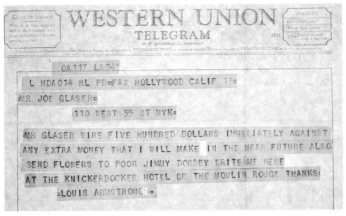

An undated telegram, probably sent in the early 1940s, from the legendary jazz musician Louis Armstrong (1901–1971) to his manager.

Long before text-messaging and e-mail, and earlier than fax machines and long-distance telephone calls, there was the telegram. Through much of the nineteenth and the first half of the twentieth centuries, sending a telegram was the easiest and fastest way of communicating with someone at a distance. European inventors and scientists experimented with various machines to send written messages as early as the 1790s. In the United States, working independently, a Yale graduate and well-known portrait painter Samuel F. B. Morse (1791–1872) received a patent for an electrical telegraph in 1837. Because so many others had worked up telegraphic systems with codes, it is difficult to credit Morse as the inventor of the telegraph. What he did essentially was, with the assistance of other scientists and instrument designers, to develop the first "user-friendly" machine with a convenient code of dots and dashes representing the alphabet and numeric system. Though there were other codes, the Morse Code quickly became the worldwide standard.

Despite some successful early demonstrations, Morse encountered difficulties for years in persuading Congress to grant him the money to lay a telegraph line between Washington, D.C., and Baltimore so he could prove once and for all the value of his idea. The central idea, of course, was that messages could be sent by means of electrical current. He and his small group of associates kept fine-tuning the system, extending the power of batteries and transmission capacity, and simplifying the machine's "finger-key" and the code so that more words could be tapped out per minute. In 1844, Congress finally approved funds. After a few errors — Morse first tried laying the wires underground and then found it worked better to string them on poles — Washington, D.C., was electrically connected with Baltimore. On May 24, 1844, Morse sent from the U.S. Supreme Court a one-sentence message, the first electrical telegram. The message, apparently chosen by the daughter of a patent official, was "What hath God wrought!" *She borrowed the exclamation from the King James Bible: "Surely there is no enchantment against Jacob, neither is there any divination against Israel: according to this time it shall be said of Jacob and of Israel, What hath God wrought!" (Num. 23:23).*

Over the next decade, Morse's telegram system grew tremendously, as America became "wired" for the first time. In 1857, the Western Union Company, which became synonymous with telegram, *was born. In January 2006, Western Union, unable to compete with the ease of e-mail, sent its last telegram. An entire verbal culture, one that often prided itself on brief, economical messages (since senders paid for telegraphs by the word) came to an end, as one technology inevitably replaced another.*

ELISSA ENGLUND

Good Grammar Gets the Girl

[THE STATE NEWS, Michigan State University/September 14, 2005]

Before You Read
Are you always careful about your grammar when you write e-mails to friends? Would you refuse to date someone who uses poor grammar?

Words to Learn

optimistic (para. 2): characterized by happiness (adj.)

pessimistic (para. 2): characterized by gloominess (adj.)

swank (para. 6): showy; rich (adj.)

nix (para. 7): to reject (v.)

In the few weeks that I've been a member of an online dating service, I've had an interesting range of people contact me. Meet Craig (not his real name). He's a 28-year-old Virgo seeking a lady who is "fun to be around." He says he finished college and is employed full-time. All in all, he seems like a pretty together guy.   1

Until you read his message. "Hi! I love to have fun weather it at work or hang out with friends," wrote Craig in his introductory conversation, which I've left with the original grammar. "I'm an optimistic because like is to short too be a pessimistic."   2

ELISSA ENGLUND *is a 2005 graduate of English from Michigan State University. She was a full-time staff member at MSU's* State News *when her annoyance with "casual online grammar" reached a critical point and inspired her to write "Good Grammar Gets the Girl." Englund, who is a night editor and occasional columnist for the* Times Herald-Record *(Middletown, New York) comments: "Most people my age don't care about grammar and the importance of clearly expressing your thoughts." She says she wrote this piece "to amuse people and get my grammar rants out to the college public!"* **For a "Student Writer at Work" interview with Englund, see page 258.**

In our second conversation, he informed me, "I don't like it when people play games and our dishonest. I have been burned to many times." Sorry, Craig. You seem a little "to dumb" to date. I'm sure Craig is actually very smart. I'm sure he's very sweet. But in the on-line dating world, that just won't cut it, babe.   3

Our society has reverted to the written word as one of the initial means of conversation. Although these love letters generally aren't written on parchment with quill pens, many first impressions are based solely on how you express yourself through the English language. With the explosion of the Internet, many couples have exchanged their first flirting words through instant messages, e-mail, and online dating services. Grammar isn't just a subject taught in seventh grade or a thing you worry about when writing a cover letter any longer. If you can't spell, use grammar, or express yourself through writing, you're going to be in trouble with the ladies.   4

If you can't spell, use grammar, or express yourself through writing, you're going to be in trouble with the ladies.

But have no fear! There are options, one of them being a nifty thing called spell check. But spell check, as I'm sure you know, can fail you. Poor Craig, for example, had no misspellings but a slew of incorrect usages. "Our" should have been "are." He mixed up "too" and "to" and "weather" and "whether." And this girl deleted him from her contact list forever.   5

Sure, maybe I'm shallow. But it makes as bad of an impression as a guy wearing a muscle shirt and daisy dukes to a swank club. It makes you seem trashy, not sweet. But I'm not totally heartless, so for all of you who are lacking in grammar hotness, I'm here. Clip out these rules. Tape them to your computer. And most important, reread something before sending it on. A lot of times, you'll catch the errors yourself. Be the Internet Romeo we all know you can be. Nobody ever rejected a guy because his grammar was too good. I promise.   6

For an annotated excerpt of this essay that highlights Englund's writing strategies, see page 257.

How to use stellar grammar to get a hot date: 7

1. With plurals, never use an apostrophe.

    Hotter than Zack Morris: "I'm looking for girls who love to laugh."

    Fewer dates than Screech Powers: "All my past girlfriend's dumped me when I cheated."

2. Possessives almost always use an apostrophe.

Singular: *Zack:* "I always treat my girlfriend's mother with respect."
Screech: "I still steal my sisters diary and read it."

Plural: *Zack:* "My friends' favorite thing about me is my sense of humor."
Screech: "My last three girlfriend's parents hated me."

3. Know the difference between "it's" and "its." "It's" is a contraction of "it is"; "its" is possessive.

Zack: "It's sexy when a girl is successful and intelligent."
Zack: "Here's a rose; I had the florist trim its thorns."
Screech: "I like when its raining because I can see through your shirt."

4. "They're" is a contraction of "they are." "There" refers to direction or location. "Their" is ownership. Likewise, "you're" is a contraction of "you are," and "your" is ownership.

Zack: "There is something about your personality that is so magnetic."
Screech: "You're dress looks great, but it would look better on my floor."

5. Have you ever read Tupac Shakur's poetry? Yeah, it's awful. Apparently, it's thug to not capitalize and nix spelling whole words to abbreviate "you" to "u," "are" to "r" and "for" to "4." But it makes you look like an eighth grader passing notes.

Zack: "I have a surprise for you when we go out tomorrow."
Screech: "i can't wait 4 us 2 get 2gethr so u can c my bed."

(Disclaimer: I always thought Screech was cuter than Zack. Plus, I hope Screech would know how to use "their," "they're" and "there" properly.)

Web **Read It Now:** Check out more student writing published by MSU's *State News* at **bedfordstmartins.com/americanow**, Chapter 7.

Vocabulary/Using a Dictionary

1. What is the root of *reverted* (para. 4)? How is reverted related to *version*?

2. What is the meaning of *slew* (para. 5)?
3. What does *stellar* (para. 7) mean?

Responding to Words in Context

1. Review Englund's essay and correct all of the grammar errors
   · made in the dialogue section. Characterize the errors. Is there a
   pattern to them? What are the main differences between how
   Zack and Screech express themselves in their writing?
2. In paragraph 4, Englund says of e-mail dating, "Although these
   love letters generally aren't written on parchment with quill pens,
   many first impressions are based solely on how you express yourself through the English language." Why use the words *parchment* and *quill pens*? What assumption is she making about the
   physical conditions of the intimate love letters or what is known
   as their textuality? How does e-mail differ from her notion of
   what love letters should be?
3. Englund goads her readers to be more romantically desirable by
   making a literary allusion, an indirect reference to literature
   when she states, "Be the Internet Romeo we all know you can
   be" (para. 6). What is an *Internet Romeo*? Do you think this is a
   good role model? Are you convinced by this allusion to follow
   Englund's rules? Why or why not?

Discussing Main Point and Meaning

1. While grammar itself may not be something that many people
   think about, Englund hopes to get you to care about sloppy
   grammar by characterizing her problem with her suitor "Craig."
   Whether or not Craig is real, he is a representation of bad grammar. How does this approach to talking about grammar affect
   you as a reader? Are you more likely to pay attention to this personalized story of a bad e-date, or would you rather have a more
   academic essay that discusses the rules of grammar? Explain your
   answer.
2. What assumptions does Englund make about Craig based on his
   grammar? Do you think she is correct? Is she fair? What assumptions do you make about a person with bad grammar?

3. Englund's article discusses how writing and dating have changed drastically because of modern technology. Many people now have online relationships and never even meet or speak to one another. Given these types of interaction, how are intimacy and writing connected? How does writing—e-mail, text-messaging, and so on—affect the intimacy of any relationship, be it one conducted online or in person?

Examining Sentences, Paragraphs, and Organization

1. Englund uses a simile to describe how bad grammar creates a particular image or persona of the writer in paragraph 6 when she states that "it makes as bad of an impression as a guy wearing a muscle shirt and daisy dukes to a swank club." What visual image do you get from this simile? What are the implications of this image? Is it an apt simile? Does this simile make you side with Englund's view of Craig?

2. Englund includes a direct address to her would-be suitor Craig: "Sorry, Craig. You seem a little 'to dumb' to date" (para. 3). Why does she directly address Craig rather than her readers? What does this address make you think or feel about Englund? About Craig?

3. When Englund lists examples of good grammar and bad grammar, she uses two characters from the television high school comedy *Saved by the Bell*. The first, Zack Morris, was considered the attractive male lead of the show, and the second, Screech Powers, was the awkward nerdy character. How effective do you think it is that she uses television characters to characterize and personalize grammar rules? How do the characters' traits and voices make you feel about the grammar rules?

Thinking Critically

1. Why do you think proper grammar and language skills are necessary? What is the importance of grammar, especially given how complex the rules are? Does how we use language affect how people see and interact with us? Explain your answer.

2. Language is constantly evolving. Although it has particular rules, the rules do change as people use language to do and describe

different things. Do you think the rules of the English language are changing? In what ways?

3. When Englund writes that our modern love letters are no longer written on parchment with a quill pen, she is not just talking about the textuality of the letter. She is also discussing the way in which writing love letters has changed. Take, for instance, this excerpt from a letter from a Civil War soldier to his wife:

> I am in hopes that I will get a whole package of letters from you in a few days. I never wanted to see you half as bad in all my life as I do now. I would give anything in the world to see you and the children. I have no idea when I will have that pleasure. . . . Write often I will get them some time. I will write every chance, do not be uneasy when you do not get letters, for when we are scouting around as we have been it is impossible to write or to send them off if we did write. Give my love to the old Lady and all the friends. My love and a thousand kisses to my own sweet Amanda and our little boys. How my heart yearns for thou that are so near and dear to me. Goodbye my own sweet wife, for the present.

Compare this with love letters you have received or written or even love songs you know. How has the way we write about love changed? What factors do you think have caused these changes?

In-Class Writing Activities

1. Englund decided not to date Craig because of the way he used words. In many ways, Englund was reading between the lines and judging Craig. Write a love letter (or e-mail) in which you try to persuade your object of affection that he or she should date you. Focus on how you present yourself as a writer and what details and evidence you should give to convince your reader to go out on a date with you. What kind of voice will you use? How will your reader judge you based on your voice and grammar?

2. Part of learning how to write has to do with learning what your shortcomings and strengths are as a writer. Take one of your recently graded papers from your English professor and review the comments your professor made. Then, write an essay in which you describe how you felt about your writing when you turned in your paper and how you view yourself as a writer after receiving the graded paper. What happened between writing the paper and

having a response from a reader? How can you improve your writing to better address the needs of your readers?

3. Englund, who obviously knows the rules of grammar, makes certain judgments about Craig throughout the article, but how does she represent herself through her writing? Reread her essay, noting particular instances where you feel strongly about Englund. Look at her word choice or diction. What does her choice of words imply about her? Look at her sentences—are they long or short, complex or simple? What do their structures, as well as the structures of her paragraphs, say about her? Finally, look at her overall argument. Does she prove her argument? Are you persuaded by her?

ANNOTATION Making Your Point with Examples

In any discussion or argument, nothing is more persuasive than a well-chosen example. We use examples often to back up a generalization with a concrete instance. The examples *show* what we mean. We can see the effectiveness of appropriate examples in the second paragraph of Elissa Englund's "Good Grammar Gets the Girl." She wants to indicate clearly to her readers that too many guys she encounters in online dating services simply can't write correctly. That's her main point, but she drives it home by showing us specific examples of someone's sloppy usage and spelling. As you can see below, good examples not only prove your point, but they also help make your writing concrete and even entertaining.

... All in all, he seems like a pretty together guy.   1

Englund quotes Craig to support her argument concretely.

Until you read his message. "Hi! I love to have fun weather it at   2 work or hang out with friends," wrote Craig in his introductory conversation, which I've left with the original grammar. "I'm an optimistic because like is to short too be a pessimistic."

Englund uses humor to further her point.

In our second conversation, he informed me, "I don't like it   3 when people play games and our dishonest. I have been burned to many times." Sorry, Craig. You seem a little "to dumb" to date. I'm sure Craig is actually very smart. I'm sure he's very sweet. But in the online dating world, that just won't cut it, babe.

—From "Good Grammar Gets the Girl" by Elissa Englund, page 251

Student Writer at Work: Elissa Englund
On Writing "Good Grammar Gets the Girl"

Q: What was the response to "Good Grammar Gets the Girl"?

A: I got some great feedback. I had two guys ask me on a date as a result of the column, promising that they were fantastic grammarians, and one friend wrote me the following e-mail as a joke, which made me incredibly happy:

> Deer Ms. England, You're column of the 14th was absolutely transpired. I especially liked the way in witch u pointed out people's common failings that even spell-czech wont catch. I hope u find many dates in the future who either lready appreciate or grow too realize the true beauty of grammer. Thank's for the laughs, witch made me disrupt the quite calm of are newsroom here in South Bend.

Q: Do you plan to write more editorials on grammar?

A: I haven't published any more of my grammar rants, but I'm a copy editor now, so I send grammar ranting e-mails to my family and friends all the time.

Q: What do you like to read?

A: I love to read the *Onion,* the *New York Times,* my own paper, the *Times Herald-Record,* and other miscellaneous papers. I read lots of news blogs online and am a cnn.com obsessive. Also, since I majored in English, I'm constantly reading novels. Right now, I'm in the middle of *You Shall Know Our Velocity,* by Dave Eggers.

Q: Any advice for college writers?

A: Get involved with your college paper. It can do wonderful things for your career, even if you don't intend to go into journalism. You can meet people who will help you in the future, and you'll improve your writing or artistic skills on a daily deadline. It's the best thing I could have done in college.

REBECCA WHEELER

"My Goldfish Name Is Scaley": There's Nothing to Correct

[DOUBLETAKE / Spring 2006]

Before You Read
Do you think your writing for school differs from how you talk? In what way?

Words to Learn

modes (para. 4): prevailing fashion or style (n.)

discourse (para. 4): connected speaking or writing (n.)

secular (para. 4): nonreligious (adj.)

interject (para. 4): interrupt (v.)

banter (para. 4): good-natured joking (n.)

acuity (para. 4): sharpness (n.)

repartee (para. 4): French, for quick and witty reply (n.)

potent (para. 4): powerful (adj.)

cadences (para. 4): rhythms in language (n.)

paradigm (para. 8): a pattern or plan (n.)

thicket (para. 9): dense bushes (n.)

dialects (para. 19): regional varieties of language with their own rules (n.)

lingua franca (para. 19): common language (n.)

REBECCA WHEELER *is an associate professor of English education at Christopher Newport University in Newport News, Virginia. Working with code-switching, African American Vernacular English, and language varieties, she attempts to bridge the achievement gap found in urban schools. She is a literacy consultant with the National Council of Teachers of English (NCTE) and has consulted with urban schools (K–16) from New York to New Orleans. Aware of the complications of aligning herself with teaching Standard English and not attempting to make vernacular English more widespread, Wheeler writes, "I strive for two goals of human justice: (1) to help teachers see students for the smart, talented, potent human beings that they are, and (2) to help create a context in which students feel self-respect—capable, confident, and potent as human beings and as strategic users of language."*

candidly (para. 20). bluntly   *vernacular* (para. 21): a native lan-
(adv.)   guage or dialect (n.)

Rajid is confused. He is troubled. Yet another paper comes back   1
from his teacher with red ink all over it. "What? She say 'Show possession!' But I did! Look! Right here! 'My goldfish name is Scaley.'
And she say 'Show plurals.' I did! Four T-shirt. That plural alright."
"She say I don't know past tense. . . . What about this—'Yesterday, I
walk to the store.' That's past! It says so, yesterday!"

His teacher is sure he does not understand possession, plurality,   2
and showing past time. But he has been using language successfully
all his life—at home. Now, at school, it seems he cannot win: His
way of speaking is "wrong," "improper," and "lazy." Their way is
right, proper, and good. And worse, they

They want to put him in special education to "fix" the way he talks.

want to put him in special education to
"fix" the way he talks. It is enough to make
anyone want to quit talking. Or writing.
They say he is supposed to give up his
mama's language. He is supposed to leave
his kin behind and learn a way of talking that feels all funny in his
mouth. And he does not see anybody—not teachers, not the school-
books, and not the tests—recognize and honor the power of his
people's language. His community is filled with speech, from the
rough and tumble play of "yo mama," to signifying, and the dozens,
to the movement and uplift of his preacher's Sunday sermons. A
neighborhood girls' jump-rope chant has quite a lot to say about the
determination of its speaker:

> Do wha'cha- wanna, Do wha'cha wanna
> Do what'cha wanna, Do wha'cha wanna

Mona Lisa Saloy, 2005 winner of the T. S. Eliot Prize for Poetry,   3
tells us that "[s]idewalk songs pass on attitudes and knowledge of
self, imitations of adult life and values, and distinct criticisms of adult
life and societal norms" (Saloy). She comments that:

> The sidewalk-song of children's folklore performs a particularly im-
> portant role in African American culture. When Black youth perform
> these sidewalk songs, they practice and learn to contribute to their
> rich African American verbal culture. By puberty if not earlier, the
> Black child must learn to "hold their own" for protection, that is,
> from verbal or physical abuse. (Saloy)

In her groundbreaking work, *Talkin and Testifyin: The Language*   4
of Black America, Geneva Smitherman tells of the intricate ways
African Americans verbally interact at home and in community using
"black modes of discourse." These modes are made up of "verbal
strategies, rhetorical devices, and folk expressive rituals," part of the
"'rich inheritance' of the African background" (1977, 103). Through
examples from songs, sacred and secular, to church sermons where
the congregants interject their responses, affirming the preacher's
word, to community banter in barber and beauty shop (104–105), to
humorous put-downs between friends where verbal acuity and wit are
highly prized (118–119), Smitherman recounts the fast-moving, complex subtleties of African Americans' verbal engagement and repartee.
And from this culture comes potent authors such as Frederick
Douglass, Maya Angelou, Malcolm X, Langston Hughes, Alice
Walker, Martin Luther King Jr. and Toni Morrison, who received the
Nobel Prize for Literature for works containing the everyday cadences
that make some well-intentioned teachers reach for the red pen.

Routinely, at the start of a college semester or of any consulting   5
workshop, I give participants a sample of sentences from public
school writing from students of all ages—from elementary, middle,
high and community college levels (e.g., *My goldfish name is Scaley.*
Mama jeep is out of gas. Ellen Goodman essay say it all. Martin
Luther King Jr. talk about freedom. Yesterday, we walk to the store).
I ask my Master of Arts in Teaching (MAT) students or public school
teachers, "What's going on in these sentences? What is your assessment of the language and the student? As a teacher, how would you
respond to this student's needs?"

Over the past five years, in my experience, student teachers, vet-   6
eran teachers, community members alike talk about how the student
is confused, doesn't understand how to show possession, has "left
off" the apostrophe -s, how the student doesn't know how to do subject verb agreement, is struggling with showing past time. Teachers
and American society say that students need to learn how to do it
"the right way."

Linguistics Offers a Research-Based Key

Professor John Rickford of Stanford University challenges us to   7
think about the children and their language differently. He argues
that we have the tools and that linguistics brings them to us. If only
we can listen. Here's another take on African American children's
writing.

Linguistics can open a world of possibilities in how we perceive African American children's language.

With linguistics comes an analytic para- 8
digm shift, a shift that can open a world of
possibilities in how we perceive and understand African American children's language.
Let's consider a *gedankenexperiment*, a thought
experiment. Here are samples of student language I have collected across five years from
five schools, ranging from elementary to
community college.

Elementary
- I went to my <u>cousin house</u>.
- And we have sweets on the weekend at <u>my mom house</u>.
- Sometimes I go to my little <u>godbrother house</u>.
- If <u>my mom old Jeep</u> is low on gas we can drive the new car around.
- The <u>dog name</u> was Bear. The <u>rabbit name</u> was Tina.
- <u>My goldfish</u> name is Scaley.
- When they were married <u>Coretta Scott last name</u> was King.
- <u>Christopher family</u> moved to Purgal.

Middle School
- Think about <u>someone use</u> of pictures.
- You was going to say <u>that boy name</u>.
- If I played on <u>Derick letter team</u> . . .
- I can't understand <u>my little sister work</u>.

Community College
- <u>Ellen Goodman essay</u> tell all about violence.
- On the television it's fun to see a <u>man eyes</u> being poked out . . .
- <u>Ms Goodman theory</u> of adding the consequences may help future generation, but not <u>today generation</u>.
- <u>Today generation</u> has already brain-washed with violence.
- There is a link between violence on TVs and violence in <u>children behavior</u>.
- . . . it is not the parents or <u>children fault</u> . . .

In the above examples, teachers see struggling students amid a   9
thicket of errors. The essence of "error" lies in the notion that someone
or something is not on some expected path. They are doing something
they "ought not" be doing, or not doing something they "ought" to be
doing. In the current instance, traditional wisdom says that the student
has "forgotten" to show possession, and has "left off" the apostrophe s.

Step back. While we appear to be neutrally and objectively de-   10
scribing the facts, actually, that's simply not so.
It's like the puzzle a colleague handed me many
years ago. After presenting me with the accom-
panying picture, my colleague asked me what it
was. (*See Fig. 1*)

Of course, I fell right in the trap and   11
replied, "It's a dandelion gone to white fluff."
"No," he replied. "Look again. What do you
actually see?" Slave to my categorizations, I
couldn't step back, couldn't disengage my automatic (and natural) tendency to see similari-

Figure 1   ties and differences, to draw inferences. He had
to tell me — "it's a circle with a long line out the
bottom and a range of lines around its circumference." That description is more neutral.

So it is with language.   12

I challenge teachers to recast their perceptions, to describe what   13
they do see, in and of itself, not in comparison to anything else.
Teachers struggle. I prompt, "Look again. What do you *actually* see?
What happens in each and every sentence before us? There's a pattern going on. What is it?"

After a time, someone will say, "two nouns sit side by side."   14

Exactly. That's the rule for possession in African American En-   15
glish. Linguists say that AAE shows possession by adjacency — by two
nouns sitting next to each other. In *My goldfish name is Scaley* — the
word goldfish sits next to the word name. In *Today generation has already been brainwashed* — the word *Today* sits next to the word *generation*. Workshop participants in New Orleans referred to "alongside
nouns," one noun sits alongside another. Second and third graders in
my work have offered the most perspicacious descriptor: In Everyday
English, we show possession by owner + owned.

This is the paradigm shift linguistics brings us — to recognize pat-   16
tern where convention diagnoses brokenness and mistake, to see

method in the traditionally diagnosed error. The implications of this one insight are staggering and transformational.

Switching, Not Correcting

Here's the next step. Teachers should understand that "there is   17
nothing to correct" when students write *My goldfish name* is *Scaley*,
but that *does not* mean they should "do nothing, sit idly by." Au contraire. This is not the story of "since all languages are equal, everybody should be able to speak however they wish." That might be true
in the best of all worlds, but we don't live there. Linguists are completely aware that in the world of business and enterprise, participants usually speak some so-called "Standard" form of the language.
However, the "Standard" language and the language of people in
power are pretty much isomorphic, identical twins. That is, whatever
the people in power speak, that will be seen as the prestige language,
the Standard. There's nothing intrinsically better in any way about
Standard English that makes it standard. It's just the language of
textbooks, reference works, the people who hold power. Standard
English has prestige because the people who speak it have prestige.

So, while any linguist will tell you that each of the nearly 6,912   18
languages on Earth (www.ethnologue.com) is structurally equal,
those same linguists will also tell you the languages are not socially or
politically equal. Clearly, some languages enjoy broader use—English or Spanish find broader use than say, Yoruba, an official language of Nigeria. Spoken broadly in Nigeria, taught in primary and
secondary school, used for government notices, in newspapers, radio
and TV, nonetheless, Yoruba won't get you too far in many international marketplaces. (Never mind the purview of any of the twenty
dialects—Oyo, Ijesha, Ila, Ijebu, Ondo, Wo, Owe, Jumu, Iworro,
Igbonna, Yagba, Gbedde, Egba, Akono, Aworo, Bunu (Bini), Ekiti,
Ilaje, Ikale, Awori—of this language).

The same holds true for the rainbow of dialects in the U.S. While   19
all dialects are structurally equal, Standard English is the language
of the marketplace, the lingua franca. It's
known by a variety of names—Standard
English, Mainstream American English
(MAE), Standard Edited English (SEE), The
Language of Wider Communication (LWC),
Business English, Professional English, The
Code of Power, etc.

> *While all dialects are structurally equal, Standard English is the language of the marketplace, the lingua franca.*

Given that societies across the globe ex-   20
pect their citizens to speak and write in the

language of power, the Standard language variety of the nation, then we expect that school systems will teach students the Standard variety. Most linguists grant this fact, quickly and candidly. Indeed, Rickford calls upon teachers to abandon failing techniques and adopt successful techniques for teaching Standard English in our schools.

Why is that so hard? Isn't it obvious that correction fails? Study after   21
study demonstrates correction to be a failing language arts practice. More than thirty years ago, Anne Piestrup showed that vernacular speakers who were corrected by their teachers actually used more, not less home speech grammar (1973). Fifteen years ago, Hanni Taylor showed that when she used traditional English department techniques, "correcting" grammar "errors," student learning faltered. Like Piestrup, Taylor's African American college students also used less Standard English and more African American English than they had started with (1991).

Teachers know that many traditional language arts approaches   22
fail African American students. Experience shows it. Decades of data show it. The federal government knows it. Witness the No Child Left Behind Act (NCLB), which requires schools to meet the academic needs of minority students. But how? What's a teacher to do?

The answer is implicit in our paradigm shift. When traditional   23
approaches assess student language as "error-filled," they misdiagnose students' writing performance. Linguistics correctly diagnoses the language facts: Students using vernacular language (*My goldfish name is Scaley*, etc.) are not making errors in Standard English, but instead, are writing correctly in the language patterns of the home dialect (Labov, 1972; Wolfram, Adger & Christian, 1999).

Students using vernacular language are not making errors, but instead, are writing correctly in the language patterns of home dialect.

Based upon this scientific understanding   24
of language, linguistics offers a two-pronged solution: Contrastive analysis and code-switching. These research proven tools are demonstrably successful in fostering Standard English mastery among minority dialect speakers. In contrastive analysis, the teacher draws upon the linguistic insights that all language is patterned and that dialects systematically contrast with each other. Accordingly, she leads students to contrast the grammatical patterns of home speech to the grammatical patterns of school speech, and so make the language contrasts explicit and conscious to the child. As the child then learns to code-switch between the language of the home and the language of the school, we add another linguistic code, Standard English, to the child's linguistic toolbox.

These techniques come straight from second language acquisition   25
research, approaches linguists have known a long time before the
days of school integration. Nearly fifty years ago, in *Linguistics
across Cultures*, ESL specialist Robert Lado explained that the patterns of people's first language (sound, word endings, and grammar)
will *transfer* into how they talk and write in a second language. A conversation I heard recently at a Chinese take-out illustrates this. A customer had asked the woman behind the counter, "Ma'am, could I
please have two forks, two plates, and two napkins?" to which the
Chinese owner replied, "Yes sir, two fork, two plate, and two nap-
kin." Here are the echoes of Chinese grammar. Since Chinese shows
plurality by number words and sentence context, that grammar pattern transferred into the woman's English exchange with her customer. *Language transfer* also applies when we are talking about a
person learning to speak or write in a second dialect. So, when an
African American student writes *I have two dog and two cat*, we
see the grammar of community language transferring into school
expression.

An ESL technique illustrated below—*contrastive analysis*—   26
helps students become consciously and rigorously aware of the grammatical differences between home speech and school speech. Then,
students can *code-switch* between language varieties. To *code-switch*
is to choose the language appropriate to the time, place, audience,
and communicative purpose. Often students will need to choose formal Standard English. Other times, as in creating dialogue, for
rhetorical effect, or for ongoing solidarity with their community, students may need to choose informal or Everyday English.

Through contrastive analysis and code-switching we *add* Stan-   27
dard English to our students' linguistic toolboxes. Research shows
that contrastive analysis succeeds in teaching Standard English to second dialect speakers.

Paradigm Shift—Walking the Walk in Virginia

Recently, I presented a workshop, *Codeswitching: Teaching*   28
Standard English in Urban Classrooms, for educators at the College
of William & Mary in Virginia. Weeks before the conference, an administrator said to me, "You're talking about explosive issues here—
Black English, African Americans, educational failure, institutional
racism. Anger. There is such anger. Aren't you afraid?"

I chuckled, replying, "You've just described my daily professional   29
terrain. No, I'm not afraid. I've learned how to walk a walk that lets

me reach many audiences all the while sidestepping anger. So, no, I'm not afraid. I'm comfortable."

    Tamisha whispers with Sharee and Shuan, her group members.   30
Xavier, Jessica, and Tylisha huddle tight. This is the tiebreaker. Their teacher, Rachel Swords, my former Education student and collaborator (Wheeler & Swords 2004, Wheeler & Swords in press), has given them a hard one. That's okay. They've been building up to this all semester. Out of the three dozen home speech patterns I have found to transfer into local student writing, students have been focusing on the top ten.

    Their task now? Discover all the informal grammar patterns in   31
the sentence and translate into formal English, Academic English.

- *All of my dad friend play basketball last summer.*

Tamisha, "Okay, I see two—*friend* uses the informal English plural   32
pattern. We know it's plural because of context—*all of.* Okay. Translate. That's *All of my dad friends. . .*"

    "But wait! Don't forget the possessive. *In my dad friend,*   33
the owner (dad) sits next to the thing owned or associated with (*friend*). That's informal possessive! It translates as . . . *my dad's friend.*"

    Too late. Xavier's hand shoots up, and Mrs. Swords hits the   34
buzzer. "Xavier, you have a translation?"

    "Sure do, Mrs. Swords," Xavier replies. "We got three informal   35
patterns: possessive, plural, and showing past time."

    "Right!" Rachel agrees. "Show us all your translation?"   36

    Tylisha presents the group's work: "*All of my dad's friends*   37
played basketball last summer."

    "Super! Xavier, Jessica and Tylisha's group wins! Good work   38
everyone! Were you close, Tamisha?" Rachel queries.

    Tamisha's group stomps their feet. They had forgotten about   39
showing past time and told Mrs. Swords so.

    Rachel walks up to the wall chart to review showing past time   40
(see Wall Chart).

    "Okay, remember, in Informal English, we show past time by   41
signal words—other words in the sentence, or maybe other words in the paragraph. Look at the left column. What signal words do we see there?" Rachel asks.

    Hands shoot up all over the third grade class: "*Yesterday*!" Tyree   42
shouts out. "*Already*," Dave contributes.

The Wall Chart

SHOWING PAST TIME
I finish___ v. I finished

INFORMAL	FORMAL
I already finish_ my paper.	I already finish<u>ed</u> my paper.
Nat Turner change_ the world.	Nat Turner chang<u>ed</u> the world.
Yesterday, I went home and turn_ on the TV.	Yesterday, I went home and turn<u>ed</u> on the TV.
The sign <u>say</u> Whites only.	The sign <u>said</u> Whites only.

THE PATTERN

Signal words
in sentence, in paragraph   Verb + -ed
Common knowledge   *(or other change in*
        shape:'said, meant', etc)

"Yes," Rachel affirms. "Exactly. There's another way. We know   43
the sentence shows past time in Informal English. Anybody remember
that?" A pause ensues.

"Yes?" Rachel calls on Kendria.   44

"Well our chart says 'common knowledge.' That means things   45
we already know."

"Exactly," Rachel agrees. "And what do we know in these sen-   46
tences that tells us the action is in the past?"

"Well, we studied Nat Turner in history. He was a long time ago.   47
Last century."

"Right!" Rachel summarizes that because of our common back-   48
ground knowledge, we know that the sentence refers to past time.
Same thing for *The sign say Whites only.*

"So, now the next step. Translation from informal to formal,   49
academic English. How do we codeswitch?"

The children affirm "add *-ed*—usually."   50

"Exactly."   51

Rachel returns to Tamisha's group. "Okay, guys, let's look at our   52
contest sentence again.

- *All of my dad friend play basketball last summer.*

"What tells us it's past time?" Rachel asks.   53

Again, hands shoot up. One child offers, "the signal words—*last*   54
summer."

"Right! That's the informal pattern for past time. So, how do we   55
code-switch it to Formal English?"

"Add *-ed!*" voices holler out.   56

And so, children engage, children talk, coming out of the silence   57
we corrected them into.

Even very young students are able to put their new understanding   58
about language to work in the classroom. Rachel circulated around
her third grade class, talking with students individually about their
writing projects. Stopping at David's desk, she was surprised. "Why
David! I thought we had talked about this! We've studied formal v.
informal language and yet here your story is filled with informal
English." David had written a storybook, *Spy Mouse and the Broken
Globe*, about a school detective. David replied, "Why Mrs. Swords. I
know about formal and informal English, but Spy Mouse doesn't."

Indeed, Spy Mouse spoke in the cadences and patterns of the   59
home language (*I won't do nothin' to you*), while eight-year-old
David chose a different variety for his author's note—Standard
English: "My name is David . . . I like to play basketball and football.
I am in the third grade. I like math and writing. I was born in Virginia." Showing an increased and conscious command of Standard
English as well as ability to codeswitch, David was able to independently articulate the reasons for his language choices, an impressive
accomplishment for any student, let alone a third grader.

We have laid down the silencing red pen. In its stead, Rachel and   60
teachers like her engage their children in criti-
cal thinking and careful analysis. Students
learn to choose their language to fit the setting, as we add the language of the school to
the language of the home. Sometimes, in narratives, children choose the language of home.
Usually, in school writing and on standardized
tests, students know to choose Formal English
patterns. Research and experience show code-
switching and contrastive analysis work.

Students learn to choose their language to fit the setting, as we add the language of the school to the language of the home.

We have said we want to teach our children the language of   61
wider communication, Standard English. Which approach shall we
take? The traditional approach that can inadvertently silence children
or the research-based, linguistic approach, code-switching and contrastive analysis that affirms the children's voices and succeeds, fostering Standard English mastery? The choice is ours and all of our fu-
tures depend on it.

Works Cited

"Ethnologue: Languages of the World." 7 July 2005. http://www.ethnologue.com.

Lado, Robert. *Linguistics across Cultures.* Ann Arbor: U of Michigan P, 1957.

Piestrup, Anne McCormick. *Black dialect interference and accommodation of reading instruction in first grade.* University of California, Berkeley: Monographs of the Language Behavior Laboratory, No. 4. 1973.

Rickford, John. Home page. July 7, 2005 http://www.standford.edu/~rickford.

Rickford, John. *Writings on the Ebonics Issue.* July 7, 2005. http://www.standford.edu/~rickford/ebonics.

Rickford, John. *Using the Vernacular to Teach the Standard.* In *Writings on the Ebonics Issue.* July 7, 2005. http://www.stanford.edu/~rickford/ebonics.

Saloy, Mona. "African American Oral Traditions in Louisiana." 7 July 2005. http://www.louisianafolklife.org/LT/Articles_Essays/creole_art_african_am_oral.html.

Smitherman, Geneva. *Talkin and Testifying: The Language of Black America.* Boston: Houghton Mifflin, 1977.

Taylor, Hanni U. *Standard English, Black English, and Bidialectalism: A Controversy.* New York: Peter Lang, 1991.

Wheeler, Rebecca S. "Code-switch to Teach Standard English." *Teaching English in the World. English Journal.* Vol. 94, No. 5. May 2005. (see www.rebecca.wheeler.net).

Wheeler, Rebecca S., and Rachel Swords (in press). *Codeswitching: Teaching Standard English in Urban Classrooms.* Urbana: National Council of Teachers of English.

Wheeler, Rebecca S., and Rachel Swords. "Codeswitching: Tools of Language and Culture Transform the Dialectally Diverse Classroom." *Language Arts.* Vol. 81 No. 6. July 2004 (see www.rebecca.wheeler.net).

Wolfram, Walt, Carolyn T. Adger, and Donna Christian, eds. *Dialects in Schools and Communities.* NJ: Lawrence Erlbaum, 1999.

Web **Read it Now:** Peruse *Slate*'s archive of articles on language and linguistics at bedfordstmartins.com/americanow, Chapter 7.

Vocabulary / Using a Dictionary

1. What does *inference* mean in paragraph 11? What is its verb form?

2. What does *perspicacious* (para. 15) mean? What root words is it derived from?

3. What does *isomorphic* (para. 17) mean?

Responding to Words in Context

1. What is a mode of discourse? What then are "black modes of discourse" (para. 4), and how are they different from the standard language?

2. When asked to describe a picture, Wheeler describes it as a dandelion before coming up with a description that is more neutral, like the one her colleague gives her in paragraph 11. What does *neutral* mean? How, according to Wheeler, can simple descriptions be neutral or not neutral?

3. Wheeler states that she is teaching her students to "code-switch between the language of the home and the language of the school" (para. 24). How is language coded? What does it mean to code-switch? Where in the essay does Wheeler show how she is code-switching for her audience?

Discussing Main Point and Meaning

1. Why, if linguists say that languages are structurally equal, are languages and dialects not treated equally? What makes one language more powerful or more accepted than another? Who makes the decision as to what language and system is the right way?

2. Why is Wheeler's administrator concerned about her conference? How is the issue of Black English an explosive issue? What does it say about our country and our educational system?

3. How can language silence a person, as Wheeler suggests in her final paragraph? How is language related to a person's identity?

Examining Sentences, Paragraphs, and Organization

1. After explaining that "teachers should understand that 'there is nothing to correct' . . . but that *does not* mean they should 'do nothing, sit idly by'" (para. 17). Wheeler emphasizes her point by using a French phrase, *au contraire*, which means "on the contrary." What is the effect of using this phrase rather than its English equivalent? How does it help to make Wheeler's argument about the languages of power?

2. After Wheeler's colleague expresses concern over her dangerous subject matter, Wheeler's next paragraph features students Tamisha, Sharee, and Shuan whispering to one another (para. 30).

What is the effect of this paragraph? How does it contrast with the statement of Wheeler's colleague?

3. Wheeler begins her essay with a student, Rajid, who is confused over his teacher's grammar instructions, and ends with students and their code-switching writing. This is known as a framework: She begins and ends with similar ideas. What is the difference between the example involving Rajid and the one involving David? How does this framework show that code-switching is an effective form of teaching English?

Thinking Critically

1. Wheeler incorporates the perspectives of various experts in her essay to show the influence of language on a person's identity. She quotes Mona Lisa Saloy, who states "[s]idewalk songs pass on attitudes and knowledge of self, imitations of adult life and values, and distinct criticisms of adult life and societal norms" (para. 3). How does language offer a person an identity? How do the songs you listen to influence your identity? Are they performing functions similar to the sidewalk songs?

2. What is the purpose of education? Should education make students conform to particular standards so they can succeed in a world that may be different from their community? Or should education equalize and celebrate differences without attempting to change students' behaviors and ways of communication? Or something else?

3. How and why does the paradigm shift that Wheeler suggests work? Can we apply it to anything other than school?

In-Class Writing Activities

1. Take a song that you know that uses AAE or informal English. Write down the lyrics. Then, code-switch and translate the lyrics into formal English. What is the difference between the two versions? How does the type of language used affect the message of the song? How would you change the formal English version to more closely resemble the original?

2. Wheeler includes a chart with many examples to show informal English and how it is used by students. With a partner, come up with examples of informal English you use or have heard used—

on television, in the movies, or in music. Then, classify the types of code-switching that are happening. Write up a lesson where you teach your classmates and your teacher how to code-switch into informal English. What rules should they follow? When do they follow them?

3. Do you think the way in which your school teaches you how to read and write is working? Write a short essay in which you look at your school's expectations, its learning techniques, and the effectiveness of its approach. Do you have other suggestions for how to learn formal English? Should teachers be teaching informal English as well? Back up your opinions with evidence and support, as Wheeler does in her essay.

Discussing the Unit

Suggested Topic for Discussion

All three of the writers included in this chapter equate language with some sort of emotional intimacy, perhaps because language is connected not only to how we view ourselves, but also to how we interact with other people. How are writing and emotional intimacy connected? Writing and identity? Why is writing such a personal experience for writers? Is it a personal experience for readers as well? How do we learn how to communicate within particular paradigms or standards?

Preparing for Class Discussion

1. The authors in this chapter have decided to communicate through written words about the use of words. How would you compare the voice of each writer? What do you think the overall purpose or thesis statement of each writer is? Which writer helped you to better understand the role of language in American life and culture?

2. Part of understanding a language is understanding individual words and how they work together. You understand the various writers in this chapter because they use the agreed-upon rules of grammar to make meaning, and none of them uses words that you cannot know the meaning of. But what happens when you

do not know the words? Whether you realize it or not, you use the rules of grammar and language to make meaning. Take, for instance, the first stanza from Lewis Carroll's "Jabberwocky":

> 'Twas brillig, and the slithy toves
> Did gyre and gimble in the wabe:
> All mimsy were the borogoves,
> And the mome raths outgrabe.

What do you think this stanza means? What words do you recognize? Why type of word (noun, verb, adjective, adverb) are the words you do not recognize? How do they make meaning with their functions? How do they make meaning with their sounds? Do you recognize any sentence patterns that also help you make sense of the words?

3. What kind of social rules do we rely on when we communicate? Some expressions are socially acceptable, but some are not. For instance, was Englund's language regarding Craig acceptable to you? Was she violating any rules of communicating? Does it make a difference whether she is communicating about an intimate encounter with a close friend or with a complete stranger? Why or why not?

From Discussion to Writing

1. A *manifesto* is a public declaration of beliefs. You've probably heard of or studied *The Communist Manifesto* by Karl Marx, although a great many other famous (and infamous) manifestos have been written. Write your own manifesto in which you list at least ten beliefs you have about language and communication. Write a paragraph for each belief, explaining why you hold it, how it works, and why it is important, as well as any other information you believe you should include to convert another person to your language beliefs.

2. Wheeler explains that what we learn in our original or home language affects how we might use another language. How have you been affected by your home language? Write your own language-learning autobiography in which you explore your first words or sentences, how you talk (and whether how you talk changes depending on who you are talking to), what you think is acceptable or unacceptable language, and why. How has your use of language changed as you have gone through school? Is your school language different from your home language? In what way?

Topics for Cross-Cultural Discussion

1. McGrath looks at the different uses of text-messaging that arise from different cultures' expectations of communication. For instance, he tells us that in China, it is embarrassing to call someone and not talk to them directly. Wheeler looks at how language is used to form identities or to rebel. How would you characterize your community's use of language? What is most commonly said? What are the rules behind communicating to particular members of your community—for instance, when asking for a favor, when complaining about something, or when asking someone out on a date? How did you learn these particular rules, and where do you think they came from?

2. Another aspect of language is what is unsaid or not allowed to be spoken. Each culture has certain taboo words and phrases. For instance, it is considered bad luck to say "good luck" to an actor. Instead, you are supposed to say "break a leg." What words or phrases are taboo in your culture? Why? How you do get around saying them?

8

Video Games: How Are They Transforming the Culture?

Ever since the Columbine Massacre in April 1999, when two Colorado high school students in a shooting rampage murdered a dozen fellow students and wounded many others before killing themselves, state and federal legislators have been searching for ways to regulate the distribution of violent video games to teenagers. An investigation after the shootings indicated that the two killers were especially fond of certain video games (along with many other forms of violent media). Attempts at restrictive legislation have been ongoing, and in 2005 to 2006, a number of bills were proposed by congressional members from both parties. One of the major pieces of legislation, the Children and Media Research Advancement Act (CAMRA), will fund a comprehensive study hoping to provide evidence linking violent media (in particular, video games) to violent behavior. The study will be conducted by the Center for Disease Control and Prevention (CDC), the prestigious Atlanta research institution known for its studies of epidemics. One reason for this extensive study is to bolster the arguments against the games since federal courts have consistently tossed out attempts at regulatory laws. One such court has said that opponents of the games "must come forward with empirical support for [their] belief that 'violent' video games cause psychological harm to minors."

Although the study is perhaps a few years from completion, it's clear that video games have become a major issue in American culture, one that touches on a number of far-ranging topics. These include the relation between media and criminal violence, the right of free expression, the federal regulation of products deemed harmful to consumers, and the special appeal of video games to males. Yet, despite so much negative public attention, video games remain a thriving business, and their appeal is growing tremendously. In "Dream Machines," one of the video industry's top creative individuals, Will Wright, explains the enormous impact of the games on an entire generation. As Wright sees them, video games invite us "to create and interact with elaborately simulated worlds, characters, and story lines. Games aren't just fantasy worlds to explore; they actually amplify our powers of imagination."

Wright is hoping that people—especially older people—will begin to realize the "positive aspects of gaming." Yet it will be difficult to persuade many adults who view the games as another product of "our toxic culture" and a leading threat to family values to accept those positive aspects. One opponent of violent video games, Rebecca Hagelin, a columnist and a vice president of a conservative foundation, is also concerned as a mother about the adverse ways the games affect children, especially boys: "Parents," she contends in "Video Game Violence and Our Sons," "must wake up to the fact that our nation's boys are being used and manipulated by an industry making billions of dollars by warping their minds." Still, the issue stubbornly remains: Do the games in fact "warp" the minds of young people? Using statistics that show Americans have become less criminally violent over the past decade, a University of Connecticut student, Brandon Nadeau, cleverly turns the conventional "games cause violence" relationship in the other direction. In "Video Games Make Society Less Violent," he believes that the same parents who are offended by the games are the ones who purchase them for their children: "I guess," Nadeau concludes, "they should be thanked for being hypocritical. After all, they are helping create a less violent society."

The chapter concludes with a look back on one of the earliest controversial games, the primitive predecessor of the Grand Theft Auto series.

WILL WRIGHT

Dream Machines

[WIRED / April 2006]

Before You Read

Why do people play video games? Are games changing to create a more personalized experience for the player? A more imaginative one? Is gaming a creative act?

Words to Learn

essence (para 2.): the most important properties that serve to identify something (n.)

empirical (para. 2): relying on or derived from observation or experiment (adj.)

hypothesis (para. 2): a tentative explanation for an observation, phenomenon, or scientific problem that can be tested by further investigation (n.)

fundamentally (para. 2): by its very nature (adv.)

cultivate (para. 7): to promote the growth of (v.)

elaborately (para. 8): done with great detail (adv.)

malleable (para. 14): changeable (adj.)

subsume (para. 14): to take in, absorb (v.)

engage (para. 16): to draw into, involve (v.)

WILL WRIGHT, *a guest editor at* Wired *magazine and cofounder of Maxis, a game development company, is also the creator of* The Sims *and myriad other games. Wright began creating games when he realized that video games were taking up much of his time. His success came while working on his first major game,* Raid on Bungling Bay, *when he realized that he enjoyed building landscapes rather than bombing them. This love led him to become an innovator in software simulation. In 2001 he was awarded a Lifetime Achievement Award at the Game Developers Choice Awards; a year later, he was inducted into the Academy of Interactive Arts and Sciences' Hall of Fame. In 2005 he was awarded the* PC Magazine *Lifetime Achievement Award.*

The human imagination is an amazing thing. As children, we 1
spend much of our time in imaginary worlds, substituting toys and
make-believe for the real surroundings that we are just beginning to
explore and understand. As we play, we learn. And as we grow, our
play gets more complicated. We add rules and goals. The result is
something we call games.

Now an entire generation has grown up with a different set of 2
games than any before it—and it plays these games in different ways.
Just watch kids with a new videogame. The last thing they do is read
the manual. Instead, they pick up the controller and start mashing
buttons to see what happens. This isn't a random process; it's the
essence of the scientific method. Through trial and error, players
build a model of the underlying game based on empirical evidence
collected through play. As the players refine this model, they begin to
master the game world. It's a rapid cycle of hypothesis, experiment,
and analysis. And it's a fundamentally different take on problem-
solving than the linear, read-the-manual-first approach of their
parents.

In an era of structured education and standardized testing, this 3
generational difference might not yet be evident. But the gamers'
mindset—the fact that they are learning in a
totally new way—means they'll treat the
world as a place for creation, not consumption. This is the true impact videogames will
have on our culture.

> The gamers' mindset
> means they'll treat the
> world as a place for
> creation, not
> consumption.

Society, however, notices only the nega- 4
tive. Most people on the far side of the
generational divide—elders—look at games
and see a list of ills (they're violent, addictive, childish, worthless).
Some of these labels may be deserved. But the positive aspects of
gaming—creativity, community, self-esteem, problem-solving—are
somehow less visible to nongamers.

I think part of this stems from the fact that watching someone 5
play a game is a different experience than actually holding the controller and playing it yourself. Vastly different. Imagine that all you
knew about movies was gleaned through observing the audience in a
theater—but that you had never watched a film. You would conclude that movies induce lethargy and junk-food binges. That may be
true, but you're missing the big picture.

So it's time to reconsider games, to recognize what's different 6
about them and how they benefit—not denigrate—culture. Consider,

Food Force video game. Launched in 2005 by the United Nations' World Food Program (WFP), Food Force teaches children about world hunger and the WFP's approach to eradicating it in the real world. According to Neil Gallagher of the WFP, the agency created the game because "children in the developed world don't know what it's like to go to bed threatened by starvation." Players take on the role of rookies and join a team of UN experts to help relieve the famine on the fictional island of Sheylan, a country plagued by drought and civil war. According to Gallagher, the game "generate[s] kids' interest and understanding about hunger, which kills more people than AIDS, malaria, and tuberculosis combined."

 Play It Now: Check out Food Force and America's Army: Rise of a Soldier at **bedfordstmartins.com/americanow**, Chapter 8.

for instance, their "possibility space": Games usually start at a well-defined state (the setup in chess, for instance) and end when a specific state is reached (the king is checkmated). Players navigate this possibility space by their choices and actions; every player's path is unique.

> *Games cultivate—and exploit—possibility space better than any other medium.*

Games cultivate—and exploit—possibility space better than any other medium. In linear storytelling, we can only imagine the

7

America's Army: Rise of a Soldier video game. Created by the U.S. Army (2000), this game gives children the opportunity to experience life as a soldier—from recruitment to boot camp to special operations and combat. Praised by U.S. soldiers for its realism, America's Army is paid for with U.S. tax dollars and distributed for free. Chris Chambers, deputy director of development for the game, said in a 2006 interview that the Army started the project "as a means of 'connecting' with America." Chambers said, "Recruiters report that the game is a valuable communications tool in connecting with young Americans.... [They] have noted that the game connects [the Army] with Gen X and Y like no other tool."

possibility space that surrounds the narrative: What if Luke had joined the Dark Side? What if Neo isn't the One? In interactive media, we can explore it.

Like the toys of our youth, modern videogames rely on the player's active involvement. We're invited to create and interact with elaborately simulated worlds, characters, and story lines. Games aren't just fantasy worlds to explore; they actually amplify our powers of imagination.   8

Think of it this way: Most technologies can be seen as an enhancement of some part of our bodies (car/legs, house/skin, TV/senses). From the start, computers have been understood as an extension of the human brain; the first computers were referred to as   9 mechanical brains and analytical engines. We saw their primary value as automated number crunchers that far exceeded our own meager abilities.

But the Internet has morphed what we used to think of as a fancy   10 calculator into a fancy telephone with email, chat groups, IM, and blogs. It turns out that we don't use computers to enhance our math skills—we use them to expand our people skills.

The same transformation is happening in games. Early computer   11 games were little toy worlds with primitive graphics and simple problems. It was up to the player's imagination to turn the tiny blobs on the screen into, say, people or tanks. As computer graphics advanced, game designers showed some Hollywood envy: They added elaborate cutscenes, epic plots, and, of course, increasingly detailed graphics. They bought into the idea that world building and storytelling are best left to professionals, and they pushed out the player. But in their rapture over computer processing, games designers forgot that there's a second processor at work: the player's imagination.

Now, rather than go Hollywood, some game designers are de-   12 ploying that second processor to break down the wall between producers and consumers. By moving away from the idea that media is something developed by the few (movie and TV studios, book publishers, game companies) and consumed in a one-size-fits-all form, we open up a world of possibilities. Instead of leaving player creativity at the door, we are inviting it back to help build, design, and populate our digital worlds.

More games now include features that let players invent some   13 aspect of their virtual world, from characters to cars. And more games entice players to become creative partners in world building, letting them mod its overall look and feel. The online communities that form around these imaginative activities are some of the most vibrant on the Web. For these players, games are not just entertainment but a vehicle for self-expression.

Games are not just entertainment but a vehicle for self-expression.

Games have the potential to subsume almost all other forms of   14 entertainment media. They can tell us stories, offer us music, give us challenges, allow us to communicate and interact with others, encourage us to make things, connect us to new communities, and let us play. Unlike most other forms of media, games are inherently malleable. Player mods are just the first step down this path.

Soon games will start to build simple models of us, the players. 15
They will learn what we like to do, what we're good at, what interests and challenges us. They will observe us. They will record the decisions we make, consider how we solve problems, and evaluate how skilled we are in various circumstances. Over time, these games will become able to modify themselves to better "fit" each individual. They will adjust their difficulty on the fly, bring in new content, and create story lines. Much of this original material will be created by other players, and the system will move it to those it determines will enjoy it most.

Games are evolving to entertain, educate, and engage us individu- 16
ally. These personalized games will reflect who we are and what we enjoy, much as our choice of books and music does now. They will allow us to express ourselves, meet others, and create things that we can only dimly imagine. They will enable us to share and combine these creations, to build vast playgrounds. And more than ever, games will be a visible, external amplification of the human imagination.

 Read It Now: To read more articles on gaming published by *Wired*, go to
bedfordstmartins.com/americanow, Chapter 8.

Vocabulary/Using a Dictionary

1. What does it mean to *automate* (para. 9) something? What other words share the prefix *auto-*?

2. What is the plural of *medium* (para 7.)? What is a medium?

3. What does it mean to *glean* (para 5.) something? What are some synonyms of *glean*?

4. What is the origin of the word *lethargy* (para. 5)? How is it related to the word *lethe*?

Responding to Words in Context

1. What does Wright mean by the term *possibility space* (para. 6)? What does his choice of the adjective *possibility* have to do with his overall argument about the value of video games?

2. What is *linear storytelling* (para. 7)? How is it different from other types of narrative—especially the narratives of games?

3. Wright explains that a video game is not just for entertainment, but that it can be "a vehicle for self-expression" (para. 13). What does it mean for something to be a *vehicle* for something else?

Discussing Main Point and Meaning

1. What is Wright's main argument? Whom is he trying to persuade? That is, who is his main audience for the essay? His secondary audience?

2. What impact does Wright think video games will have on culture? How does his perspective differ from that of nongamers?

3. How does Wright support his claim that gaming is really self-expression?

4. How do gamers personalize their gaming experiences? How does Wright predict that games will evolve?

Examining Sentences, Paragraphs, and Organization

1. To open his essay, Wright describes the role of imagination in play. How does he use this to structure the rest of his essay?

2. In paragraph 4, how does Wright mention the possible negatives of video games? Why does he provide these points this way?

3. How does Wright bring the essay to a close? How does his closing paragraph relate to the rest of the essay?

Thinking Critically

1. Wright makes the point that the reality of participating in an activity (such as playing video games or watching movies) can be vastly different than the impression gained by simply watching the participants. Is this true of all activities, or only some? What would be some differences between activities that are or are not like this?

2. The essay states that the video game generation has grown up not just playing a different set of games, but playing them in different ways. Why might this be the case?

3. What is your experience with gaming? Do you agree that gaming is a positive activity? A creative one? Explain.

In-Class Writing Activities

1. Wright's essay focuses heavily on one positive aspect of video games. Are there any other positive aspects of video games that he has not mentioned? Choose one and describe it. Why is it positive? Is it frequently overlooked? Is it unique to video games?

2. How have games changed over time? How are the games Wright describes different from those of the previous generation? Is the difference entirely technological, or are there other differences that are completely separate from the technological divide?

REBECCA HAGELIN

Video Game Violence and Our Sons

[TOWNHALL.COM / March 28, 2006]

Before You Read

Do violent video games lead to violent acts? Can a cause-and-effect case be made? Do minors need to be protected from the effects of some video games?

Words to Learn

diversions (para. 2): things that relax the mind and entertain (n.)

acquire (para. 6): to gain possession of (v.)

snuffed (para. 7): put to a sudden end; extinguished (v.)

regulating (para. 7): controlling or directing (v.)

REBECCA HAGELIN *is vice president of the Heritage Foundation, a conservative group whose vision (as quoted from the group's Web site, www .heritage.org) is to "create an America where freedom, opportunity, prosperity, and civil society flourish." Hagelin also writes a weekly column for WorldNetDaily.com and Townhall.com called "Heat Beat" in which she looks at social issues through her perspective as a mother.*

anomalies (para. 8): exceptions to the rule (n.)

warp (para. 8): to twist out of shape (v.)

psyches (para. 8): minds; psychological selves; souls (n.)

scoff (para. 8): to mock (v.)

"Life is like a video game. Everyone has to die sometime."   1

If you spent part of your youth playing "Pac-Man" and "Space 2 Invaders," such a statement must seem bizarre. Video games were . . . well, games — innocent diversions that did nothing worse than eat up dotted lines and too much of our allowances. A waste of time? Perhaps. But nobody got hurt.

At least, they didn't used to be.   3

The opening statement above was spoken by Devin Moore, a 4 teenager who murdered three people — two police officers and a 911 dispatcher — in a Fayettesville, Alabama, police station in 2003. Arrested on suspicion of car theft, Moore was brought in for booking and ended up on a bloody rampage.

He lunged at Officer Arnold Strickland, grabbed his gun and shot 5 him twice. Officer James Crump, who responded to the sound of the gunfire, was shot three times. And before he ran outside with police car keys he snatched, Moore put five bullets in Dispatcher Ace Mealer. Was this the first time Moore had committed such a heinous crime? Yes and no.

Moore was a huge fan of a notorious video game called Grand 6 Theft Auto. As the title suggests, the goal is to steal cars. If that's all there was to the "game" it would be bad enough, but it gets worse: The way to acquire and hold on to the cars is to kill the police officers who try to stop you. And the sick minds behind the game give you plenty of choices — shooting them with a rifle, cutting them up with a chainsaw, setting them on fire, decapitation. If you shoot an officer, you get extra points for shooting him in the head. It's no surprise, then, that all of Moore's real-life victims had their heads blown off.

According to court records, Moore spent hundreds of hours play- 7 ing Grand Theft, which has been described as "a murder simulator." But this time, his victims weren't a collection of animated pixels on a TV screen. They were flesh-and-blood human beings whose lives were snuffed out in seconds. They had families who continue to mourn their loss — such as Steve Strickland, Officer Strickland's brother. Tomorrow, he will testify before the U.S. Senate Judiciary Committee's Subcommittee on the Constitution, Civil Rights and

Property. Chaired by Senator Sam Brownback, R-Kansas, the purpose of the hearing is to examine the constitutionality of state laws regulating the sale of ultra-violent video games to children. Three psychologists will testify about the potential link between playing violent video games and copycat violence, and whether the games contribute to aggressive behavior.

With the ever-expanding use of technology by our children, such   8
hearings are critical. We must determine if Moore and other murderers like him are anomalies or if ultra-violent video games dangerously warp the psyches of our youth. Those tempted to scoff at the connection between video games and behavior should bear a couple of things in mind. First, video games are not passive or spectator media. While playing the game, teenage boys and young men, the largest users of video games, actually become the characters who cut up their victims with chainsaws, set them on fire, or chop off their heads.

> *Users become the characters who cut up their victims with chainsaws, set them on fire, or chop off their heads.*

According to Dr. Elizabeth Carll of the American Psychological   9
Association (who also will testify tomorrow), this active participation enhances the "learning" experience. And video games are often played repeatedly for hours on end—so, hour after hour, teens playing games such as Grand Theft Auto "learn" how to kill police officers and earn points for their barbarianism.

The second fact to keep in mind is that teenagers' brains are still   10
developing and are extremely impressionable. The parents of teens hardly need reminding that for all their joys, teens often lack judgment, critical thinking skills, and foresight. Some are better than others, yes, but many (like Moore) are startlingly deficient. In short: Put a "murder simulator" in their hands, and you just might be asking for trouble. But don't put words in my mouth—I am not saying that every kid who plays a violent video game will become a criminal.

And as a staunch conservative who believes that "the govern-   11
ment that governs least governs best," I'm not advocating a plethora of laws that may have a chilling effect on free speech. I do, however, recognize that it is sometimes necessary to provide special protections for minors from harmful materials—take pornography and alcohol, for example. As a mother, I also believe that our nation must examine how the products of our toxic culture affect the civility and safety of our children and of our society. We owe it to the students who

died at Columbine; we owe it to Devin Moore's victims; we owe it to our own children.

But armed with the truth, and a God-given mandate to train our   12 own children, we must never depend on government to take care of our kids or raise them. Parents must wake up to the fact that our nation's boys are being used and manipulated by an industry making billions of dollars by warping their minds. As I outline in my book, *Home Invasion: Protecting Your Family in a Culture That's Gone Stark Raving Mad*, it doesn't take an act of Congress to take back your home—it takes active, loving, informed parenting. It takes setting boundaries and sticking with them. It takes understanding our kids, and understanding that our kids need us to guide them. Senator Brownback is taking a bold step and doing his job as an elected official in exploring the effects of video game violence—it's up to parents to use the information to protect our sons and our society.

> *Boys are being used and manipulated by an industry making billions of dollars by warping their minds.*

 Read It Now: To read conservative perspectives on gaming and other topics by Townhall.com columnists, go to **bedfordstmartins.com/americanow**, Chapter 8.

Vocabulary / Using a Dictionary

1. What is a *rampage* (para. 4)? What are the origins of this word?
2. What does it mean to be *animated* (para. 7)? What does the word *animate* have to do with the word *anima*?
3. What happens when someone *testifies* (para. 7)? What are some synonyms of *testify*?

Responding to Words in Context

1. What words could have been used instead of *bloody rampage* (para. 4)? Why do you think Hagelin chose this phrase?
2. What are the implications of the phrase *God-given mandate* (para. 12)?
3. Throughout her essay, Hagelin chooses some vivid words and terms (such as *bloody rampage* in para. 4 and *heinous* in para. 5).

Identify a few other vivid words in the essay. How do they contribute to (or detract from) the tone and effectiveness of the author's main argument?

Discussing Main Point and Meaning

1. How does the author reconcile laws against violence in video games with free speech? Do you think this is a valid position?
2. Do you agree with the author's position on the role of parents in choosing activities for a child? Why or why not?
3. How does the author view the greater context of our culture? What are her opinions and politics? How do they affect the essay?

Examining Sentences, Paragraphs, and Organization

1. How does Hagelin begin her essay? Why does she use this technique?
2. The author mentions Dr. Elizabeth Carll by name but does not quote her. How does she convey Dr. Carll's opinion and information? Why does the author place the word *learning* within quotation marks?

Thinking Critically

1. Who do you think is the intended audience for this essay? What tells you this?
2. The author latches onto the phrase *murder simulator* (paras. 7, 10). Why do you think she does this?
3. What evidence does Hagelin provide—about game features and the gamers themselves—to support her argument? Do you agree with her? Why or why not?
4. Hagelin writes in paragraph 6 that the creators of Grand Theft Auto have "sick minds." Do you agree? What arguments, if any, could be made in favor of violent video games?
5. In paragraph 11, Hagelin gives her perspective as a mother and also refers to victims of Columbine and of Devin Moore. Is this effective? Explain.

In-Class Writing Activities

1. Consider what kinds of laws can be enacted against violence and video games. How can gaming be legislated? What kinds of pitfalls might there be?

2. How much of a choice in their recreation do you think children should have? How would this vary by age? Do you think the level of control that the author describes is too little, too much, or just right? Are there any special circumstances that should be considered? Explain.

BRANDON NADEAU

Video Games Make Society Less Violent

[THE DAILY CAMPUS, The University of Connecticut / October 21, 2005]

Before You Read

Should we thank PlayStation for the decrease in violent crime? How much should we rely on the statistical data of studies on the relationship between video games and violence?

BRANDON NADEAU *is an anthropology student in his sophomore year at the University of Connecticut and a weekly columnist for UConn's* Daily Campus. *Nadeau wrote "Video Games Make Society Less Violent" to address prevailing attitudes about the dangers of video games. "I wanted to provide a counter argument to the false accusations in the media at the time," says Nadeau. One of his main complaints about the media is that when journalists address the alleged connection between video games and violence, they "don't use facts and figures; they live off sensationalism."* **For a "Student Writer at Work" interview with Nadeau, see page 296.**

Words to Learn

satire (para. 2): irony used to attack foolish beliefs and attitudes (n.)

ample (para. 2): of a large size or amount (adj.)

mainstream (para. 3): representing the prevailing attitudes of a society (adj.)

refute (para. 4): to prove to be false (v.)

compelling (para. 4): drivingly forceful (adj.)

amicable (para. 5): sociable (adj.)

advocates (para. 7): those who speak or argue in favor of (n.)

hypocritical (para. 7): claiming to hold feelings or beliefs that you really do not (adj.)

Jack Thompson, a Miami, Florida, medical malpractice lawyer, has spent more than ten years protesting video game violence. Recently, however, he offered $10,000 to anyone who would make and market one of the most violent video games I have ever heard of.   1

This, of course, is Thompson's idea of satire. He hates video game violence and uses his ample hate to try to stop any form of violence entering the games. Thompson has hate and little else to go on, though. Thompson is the man who claimed that "Halo" inspired the Beltway Snipers in 2002 because "Halo" was a sniper rifle simulation. He also got some more airtime when he claimed "The Sims 2" contained a nude patch. His main point is that video games inspire violent behavior in people.   2

Thompson doesn't have any facts on his side. Actually, they are all against him. Since video games became a mainstream industry, around the time the PlayStation came out in 1995, the violent crime rate has decreased significantly. By the time one of Thompson's favorite targets, "Grand Theft Auto 3," was released, the violent crime rate was 30 percent lower than it had been twenty years earlier. Oddly enough, the rate has decreased every year since 1995, resulting in a new record-low rate in violent crime every year.   3

This alone seems enough to refute any claim Thompson or the rest of the antivideo lobby has about the games' influence on real life. But more compelling is the fact that the audience Thompson claims is the most heavily influenced (teenagers) has seen an extremely sharp decline in violent crime since the PlayStation was put on the market. It appears the rate was highest in the "Nintendo   4

Since video games became a mainstream industry, the violent crime rate has decreased significantly.

Era," a time when video game violence was at a minimum. (Nintendo actually had a series of rules to make sure games were fairly nonviolent, such as a "no blood" rule for any game.)

Studies on how video game violence influences real-world vio-   5
lence have had mixed results. One study in particular, where gamers were asked to play a game for hours on end, showed the players were more friendly and amicable, as well as slower to rile, than before the game was played. The researchers compared this to when someone finished watching a violent movie—the viewers were almost the exact opposite of the gamers. The reason for this, the researchers said, was that the games gave people something to do, while movies made them sit and watch; they weren't in control of what was happening, and this made them angry.

Maybe the best evidence I have against the entire "violence in-   6
spires violence" movement is myself. I have played games my entire life, everything from "Super Mario Brothers" to "Manhunt" and "Halo." Yet, I have never committed a violent act. I have the equipment to do something (pellet guns, pocket knives etc.), yet I have never used them to hurt someone or something. When I shoot someone in a game, I don't think, "That would be cool to do." Actually, I don't think about it at all, it's harmless entertainment; six seconds from then, I could be killed and I know I'll come back in a few more seconds. To anyone mentally stable enough to play a complex game, it is apparent it is not reality and should not be imitated.

> *When I shoot someone in a game, I don't think, "That would be cool to do."*

In the end, video game violence has been given a bad spin by the   7
media and anti-violence advocates. Peddling violent games to children is a dangerous prospect, which is why there is a ratings board that restricts which age groups can buy which games. The same parents who hate these games are the ones who are buying them for their children. I guess they should be thanked for being hypocritical. After all, they are helping create a less violent society.

For an annotated excerpt of this essay that highlights Nadeau's writing strategies, see page 294.

Web **Read It Now:** To check out UConn's *Daily Campus* for more student views on gaming and other issues, go to bedfordstmartins.com/americanow.com, Chapter 8.

Vocabulary / Using a Dictionary

1. What does *malpractice* (para. 1) mean? What other words begin with *mal-*?
2. What is the difference between *hypocrisy* and *hypocritical* (para. 7)?
3. What is *peddling* (para. 7)? What other word might the author have chosen to convey the same meaning and tone?

Responding to Words in Context

1. What does it mean to say that games *inspire* (para. 2) violent behavior? Why do you think Nadeau chose the word *inspired* rather than cause, for example?
2. Is the word *evidence* (para. 6) similar to *proof* or *facts*? Are they the same? Can they be used interchangeably?

Discussing Main Point and Meaning

1. What specific points does Nadeau use to refute Jack Thompson and to back up his own points about video games?
2. What do you think the author means by saying that video games are a "mainstream industry" (para. 3)?
3. According to Nadeau's essay, since the mainstreaming of video games in 1995, what has happened to the violent crime rate?
4. Do you agree that "the same parents who hate these games are the ones who are buying them for their children" (para. 7)? Is this an accurate statement? Why or why not?

Examining Sentences, Paragraphs, and Organization

1. How does Nadeau lead the essay to his main point?
2. Does Nadeau bring his personal experience into the essay smoothly and effectively? Explain.
3. When Nadeau concludes his essay, has he proven a point? How does he reiterate his claims in the last paragraph?

Thinking Critically

1. Nadeau notes in paragraph 3 that all the facts are against Thompson. How does he back this up? Do you agree with Nadeau on this? Why or why not?

2. How would you refute Nadeau's arguments? Can they be argued against?

3. Consider Nadeau's use of examples throughout the essay. How would the essay have been different if he had included direct quotations from Jack Thompson? Is Nadeau specific enough, for example, when he refers to trends and studies? Does he provide enough detail, or would more detail clutter his essay? Would citations have been helpful or distracting? Explain.

In-Class Writing Activities

1. Describe your experiences with video games. Are they similar to Nadeau's? Do you find yourself agreeing with him because of this, or do you take a different stance?

2. Could there be reasons for the drop in the crime rate other than video games? Think of some other things in recent years that could have contributed to it and describe them.

3. Nadeau writes in paragraph 4 that Nintendo once "had a series of rules to make sure games were fairly nonviolent, such as a 'no blood' rule for any game." Would gaming be less violent if a "no blood" rule were still in place?

ANNOTATION The Art of Argument: Arranging Evidence

When we construct an opinion paper, we need, of course, to offer reasons and evidence supporting our position. But to make our position fully persuasive, we need to arrange the reasons and evidence effectively. In many potentially good opinion essays, the writer fails to position his or her evidence in the most convincing order. In his attempt to refute the arguments of lobbyists like Jack Thompson, who claim that violent video games lead to violent behavior, University of Connecticut student **Brandon Nadeau** provides a solid model of the way evidence can be effectively organized in his essay "**Video Games Make Society Less Violent.**" Observe that in the first paragraph below, Nadeau offers statistical support that shows violent crime has decreased significantly since video games became a major industry in 1995. In other words, if video games are causing violent behavior, why is the rate of violent crimes dropping? But Nadeau doesn't stop there. In his next paragraph, after acknowledging that the statistics he supplies would alone seem "enough to refute" the anti-game lobby's contentions, he introduces an even "more compelling" fact: The rate of violent crime among teenagers—the very audience the lobbyists worry about—has dropped significantly since 1995. This one-two punch represents a highly effective method of refutation. Consider how less compelling his position would be had he reversed the order of statistical evidence or left out the second piece of data entirely.

Nadeau first addresses Thompson's claim with crime statistics.

He goes further by providing most important statistic.

Thompson doesn't have any facts on his side. Actually, they are all against him. Since video games became a mainstream industry, around the time the PlayStation came out in 1995, the violent crime rate has decreased significantly. By the time one of Thompson's favorite targets, "Grand Theft Auto 3," was released, the violent crime rate was 30 percent lower than it had been twenty years earlier. Oddly enough, the rate has decreased every year since 1995, resulting in a new record-low rate in violent crime every year.   1

This alone seems enough to refute any claim Thompson or the rest of the antivideo lobby has about the games' influence on real life. But more compelling is the fact that the audience Thompson claims is the most heavily influenced (teenagers) has seen an extremely sharp decline in violent crime since the PlayStation was put on the market. It appears the rate was highest in the "Nintendo Era," a time when video game violence was at a minimum. (Nintendo actually had a series of rules to make sure games were fairly nonviolent, such as a "no blood" rule for any game.)   2

— From "Video Games Make Society Less Violent" by Brandon Nadeau, page 290

Student Writer at Work: Brandon Nadeau
On Writing "Video Games Make Society Less Violent"

Q: When you wrote this piece for the UConn *Daily Campus,* who was the audience you were hoping most to reach?

A: Uninformed students, professors, and people interested in knowing the truth about video games.

Q: What kind of response did you get?

A: Most people told me they liked it. One or two tried to counter my argument with things they had heard on TV—but they had no factual backing. It's hard to change minds, though, as we're all a little thick-headed when it comes to what we believe.

Q: Have you written about video games since then?

A: I might soon, but no one is attacking video games as hard as they used to thanks to a toned-down year in terms of real life violence. A little while ago, though, one of my fellow *Daily Campus* writers wrote a piece on a specific video game. In the article she stated that although she had never actually played the game, she believed it would make people act like the characters in it. That's the kind of person I was trying to educate with my article.

Q: What have you discovered as a writer that you'd want to share with others?

A: The key to writing well on some topics is to get angry. The more passionate about something you are, the better your writing becomes as long as you can keep your opinions in check with reality.

AMERICA THEN . . . 1976

Death Race, the Beginning of Video Game Censorship

Given the primitive graphics of the first video games—such as Computer Space (1971) or Pong (1972)—the level of realism was so low that violence and sexuality were not issues. For a few years, men

The poster for the 1975 cult film that inspired Death Race (1976), the controversial arcade game that was the predecessor to today's Grand Theft Auto.

and women in bars across America were thrilled simply to insert quarters into an arcade machine and try to score points by maneuvering small paddles against a little square "ball" that ricocheted harmlessly back and forth while making a pleasing "pong" sound.

But it didn't take long for public protests to build against the fledgling video game industry. The predecessor of the Grand Theft Auto series was a 1976 arcade game called Death Race. The game was named after the 1975 cult film Death Race 2000, *starring David Carradine and Sylvester Stallone. "In the year 2000," the movie ads read, "hit and run driving is no longer a felony. It's the national sport!" With the Death Race game, Americans first realized that interactive games played by young people could be designed to simulate antisocial and criminal behavior. The issue ever since has been: Does simulated* violence *stimulate* violence? *Despite its rudimentary black and white graphics and content—the purpose of the game was to score points by driving over stick-figure "gremlins" and turning them into tombstone crosses—Death Race quickly became a national controversy that received enormous media attention. Parent groups, the*

National Safety Council, and various law enforcement associations condemned the game for promoting reckless driving and homicidal behavior (the fact that the game's first title had been Pedestrians *didn't help).*

A Long Island mother and PTA president, Ronnie Lamm, focused on Death Race *in what was apparently the first organized protest against video game violence. After an appearance on the then popular* Donahue *talk show, her cause was taken up by the mainstream media. The controversy culminated in a major segment on* 60 Minutes *that examined the psychological impact of video games on young children.* Death Race *was soon taken off the market. For today's video arcade collectors, it is one of the hardest games to find.*

Discussing the Unit

Suggested Topic for Discussion

Views on the relationship between video game violence and real-life violence vary from person to person and across age groups. The views expressed in this chapter likewise vary a great deal. Consider your experiences with or observations about violent video games. Do you have any opinions about their relationship to real-life violence? Can you be swayed in one direction or the other? What would it take to convince you, and why? Do you think the idea that gaming leads to violence is a new assumption? Have other media been associated with violence?

Preparing for Class Discussion

1. Hagelin takes a decidedly moral stance in her opposition to video games, and Nadeau takes a stance based on empirical evidence. Is one of these essays more well founded than the other? Why? If one does hold more weight with you, does that invalidate the arguments that the other raises?

2. Wright raises a number of compelling points about the creative and positive potential of games. How can these productive uses affect our culture?

From Discussion to Writing

1. Choose a stance for or against video games. Using information taken from the essays in this chapter as well as from your own experiences, support your position. Do not feel as if you have to stay focused on the violence in the games. Feel free to explore other aspects of them as well.

2. Are the arguments surrounding video games new ones? Do you think previous forms of entertainment or media have caused similar arguments in the past? What other types of entertainment may have been controversial when they were first introduced before becoming commonplace today?

Topics for Cross-Cultural Discussion

1. Wright's essay focuses heavily on the difference between the games and activities of the newer generation as opposed to those of their parents. Do these differences indicate enough of a divide in the minds of the younger and older generations so that they can be considered *culturally* different? Why or why not?

2. Can the "possibility space" and adaptive nature of video games that Wright discusses be used to spread common ideas through various cultures and attempt to bridge the gaps? Would the games themselves need to be changed for different cultures?

9

Do We Need an Ethics of Buying?

Has consumption grown out of control? Has shopping become not a practical necessity but a genuine addiction? Americans are digging themselves deeper and deeper into debt—but for what? In "Pie in the Sky," the essayist and environmentalist Bill McKibben worries that "we've officially run out not only of things that we need, but even of things that we might plausibly desire." As he pages through a popular in-flight catalogue, he wonders who actually needs "a giant-capacity mailbox that holds up to two weeks of mail" or a shower "soap dispenser with infrared sensor technology." Products like these have clearly inspired the edgy anti-advertising magazine *Adbusters* to declare a new national holiday: You can celebrate "Buy Nothing Day" by adhering to a "24 hour moratorium on consumer spending."

In our current consumer world, especially in the purchase of designer clothing and accessories, logos and brand names have taken on almost magical significance, as many people are willing to pay considerably more money simply to display a prestigious designer's signature look. Handbags made by Burberry, Louis Vuitton, Coach, Dior, Chanel, or Gucci can be outrageously expensive, which has led to the enormous popularity of counterfeits ("knock-offs") that can be bought on the street for very little. Sometimes, as Jan Goodwin reports in "The Human Cost of Fakes," the counterfeits are so well done that it takes an expert eye to detect the difference between the knock-off and the real thing. Although Goodwin is sensitive to the huge costs to the world economy caused by fake brand name goods, she is more concerned with the exploitation of child labor that is behind the global counterfeit business: "If you buy fakes," she writes, citing a human rights activist, "even of high-price name brands, you run a risk of buying something that has been produced by a child forced to work under horrendous conditions." "Thank God for Chinatown," confesses Sarah J. Gernhauser, a Louisiana State University journalism major specializing in entertainment. Visiting Manhattan, she discovers "knock-off heaven," where—giving into temptation—she buys a fake Coach purse and matching wallet, but not without a subsequent "guilty conscience."

In 1998, American college students learned how powerful they could be as they joined in solidarity with labor activists to combat the deplorable conditions of the workers who make the brand-name clothing sold in college stores throughout the nation. In forming the United Students Against Sweatshops (USAS), they launched one of the most powerful reforms in the apparel industry in recent history. In the pamphlet, "Solidarity: United Students Against Sweatshops," USAS members clearly announce the organization's identity and basic principles. Not all students, or even all activists, are inclined to agree with the organization's methods, however. In "A Call for More Sweatshop Labor," one Columbia University student, Peter Law, echoes the concerns of many who believe that the exploitative conditions of textile sweatshops are offset by the economic opportunities and revenue they offer developing countries. If, Law suggests, the developed world "stopped buying textile goods from developing nations in order to end sweatshop labor, it would be tantamount to a withdrawal of hundreds of billions of dollars in annual aid to those countries."

The chapter concludes with a brief examination of the groundbreaking book that made Americans aware of their powerful and irrational desire for "conspicuous consumption."

Do We Shop Too Much?

Bill McKibben, Pie in the Sky

Adbusters, The Evolution of Buy Nothing Day

Before You Read

Have you ever bought a product that you didn't need and would probably never use? Is American consumption out of control? Could you survive for twenty-four hours without buying anything?

Words to Learn [McKibben]

deciphering (para. 1): decoding (v.)

confines (para. 1): limits (n.)

tresses (para. 2): long locks of hair (n.)

ions (para. 2): electrically charged particles (n.)

plausibly (para. 3): seemingly likely or credible (adv.)

synthetic (para. 5): fake; not made of a natural material (adj.)

perchance (para. 5): by chance (adv.)

intermittent (para. 9): stopping and starting at regular intervals (adj.)

facade (para. 10): the front of a building (n.)

caddies (para. 11): containers (n.)

eons (para. 12): long periods of time (n.)

marinating (para. 12): soaking food in a flavorful liquid (v.)

marooned (para. 13): abandoned (v.)

vexing (para. 13): annoying (adj.)

Words to Learn [Adbusters]

dinghies (para. 1): small boats or life rafts (n.)

tree-huggers (para. 1) slang term for *environmentalists*, usually derogatory (n.)

geopolitical (para. 2) relating to factors such as geography, eco-

nomics, and demography that influence politics (adj.)

rabid (para. 2) raging; uncontrollable (adj.)

firebrand (para. 2) agitator; someone or something that creates unrest or strife to promote a cause (n.)

BILL McKIBBEN

Pie in the Sky

[ORION / March / April 2006]

Question: should anyone who requires a "revolutionary new   1
laser technology system" in order to figure out if they're parking in
the right spot inside their own garage really be allowed behind the
wheel in the first place? Compared with the other tasks of a driver —
making right-hand turns, making left-hand turns, deciphering the
red-amber-green vernacular of a stoplight — safely positioning your
auto within the confines of your own garage seems like a fairly
straightforward task, the kind of thing that might not require a laser.

But you'd be surprised how useful lasers can be. The Hairmax   2
Laser Comb, for instance, used only fifteen minutes a day, three times
a week, results in noticeably thicker locks and tresses. And not just
lasers. Ions are also surprisingly useful — confusingly, negative ions.
A lamp made of salt crystal mined from the Himalayas emits them,
aiding you in the fight against "dust mites" and also "depression."

We've officially run out not only of things that we need, but even of things that we might plausibly desire.

If there's any piece of writing that de-   3
fines our culture, I submit it's the SkyMall
catalogue, available in the seatback pocket of
every airplane in North America. To browse
its pages is to understand the essential secret
of American consumer life: We've officially
run out not only of things that we need, but
even of things that we might plausibly desire.

BILL McKIBBEN *is an author, professor, and environmentalist who lives in the Adirondacks with his wife, author Sue Halprin, and their daughter. McKibben is a former staff writer for the* New Yorker *and a contributor to publications including the* New York Times, Harpers, *the* Atlantic Monthly, *and* Outside *magazine. He writes often on environmental issues, including global warming, overpopulation, and consumerism. An active Methodist and Sunday school teacher, much of his work is informed by his spiritual leanings.*

But we in the airline traveling class still have a few problems to   4
solve in our lives. Judging from the joys on offer, our particular worries at the moment might be categorized as follows:

I'm overworked and overtired. In which case, I need a $4,000   5
massaging recliner with voice control, synthetic leather ("softer, more
plush than leather"), and thirty-three airbags—a machine that "pam-
pers your body and soothes your soul." And if perchance I drift off to
sleep, "the peaceful progression wake-up clock" will rouse me with
infinite care. "Thirty minutes before wake-up time, the light glows
softly, brightening over the next half hour, while faint aromatherapy
scents release into the air. Fifteen minutes before wake up, the clock
generates one of six soft nature sounds." In case that isn't quite
enough, I might want to back it up with the "sensory assault alarm
clock," whose large, wired vibrating pad placed under the mattress
shakes you awake in time to turn off the clock before it emits a
ninety-five-decibel alarm and starts flashing a strobe light.

I have an immense supply of trousers, and hence require the   6
closet organizer trouser rack to keep twenty pairs of slacks neatly
hung and readily accessible. The five-eighths-inch-diameter birch
dowels "reduce creasing of even fine fabrics," and "nylon washers
between the dowels ensure smooth swing motion."

I distrust my neighbors and government, and so would benefit   7
from a giant-capacity mailbox that holds up to two weeks of mail
(catalogues, presumably). "Don't bother a neighbor to get your mail,
and don't tell the post office you'll be away."

I am extremely, extremely clean. I'm therefore thankful that my   8
toothbrush has been ultravioletly cleansed overnight to remove the
"millions of germs" that would otherwise accumulate, and my room
is protected against "airborne bacteria, viruses, and germs" by a
Germ Guardian machine, "proven by a Harvard researcher," which
"takes ultraviolet C energy and multiplies its germ-killing power in
our exclusive Intensifier Chamber." Also, I have another very similar-
looking machine "now with exclusive Ozoneguard" in case any
ozone is nearby. And a soap dispenser with infrared sensor technology for my shower, a "no-touch approach that dramatically reduces
the chance of spreading germs."

I have way too many watches, and therefore might benefit from a   9
$300 case that will shake them all with "intermittent timers and di-
rectional controls" to mimic the action of a human wrist and hence
keep them fully wound at all times.

I have plugged in so many things that the planet has warmed con-   10
siderably, reducing the chances that my children will experience a nat-
ural winter. So I have purchased a "weatherproof light projection box
that rests on your front lawn and transforms the entire facade of your
house into an illuminated snowscape. The box creates the illusion of
gently falling snow flurries by directing a bright white beam onto a ro-
tating mirrorball." Flake size and fall rate are, pleasingly, adjustable. I
have opted also to purchase an "exclusive heavy duty vinyl snow
castle" that will "set up almost anywhere in just minutes with the included electric pump." A real snow castle would, SkyMall notes,
"take hours to build and require lots of snow," but this version "encourages children to use their imaginations while having fun."

I have an enormous number of remote controls, and hence need   11
caddies to store them, small "buddy lights" to illuminate them, and
locator devices to find them when I have mislaid them.

I may be devolving. Though for eons my ancestors have grilled   12
meat over flames, I am no longer very clear on the concept and so
would like a digital barbecue fork that I can stick into my burger or
steak and receive a readout indicating whether it is currently rare,
medium, or well done. Also, it would help a lot to have all the lights
already strung on my artificial Christmas tree, and the difficult task
of marinating would be much easier if I had a $199.95 marinating
machine. Frankly, I've lately found grilled cheese sandwiches more
trouble than I want, but with my dishwasher-safe Toastabag I can
simply place a slice of cheese between two slices of bread and pop it
in my toaster. (Depressing the toaster lever still requires my thoughtful attention, as does chewing the resulting treat.)

There are a few problems SkyMall can't solve (the lack of com-   13
munity that comes when you live in a giant stuff-filled house marooned on its half-acre lot, the lack of security that comes when your
country is spending its money on remote-control golf balls instead of,
say, healthcare and retirement savings). And there's always the vexing question of what the people who are making these items think
about the people who will buy them.

(I was in a shower curtain factory in rural China last year where   14
the very nice people sewing the curtains told another visitor that they'd
never actually encountered a shower curtain outside the factory. If
that's true for a shower curtain, one wonders what their fellow workers make of the traveling wine trolley, the pop-up hot dog cooker, the
hand-held paper shredder with wood-grain plastic handle.)

But this kind of talk sounds tired, clichéd, left over from the '60s.   15
Everyone knows that the most important thing we can do is grow the
economy. When you buy the Designated Driver, a faux golf club that
you store in your bag to dispense forty-eight
ounces of cold beverages, then you grow the
economy. No doubt about it. Also, the Vin-
tage Express Aging Accelerator that ages
your bottle of wine ten years in ten seconds
by surrounding it with "extremely powerful
Neodymium magnets to replicate the Earth's
magnetic field." Only a real jerk or a Christian or something would
point out that there might possibly be items in this world that it would
make more sense to spend our money on. (Insecticide-impregnated
bednets to stop the spread of malaria run about five dollars. If only
they came in self-erecting pastel versions that would also rouse you
out of bed with gentle nature sounds.)

> *Everyone knows that the most important thing we can do is grow the economy.*

ADBUSTERS

The Evolution of Buy Nothing Day

[ADBUSTERS/March/April 2006]

Thirteen years ago, Buy Nothing Day was born from the same   1
west-coast Canadian environmentalism that launched Greenpeace
and pitched hippies against loggers, dinghies against whaling ships:
the realization that over-consumption was fed by the 3,000 daily
marketing messages dripped into our subconsciousness by the corporate mass media. Mental environmentalists, media activists, and tree-
huggers joined forces and Buy Nothing Day blossomed.

Most recently, in the wake of several horrific acts of interna-   2
tional terrorism, Buy Nothing Day underwent its most radical
transformation—forging a harder geopolitical edge—as a new band
of strategists began to raise fears about what rabid over-consumption
was doing to our very chances of survival. Could the hatred that
fueled 9/11 have anything to do with the staggering inequalities
between the world's rich and poor? Was over-consumption one of
the root causes of terror? They [the Buy Nothing Day organization]
thought so, and . . . Buy Nothing Day has become a political
firebrand.

ADBUSTERS *is a not-for-profit magazine with an activist bent. The magazine, whose articles and visuals often parody marketing and other types of
media, hopes to change existing power structures through its new social activist movement of the information age. According to its Web site (www
.adbusters.org), Adbusters is ultimately "an ecological magazine, dedicated
to examining the relationship between human beings and their physical and
mental environment. We want a world in which the economy and ecology
resonate in balance. We try to coax people from spectator to participant in
this quest. We want folks to get mad about corporate disinformation, injustices in the global economy, and any industry that pollutes our physical or
mental commons."*

Founded by Canadian artist Ted Dave and promoted by *Adbusters* magazine, "Buy Nothing Day" is an annual international day of protest against consumerism, during which participants do not purchase anything for twenty-four hours. In the United States, "Buy Nothing Day" is held on the day after Thanksgiving, one of the busiest shopping days of the year.

Web **Read/Hear/See It Now:** Read select articles, listen to interviews, and watch documentary videos by contributors to *Orion: The Magazine of Culture, Creativity, and Change* and see what *Adbusters* is all about at **bedfordstmartins.com/americanow**, Chapter 9.

Vocabulary / Using a Dictionary

1. What is the root of the word *deciphering* (McKibben, para. 1)? What does *decipher* have to do with the word *cipher*?

2. McKibben uses the term *depression* in paragraph 2 and *depressing* in paragraph 12. What are the different meanings of these two words? How are these words related?

3. How is *plausible* (McKibben, para. 3) related to *implausible*?

4. What does *illuminated* mean (McKibben, para. 10)? How is it related to *lumens*?

5. What is the root word of *consumption* (*Adbusters*, para. 2)? When and how did this word originate?

Responding to Words and Images in Context

1. What does the word *vernacular* mean (McKibben, para. 1)? How can a stoplight have its own vernacular? How does this relate to the idea of culture?

2. In paragraph 12, McKibben states, "I may be devolving." How is *devolving* related to the word *evolving*? What does it mean to devolve? What does this use of the term tell you about McKibben and his point?

3. In his final paragraph, McKibben states that "everyone knows that the most important thing we can do is grow the economy. When you buy the Designated Driver, a faux golf club that you store in your bag to dispense forty-eight ounces of cold beverages, then you grow the economy. No doubt about it." In this context, what do you think he means when he states, "No doubt about it"?

4. The *Adbusters* "Buy Nothing Day" poster features a particular image as the "A" in Day. Where have you seen that image before? Why do you think the poster's designers choose to use it as the A? What is its significance?

5. What is the meaning of "rabid over-consumption" (*Adbusters*, para. 2)? What is the effect of the word *rabid*? What other words might have been chosen?

Discussing Main Point and Meaning

1. The title of McKibben's essay — "Pie in the Sky" — has its origins in a 1911 labor song, "The Preacher and the Slave":

> You will eat, bye and bye,
> In that glorious land above the sky;
> Work and pray, live on hay,
> You'll get pie in the sky when you die.

What do you think the phrase "pie in the sky" means in the song? How does McKibben use this phrase to talk about the Sky-Mall catalogue? How is the *Adbusters* poster responding to the idea of pie in the sky?

2. The *Adbusters* text states that in light of recent terrorist attacks, Buy Nothing Day is more important than ever. It refers to the 9/11 (2001) attacks during which terrorists hijacked four planes and flew them into the World Trade Center Towers and the Pentagon, killing more than three thousand people. *Adbusters* makes the claim that American consumerism—which creates intolerable workplace conditions in developing nations—has helped create great animosity toward Americans. How does *Adbusters* argument affect your attitude toward the SkyMall catalogue and its contents?

3. McKibben, in his humorous critique of consumerism, is particularly sarcastic in paragraph 15 when he states that "only a real jerk or a Christian or something would point out that there might possibly be items in this world that it would make more sense to spend our money on." What does McKibben really mean by that statement? How does it affect your reading of his argument?

4. McKibben's essay seems to speak directly to the *Adbusters* poster in that both critique crass consumerism or consumerism that is undignified. What are the differences in what McKibben and *Adbusters* expect consumers to do? How do they persuade you—either through the visual or verbal argument—to do what they suggest?

Examining Sentences, Paragraphs, and Organization

1. Transitional words are words that are used to make smooth connections between ideas (for example, *but, and, or*). In each paragraph in which McKibben looks at a product from the SkyMall catalogue, he uses transitional words to go from "problem" to solution. Underline the different transitional words he uses and examine how they make the connections between problems and solutions smoother. Do they work to "sell" the product, or do

they simply disguise the disconnect between the two ideas? Explain your answer.

2. In paragraph 14, McKibben includes parenthetical information. Information that is parenthetical is usually secondary information; in this case McKibben notes that rural workers in China have never encountered a shower curtain outside the factory. Why do you think he offers this information in this way? What is the effect on his argument?

3. Throughout his essay, McKibben uses a sarcastic tone to argue that consumerism is affecting the planet—beginning with the question of whether those who need a laser-guided parking system should be allowed to drive. What paragraph represents the climax of McKibbon's argument? Explain why. Is his use of tone an effective way of making his point?

4. Examine the use of questions in the second paragraph of the *Adbusters* text. What is the rhetorical effect of using questions instead of simply making statements? How does this contribute to the main argument presented by *Adbusters*?

Thinking Critically

1. What does it mean to consume? How can our habits of consumption provide a picture of our ethical responsibilities? How would McKibben define consumers' ethical responsibilities? What do the creators of *Adbusters* think our consumer responsibilities are?

2. McKibben states, "if there's any piece of writing that defines our culture, I submit it's the SkyMall catalogue" (para. 3). How can a catalogue define our culture? What do the catalogues you read say about culture? What does the SkyMall catalogue, according to McKibben, say about our culture? What does *Adbusters*, which is known for its parodies of advertisements, say about our culture?

3. McKibben argues that consumerism is damaging to our environment, to our community, and to our individual selves, but he also implies that consumerism has beneficial effects such as growing the economy and providing jobs to workers such as those in rural China, who manufacture the products we buy. Do you think consumerism is a good or bad thing? Given your response, how do you respond to the "Buy Nothing Day" poster? Do you agree with it? What would the ramifications of buying nothing be? Who would be affected?

4. McKibben points out that workers who make the products we buy may never have the chance to buy the products or even have a use for them. *Adbusters* assumes that if we do not buy products, people will be better off. Pick a product that you buy and research it. Determine who manufactures it, how much its workers earn, who else buys it. Then, write a report in which you discuss your findings. If nobody bought the product, who would be affected?

In-Class Writing Activities

1. Read through one of your favorite catalogues and bring to class an advertisement that you find interesting. Then, write a short essay in which you analyze the advertisement with the following questions in mind: Who is the audience of the advertisement? How does it use words and images to convince its audience that they need this product? What does the ad imply about its potential purchaser? Is it persuasive? Why or why not?

2. Take a look around your classroom and then list or catalogue some of the items that you think define who you and your classmates are or how you live. Then, following the model of McKibben's numbered paragraphs, write the problem that these products solve and highlight their selling points. Try to "sell" the items to a particular audience, paying close attention to their needs and wants.

PAIRED READINGS

Are Designer Knock-Offs Ethical?

Jan Goodwin, The Human Cost of Fakes

Sarah J. Gernhauser, The Morality of Designer Knock-Offs

Before You Read

Have you ever bought a designer "knock-off" product? If so, why? Where did you buy it? Do you think the original designer product is worth the price? Who do you think is affected by your counterfeit purchase?

Words to Learn [Goodwin]

canapés (para. 1): appetizers of bread and spread such as caviar or cheese (n.)

coveted (para. 4): desired; wanted (adj.)

incapacitated (para. 7): to be without normal abilities (adj.)

toiled (para. 7): worked long and hard (v.)

ramshackle (para. 7): ready to collapse; rickety (adj.)

compounding (para. 10): adding to (v.)

Word to Learn [Gernhauser]

femme (para. 1): French for "female" (adj.)

salivates (para. 3): produces an excess of saliva; drools (v.)

faux (para. 3): fake (adj.)

gorged (para. 5): overate (v.)

Atkins (para. 5): a popular low-carbohydrate diet developed by Robert C. Atkins (n.)

counterfeit (para. 5): fake (adj./n.)

vendor (para. 7): seller (n.)

naive (para. 9): inexperienced (adj.)

JAN GOODWIN

The Human Cost of Fakes

[HARPER'S BAZAAR/January 2006]

We've all become used to seeing fakes for sale on the sidewalks,   1
but as counterfeiters have grown ever more skilled at reproducing
luxury goods, more and more of us risk being the victims of unwit-
tingly purchasing a knockoff. Just ask my fashionable colleague who
had this rude awakening at a recent cocktail party: She was nibbling
on canapés, a designer bag in the crook of her arm, when a publicist
for the brand came over to chat and asked her where she'd bought
her handbag. My colleague had received it from her boyfriend—a
much-loved first-anniversary gift—and he'd found it online at a great
price. "That bag is a fake," the publicist informed her. My colleague
asked her how she could tell and was shown the subtle difference in
stitching—almost invisible to the naked eye—that separated her
handbag from the genuine thing. She was mortified.

Design houses are constantly plagued by high-end fakes being   2
sold on e-commerce sites. Tiffany & Co. is currently suing eBay, the
world's largest online auction site, for allowing the sale of counterfeits, and Gucci filed suit against some 30 websites in the United
States last year and is currently tackling at least 100 more.

"There isn't a day we don't receive calls from customers com-   3
plaining that they have purchased products from unscrupulous sellers
on websites and received products that do not look real or are falling
apart," says Jonathan Moss, legal counsel for Gucci in the United
States. "It's the biggest problem by far for us."

Today it is estimated that intellectual-property theft—the busi-   4
ness of counterfeit and pirated goods—costs the world economy a

JAN GOODWIN, *prize-winning journalist and author of* The Price of
Honor: Muslim Women Lift the Veil of Silence on the Islamic World *(1994),
uses much of her writing to explore international issues such as the war in
Bosnia and the Taliban's oppression of women and to expose how women
and other minorities are treated.*

whopping $600 billion a year. Losses to U.S. businesses alone come to $200 billion to $250 billion, according to Kevin Delli-Colli, deputy assistant director of financial and trade investigations at U.S. Immigration and Customs Enforcement. Roughly two-thirds of these fakes—including copies of such coveted brands as Cartier, Dior, Hermès, Louis Vuitton, Rolex, and Van Cleef & Arpels—are produced in China, making it the counterfeit capital of the world. Along with Korea and Taiwan, China is now specializing in triple-A mirror-image knock-offs so close to perfect, even the experts have trouble identifying them as fakes.

Shanghai and Beijing are rapidly becoming the glittering cities of the future, where the more than 250,000 Chinese "dollar millionaires" can now live a life of luxury. International accounting firm Ernst & Young predicts that within a decade, China will surpass the United States as the world's second-largest consumer of luxury goods (Japan is the largest). Yet, at the same time, China's economic restructuring has seen massive unemployment and the collapse of the rural economy. And with the rapid rise of school fees, which can sometimes exceed what a farmer earns in a year, it has become impossible for many children to continue their education. As a result, parents have little choice but to send their sons and daughters to work, not realizing how deplorable conditions for them may be.

"If you buy fakes, even of high-price name brands, you run a risk of buying something that has been produced by a child forced to work under horrendous conditions," says Sharon Hom, executive director of the New York–based organization Human Rights in China. According to one study by the International Labour Organization, some 44.6 million 10- to 14-year-olds were working in Asia a decade ago. "The number is much higher now," says Hom, a Hong Kong–born lawyer. In some enterprises in China, recent reports indicate that child workers make up as much as 20 percent of the workforce.

> If you buy fakes, you run the risk of buying something produced by a child forced to work under horrendous conditions.

Wang Yajuan was one of these workers. Because her father was incapacitated from heart disease and the family needed help with his hefty medical bills, she was working at a textile factory, near Shijiazhuang City, Hebei Province, when she was 14. Along with other children, she toiled at least 12 hours a day, 7 days a week, and slept in a ramshackle factory dorm, unheated in the frigid winter. Exhausted

5

6

7

after their long workday, Yajuan and her four roommates lit a primitive charcoal stove one night in December 2004 and went to sleep in the poorly ventilated room. In the morning they were found unconscious from inhaling charcoal fumes and declared dead. The factory owner ordered that the girls' bodies be sealed in coffins immediately and sent off for cremation. A later investigation revealed that at least two of the girls had still been alive when they were entombed.

Despite the local government's effort to suppress what had happened, news of the tragedy leaked out, highlighting the issue of underage workers in China. Their circumstances often tantamount to slave labor, most employees earn a fraction of the minimum wage, if they are paid at all. Their hours may start as early as 7 A.M. and not end until the following day, according to the China Labour Bulletin, an activist organization in Hong Kong. Children as young as 12 and 13 are expected to work these brutal hours, day in and day out, with sometimes only one day off a year. 8

Even state schools contribute to this crisis. More than a decade ago, with the encouragement of the government, local authorities began instituting mandatory "work and study" programs to fund undersubsidized schools. Children as young as 7 can be required to work from 6 A.M. until dark; if they don't comply, they may be denied diplomas or fined. "Tragically there have been accidents with heavy machinery resulting in injury and death," reports Hom. 9

> The circumstances of underage workers are often tantamount to slave labor. Children as young as 7 can be required to work from 6 A.M. until dark.

In China it is illegal for children under 16 to work, but the laws are not always enforced. Compounding the matter are regulations issued in 2000 by the Ministry of Labor and Social Security mandating that child-labor statistics, like many other labor statistics, be classified as state secrets. 10

The implementation of anticounterfeiting laws is similarly hampered. "The laws are on the books in Beijing, but local authorities in this sprawling country usually lack the resources and motivation to enforce them," says Bruce Lehman, a lawyer and chairman of the International Intellectual Property Institute in Washington, D.C. "Another problem is, under Chinese law, it is criminal to make counterfeit goods, but not to export them." 11

Under international pressure, the Chinese Supreme People's Court and Procuratorate jointly issued new standards against intellectual-property crimes in December 2004, but there's still a long 12 way to go. "There has been an increase in prosecutions and convictions, but the base was low, so an increase in convictions of 50 percent is still not enough to have much of an impact," says Joe Simone, a lawyer and spokesman for the Luxury Goods Industry Working Group of the Quality Brands Protection Committee, based in Beijing, which counts among its members Burberry, Chanel, Gucci, Louis Vuitton, and Prada. These commercial rivals have joined together to take on Beijing's New Silk Alley Market. With five stories and more than 1600 outlets, it is a notorious market for fake name-brand clothing, leather goods, watches, and jewelry. Silk Alley is so infamous, the city's official website lists it as a place to shop for souvenirs. The watches alone take up a space the length of a football field.

But the market's days may be numbered as designer companies try   13
a new tactic. "Our civil trial against Silk Alley's landlord started in September, and we have prepared the evidence for a number of other cases," explains Simone. "We are sending a shot over the bow to landlords everywhere in China. The people who run these factories are scumbags, hiring children, locking employees in production areas where there have been fires and they can't get out. And the landlords are just as responsible. Now they are being exposed, and they don't like it."

SARAH J. GERNHAUSER

The Morality of Designer Knock-Offs

[THE DAILY REVEILLE, Louisiana State University/January 18, 2005]

The idea of one day reaching the level of success at which I can   1
spend exorbitant amounts of money on designer clothing, purses, wallets and jewelry is a goal that I, along with many of my femme friends, hope to achieve. However, in this glorious day of the

---

SARAH J. GERNHAUSER *was an entertainment columnist for the* Daily Reveille *at Louisiana State University when she wrote "The Morality of Designer Knock-Offs."*

twenty-first century, I can find these normally expensive items at a
far lower cost.

Thank God for Chinatown.   2

For those of you who may be ready to turn the page and look for   3
the crossword puzzle, allow me to explain the relevance of this column.
Chinatown, located in lower Manhattan, is notorious for its wall-
to-wall imitation designer purses, wallets, watches—and for those
testosterone-packed men, car parts and stereo systems. It is a Mecca
for the college student who salivates over these items in the pages of
Vogue, but unfortunately, due to the lack of a suitable paycheck, must
settle for a faux bag until the days of Biology and English are over.

My motto has always been "If you can't make it, just fake it."   4
There's no shame in carrying around a fake Louis Vuitton bowling
bag or Dooney and Burke saddle purse (unless of course the leather coloring is so off it's obviously vinyl). But before I continue with my story, allow me to clarify my designer-obsessed mindset. I love Gucci and Prada, but if I reached the level of financial success at which I could actually own the purses and dresses whose pictures adorn my bedroom walls, I would definitely match the amount I spent on the $5,000 leather Gucci clutch and send it to the less fortunate. My heart is not made out of Coach leather; I understand the responsibility and priorities money carries.

My heart is not made of Coach leather; I understand the responsibility and priorities money carries.

I visited Manhattan over the holiday break, and as I am sure you   5
suspected, Canal Street was the first place I visited after I gorged myself on an Atkins nightmare of pizza and cheesecake. Due to the
flooding of counterfeit designer items and an increase in the black
market, the New York City Police Department instituted the "Canal
Street Initiative." This program no longer allows the Chinatown
shops to show the designer name on the bag it imitates. So unless you
want a tote with "Frada" stamped on the cheap leather, you have to
ask the workers if they keep any designer counterfeits in stock.

A little effort on your part can go a long way down these   6
Manhattan streets—or in my case, an aggressive seller, who guided
me far away from a packed Canal Street. I apparently have the words
"Sucker for Louis Vuitton" written across my forehead, since I was
approached by at least two workers in each shop with bargain prices
for these purses. After refusing many offers, I fell into the hands of
one very enthusiastic and aggressive seller.

I should have just kept walking, but instead I followed this ven- 7
dor four city blocks from his shop and around a corner to a Chinese
restaurant, where I was greeted by a petite Asian girl. After the two
conversed in a language I will never understand, I was taken up a
hidden staircase into an attic. Chanel and Louis would have thrown
up in the room that greeted me. From one wall to the next were
purses, umbrellas, wallets and even dog carriers with the logos of
Burberry, Coach, Louis Vuitton and more.

> *All I can think is how bad I feel for these designers who spend their lives attempting to make their products elite.*

So here I am in knock-off heaven, and 8
all I can think is how bad I feel for these designers who spend their entire lives attempting to make their products elite—and I am
bargaining a Fendi sac bag down from its
original price. Unfortunately, I gave in to my
lust and purchased items from the Chinese
restaurant by day, the counterfeit designer
purse market by night.

I know, shame on me. And to make 9
matters worse, once I got home, I began to do research on counterfeit
purses. According to Kevin Doughty, a private counterfeit expert and
founder of CounterTech Investigations, New York City alone loses
approximately $350 million and 25,000 jobs a year due to the coun-
terfeit market. Talk about a guilty conscience. I can prance around
campus with my matching Coach purse and wallet while people lose
their jobs. And the idea of that makes me sick. One day, the fake
leather straps on my purse will fade and begin to break, but the counterfeit market that extends across the country will continue to attract
naive designer-obsessed college students like myself.

Now, I look at my purse and realize all that glitters is definitely 10
not gold, and I am looking forward to saving up for my real Prada
clutch. Adieu, Chinatown.

Web **Read It Now:** For more views on consumerism and other topics by students at
Louisiana State, go to **bedfordstmartins.com/americanow**, Chapter 9.

Vocabulary/Using a Dictionary

1. Goodwin uses the word *unscrupulous* to describe sellers of counterfeits (para. 3). What is the connotation of *unscrupulous*? How
   does it differ from the word *dishonest*?

2. According to Goodwin, "Silk Alley is . . . infamous" (para. 12). What does *infamous* mean? How is it related to *famous*?

3. How is *exorbitant* (Gernhauser, para. 1) related to *orbit*?

4. Gernhauser complains that she has a "guilty conscience" from buying knock-offs (para. 9). What does *conscience* mean? How is it related to the word *science*?

Responding to Words in Context

1. Goodwin says that her friend was *mortified* when she found out her bag was fake (para. 1). What does *mortified* mean? After reading about Wang Yajuan and her death (para. 7), do you think *mortified* is the right term?

2. According to Goodwin, counterfeiting is against the law because it is "intellectual-property theft" (para. 4). What is intellectual property? How can one steal intellectual property? How is a copy of a designer bag intellectual-property theft?

3. In paragraph 3, Gernhauser states that Chinatown is a "Mecca."
 • What does she mean by *Mecca*? Do you think this use of a religious term is derogatory? Explain.

4. In paragraph 5, Gernhauser states that she "gorged" on pizza and cheesecake before she visited Chinatown to shop. How do her eating habits relate to her shopping habits?

5. In paragraph 10, Gernhauser uses the cliché "all that glitters is not gold." What does she mean by that? What are the origins of this saying?

Discussing Main Point and Meaning

1. Despite opening her essay in the context of a cocktail party, Goodwin attempts to show how money can cause problems. How does the wealth she describes compare with the poverty she describes? How are the two related?

2. According to the Goodwin essay, why would the Chinese government want to suppress the news of the young workers' deaths? What do the government's actions imply about its attitude toward the counterfeit market?

3. Why does Gernhauser purchase counterfeit products? According to this essay, what do these products offer her and other consumers? What don't they offer?

4. Gernhauser states, "I understand the responsibility and priorities money carries" (para. 4). What do you think she means by this? What do you think are the "responsibilities and priorities" of money? Are they similar to what Goodwin believes them to be?

Examining Sentences, Paragraphs, and Organization

1. In paragraph 7, Gernhauser describes her "knock-off heaven" by stating, "Chanel and Louis would have thrown up in the room that greeted me." How does this sentence describe her relationship with the designers and their products? How does this affect her overall argument? How does it make you feel about counterfeit objects? About designer objects?

2. Although Goodwin's article is about the human cost of fakes, she begins her article with an anecdote about her friend at a cocktail party and not about the child laborers who are forced to work in deplorable conditions. Look at the word choice in her opening paragraph. Why do you think she begins this way? What are your expectations, as a reader, for the rest of the essay?

3. Gernhauser organizes her essay around Chinatown. She first begins by stating, "Thank God for Chinatown" (para. 2) and then finishes with "Adieu, Chinatown" (para. 10). By using Chinatown as the location of her story, she creates a framework that gives her readers boundaries they can use to understand and relate to her argument. How does this framework help ground her argument? How does she represent Chinatown throughout her essay? Do you think this is an effective framework?

Thinking Critically

1. Goodwin writes that the Internet has made counterfeiting more common: People who pay for the real thing on eBay and Froogle often receive counterfeit products in return. Counterfeit drugs — those that are really sugar pills or saline solutions — or counterfeit technologies that do not perform as they should are considered bad products because they can endanger people's lives; they are not what they seem to be. But are counterfeit clothing and accessories — which attempt to sell an image — bad things? If you get what you pay for, is it acceptable practice to buy cheaper, lower-quality goods? Does it matter how those goods affect the workers and the environment?

2. When she is bargaining to get a cheaper price on a purse, Gernhauser begins to feel bad "for these designers who spend their entire lives attempting to make their products elite" (para. 8). What makes a product elite? Is an elite product worth its hefty tag? Is it moral to charge $800 for a pair of Jimmy Choo shoes?

3. Who is responsible for the problem of counterfeit goods? Goodwin's article points to the business practices of the governments of developing countries where most of the counterfeiting is done. Are they responsible? Are the landlords and factory workers responsible? Or are the people who are willing to buy counterfeit products and who continue to make the market grow? What responsibility, if any, can be assigned to designers of elite high-priced goods?

In-Class Writing Activities

1. Gernhauser shops for elite designer products because she wants to look a certain way—she is image-conscious to the point where her motto is, "If you can't make it, just fake it" (para. 4). Write an essay in which you explore and analyze what it means to wear designer clothing. Who wears Gucci and Prada? What do the products say about them? Do you wear designer clothing? Why or why not?

2. Who exactly is responsible for counterfeiting, and how can you, a consumer, stop practices that harm children? What company or business practices do you find unethical and believe should change? Perhaps a clothing company abuses child labor, a food company treats animals inhumanely, or automobile manufacturers do not make energy-efficient cars. How should the company change its practices? Write a letter of protest to the company in which you argue that its practices are unethical. Offer solutions the company can follow.

3. Gernhauser uses Chinatown as a framework to show what counterfeiting is like—something foreign and hidden to her, not an actual part of her normal, everyday routine. Go to a shop or mall that you frequent. Take notes on what it looks like, who visits it, what it sells. How would you characterize it? How does this place represent particular habits of its consumers? What does it represent about society?

What Should We Do about Sweatshops?

United Students Against Sweatshops, Solidarity Manifesto

Peter Law, A Call for More Sweatshop Labor

Before You Read and View

What are workers' rights? Have you ever thought about the people who make your clothes? Would you buy from a company that abused its workers or paid them poorly?

Words to Learn [USAS]

grassroots (panel 2, para. 1): basic, fundamental; at the level of the individual (adj.)

progressive (panel 3, para. 1): to have political leanings that in-

volve new ideas, education, and self-expression (adj.)

ideological (panel 3, para. 3): relating to a system or set of beliefs (adj.)

Words to Learn [Law]

Alma Mater (para. 1): Latin for "fostering mother"; a school that one has attended and/or graduated from (n.)

chauvinistic (para. 2): describing an attitude of superiority (mainly of men toward women) (adj.)

textile (para. 3): cloth or woven material (n.)

tantamount (para. 3): equivalent (adj.)

UNITED STUDENTS AGAINST SWEATSHOPS

Solidarity Manifesto

[STUDENTSAGAINSTSWEATSHOPS.ORG / 2005]

UNITED STUDENTS AGAINST SWEATSHOPS *(USAS) was created in the late 1990s in response to a growing awareness that university and sports apparel was being manufactured in sweatshops. Student groups across the nation formed USAS to enter into a conversation regarding global trade and labor practices. They created a code of conduct that called for public disclosure, living wages, and women's rights, and staged sit-ins and demonstrations to publicize their fight. The following mission statement is found at the USAS Web site at www.studentsagainstsweatshops.org.*

United Students Against Sweatshops

If you've come to help me, you are wasting your time. But if you've come because your liberation is bound up with mine, then let us work together.
—Lilla Watson

www.studentsagainstsweatshops.org

202 NO SWEAT

WHO WE ARE

United Students Against Sweatshops is a grassroots network of over 200 high school, college, and university groups organizing campaigns in solidarity with workers on our campuses, in our communities and internationally.

USAS' three cornerstone campaigns are the Sweat-Free Campus Campaign, the Ethical Contracting Campaign, and the Campus Living Wage Campaign.

USAS is also building diverse student/youth power, fighting oppression and working for more democratic campuses. Students win campaigns through direct action organizing.

NATIONAL STAFF

Hevily Ambriz Espinoza, National Organizer
hevily@usasnet.org, 202 NO SWEAT or 805-754-0257

Gladys Cisneros, National Organizer
gladys@usasnet.org, 202 NO SWEAT or 202-270-5281

Zack Knorr, National Organizer
zack@usasnet.org, 202 NOSWEAT or 951-368-8004

For all questions, and to get involved, drop any of us an email or write us all at: *organize@usasnet.org*

OUR PRINCIPLES OF UNITY

1. **We work in solidarity with working people's struggles.** In order to best accomplish this and in recognition of the interconnections between local and global struggles, we strive to build relationships with other progressive movements and cooperate in coalition with other groups struggling for justice within all communities—campus, local, regional, and international.

2. **We struggle against racism, sexism, homophobia, heterosexism, classism, and other forms of oppression within our society, within our organizations, and within ourselves.** Not only are we collectively confronting these prejudices as inherent defects of the global economy which creates sweatshops, but we also recognize the need for individuals to confront the prejudices they have internalized as the result of living and learning in a flawed and oppressive society.

3. **We are working in coalition to build a grassroots student movement that challenges corporate power and that fights for economic justice.** This coalition is loosely defined, thus we strive to act in coordination with one another to mobilize resources and build a national network while reserving the autonomy of individuals and campuses. We do not impose a single ideological position, practice, or approach; rather, we aim to support one another in a spirit of respect for difference, shared purpose and hope.

4. **We strive to act democratically.** With the understanding that we live and learn in a state of imperfect government, we attempt to achieve truer democracy in making decisions which affect our collective work. Furthermore, we strive to empower one another as individuals and as a collective through trust, patience, and an open spirit.

TO AFFILIATE WITH **USAS,** *EMAIL* *ORGANIZE@USASNET.ORG WITH YOUR RELEVANT CONTACT INFORMATION AND A STATEMENT THAT THE GROUP AGREES WITH OUR PRINCIPLES OF UNITY.*

www.studentsagainstsweatshops.org

PETER LAW

A Call for More Sweatshop Labor

[THE COLUMBIA DAILY SPECTATOR, Columbia University/January 26, 2005]

A few weeks ago, I witnessed a loud, forceful, and misguided   1
protest against sweatshop labor by Columbia students from the feet
of Alma Mater. I am sorry she had to share her sunny afternoon with
such a farcical scene. As far as I could hear from my room, the students were conducting a mock fashion show of cheap garments produced under deplorable conditions in countries such as Pakistan,
Guatemala, and Madagascar. The students railed against the unfair
labor practices, harsh management, lack of unionization, and wages
as low as $3 a day that go into the production of our own sweaters,
shorts, and underwear. Worst of all, most of the workers who are
being abused are, as the students would put it, defenseless women. I
admit I am also outraged — at the students.

> *A job making sweaters for rich people in America is a ticket out of poverty and disease.*

In their quest to achieve cosmic and so-   2
cial justice for every person, plant, and animal on the planet, the students against
sweatshop labor fail to recognize that a job,
even one that pays $3 a day, is better than
starvation. For a woman in a repressive or
chauvinistic society, a job making sweaters

PETER LAW *is a sophomore studying economics and political science at* Columbia University. *He wrote "A Call for More Sweatshop Labor" for his campus paper when he was a freshman. "The opinion pages of the* Columbia Daily Spectator," *Law says, "are filled day in and day out with op-eds coming from the leftmost half of the political spectrum. I hoped that my story would provide some variety to that body of work and spark campus debate and discussion about what truly constitutes 'sustainable' economic development and the best ways for a country to pull itself out of poverty. Universities are a place for learning, and that end is not served if the only ideas presented on campus are different only in degree."* For a "Student Writer at Work" *interview with Law, see page 335.*

for rich people in America is a ticket out of poverty and disease. If women in Laos find it difficult to escape the domination of their husbands, fathers, or brothers while they have a job, how are they going to do so without one?

If Columbia University and the rest of the developed world   3 stopped buying textile goods from developing nations in order to end sweatshop labor, it would be tantamount to a withdrawal of hundreds of billions of dollars in annual aid to those countries. The CIA World Fact Book reports that twenty countries have textiles as their primary export, and for another twenty textiles is a major industry. What would these countries do without the textile industry? What would be the impact on terrorism if millions of Pakistanis, Afghans, or Indians lost their jobs making clothes for the developed world?

The students complained that sweatshop workers cannot even af-   4 ford to purchase the goods they produce. This is true, and it is partly because highly inefficient protective tariffs abound in both the developed and developing worlds on clothing and other textile products. It is also because textile workers are indeed poor, but they need not always be that way.

Textile workers are indeed poor, but they need not always be that way.

Millions of British and American poor worked in horrible condi-   5 tions in textile mills or in the textile industry around the turn of the last century. Textiles helped make both our countries rich. As countries grow wealthier, their workers enjoy better working conditions because the country can afford them. Unions, paid lunch hours, and mandatory rest periods are luxuries that the developed world can impose upon its companies, but would break the struggling enterprises of the developing world. In China, for example, there is actually a small but growing scarcity of skilled labor, and accordingly many sweatshop-employed women are demanding and receiving higher wages and luxuries such as paid lunches and even factory libraries.

Progress like this cannot be made if people do not buy sweat-   6 shop-produced goods. Labor practices change because of the dictates of the market, not the dictates of outraged students of the left. Not buying goods produced with cheap labor would only force companies to make that labor even cheaper, and would likely worsen the working conditions for millions of workers around the

For an annotated excerpt of this essay that highlights Law's writing strategies, see page 334.

world. A better plan would be to do the opposite—instead of boycotting sweatshop textiles, check the label the next time you shop and make sure your clothes come from the developing world! The people of Mauritius need the money more than South Carolinians or Northern Italians—spread the wealth!

Web **Read It Now:** Find out more about the United Students Against Sweatshops and read more editorials by Columbia University students at bedfordstmartins.com/americanow, Chapter 9.

Vocabulary / Using a Dictionary

1. What does *autonomy* mean (USAS, panel 3, para. 3)? What are the two roots of this word? What does *autonomy* have to do with the self?

2. What does *deplorable* mean (Law, para. 1)? What is the meaning of its Latin root, *plorare*? How are these two terms related?

3. What are *dictates* (Law, para. 6)? How is that word related to *dictator*?

Responding to Words in Context

1. USAS states that one of its principles is "to act democratically" (panel 3, para. 4). What does it mean to act democratically? How might it be possible to act democratically in regard to sweatshop labor practices?

2. In paragraph 1, Law calls the protests at Columbia "farcical," an adjective that is derived from the word *farce*. What is a farce? How, according to Law, is the protest farcical? Do you agree with his description of the protest?

3. In paragraph 5, Law states that market forces are altering labor practices in developing countries. As more people buy sweatshop goods, more money is poured into those countries' economies, and the workers reap the benefits of "higher wages and luxuries such as paid lunches and even factory libraries." What is your definition of *luxury*? Do you think paid lunches are luxuries? What would you consider a luxury at your own workplace?

Discussing Main Point and Meaning

1. USAS and Law produce different arguments regarding sweatshop labor, although both seem to agree that labor practices should not result in people being abused or dominated by others. In its second principle, USAS states that it struggles "against racism, sexism, homophobia, heterosexism, classism, and other forms of oppression" while Law states that sweatshop labor helps women "escape the domination of their husbands, fathers, or brothers" (para. 2). How are sweatshop labor and these issues of discrimination related? How does sweatshop labor take advantage of these issues? How can it fight these issues?

2. USAS's manifesto features a quote from Lilla Watson, an aboriginal activist: "If you've come to help me, you are wasting your time. But if you've come because your liberation is bound up with mine, then let us work together." What does this statement mean? How do both USAS's and Law's essay speak to this statement?

3. Although his essay is short, Law attempts to show the larger ramifications of buying textiles from developing nations, and asks, "What would be the impact on terrorism if millions of Pakistanis, Afghans, or Indians lost their jobs making clothes for the developed world?" (para. 3). How are sweatshop labor and terrorism related?

Examining Sentences, Paragraphs, and Organization

1. In "A Call for More Sweatshop Labor," Law ends his first paragraph by stating, "Worst of all, most of the workers who are being abused are, as the students would put it, defenseless women. I admit I am also outraged—at the students." How does this statement in Law's first paragraph affect your expectations of the essay? Does it make you want to continue reading? Why or why not?

2. Tone, or voice, is how authors come across to their audience. An author's tone can be outraged, depressed, excited, sad, and so on, based on word choice, sentence structure, and overall topic. How does the tone of the "principles of unity" (panel 3) in USAS's manifesto differ from the tone of Law's second paragraph? In many ways, Law is speaking directly to USAS. If they were actually debating each other, which tone do you believe would be the more effective for this argument? Why?

3. A good argument often has a call-for-action (or CFA) that urges its readers to do something. What is the CFA of USAS? What is Law's CFA? Where do you find the CFA in each of these readings? How do the essays organize themselves to persuade readers to take action? Are they effective? Why or why not?

Thinking Critically

1. What are the working conditions for those who are involved in making your clothing? Your iPod? Your car? Are these conditions acceptable or should they be changed?

2. Given that we now live in a global economy—in which certain countries create low-cost goods for other countries and American workers are now competing with them and creating low-cost manufactured goods—should we establish a global system of labor laws that benefits all people?

3. The American economy had a very violent history in the late nineteenth and early twentieth centuries as it became industrialized. Workers had to fight for the right to unionize, for a shorter work week, and for the shorter workdays that we now enjoy. What are the rights that workers can and should expect? Why are these rights important?

In-Class Writing Activities

1. Using the USAS's manifesto as a model, create your own manifesto as a student or as an employee. Write a paragraph describing who you are and the various goals you have for your school or employer. What rights are you fighting for? Pay attention to tone—how will you convince your audience that your goals are the right goals for student workers? What evidence will you use to support your argument?

2. As both Law and USAS point out, it is important to provide readers with a call for action—something that you want readers and citizens to do to help make the world a better place. Based on these two readings and on your class discussions, formulate a call for action regarding labor practices on your campus, addressed to the students at your school. Then, in an editorial for your student newspaper, write up that call for action, making sure to convince your readers that your ideas will ensure fair labor practices and goods for all.

3. Part of the responsibility of fair labor rests on the consumers: How much are you willing to pay for your goods? What companies are you willing to patronize? Part of the responsibility rests with the company itself: How does a company make a profit while making sure it treats its workers fairly? What is the right amount of pay? In the early 1900s, Henry Ford made sure he paid his workers enough that they could afford to buy Ford cars. Come up with a manufacturing business you would like to run. You can manufacture clothes, electronics, or any other type of goods. Write up your company plan. What is your responsibility as a company to your workers? To your customers? What safeguards will you put in effect to make sure you meet your responsibilities? What wages and luxuries will you give your workers?

ANNOTATION **Effective Persuasion: Recommending**
a Course of Action

The primary purpose of a persuasive essay is to change someone's thinking or course of action. On election day, a newspaper editorial will encourage
its readers to vote for a particular candidate; in the same paper, a film review
may discourage moviegoers from attending a certain film the reviewer finds
"pointless, trivial, and embarrassingly dumb"; and an opinion column in that
paper may try to persuade parents to avoid buying fast food for their children. All of these pieces will offer reasons for their views, but they will also
urge their readers to take some form of action. In **"A Call for More Sweatshop Labor,"** a Columbia University student, **Peter Law,** provides an excellent illustration of how a writer can persuasively conclude an essay by recommending a course of action. In this case, Law suggests that students quit one
form of action (boycotting sweatshop clothing) and take up a totally opposite action (buying only sweatshop clothing). What's effective about his
essay—whether one agrees with it or not—is the way he systematically
moves his argument from a set of reasons supporting his position to a direct
call for action.

Law argues that boycotts worsen conditions for workers.

Progress like this cannot be made if people do not buy sweat-
shop-produced goods. Labor practices change because of the dictates of the market, not the dictates of outraged students of the left.
Not buying goods produced with cheap labor would only force
companies to make that labor even cheaper, and would likely
worsen the working conditions for millions of workers around the

*He calls for stu-
dents to end boy-
cott and instead
buy only sweat-
shop clothes.*

world. A better plan would be to do the opposite—instead of
boycotting sweatshop textiles, check the label the next time you
shop and make sure your clothes come from the developing
world! The people of Mauritius need the money more than South
Carolinians or Northern Italians—spread the wealth!

—From "A Call for More Sweatshop Labor" by Peter Law,
      p. 328

Student Writer at Work: Peter Law
On Writing "A Call for More Sweatshop Labor"

Q: What inspired you to write this piece?

A: As a bright-eyed college Republican arriving at far-left Columbia University in the city of New York, I was eager at the start of my freshman year to test the waters and see what type of reaction a strongly conservative piece would receive. The mock fashion show staged by Columbia's anti-sweatshop labor campaigners, which was described in my article, gave me an extra push.

Q: What kind of feedback did you get?

A: For all of their talk of tolerance, Columbia's student body is remarkably unkind to those who offend their conceptions of political orthodoxy. Several people wrote letters to the editor in response to my piece, two people wrote a joint op-ed, a few people e-mailed me, and one person called me to leave an angry voice message attacking me for being heartless.

Q: Did any of that change your mind about sweatshop labor?

A: My views have not changed. I still believe that the surest path to national economic development is by progressively climbing up the economic ladder from engaging in low-skill, low-wage industries to high-skill, high-wage ones. A country cannot go from subsistence farming to designing computer chips overnight. It is easy for people in the developed world to demand that employers in the developing world pay "living" wages and provide "fair" working conditions, but it is next to impossible for a business in a highly competitive field like textiles to do so in a developing country and stay competitive. What constitutes "living" or "fair" in the U.S. differs widely from what those terms entail in the developing world. To require businesses in the developing world to operate at developed world standards would only serve to hurt businesses and people.

Q: Do you have any advice for fellow student writers?

A: Always start with a thesis and a plan for how to prove it! You don't need a full outline before you start writing (at least in my opinion), but you do need a creative, forceful argument and at least a feeling for how you will support it with concrete evidence.

The Powerful Theory of Conspicuous Consumption

If any one principle of consumption holds true for today's America, it is this: People no longer buy something merely because they need it; they buy it because it's available. How this principle of consumption became a major factor in American life and economy is a fascinating story that begins sometime in the 1880s, with the rise of advertising, the birth of large department stores, the success of the Industrial Revolution, and the rapid expansion of mass media. It is, in effect, a story about the invention of the modern "consumer," a largely irrational creature hardly imagined in classic economics. This new phenomenon was brilliantly identified by a maverick economist named Thorstein Veblen in a 1899 book called The Theory of the Leisure Class.

Veblen (1857–1929), the American-born son of Norwegian immigrant parents, was one of the first to point out—long before radio, television, mega shopping malls, and the Internet—the enormous power of what he memorably called "conspicuous consumption"—the desire to demonstrate one's prestige and status based on one's material acquisitions. And long before Madison Avenue discovered the power of envy (the modern consumer may be defined as someone who desperately wants whatever others possess), Veblen argued that after self-preservation, "emulation is probably the strongest of economic motives." Veblen saw emulation as wasteful and irrational; he once said that "man is not a logical animal, particularly in his economic activity."

His economic theory still retains a remarkable explanatory power and is the precursor to such best-selling books as Freakonomics *(2005), which attempt to explain the "hidden side of everything." Although Veblen would never have imagined such an item of apparel, he would nevertheless be able to explain through his theory why someone would pay hundreds of dollars for designer-ripped blue jeans. He had a keen eye for detecting "conspicuous waste." He saw that people tended to place enormous value on useless objects and skills, often because these were evidence of one's capacity for "waste-*

Thorstein Veblen (1857–1929), creator of the theory of conspicuous consumption.   The Granger Collection, New York.

ful expenditure." Too many things that we spend time and money on lavishly he considered simply "decorative" and as having no useful function; for example, he satirizes the affluent American male's preoccupation with his "lawn," which is merely a cow pasture that must be kept closely cropped but without benefit of a cow. At one point he amusingly contrasts Americans' preference for dogs over cats. Why? Dogs are more useless and expensive to keep and therefore are afforded a higher stature as domestic pets.

Veblen received an undergraduate degree in economics from Carleton College and then took a PhD in philosophy at Yale. But his disposition and his unorthodox economic theories kept him moving from one academic position to another. In 1919 he helped develop the now famous New School for Social Research in New York City. Besides The Theory of the Leisure Class, *he published over ten books and many articles.*

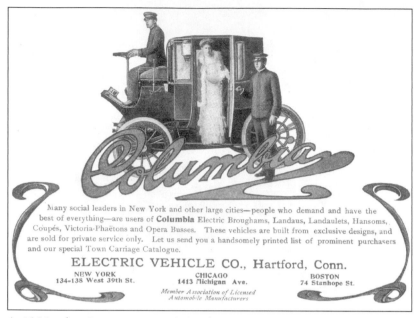

Many social leaders in New York and other large cities—people who demand and have the best of everything—are users of **Columbia** Electric Broughams, Landaus, Landaulets, Hansoms, Coupés, Victoria-Phaëtons and Opera Busses. These vehicles are built from exclusive designs, and are sold for private service only. Let us send you a handsomely printed list of prominent purchasers and our special Town Carriage Catalogue.

ELECTRIC VEHICLE CO., Hartford, Conn.

NEW YORK
134-138 West 39th St.

CHICAGO
1413 Michigan Ave.

BOSTON
74 Stanhope St.

*Member Association of Licensed
Automobile Manufacturers*

A 1904 advertisement promoting a luxury car.   The Granger Collection, New York.

Discussing the Unit

Suggested Topic for Discussion

Money is power. Arguably, whoever has the most money has the power to change the world. Consider how much money was spent on the last U.S. presidential election: over $528 million. The winner spent $40 million more than his closest opponent. In this scenario, what can an individual consumer do? This chapter hopes to get you thinking about what you, as someone with money or someone with limited funds, can do to exercise the responsibilities that come along with it. Is it ethical to buy one product over another? What does it mean to buy a product? Who is affected by what you buy? What products do Americans buy, and what does this say about us as a culture? Should we shop more responsibly? If so, how?

Preparing for Class Discussion

1. What does each of the writers believe are good consumer and business practices? Some of them, like Law and Goodwin, seem to be at odds, but are they? And what would happen to other nation's economies—especially the poorest—if suddenly we bought nothing? Although what writers think may not always be explicit as, say, USAS's manifesto, their ideas are often implied through the contrasting situations they show and through their calls for action. Write down lists of good consumer habits based on each reading. Which ones are opposites? Which ones overlap? Where is the middle ground? How can we reach it?

2. The readings in this chapter cover some products you may not buy—authentic Prada bags and inflatable castles from Sky-Mall—and some you may—college sweatshirts and other paraphernalia. How does what you individually buy affect others? Keep a shopping diary for a week. What did you buy? Where? Why? How much did you spend? Was it (a) a necessary purchase, (b) a luxury purchase, (c) an impulse purchase? Then, in a separate diary, write about a day on which you buy nothing. Write up your findings about your consumer habits in a short essay.

3. Can a nation that runs on sweatshops and cheap labor be considered a democracy? Does the United States—or any other nation benefiting from the labor of such countries—have a responsibility to improve the conditions and rights of the workers there? Why or why not? And what about conditions in the United States, say, for migrant workers? What, if anything, should nations do to improve working conditions for all people?

From Discussion to Writing

1. Based on the above questions and the readings, what are the responsibilities that come with having money? What do you think are your individual responsibilities when shopping? Write a short essay—using evidence from the readings and from your own "consumerism" diary—in which you outline the ethics of buying. Remember to include a call for action for your readers.

2. Part of the problem with trade and consumerism, as Goodwin's article points out, is the secrecy that often goes along with bad

business practices. Consumers do not always know what or from whom they are buying. After doing some research of a company whose products you buy, write a report (or an exposé) that addresses these questions: Does the company have good or bad business practices? What is its philosophy regarding its workers?

Topics for Cross-Cultural Discussion

1. Each nation—even each city—relies on a particular industry to keep its economy running, whether it is the automobile industry in Detroit or the electronics industry in Tokyo. Discuss among your classmates the largest industry in your hometown. Who works there? What is made there? How are the workers treated? What, if anything, would you change about the various business practices in your hometown?

2. Does shopping have any cultural significance for your family or community? Do you shop with family or with friends? What rituals or habits are invoked when you shop, and why? Why do you have these habits and these ideas about shopping? How were they formed?

10

The News Media: Are Opinions Replacing Facts?

At one time, the media and the general public accepted a distinction between fact and opinion. Fact was accepted as undisputed information or a real occurrence; it was based on evidence and statements that could be logically or scientifically established as true (for example, it's a scientific fact that the earth revolves around the sun, even though we don't personally see or feel this). Opinion, on the other hand, was regarded as a belief or viewpoint that might be held with confidence but could be subjected to dispute. In other words, opinion was open to doubt and susceptible to successful challenge. (For more discussion on this distinction, see the introduction, pp. 3–6.) Although some philosophers and scientists have long contested this neat distinction, the difference between fact and opinion (or objectivity and subjectivity) has remained for a long time a central guideline for newsrooms and media analysis.

In recent years, however, this old distinction has become increasingly blurred, as more and more news outlets have turned to so-called opinion journalism. The reasons behind this trend are complex, but anyone who follows news production closely is aware of the ways opinion has dominated coverage, from the popularity of networks featuring the subjective and often extreme views of opposing pundits to outright political bias and "spin." As the president of ABC News, David Westin, suggests in "The Truth about TV News," "Opinion is interesting—and valuable—only if it is based on facts." Yet is most of the daily news you receive coming from the reverse direction—that is, the "facts" are based only on opinion?

Perhaps "opinion journalism" is actually the better model for the future, maintains a veteran journalist who knows nearly every facet of the news and commentary business. In "The Twilight of Objectivity," Michael Kinsley looks at the way cable news has been succeeding as a result of its highly emotional and personal displays of political perspectives. He wonders if it's time for the traditional American newspaper—now seriously threatened by blogs and podcasts—to learn from cable news and abandon its goals of objectivity. "Opinion journalism," Kinsley argues, "can be more honest than objective-style journalism, because it doesn't have to hide its point of view."

Both Westin and Kinsley are keenly aware of the power that informed (and not-so-informed) opinion exerts on today's Americans, who often seem more interested in what they should *think* about an issue than what they should *know* about it. One consequence of this trend is, as Mississippi State University student Jason Browne suggests, that everyone now feels obligated to have an opinion on everything. In "If You Don't Have an Opinion, Relax," he wonders why this is so and advises fellow students that it's probably better not to have an opinion than to "fake one." "There's no shame in being undecided," he concludes. The chapter ends by showing how a *New Yorker* cartoonist, William Haefeli, depicts the way the power of opinion has entered our everyday lives.

DAVID WESTIN

The Truth about TV News

[THE COLUMBIA JOURNALISM REVIEW / March / April 2005]

Before You Read

Should news programs offer opinions or just facts? How does a news-caster's reference to his or her personal opinion affect your response to a newscast?

Words to Learn

apocalyptic (para. 1): predicting doom (adj.)

craven (para. 13): cowardly (adj.)

sweeps (para. 13): measurement periods of the Nielsen media research company, which records national ratings (n.)

monolithic (para. 14): massively uniform (adj.)

inveterately (para. 18): habitually (adv.)

inductions (para. 18): conclusions reached by a logical process (n.)

republic (para. 21): a state controlled by citizens; a commonwealth (n.)

The anchor changes at NBC and CBS News, combined with the emergence of Fox News, have brought up, again, apocalyptic thoughts about traditional television news. Network news will never be the same. Viewers are turning away from the evening programs.

1

DAVID WESTIN *has been the president of ABC News since 1997. With a background in law and a degree from the University of Michigan, Westin has also served as general counsel for ABC. He is responsible for all news on the network, including* World News Tonight, Nightline, Good Morning America, 20/20, Primetime, *and* This Week with George Stephanopoulos. *His additional responsibilities for ABC include overseeing ABC News Radio and ABC.com. Westin cites* Nightline *as one of ABC's best news programs. That broadcast, he says, presents "context and meaning and perspective. . . . [T]hat is where ABC needs to focus its efforts in the future."*

Cable can cover the big events. The Internet is quicker and livelier. All three networks are going the way of the dinosaur.

It will surprise no one that, despite such doomsayers, I see a   2
bright future ahead for network news, a future that can be even brighter than our past. There is a real and present danger, but it's not the changing technology and the increase in news outlets that everyone likes to talk about. To the contrary, I believe the new world offers us exciting opportunities to reach our audiences, as we find ways to deliver news that is available to people when and where they want it. For me, the real danger we face lies not in how we provide the news, but in what we are providing.

As we've watched an explosion in news outlets, we've seen a simultaneous   3
explosion in the opinions being expressed every minute of every day over these "news" outlets. This rush to present opinion is beginning to drown out our reporting of facts. The clash of ideas is moving to center stage, while the search for truth is being pushed into the wings.

> *This rush to present opinion is beginning to drown out our reporting of facts.*

There are powerful business reasons for the embrace we're seeing   4
of opinion journalism on TV. It's vivid, it's entertaining, and—let's face it—it's less expensive than reporting out a difficult story. Opinion offers a quick, efficient, and effective way to attract an audience in a cluttered world.

Seeking to report the factual truth of a matter, on the other hand,   5
can be hard work, expensive, and inefficient. It requires developing or hiring reporters who truly know what they're reporting about. It requires following leads that may go nowhere. The emphasis on opinion is therefore understandable. But I have two concerns about where we are headed.

First, and perhaps most obvious, the more we fill up our reports   6
with opinion, the less time we have for reporting facts. It's all well and good, for example, to have people who know what they're talking about give their views, for example, about whether we're doing what we should be doing to make our ports safer. But before we get to that discussion, shouldn't we spend some time finding out what security and risks already exist at U.S. ports? It may be interesting to hear a heated debate about health care in the United States, but shouldn't we know where we stand now, what the future is likely to hold, and what the options might be? Emphasizing opinion to the exclusion of factual reporting undermines the very value of the opinions

being expressed. Opinion is interesting—and valuable—only if it is based on facts.

There's a second, far more disturbing, problem with the expansion of opinion in television news. It can create the impression among the audience that everything they're seeing is an expression of someone's opinion. Many outlets fail to do a good job of distinguishing between opinion and fact. As a result, audiences see people who look like one another on sets that look alike with similar graphics either expressing strong opinions or reporting the facts. Is it any wonder that the audience starts to believe that it's all the same? 7

Unless we're careful, we who are charged with reporting the news could lose sight of truth as our ultimate goal. We could end up in a world where, implicitly, none of us—not the audience and not the reporters—even believe any longer in the truth. 8

We could end up in a world where none of us believe any longer in the truth.

This may seem a radical—even a ridiculous—suggestion. How could it be that we would give up our belief in the truth? But look at some of the reporting we see on television today. Increasingly, some reporters don't even ask whether something is true or false. They jump over this basic question and go straight to an analysis of who's doing the talking and why. What is their affiliation? What hidden motive may they have for saying what they're saying? It's all about strategy and the political game rather than the facts underlying a debate. 9

Take, for example, the much-publicized Swift Boat Veterans for Truth. When their advertisements hit the airwaves last August, there was enormous media coverage of what they said, followed quickly by a thorough examination of who these people were and what motives they had, and then by comments from the Kerry campaign. But whether or not one agreed with the group's ultimate conclusions about Senator John Kerry, here was someone asserting claims of fact—claims that are susceptible to being proven right or wrong. Yet how much of the media attention was directed to the basic question: Were the accounts of what happened in Vietnam thirty-five years ago true or false? 10

The question of whether anyone can discern the "truth" about what happened thirty-five years ago—or even what is happening today—is one that has occupied philosophers for years. But as interesting as that academic question may be, those of us in network news don't have the luxury of giving up on our goal of truth-telling. 11

A different example comes from ABC News: one year after Presi-   12
dent Bush declared the end of major hostilities in Iraq, *Nightline* devoted an entire program to reading the names of American service
personnel killed to that point. Here there was no dispute about the
facts. These men and women had all given their lives in the continuing Iraq hostilities. The idea, while powerful, was not entirely original. *Life* magazine had done something similar in the 1960s when it
published the pictures of American service people killed during a
single week in Vietnam.

When we announced we would be doing this, we were immedi-   13
ately greeted with a chorus of skepticism and criticism from people
who claimed we were motivated by antiwar sentiment. Sinclair
Broadcast Group refused to air the *Nightline* program on its ABC af-
filiates. One TV critic even claimed we were doing it as a "craven ratings stunt for sweeps."

There was no monolithic antiwar sentiment underlying the   14
Nightline broadcast. I do not know the sentiments of all the dozens
of people who worked on the broadcast; I'd
be surprised if some were not opposed to the
war. A plurality of Americans were. But Ted
Koppel said openly during the broadcast
that he was not opposed to the war. And I
can tell you that the reason I approved the
broadcast was my belief that part of the
truth we needed to report about Iraq was a
complete accounting of the price the nation was paying.

Part of the truth we needed to report about Iraq was a complete accounting of the price the nation was paying.

But whatever our collective motives, the much more important   15
question is why those motives really mattered in the first place. We
heard from many viewers. Some found the reading of the names a fitting tribute to young men and women who gave their lives for their
country. Others found it a needlessly painful reminder of the price
being paid on our behalf—and objected that we did not include a re-
counting of events that led up to the Iraq invasion. But how people
reacted to the broadcast seemed to depend more on the views of
those watching than it did on the imputed motives of those putting
the broadcast on the air.

I made this point at the time to a senior White House official. He   16
disagreed. He felt that our airing the program became a statement
against the war, not because of what we said but because many
people assumed our attitude was antiwar. To make the point clear, I
asked him whether he would have had a different view if Fox News

had put on the very same broadcast. He said that would be an entirely different case.

This was a fascinating and powerful response. The imputing of   17
motives, even where there is no conflict over the facts, tends to distract from the fundamental and essential question: What is the truth?

One of my favorite quotes comes from the late Harvard philoso-   18
pher Willard Van Orman Quine: "Creatures inveterately wrong in their inductions have a pathetic but praiseworthy tendency to die before reproducing their kind." It's been abundantly clear, at least since September 11, 2001, that, if Americans get it wrong at this point in our country's history, our survival may be at risk. And when I talk about getting it "wrong," I don't mean only our policies or opinions. I mean the underlying truth of our situation in the world.

This requires real journalism, and it will not be easy. It will re-   19
quire that some of us in the news business put ourselves in harm's way, as my colleagues are doing in Iraq. It will require continued and increased investment in things such as investigative work, beat reporting, and documentaries—an investment that some of us make daily but that others have trouble with in a universe of increased competition and reduced audiences.

Note that I talk in terms of an "investment," which by definition   20
requires some faith that our audiences really want a responsible, reliable news report. And that faith must come from our owners, from news management, and from our newsrooms and reporters. If our faith is well-placed, then our investment will pay off in the form of loyal attention from people who come to us, day in and day out, simply because we present the truth, not mere opinion.

If we are willing to redouble our commitment to finding the   21
truth—no matter how difficult—and reporting it to the American people, then network news will remain an important part of the republic we serve. And no one will doubt our future.

Web **Read It Now:** Read more perspectives published in the *Columbia Journalism Review* and check out ABC's profile of David Westin and links to the network's news programs at **bedfordstmartins.com/americanow**, Chapter 10.

Vocabulary / Using a Dictionary

1. In his opening paragraph, Westin uses the word *apocalyptic*. What is the apocalypse?

2. What is the Latin meaning of *affiliation* (para. 9)? How does this meaning relate to its contemporary definition?
3. What is the root word and origin of *monolithic* (para. 14)?
4. What is the root word and meaning of *pathetic* (para. 18)?

Responding to Words in Context

1. What does Westin mean when he asserts that the major networks are "going the way of the dinosaur" (para. 1)?
2. What is the meaning of the reference "cluttered world" (para. 4)? According to this reference, how is the world "cluttered"?
3. In paragraph 11, the writer places the word *truth* in quotation marks. What implication or suggestion do the quotation marks have?
4. Westin quotes the phrase "wrong in their inductions" in paragraph 18. What is the meaning of *inductions* in this reference?

Discussing Main Point and Meaning

1. In paragraph 4, the author identifies "opinion journalism" as a significant problem. For Westin, what problems are associated with this form of journalism?
2. In paragraphs 12 through 15, Westin describes responses to an ABC *Nightline* feature that listed the names of American service personnel killed in Iraq. According to Westin, this program had no political or antiwar motive, yet senior White House officials disagreed with him. Why were these officials concerned about the program?
3. In paragraph 18, Westin asserts that "if Americans get it wrong at this point in our country's history, our survival may be at risk. And when I talk about getting it 'wrong,' I don't mean only our policies or opinions. I mean the underlying truth of our situation in the world." What does he mean by this statement and the reference to "getting it wrong"?

Examining Sentences, Paragraphs, and Organization

1. Westin begins his essay by acknowledging problems that confront news organizations, but he then asserts that he sees a "bright

future" for network news. For Westin, what is the "real and present danger" that he describes in the next few paragraphs?

2. What reasons does Westin cite to explain the spread of "opinion journalism"?

3. What is the significance of Westin's reference to the Swift Boat Veterans for Truth in paragraph 10? How does this example affect his overall argument?

4. What does Westin mean in paragraph 19 when he uses the phrase "real journalism"?

Thinking Critically

1. In paragraph 15, Westin, in evaluating responses to ABC's *Nightline* program, states that reactions "seemed to depend more on the views of those watching than it did on the imputed motives" of those who produced the program. What does he mean? What is an "imputed motive"?

2. In paragraph 6, Westin speculates on the role of opinion in reporting the news and refers specifically to news reports regarding security at U.S. ports. According to the writer, what happens when such reports rely too much on opinion? When does he believe that opinion is useful or valuable?

3. Westin believes that when journalists rely too much on opinion, truth is compromised. How convincing is his argument about truth? Evaluate his reasoning. Do you agree with him? Why or why not?

4. When was the last time that you watched a national news broadcast on one of the major TV networks? To respond to the questions in this unit, it's important to be familiar with the TV news media, which represents many Americans' primary source of information about the world. For this assignment, watch the network news for an entire week. Take notes that include the station you are watching along with some of the featured topics. Afterward, review your notes and attempt to identify what is news and what is opinion.

In-Class Writing Activities

1. In evaluating Westin's ideas, consider some of the news programs that you've watched in the last year. Recall some news features

that contained elements of opinion. What do you believe was the impact of these opinions? Write a short essay in which you analyze the effect of opinion on those news reports.

2. In making a case against "opinion journalism," Westin uses logic, his own experience, and examples from the news to support his argument. How effective is his argument? Write a short essay that lists the strong points as well as any weaknesses of this argument. Can you think of ways in which Westin's argument might have been improved?

MICHAEL KINSLEY

The Twilight of Objectivity

[THE WASHINGTON POST / March 31, 2006]

Before You Read

Is "opinion journalism" better than objective reporting? Should newspapers follow the examples of news programs on television and news sites on the Web—and present more personal perspectives than facts?

Words to Learn

palsy-walsy (para. 1): slang for overly familiar or friendly (adj.)

populist (para. 1): advocating for the rights and interests of ordinary people (adj.)

MICHAEL KINSLEY *has written for all forms of media—for magazines and newspapers, including the* Los Angeles Times, *the* New Republic, *and* Harper's *magazine; for television, where he was cohost of CNN's* Crossfire; *and for the Internet as a founding editor of the online journal* Slate. *As an opinion writer, Kinsley believes, "If you're going to peddle opinions for a living, self-assurance is essential. If you don't have it, you need to bluff."*

xenophobe (para. 1): a person who fears or hates foreigners (n.)

outsize (para. 1): larger in size than usual (adj.)

overwrought (para. 2): overly upset, emotional, or agitated (adj.)

messiah (para. 3): somebody regarded as or claiming to be a savior (n.)

raucous (para. 3): loud, hoarse, or unpleasant sounding (adj.)

purportedly (para. 5): claimed or supposed to be, but without evidence (adv.)

counterparts (para. 7): people or things that have similar characteristics to other people or things (n.)

arbitrary (para. 7): based solely on wishes, feelings, or perceptions rather than facts (adj.)

CNN's Lou Dobbs—formerly a mild-mannered news anchor noted for his palsy-walsy interviews with corporate CEOs—has turned into a raving populist xenophobe. Ratings are up. It's like watching one of those "makeover" shows that turn nerds into fops or bathrooms into ballrooms. According to the *New York Times*, this demonstrates "that what works in cable television news is not an objective analysis of the day's events" but "a specific point of view on a sizzling-hot topic." Nicholas Lemann made the same point in a recent *New Yorker* profile of Bill O'Reilly. Cable, he wrote "is increasingly a medium of outsize, super-opinionated franchise personalities." 1

> "[Cable] is increasingly a medium of outsize, super-opinionated franchise personalities."

The head of CNN/US, Jonathan Klein, said that Lou Dobbs's license to emote is "sui generis" among CNN anchors, but that is obviously not true. Consider Anderson Cooper, CNN's rising star. His career was made when he exploded in self-righteous anger and gave Louisiana Senator Mary Landrieu an emotional tongue-lashing about the inadequate relief effort after Hurricane Katrina. Klein has said that Cooper has "a refreshing way of being the anti-anchor . . . getting involved the way you might." In short, he's acting like a human being, albeit a somewhat overwrought one. 2

And now on CNN and elsewhere, you can see other anchors struggling to act like human beings, with varying degrees of success. Only five months before anointing Cooper as CNN's new messiah (nothing human is alien to Anderson Cooper; nothing alien is human to Lou Dobbs), Klein killed CNN's long-running debate show *Crossfire*, on the grounds that viewers wanted information and not 3 opinions. Klein said he agreed "wholeheartedly" with Jon Stewart's widely discussed and uncharacteristically stuffy remark that *Crossfire* and similar shows were "hurting America" with their occasionally raucous displays of emotional commitment to a political point of view.

But that is just a personal gripe (I worked at *Crossfire* for six   4
years). More important is that Klein is right in sensing, on second thought, that objectivity is not a horse to bet the network on. Or the newspaper either.

The newspaper industry is having a psychic meltdown over the   5
threat posed by the Internet. No one seriously doubts anymore that the Internet will fundamentally change the news business. The uncertainty is whether it will change only the method of delivering the product or will also change the nature of the product. Will people want, in any form, a collection of articles, written by professional journalists from a detached and purportedly objective point of view? Or are blogs and podcasts the cutting edge of a new model—more personalized, more interactive, more opinionated, more communal, less objective?

Are blogs and podcasts the cutting edge of a new model—more personalized, less objective?

It might even be a healthy development for American newspapers   6
to abandon the conceit of objectivity. This is not unknown territory. Most of the world's newspapers, in fact, already make no pretense of objectivity in the American sense. But readers of the good ones (such as the *Guardian* or the *Financial Times* of London) come away as well informed as the readers of any "objective" American newspaper. Another model, right here in America, is the newsmagazine, all of which produce much outstanding journalism with little pretense of objectivity.

Most of the world's newspapers already make no pretense of objectivity in the American sense.

Opinion journalism can be more honest than objective-style   7
journalism, because it doesn't have to hide its point of view. All observations are subjective. Writers freed of artificial objectivity can try to determine the whole truth about their subject and then tell it whole to the world. Their "objective" counterparts have to sort their subjective observations into two arbitrary piles: truths that are objective as well, and truths that are just an opinion. That second pile

of truths cannot be published, except perhaps as a quote from someone else.

Without the pretense of objectivity, the fundamental journalist's   8
obligation of factual accuracy would remain. Opinion journalism brings new ethical obligations as well. These can be summarized in two words: intellectual honesty. Are you writing or saying what you really think? Have you tested it against the available counterarguments? Will you stand by an expressed principle in different situations, when it leads to an unpleasing conclusion? Are you open to new evidence or an argument that might change your mind? Do you retain at least a tiny, healthy sliver of a doubt about the argument you choose to make?

Much of today's opinion journalism, especially on TV, is not a   9
great advertisement for the notion that American journalism could be improved by more opinion and less effort at objectivity. But that's because the conditions under which much opinion journalism is practiced today make honesty harder, and doubt practically impossible.

Unless, of course, I am completely wrong.   10

 Read It Now: Read more views by Kinsley and others at the *Washington Post* and *Slate* at **bedfordstmartins.com/americanow**, Chapter 10.

Vocabulary / Using a Dictionary

1. Use your dictionary to determine the root words of *xenophobe* (para. 1).

2. What is the meaning of the root word of *emote* (para. 2)? What commonly used noun does it derive from?

3. What is the root word and origin of *communal* (para. 5)? What other words can be formed from this root?

Responding to Words in Context

1. In referring to the personnel on cable networks, Kinsley cites Nicholas Lemann's term *franchise personalities* (para. 1). What is the meaning of this phrase?

2. If the Latin phrase *sui generis* means "one of a kind," what does the writer suggest when he asserts that "Dobbs's license to emote is 'sui generis' among CNN anchors" (para. 2)?

3. The writer refers to the *anointing* of Anderson Cooper at CNN as a *new messiah* (para. 3). What meaning and suggestions do these two references have?

4. Kinsley cites Jonathan Klein's statement that Anderson Cooper has "'a refreshing way of being the anti-anchor'" (para. 2). What are the implications of the term *anti-anchor*?

5. In referring to the current state of the newspaper industry, Kinsley uses the phrase *psychic meltdown* (para. 5). What does this phrase indicate?

Discussing Main Point and Meaning

1. Kinsley mentions that CNN's Jonathan Klein cancelled the debate show *Crossfire* (para. 3). What reasons did Klein give for terminating this program? How did those views change afterward?

2. In evaluating influences on the contemporary news industry, Kinsley refers to the impact of the Internet (para. 5). What influences does he believe the Internet is having on the newspaper industry?

3. In referring to objectivity in news reporting, Kinsley uses the phrases *conceit of objectivity* (para. 6) and *pretense of objectivity* (paras. 6, 8). What do these phrases suggest? Are they intended to express similar or different meanings? How do they connect to the larger main points of the essay?

Examining Sentences, Paragraphs, and Organization

1. Kinsley, who makes a case for opinion journalism, begins his essay with a reference to Lou Dobbs of CNN. Why does Kinsley begin with this reference? Why is Dobbs likened to the "makeover" shows that abound on television?

2. In his characterization of network news anchors, Kinsley states that they are "struggling to act like human beings" (para. 3). What does this simile express about the style or behavior of news anchors?

3. In paragraph 7, Kinsley asserts that opinion journalism can be more honest than objective-style journalism. How does the writer support this claim?

4. According to Kinsley in paragraph 8, what are the "new ethical obligations" to which opinion journalists must adhere? What questions does he think these journalists should consider?

Thinking Critically

1. In seeking to support his argument against traditional "objective-style journalism" (para. 6), Kinsley refers to London's *Guardian* and *Financial Times* as examples. Evaluate the effectiveness of these supports. As stated, how much do they contribute to his argument?

2. In paragraph 2, Kinsley cites CNN head Jonathan Klein's remarks about Anderson Cooper. Kinsley refers to Cooper as "acting like a human being." Given the context, what does this remark say about Cooper and changes within the news media?

3. Consider the final words of Kinsley's essay: "Unless, of course, I am completely wrong" (para. 10). How does this statement relate to his ideas of the opinion journalist's ethical obligations? Does this line add or detract from his overall argument? Explain.

In-Class Writing Activities

1. How effective is Kinsley in advocating opinion-based reporting? Write an essay that evaluates not the merits of the topic itself but Kinsley's argument in favor of a form of journalism that relies on the opinions of the reporter. As a student of writing, what do you perceive as the major strengths of this argument? What are its weaker elements?

2. Kinsley begins his article by citing a *New York Times* feature that states "what works in cable television news is not an objective analysis of the day's events" but "a specific point of view on a sizzling-hot topic" (para. 1). Evaluate this claim. Why would Americans be more interested in someone's point of view than in an objective description of current events? Write an essay in which you analyze this comment.

3. Assume for the purposes of this assignment that newspapers and media outlets have accepted Kinsley's advice and shifted to a model based on opinion over objectivity. Imagine the nature of news reporting that relied on this model of journalism. Try to identity some of the most obvious and immediate changes that might result. Would an audience be better served? In what ways? What problems might result from this model?

JASON BROWNE

If You Don't Have an Opinion, Relax

[THE REFLECTOR ONLINE, Mississippi State University/April 19, 2005]

Before You Read

Have you felt compelled to express an opinion on an issue that you really didn't care or know much about? Should students be expected to express their ideas about current topics?

Words to Learn

extinct (para. 2): having died or ceased to exist (adj.)

stigmatizes (para. 2): marks as socially undesirable (v.)

zenith (para. 3): the high point or climax of something (n.)

vilify (para. 5): to make malicious or abusive statements about someone (v.)

oppressive (para. 5): harshly dominating or stifling (adj.)

touts (para. 5): praises, offers, or advertises something (v.)

decipher (para. 6): to determine what a word or piece of writing says (v.)

zealot (para. 7): someone who shows excessive interest or belief in a cause (n.)

JASON BROWNE *wrote this editorial for the* Reflector Online *when he was a weekly staff writer and opinion columnist for the paper. At the time, he was a senior at Mississippi State University; he has since graduated and holds a degree in Communication with an emphasis in Journalism. Browne, who seeks a writing-focused career, is interested in "politics, religion, and lifestyles" and is a regular reader and viewer of* CNN.com *and* MTV News. *His advice for student writers: "Write about things that you're genuinely interested in. It will be obvious in your work."* **For a "Student Writer at Work" interview with Browne, see page 362.**

Fence sitting has become a lost art in America. Every day we're   1
being yelled at from a thousand different directions to think about a
million different things. But it's not enough anymore that we just
consider the issues; we're expected to choose a side as well. And the
media, which are split down the middle on practically every facet of
American life, seem to agree that you should have an opinion on
everything. But you can't make someone care about something.
Can you?

Perhaps it's not completely accurate to say that fence sitting is ex-   2
tinct in America; there will always be those who don't care about
anything that doesn't directly affect their
lives. But the media has succeeded in creating an atmosphere that stigmatizes indifference and people are afraid to admit they
don't care. A more appropriate phrasing
may be that fence sitting has been forced underground.

**People are afraid to
admit they don't care.**

This is especially true in an academic setting. College students are   3
at the zenith of susceptibility to taking up causes: old enough to be
concerned, young enough to sustain the fight, and educated enough
to develop compelling arguments. Thus, in an environment where
one is expected not only to be up on current events, but to have an
original take on them, those without an opinion may be tempted to
take someone else's rather than admit to having none.

Furthermore, in a college setting there is added pressure to act   4
on your beliefs. How many times in the past year has a fellow student urged you to take an active interest in politics? But even after
the calls to action, the voice of the fence sitters is just as loud as any
group's. See the evidence: this year the turnout for Student Assembly
elections fell 50 percent from last year. And last year only 3,000
people voted.

There's absolutely nothing wrong with being concerned with is-   5
sues. But there's no need to vilify those who don't care. Doesn't the
Constitution, which protects our right to speak our mind, also protect our right not to speak at all? Wouldn't a government that forced
everybody to speak up be just as oppressive
as a government that forced everybody to be
silent? And politicians understand this fact.
When President Bush touts our right to practice whatever religion we choose, he always
throws in "or to practice no religion at all."

For an annotated excerpt of
this essay that highlights
Browne's writing strategies,
see page 361.

By William Haefeli, the *New Yorker*, January 9, 2006.

But fence sitting runs much deeper than just politics. I was   6
touched by Terry Schiavo's situation, just as most of you probably
were, but I never chose a position on the issue. The same goes for the
war in Iraq. With all the reasons and rhetoric flying back and forth
it's difficult to decipher how necessary America's presence in Iraq
truly is. The truth about the war, as usual, is probably somewhere in
the middle.

WILLIAM HAEFELI, a cartoonist for the New Yorker, *first began reading
the magazine when he was eight—but only for its cartoons. He attended
Duke University as a psychology major, but changed his focus and began
taking art classes, even though he was often steered away from drawing. It
wasn't until he was working in the advertising industry, drawing logos for a
lactating machine for cows, that he realized he needed to follow his dream of
cartooning. Haefeli, whose cartoons look closely at relationships, draws only
as much as he needs for the joke: "I consider myself more of a writer. Good
writing tells me what the drawing needs to be. If I have no idea, I don't know
what to draw."*

However, the war has managed to bring out the zealot in too   7
many otherwise moderate individuals. Tolerance and respect for differing opinions seem to have fallen by the wayside as more people assume a do-or-die attitude about their own point of view. So if you
have an opinion, great. But if you don't have one, please don't fake
one. There's no shame in being undecided.

 Read It Now: Read more opinions by Browne and other MSU students at
bedfordstmartins.com/americanow, Chapter 10.

Vocabulary / Using a Dictionary

1.   What is the origin and root of the word *stigmatize* (para. 2)?
2.   What is the root word from which *vilify* derives (para. 5)? What
     are some related words?
3.   What is the root word and origin of the word r*hetoric* (para. 6).

Responding to Words in Context

1.   Consider Browne's use of the phrase *fence sitting* in paragraph 2.
     What does he mean when he asserts that fence sitting has been
     "forced underground"?
2.   What docs the writer mean when he asserts that "college students
     are at the zenith of susceptibility to taking up causes" (para. 3)?
3.   In paragraph 7, Browne refers to those who have a "do-or-die"
     attitude about their own points of view. What is the meaning of
     this reference?

Discussing Main Point and Meaning

1.   What is Browne's characterization of the media in paragraphs 1
     and 2?
2.   In describing the plight of fence sitters, what does the writer
     mean when he states that they have been "forced underground"
     (para. 2)?
3.   In referring to the war in Iraq, how does Browne describe its im-
     pact on "otherwise moderate individuals" (para. 7)?

Examining Sentences, Paragraphs, and Organization

1. Browne begins his first paragraph with a collective first-person point of view; he refers to himself as *we*. Who does the writer appear to include in this point of view? What are the implications of using *we* and not the first-person singular *I*? How does the *we* point of view affect you as a reader?

2. In paragraph 3, how does Browne describe the predicament of college students? In what ways does he feel students are susceptible?

3. According to Browne, what are some results of the pressure on college students to "act on [their] beliefs" (para. 4)?

4. In what manner does Browne use the Constitution to support his point of view (para. 5)?

Thinking Critically

1. Does your response to this essay differ because it was written by a college student? Why or why not?

2. Browne describes himself as one who doesn't care about contemporary issues and asserts that those who "don't care" shouldn't be vilified (para. 5). Does this form of indifference represent the same thing as being neutral (which is an unwillingness to favor one side or another)? Explain.

In-Class Writing Activities

1. In his essay, Browne seeks to defend students who have no point of view on current affairs and issues. Do you agree with him? Why or why not? Write a short composition in which you take and support a clear position.

2. Do you hold opinions on the issues we face today as a society? Why or why not? Which current social issues, if any, do you care about most? Explain.

3. Consider the reasons why some students might refrain from taking a position on a given topic. Why do you suppose that they prefer to remain indifferent? Write an essay in which you explore the cause of this indifference, using specific examples to make a point. To assist you in connecting with this topic, place it in the context of the college where you attend classes.

ANNOTATION Using Parallel Structures

By using parallel structures, writers can make their sentences and paragraphs more coherent and memorable. Observe how President John F. Kennedy famously employed parallelism in his Inaugural Address (January 20, 1961): "Let every nation know, whether it wishes us *well or ill*, that we shall *pay any price, bear any burden, meet any hardship, support any friend, oppose any foe* to assure the *survival and success* of liberty." As you can see from this prime example, parallel structures are built by pairing ideas, balancing clauses, repeating key words and phrases, and using the same verb form. Note, too, that Kennedy is careful to balance sounds and rhythms at the same time.

You will see below how a Mississippi State student, **Jason Browne**, effectively draws on parallel structures for emphasis and coherence in his essay "**If You Don't Have an Opinion, Relax.**" Parallel structures inform the entire paragraph below, as he uses them to balance clauses and pair ideas. His first use of parallelism (in his second sentence) is especially effective for clarity and emphasis. It makes a memorable point and wholly supports his contention that college students are especially inclined to support causes. In the paragraph's last sentence, he uses parallel structures less openly, but if you go back over the sentence you will see it consists of two different parallel constructions, both commonly used by writers, "not only . . . but" and "rather than."

Browne uses parallel construction—"_ enough to _" for clarity and emphasis.

Browne's final sentence is also parallel, adding to the balance and effectiveness of the paragraph.

This is especially true in an academic setting. College students are at the zenith of susceptibility to taking up causes: old enough to be concerned, young enough to sustain the fight, and educated enough to develop compelling arguments. Thus, in an environment where one is expected not only to be up on current events, but to have an original take on them, those without an opinion may be tempted to take someone else's rather than admit to having none.

—From "If You Don't Have an Opinion, Relax" by Jason Browne, page 356

Student Writer at Work: Jason Browne
On Writing "If You Don't Have an Opinion, Relax"

Q: What audience did you have in mind when you wrote this piece for Mississippi State's *Reflector*?

A: College students of all political affiliations.

Q: What motivated you?

A: I wanted to ease anxiety over the pressure to be informed and intellectually invested in every current issue in the headlines. I was inspired to write this primarily by radio talk show hosts—such as Bill O'Reilly and Sean Hannity—who seem to demand that every American citizen should take sides on each and every issue for the sake of determining who is right and who is wrong.

Q: How would you compare your opinions to those of other students on campus?

A: I consider myself a voice of moderation. I don't endorse mounting a soapbox every time an individual is enlightened on a "significant" issue, nor do I endorse ignoring the news in an attempt to put the world on mute.

Discussing the Unit

Suggested Topic for Discussion

The readings in this chapter pose a variety of compelling questions: What is the role of the news media in our changing society? What do Americans expect of the media? How has technology affected news coverage of essential events? How should the term *news media* be interpreted? Finally, what is the place of personal opinion in our conceptions of the news?

Preparing for Class Discussion

1. The three essays in this unit each reflect distinctly different opinions. Westin, as president of ABC News, expresses perhaps the most traditional vision of the news media. Westin, though he ac-

knowledges the recent changes in broadcast news, including threats posed by the Internet, nevertheless claims to see a bright future for the broadcast media. The one development that he perceives as a threat assumes the form of opinion journalism—the "explosion of opinions" that has assumed greater popularity in recent years. Westin views opinion journalism as antithetical to truth and provides examples from his own experience that result in distortions of the truth. In evaluating his essay, identify and consider the possible problems or weaknesses with Westin's argument.

2.   The essay authored by columnist Michael Kinsley, while not personally directed at Westin, contrasts sharply with the other's ideas. As a former writer for the cable news program *Crossfire*, Kinsley provides readers with detailed examples describing CNN's approach to opinion journalism. Kinsley believes that opinion can be more "honest" than objective-style journalism and cites examples of English newspapers that have achieved popularity as a result of their embrace of opinion. In considering Kinsley's thesis, think about what it might lack. In what ways do you disagree with his vision of the news?

3.   While the first two readings in this chapter deal with the same topic from distinctly different vantage points—and represent a potential for traditional "pro/con" debate—the third essay simply asserts the writer's right not to have an opinion—to remain indifferent. The juxtaposition of Browne's somewhat casual declaration with more partisan and emotional essays provides some degree of irony. As media executives agonize over possible strategies for engaging and responding to a diminishing audience, Browne dismisses the topic and declares his lack of interest in the opinions that the other two writers so highly value. What is the role of opinion, not just in the news media but in American life? How important should it be? What does the expression of opinion have to do with democracy?

From Discussion to Writing

1.   The first two writers, Westin and Kinsley, express contrasting opinions regarding the nature of the news media. For Westin, truth—in the form of fact—represents the most significant element of the news media. By contrast, Kinsley asserts that

objectivity is a pretense and all journalists are to some degree governed by subjective views, either their own opinions or the opinions of others. In considering these distinctly different viewpoints, decide which model is most appealing to you and write an argumentative essay that favors one model over the other. Review the essential facts on which the essays are based and develop an argument in which you favor one model and criticize the opposing view. In developing and supporting your position, do not limit your ideas to those included in the essays, but go beyond the text and seek information—including interviews and discussion with peers and teachers—that you might incorporate into the body of your paper.

2. After reviewing the views of Westin and Kinsley, carefully annotate the quotes they employ to illustrate and clarify their positions. Consider how each might respond to the other's ideas. Without engaging in speculation and making guesses regarding what each writer might say, write a critique of Westin based on the ideas and statements of Kinsley; then reverse your approach and use Kinsley's ideas and comments to critique Westin. Because these writers represent such distinctly different views, such a critique should flow naturally from your reading. In developing the body of your essay, use quotes and specific facts as well as clearly supported inferences to support your main ideas.

3. Consider the philosophy of Browne, a student who seems turned off by or disillusioned with the current news media to the extent that he is unwilling to take a position. Given that we live in a democracy in which the views of each citizen help to elect leaders and determine public policy, how does Browne's ideology of "fence sitting" affect the world around him? Does he have at least a moral, if not a legal, obligation to develop an opinion and become engaged in key issues? Write an essay in which you analyze Browne's position, focusing on the impact of this indifference on the larger society. In developing support within your essay, attempt to identify the impact of this behavior as it might relate to specific issues and topics with which you are familiar, perhaps referencing issues and events on your campus.

Topics for Cross-Cultural Discussion

1. At a crucial point in Kinsley's essay, he cites international newspapers, the *Guardian* and the *Financial Times*, as valid models of

opinion-based journalism. Kinsley also states that "most of the world's newspapers" make no pretense of objectivity. To affirm the truth of the writer's remarks and to examine other models of opinion journalism, locate examples of these publications and evaluate them according to their effectiveness and quality.

2. Survey students from multiple cultures to determine how they define the news—and specifically, the balance of factual reporting and opinion. Use models from several different cultures to expand your analysis of this topic as it relates to the use of opinion and fact. Finally, ask students from other cultures for their views on the question of whether news should present fact or opinion.

11

Are Science and
Religion Compatible?

   Debates about the differing ways that religion and science explain the creation of the universe and the emergence of human life have been going on for centuries. Not all scientists are opposed to religion, nor are all religious individuals anti-science. One of the greatest scientific intellects of the twentieth century, Alfred Einstein, once said that "science without religion is lame; religion without science is blind." But, as history shows, every now and then the fragile truce between religion and science is disrupted by a controversy that pits science against religion and makes it seem as though these two ways of viewing the world can never be reconciled.

   The debates have grown more frequent ever since the evolutionary writings of Charles Darwin. One of the earliest and most memorable of these debates was the highly publicized John Thomas Scopes trial of 1925 (popularly known as the Monkey Trial). In many ways, this landmark trial, which ran for less than two scorching summer weeks in Tennessee, established the tone and level of discourse for much subsequent debate between American scientists and religionists. To set an important context for discussion, the chapter begins with a summary of that trial in "America Then . . . 1925."

   Flash forward eighty years: Some things haven't changed. Supporters of religion and the Christian Bible are no longer objecting to evolution being taught in biology class, but they are concerned that the story of Genesis is not receiving sufficient attention as a rival explanation of creation. But this time around, the word *creation* is being replaced by a term that appears to possess greater scientific value: *intelligent design*. To put it simply, the basic concept of intelligent design is that the natural world is far too complex to have evolved by random accidental events. This religious view of the world is held by millions of Americans who have little interest in scientific matters.

In late 2005, two events made it appear that the Scopes trial had returned—but with an entirely new cast of characters and slightly new arguments. This time the states were Pennsylvania and Kansas. In Pennsylvania, a federal judge decided that a school district could not alter the science curriculum to include intelligent design since, as the judge viewed it, this would be simply a thinly veiled attempt to advance creationism and endorse a religious view prohibited by the First Amendment. In Kansas, where the issue has been hotly debated for years, the state board of education voted 6 to 4 to introduce new science standards that challenge evolution and allow the option of teaching rival theories.

A few months earlier, President Bush fueled the national debate and helped promote the cause of intelligent design when he was quoted as saying that both sides ought to be properly taught. Bush was referring to what is called the "teach the controversy" policy, which encourages science teachers to cover both sides of the argument. Some educators, such as John Angus Campbell and Stephen C. Meyer, find this a healthy educational attitude. In "Evolution: Debate It," they argue that Darwin's evolutionary theory should be taught as "a credible, but contestable, argument" and that teachers should advance "scientific arguments for, and against, contemporary evolutionary theory."

Yet other educators, including many science teachers, see this argument as a way to introduce religious beliefs (whether they center around the creationist's God or the more modern Designer) into the biology or geology classroom. Their criticism is also based on the idea of a legitimate "controversy," which in a normal discussion would endow each side with an equal credibility. But many scientists see evolution and natural selection as irrefutable and believe that teaching both sides of the argument is equivalent to, say, spending one-half of a semester seriously debating whether the earth is flat or whether the sun revolves around the earth. In "Evolution: Just Teach

It," two top members of the National Center for Science Education remain skeptical of the "teach the controversy" policy, which they regard as essentially "propaganda that evolution is a theory in crisis."

We hear a great deal on this topic from scientists, educators, and political commentators, but what is the impact on individual students? Can someone who believes in intelligent design still pursue a career in the hard sciences? Can a college student majoring in science retain his religious beliefs despite what goes on in the classroom? In "Age-Old Debate: Creationist Students in the Science Classroom," Chase Mitchell, an Auburn University newspaper editor, reports on a freshman geology student who is intent on passing the course, even though "he doesn't believe what the professor is saying."

The chapter concludes with a look at how a belief in intelligent design could lead to a personal dilemma. One of the nation's most popular comic artists, G. B. Trudeau, imagines what might happen when a creationist gets some unpleasant news from his physician.

AMERICA THEN . . . 1925

The Scopes Monkey Trial

One of the earliest battles in what Americans now call the "Culture Wars"—the nationally divisive conflicts surrounding religion, sexuality, morality, patriotism, education, and personal and social values—occurred in 1925 during two blistering hot weeks in the small town of Dayton, Tennessee. In February of that year, a state law (the Butler Act) was enacted that declared it illegal for any public school "to teach any theory that denies the story of the divine creation of man as taught in the Bible, and to teach instead that man has descended from a lower order of animals." Within a few months, Tennessee found a culprit: a science teacher at Dayton's Rhea County High School, John Thomas Scopes. No sooner was the twenty-four-year-old teacher arrested for teaching evolution in a biology class than the recently formed American Civil Liberties Union (ACLU) rallied to his defense.

"The Monkey Trial" (as the media instantly termed it) moved quickly, beginning on July 10 and ending on July 21. The head of the

John Scopes (above left). High school teacher and football coach John Scopes (1900–1970) said, "If you limit a teacher to only one side of anything, the whole country will eventually have only one thought. . . . I believe in teaching every aspect of every problem or theory." *Clarence Darrow and William Jennings Bryan* (above right). An attorney and a leading member of the American Civil Liberties Union, Clarence Darrow (1857–1938) defended John Scopes and the teaching of evolution at the famous Dayton, Tennessee, trial, arguing against William Jennings Bryan (1860–1925), the famous orator known as the "Great Commoner" for his belief in the goodness of the common man. Bryan, who opposed the teaching of evolution in public schools, aided the state prosecutor at the trial.

defense team was Clarence Darrow, one of the nation's most prominent trial lawyers and well known for his agnostic views; the head of prosecution was the elder statesman and nationally famous populist, William Jennings Bryan. Known as the "Great Commoner," Bryan had run unsuccessfully for president of the United States three times as a progressive and pacifist Democrat. The trial turned out to be more of a staged philosophical debate than a courtroom proceeding as both sides displayed their signature oratorical skills—Darrow attempting to demolish religious superstition and Bryan intending to uphold the traditional virtues of old-time religion. As Bryan announced before the trial, "The contest between evolution and Christianity is a duel to the death. If evolution wins, Christianity goes." The trial offered ready-made polarizing views. Darrow represented

Anti-Evolution League. Outside the Dayton Courthouse, where the Scopes trial was conducted, evangelist T. T. Martin sold copies of his anti-evolution book, *Hell and the High School* (1923), in which he drew a connection between evolutionism and the "revolt of Youth" of the 1920s.

the intellectual elite and freethinking urban American who valued scientific progress and academic freedom, while Bryan stood for the ordinary citizen, rural traditions, and age-old values. Sophisticated northern newspapers and magazines (such as the New Yorker*) had a field day ridiculing the state of Tennessee—"to which even the most primitive form of civilization has never penetrated"—and by extension the entire fundamentalist South.*

As the trial proceeded, the prosecution called on a number of Scopes's students to confirm that he had taught evolutionary theory, but the defense was able to counter that Scopes simply taught out of a state-approved textbook that was readily available. Bryan, however, used that textbook to declare that evolutionism would lead only to atheism and moral corruption. Denied by the judge the use of "expert testimony" from scientists, the defense, in a surprise move, invited Bryan to the stand as an expert witness on the Bible. Bryan accepted this unorthodox move, but it proved to be a tactical error when Darrow sarcastically forced him into a maze of contradictory statements based on a literal reading of Genesis. The debating points could have been made in any college classroom, and the following day the judge, realizing Bryan's testimony was hardly relevant to the case, expunged it from the trial record. It took the jury only several minutes to return a guilty verdict. After all the rhetorical fireworks, the case was rather simple: The Butler Act was constitutionally enacted state law, and Scopes had violated it.

This incredibly dramatic trial ended quite anticlimatically for two reasons: one as a result of defense strategy and the other because of a technicality. Darrow decided not to offer a concluding argument because he knew that this would procedurally bar the prosecution from delivering one. This deprived Bryan of delivering a major speech he had prepared for the occasion. The technicality arose when the judge ordered Scopes to pay a $100 fine. According to state law, the amount of the fine could be determined only by the jury. An appeals court eventually reversed the decision two and a half years later, but Scopes—who by then had quit teaching—was never retried. Within days after the trial, an exhausted Bryan, though three years younger than his arch-enemy Darrow, was dead, his illustrious political reputation forever distorted by the role he enacted over a few hot summer days in a small Tennessee town.

Web **Read It Now:** Learn more about the Scopes trial from a professor of law at the University of Missouri and find out more about the ACLU at **bedfordstmartins.com/americanow**, Chapter 11.

The Intelligent Design Debate

John Angus Campbell and Stephen C. Meyer, Evolution: Debate It

Eugenie C. Scott and Glenn Branch, Evolution: Just Teach It

Before You Read

Where is the essential divide between intelligent design and scientific theory? Why do you think the question of creationism versus evolutionism is still such a difficult one for people to discuss—much less agree upon? What should be taught in public school classrooms?

Words to Learn [Campbell and Meyer]

orthodoxy (para. 4): adherence to the conventional standards of an institution or group (n.)

fosters (para. 5): promotes the growth of (v.)

embryologist (para. 9): a specialist in the field of early development and growth of living creatures (n.)

Words to Learn [Scott and Branch]

sectarian (para. 4): pertaining to a sect (a group of people who adhere to the same doctrine or religious beliefs); narrowly confined or limited in interest, purpose, scope (adj.)

proponents (para. 6): those who argue in support of something (n.)

phenomena (para. 6): occurrences or facts that are perceivable by the senses (n.)

flagellum (para. 6): a whiplike appendage that allows the locomotion of certain cells and other microorganisms (n.)

pedagogical (para. 11): relating to the art or profession of teaching (adj.)

propaganda (para. 12): material disseminated by the advocates or opponents of a doctrine or cause (n.)

spurious (para. 13): false (adj.)

JOHN ANGUS CAMPBELL
AND STEPHEN C. MEYER

Evolution: Debate It

[USA TODAY.COM/August 14, 2005]

The sky is falling.   1

Or so you might think if you have been reading reports about the   2
Kansas State Board of Education's proposed policy on teaching evolution. Though many have portrayed the hearings that led to the
Kansas policy as a rerun of the Scopes trial, the reality is much different. Rather than prohibiting teachers from teaching about evolution
(as Tennessee law did for John Scopes in 1925), Kansas is poised to
adopt a policy that would enable students to learn more about the
topic.

Specifically, the Kansas policy would require students to learn   3
not only the full scientific case for contemporary evolutionary theory,
called "neo-Darwinism," but also the current criticisms of the theory
as they appear in scientific literature. The Kansas policy would not
require, or prohibit, discussing the theory of "intelligent design,"
which has been so much in the news since President Bush spoke
about it earlier this month.°

Though Zobgy polls show that 71 percent of the public favors a   4
policy like the Kansas one, defenders of teaching only the case for

°In August 2005.

JOHN ANGUS CAMPBELL *is director of graduate studies at the University of
Memphis's Department of Communication. His work has helped to establish
the "rhetoric of science," which looks at science as a method of communication and persuasion. Campbell believes that "teaching science as argument
helps students understand the nature of science." Campbell edited* Darwin-
ism, Design, and Public Education *(2003) with* STEPHEN C. MEYER. *Meyer is
the director and Senior Fellow of the Center for Science and Culture at the
Discovery Institute in Seattle, which advocates the concept of intelligent
design. Meyer favors a "teach the controversy" strategy of intelligent design
and evolution.*

Darwinian orthodoxy regard it with suspicion. For them, the Kansas policy illustrates the folly of determining the science curriculum within the democratic process.

Moving Forward

The two of us disagree about the status of Darwin's theory. Even 5
so, we think there is a way to teach evolution that advances science education, fosters civil discourse and also respects public opinion. We encourage teach-

Students should learn the scientific arguments for, and against, contemporary evolutionary theory.

ers to present the case for Darwin's theory of evolution as Darwin himself did: as a cred-ible, but contestable, argument. Rather than teaching evolution as an incontrovertible "truth," teachers should present the argu-ments for modern neo-Darwinism and en-courage students to evaluate these arguments critically. In short, stu-dents should learn the scientific arguments for, and against, contemporary evolutionary theory.

There are good reasons for teaching science, and Darwinian evo- 6
lution, this way. Teaching scientific controversies and arguments helps students understand the nature of science. Contrary to the "men in white coats" stereotype, with scientists as data-collecting au-tomatons, scientists argue about how best to interpret evidence. Stu-dents who learn the arguments for and against a theory are learning how science works. Teaching current scientific arguments about a theory also gives students an understanding of the status of a theory. And, in the case of neo-Darwinism, there are significant scientific criticisms of the theory students should know about.

Some scientists think the fossil record challenges the Darwinian 7
idea that all organisms share a common ancestor. Events such as the "Cambrian explosion" show that new forms of life appear suddenly in the fossil record without evidence of connection to earlier forms — contradicting Darwin's picture of the history of life as a fully-connected branching tree.

Many scientists also doubt the ability of Darwin's mechanism of 8
natural selection to produce the major innovations — the new organs and body plans — that arise during life's history.

Recently, four hundred Ph.D.-level scientists, including a distin- 9
guished embryologist and member of the Russian Academy of Sci-ences, signed a statement questioning the creative power of the nat-ural selection/mutation mechanism.

The Evolution Debate

Neo-Darwinism The modern version of the theory of evolution. It affirms that all living organisms descended from original common ancestors, but it includes the infusion of newer molecular genetic and developmental theory.

Theory of evolution The theory that all species of plants and animals descended from a common ancestor. It also asserts that the process of natural selection plays a large role in the diversification of life over time.

Intelligent design A new and developing theory that says certain features of living systems are best explained by an intelligent cause rather than an undirected mechanism. While ID does not reject evolution as change over time, or common ancestry, it does challenge the idea that life arose by undirected processes of natural selection.

Creationism The religious concept that a supernatural creator produced the universe and life directly. It's often based upon the Bible's Book of Genesis.

Source: Webster's New World College Dictionary, John Angus Campbell, Stephen C. Meyer, Eugenie C. Scott, and Glenn Branch.

In May, fifteen such doubting scientists from universities such as Cornell, Wisconsin, Georgia and Italy's Perugia came to encourage the Kansas board to let students learn about the evidence challenging (as well as supporting) evolutionary theory.   10

Some scientists also doubt the Darwinian idea that living things merely "appear" designed. Instead, they think living systems display indicators of actual or "intelligent" design. Prominent scientists such as biochemist Michael Behe and biophysicist Dean Kenyon have cited intriguing evidence to support this theory, such as the presence of digital code, complex circuits and miniature motors in living cells.   11

Additionally, mathematician William Dembski has developed a statistical method for identifying tell-tale signs of intelligence. Dembski's method of design detection confirms our common sense intuition that digital information—including that found encoded within the DNA inside the cell—points to an intelligent source.   12

Teachers should be free to discuss alternatives [to evolution] if they are based upon scientific evidence, not scriptural texts.

Because intelligent design is a new theory, we, like Kansas' board, don't think students should be required to learn it. But we do think teachers should be free to discuss   13 such alternatives if they are based upon scientific evidence, not scriptural texts.

So what should the public do when competent experts disagree   14
about whether evidence supports a theory, as they do in the case of
Darwinian evolution? Our answer: Teach the competing arguments.

"One Long Argument"

To his great credit, Darwin addressed every competing argument   15
he could in *The Origin of Species*. When evolution is taught as
Darwin presented it—as "one long argument" resting on a large and
diverse body of facts, but nevertheless as an argument from which
thoughtful people (and scientists) can dissent—fewer parents will object to their children learning about it.

As John Scopes said, "If you limit a teacher to only one side of   16
anything, the whole country will eventually have only one thought....
I believe in teaching every aspect of every problem or theory."

EUGENIE C. SCOTT AND GLENN BRANCH

Evolution: Just Teach It

[USA TODAY.COM/August 14, 2005]

In the beginning, creationists tried to ban the teaching of evolution   1
altogether. Most famously, eighty years ago, John Scopes was tried for
breaking a Tennessee law outlawing such instruction. He was found

---

EUGENIE C. SCOTT *is the executive director of the National Center for Science Education (NCSE), which advocates teaching evolution in public school. Scott has been involved in the creationism/evolution controversy for over twenty years and has received numerous awards from various scientific organizations. She believes that science explains the natural world through the laws of matter and energy: "I believe there is nothing beyond matter and energy."*

GLENN BRANCH *is also involved with the NCSE as deputy director. "It doesn't matter if [intelligent design proponents] label it philosophy, science or home economics," Branch says, "for [intelligent design] to be endorsed as scientifically credible is a violation of church-state separation."*

guilty, and evolution effectively disappeared from the high school curriculum shortly thereafter, though it continued to be taught in universities.

But when university scientists began writing high school biology   2
textbooks in the late 1950s and early '60s, evolution returned to the curriculum, provoking a second outbreak of anti-evolutionism during the '70s and '80s.

Creationism was repackaged as "creation science" in the hope   3
that it would be taught along with evolution.

The 1982 decision showed that laws [for equal time for creation science] violated the First Amendment by promoting a sectarian religious idea inappropriate for the public school science classrooms.

In the '70s and '80s, at least twenty-six   4
states tried to legislate equal time for creation science with evolution, bringing the courts back in. The 1982 U.S. district court decision in *McLean v. Arkansas—Scopes II*—showed that such laws violated the First Amendment's Establishment Clause by promoting a sectarian religious idea inappropriate for the public school science classrooms. In 1987, the Supreme Court reached the same decision in *Edwards v. Aguillard.*

Such decisions doomed creation science   5
in the public schools, but they opened a niche for a repackaging of creationism: "intelligent design" (ID).

Like creation science, ID was presented as a scientific "alterna-   6
tive" to evolution, though its scientific content was intentionally vague. Its proponents claimed to have a method to identify natural phenomena that are, supposedly, incapable of being explained by evolution. ID advocates contend that "irreducibly complex" structures such as the bacterial flagellum can only be explained by appealing to the action of an intelligent agent.

To secure a wide base of creationist supporters, ID advocates are   7
coy about when and how such actions occurred. Because creation science, which insists on a 6,000-year-old Earth, is still the dominant form of anti-evolutionism, ID can't afford to take a stand to the contrary. Nonetheless, the mainstream of the ID movement is sympathetic to what theologians call progressive creationism, where God creates in fits and starts over time, rather than in six days. It's still creationism, and so is ID.

All Signs Point to "God"

To avoid this accusation, and thus circumvent the Establishment   8
Clause, ID advocates are also coy about the identity of the designer, claiming that it doesn't have to be God. But, token allusions to the

possibility of extraterrestrial or time-traveling biochemists notwithstanding, no one is fooled into thinking that the designer is not the Designer: God.

Initially, ID proponents encouraged the teaching of ID in the   9
public schools, but lately they've had second thoughts. They likely have figured out that if a school district required the teaching of ID, a judge would inevitably ask, "By the way, who's the 'intelligent designer'? Sounds a lot like God." And the jig will be up.

To avoid this legal predicament, the ID movement's leaders have   10
shifted strategy, encouraging school districts and teachers not to teach ID but to teach "evidence against evolution" or "the controversy." This message comes too late for Dover, Pennsylvania, where last fall the school board passed a policy requiring the teaching of ID. In September, Dover's ID policy will go on trial, in what might aptly be called *Scopes III.*

Elsewhere—in Kansas, for example, where a creationist majority   11
on the State Board of Education is monkeying with the state's science standards—"teach the controversy" is the

> *"Teach the controversy" is the new rallying cry of creationists.*

new rallying cry of creationists. The hope is that if students are taught that evolution is suspect, they will automatically embrace creationism. But "teach the controversy" is not a pedagogical device that will help them in college: Evolution is taught matter-of-factly at the nation's most prestigious universities, including religious institutions such as Brigham Young, Baylor and Notre Dame.

The propaganda that evolution is a theory in crisis is hardly new.   12
In 1925, William Jennings Bryan falsely contended that evolutionary science was on the verge of collapse, as his heirs argue today. Yet the evidence for evolution is stronger than ever.

Historically, improvements in the teaching of evolution are in-   13
evitably followed by a backlash. When anti-evolutionists couldn't ban evolution, they tried to get creationism taught alongside it. When the courts said creationism couldn't be taught in public schools, anti-evolutionists called for teaching spurious "evidence against evolution" in the hope that students would come to mistrust evolution and accept creationism by default.

What's Happening in Classrooms

What ought to be taught in high school science class? The basic   14
methods and results of the consensus view of the scientific community. Evolution is part, and a vital part, of this consensus; creation

science and intelligent design are not. Students should understand evolution, both if they are going on to college and for general scientific literacy. But in too many places across the country, students are not learning it.

And that's a problem, because it is widely recognized that the twenty-first century will be the century of biology, in which genomic, medical and biotechnological discoveries are bound to revolutionize our economy and our lives — and those of our children. America needs to produce the scientists who will pioneer in these fields, which means maintaining and improving the quality of science education — including a healthy dose of evolution, uncompromised by sectarian dogma, bad science and fake "critical analysis." Because those high school kids in India, China, Korea and Singapore are learning evolution, even if ours aren't. 15

Web **Read It Now:** Learn more about evolution from PBS and the National Center for Science Education and about the theory of intelligent design from the Discovery Institute by visiting **bedfordstmartins.com/americanow,** Chapter 11.

Vocabulary / Using a Dictionary

1. What do you think *neo-Darwinism* means (Campbell/Meyer, para. 3)? What other words include the prefix *neo-*?

2. What is an *automaton* (Campbell/Meyer, para. 6)? What other words include the prefix *auto-*?

3. What does it mean to be *coy* about something (Scott/Branch, para. 7)? What implication does using this word have?

Responding to Words in Context

1. Campbell and Meyer refer to scientists as *automatons* (para. 6); what image of scientists does this create for you? Why did the writers choose this word?

2. Darwin called evolution "one long argument" (Campbell/Meyer, para. 15). How does this use of the word *argument* relate to the more common definition of it?

3. Scott and Branch note that equating an "intelligent designer" with God would mean that "the jig will be up" (para. 9). What do they mean by this? What does using this phrase imply?

Discussing Main Point and Meaning

1. Scott and Branch describe creationism as having been "repackaged as creation science" (para. 3), which in turn was repackaged as "intelligent design" (para. 5). What do they mean by these statements?
2. How do Campbell and Meyer open their essay? Why do you think they do this? What do they hope to accomplish?
3. What do Scott and Branch close their essay with? Why would they use this ending?
4. On what major ideas do Scott/Branch and Campbell/Meyer disagree?

Examining Sentences, Paragraphs, and Organization

1. Why do Scott and Branch use quotes in the initial references to creation science and intelligent design? Is this punctuation grammatically necessary, or does it serve another purpose?
2. Comment on the use of headings in both essays. What do they accomplish?
3. How do Campbell and Meyer move from point to point in the body of their essay? Is it organized in any particular way?

Thinking Critically

1. Consider how Campbell and Meyer argue their side of the debate. Do they hold their position to be correct and the opposing views incorrect, or do they take a different tack?
2. Scott and Branch take a different approach to defending their side of the debate. What tactics do they use? What points are addressed, and what are ignored? What does this tell you about their position?

In-Class Writing Activities

1. Look over the glossary of terms originally printed with both essays (see p. 375). Does one of these positions appeal to you more than any other? Why or why not? Take into account your experiences as well as points raised in the two essays.

2. Comparing the two essays, do you believe that each addresses the points raised in the other? Or are the writers addressing different questions in order to persuade their readers? What evidence do you have for your belief?

===

CHASE MITCHELL

Age-Old Debate: Creationist Students in the Science Classroom

[THE AUBURN PLAINSMAN, Auburn University/October 13, 2005]

Before You Read

Suppose a student believes in something that is contrary to what is being taught in a course—evolution, for example? What difficulties might the student have? Likewise, think about the difficulties that a teacher might have instructing students whose beliefs differ from the course material. Is there any way to resolve this?

Words to Learn

curriculum (para. 1): the courses of study offered by an educational institution (n.)

vestigial (para. 3): functionless; left over from an earlier time (adj.)

CHASE MITCHELL *is a journalism major at Auburn University and campus editor for the* Auburn Plainsman. *He wrote "Age-Old Debate" because he wanted to look at both sides of the evolution/intelligent design debate. "I wanted to see what it was like for a student in a college-level course who must write down answers he or she believes to be wrong in order to make a passing grade," says Mitchell. "I also wanted to get a professor's opinion on the debate, and find out if it's one that should even exist in a college classroom." Mitchell comments on writing: "Never let yourself be a boring read. Anything can be interesting, as long as you find a way to inject your own style and substance into your work."*

futile (para. 5): ineffective; useless (adj.)

parameters (para. 5): boundaries (n.)

methodology (para. 5): means, technique, or procedure (n.)

When David Smith walks into his geology class, he sits down, listens closely to the day's lecture and pores over his notes, just like any other studious college freshman. The only problem is, he doesn't believe what the professor is saying—literally. Smith is a Creationist, and his religious views often clash with the course curriculum. "I actually had a test today," Smith said, "and I was sitting there taking the test, thinking, 'I know this is wrong, but I've still got to make the grade,' so it's a struggle."

1

An engineering major, Smith believes the Earth and everything on it was created by God in six days only a few thousand years ago. Traditional science, on the other hand, upholds Charles Darwin's theory that evolution and natural selection shaped life on Earth over the course of millions of years. College science courses typically support the same point of view.

2

> Smith believes that the Earth and everything on it was created by God in six days only a few thousand years ago.

"You have things in biology textbooks, like that humans have vestigial organs," Smith said. "That's just wrong—medically and scientifically wrong. And it's used to support evolution." He said students who think as he does shouldn't be force fed ideas they don't agree with. "[Professors] are just trying to find any evidence they can to support this theory," Smith said.

3

Jody Graham, associate professor of philosophy, said she is no stranger to the topic of religion versus science. Her class often ends up on the subject, she said, because many historical philosophers have wrestled with the same issue. "For instance, Galileo said that the Bible is not doing science," she added, "and to think that there's a conflict is to misinterpret what the Bible is supposed to be doing."

4

Creationists use a scientific theory, often referred to as "intelligent design," to put a scientific face on their belief that a single deity is responsible for all life on Earth. Graham pointed out that some philosophers have said it's futile to try and blend the two. "Intelligent design is a way to challenge evolution within scientific parameters," she said, "whereas some people are going to say biblical accounts aren't even supposed to be in the scientific methodology, so it's a mistake to think that they're in conflict."

5

"Creationist students have difficulty taking classes that conflict with their beliefs." (original caption from *The Auburn Plainsman*).   Cartoon by Andrew Thomson.

Graham said not all, but some students might have closed off their minds to the theory of evolution without thoroughly examining the scientific evidence that supports it: "I do think that some students try to hold this intelligent design theory without really trying to talk about it." But Smith pointed out that he has researched the subject tirelessly, and that he enjoys discussing the topic with his professors. "The creation/evolution debate is something that lights my fire," he said. "I enjoy it, and I'm really passionate about that."   6

"Some students try to hold this intelligent design theory without really trying to talk about it."

Smith often consults *The Evolution Cruncher* by Vance Ferrell, a 900-page book that Smith calls "an encyclopedia for Creationists." "I'm working my way through it," he said. "It's kind of difficult reading, but there's a lot of good information in there." After learning more about the subject, Smith noted, he decided the evidence supporting evolution is unreliable. He also maintained there is fossil evidence available to support everything from the Great Flood to dinosaurs co-existing with human beings.   7

Creation scientists believe that dinosaurs were created on the same day as everything else in the animal kingdom, but that they were wiped out during the Great Flood because they weren't smart enough to survive. Smith said he knows some Christians who say evolution and creation can be compatible. He disagrees. "A lot of people believe   8 that the Bible should be interpreted so that evolution can fit," he observed. "Those people will slide in millions of years in the first few verses of Genesis. I believe that's not theologically correct."

Smith said some people view Genesis as being more metaphorical   9
rather than literal. In their opinion, the six "days" in which Christians say God created the Earth actually symbolize millions of years. Smith sees a problem with that reasoning. "The Bible says six days and in no other place in the Bible does it say 'days' and really mean millions of years. It'll say Jesus was in the tomb for three days, does that mean he was there for three million years? No, it means three days."

Smith thinks that if Christians who believe in evolution would   10
take a look at intelligent design, "a lot of people would change their minds." He added that, in the future, he'd like to see courses offer both theories and allow students to choose which one they want to believe. Graham said her class does not discourage any particular religious views, but that she does ask the students to at least question their beliefs. "I do get the sense that there isn't a forum for the students to engage in the question about evolution versus creationism," she remarked. "Perhaps that's the case, and perhaps we need to address that."

For an annotated excerpt of this essay that highlights Mitchell's writing strategies, see page 386.

 Read It Now: Read more editorials by Mitchell and other Auburn University students at **bedfordstmartins.com/americanow**, Chapter 11.

Vocabulary / Using a Dictionary

1. What does it mean to *misinterpret* something (para. 4)? What other words use the prefix *mis-*?

2. What does it mean to be *metaphorical* (para. 9)? What does it mean to be *literal* (para. 9)? How do these two words relate to each other?

Responding to Words in Context

1. Why does Mitchell use the phrase *scientific theory* (para. 5) instead of just *theory*? Is there a difference?

2. What does it mean to do something *thoroughly* (para. 6)? Why does the author use the phrase *thoroughly examining* instead of just *examining?*

Discussing Main Point and Meaning

1. What, if any, is Mitchell's main thesis statement? What does the main thrust of the essay seem to be?
2. David Smith is quoted as saying that professors "are just trying to find any evidence they can to support" the theory of evolution (para. 3). What kind of impression does this give you, either of the professors spoken of or of David Smith? Do you think that this quote helps or hinders Smith's point?

Examining Sentences, Paragraphs, and Organization

1. How does the author open his essay? Why do you think he does this?
2. In what way does Mitchell incorporate quotations from others? How are they organized? Are they effective? Why or why not?
3. In closing his essay, Mitchell uses two different viewpoints. How is this handled within the paragraph, and what effect does the closing have on you as a reader?

Thinking Critically

1. Mitchell describes two separate stances in this essay — one is scientific, the other religious. Can they be put side by side, or are they not alike enough for such a direct comparison?
2. David Smith states in the essay that there are facts in biology textbooks that are "just wrong." Is this plausible? Why would Smith make this claim?

In-Class Writing Activities

1. In this essay, Associate Professor of Philosophy Jody Graham notes that "some students might have closed off their minds to the theory of evolution" before they even examine the evidence (para. 6). Do you agree? What reasons might people have to

dismiss something out of hand without investigating it first? Think beyond this argument to others you have seen or heard.

2. Consider the proposed idea to have courses offer both the theory of evolution and the idea of intelligent design. Do you agree or disagree with this? Why? Can you think of any problems this idea could create?

ANNOTATION Using Quotations

Two types of quotations are routinely seen in nonfiction. One type, more common in essays and criticism, is the use of a famous or previously published quote. For example, a writer might begin an essay: "As Franklin D. Roosevelt once said, "'We have nothing to fear but fear itself.'" A book like Bartlett's *Familiar Quotations* is a rich source of memorable quotes and has been used by several generations of writers, artists, celebrities, and political figures. More commonly seen in journalism, however, are the quotations gathered from live interviews. In writing news or feature stories, the journalist usually needs to collect interviews from a number of people — experts, eyewitnesses, accident victims, and so on — who will have something relevant to say about a topic. But gathering the interviews is only one part of the process. The writer then needs to integrate the quotations so they work effectively within the body of the essay.

In "Age-Old Debate: Creationist Students in the Science Classroom," Auburn University student **Chase Mitchell** organized his entire piece around two interviews — one with an engineering freshman who accepts intelligent design and the other with a philosophy professor who believes students should be more scientifically open-minded. Note how Mitchell skillfully incorporates quotes from the separate interviews, allowing each person to represent a position. Note, too, that he does so without inserting — either directly or indirectly — his opinions into the essay. The quotations alone drive the essay and in each paragraph supply the momentum. The reader is left with the impression that the two subjects are actually speaking to each other and bouncing thoughts off each other, yet nowhere does Mitchell acknowledge that student and professor are in any way connected outside of the essay.

Mitchell provides the professor's view in her own words, without taking a position himself.

By offering the student's (Smith's) own words, Mitchell puts the two perspectives in conversation with each other.

Creationists use a scientific theory, often referred to as "intelli- 1
gent design," to put a scientific face on their belief that a single
deity is responsible for all life on Earth. Graham pointed out that
some philosophers have said it's futile to try and blend the two.
"Intelligent design is a way to challenge evolution within scientific
parameters," she said, "whereas some people are going to say
biblical accounts aren't even supposed to be in the scientific
methodology, so it's a mistake to think that they're in conflict."

Graham said not all, but some students might have closed off 2
their minds to the theory of evolution without thoroughly examining
the scientific evidence that supports it: "I do think that some students try to hold this intelligent design theory without really trying to
talk about it." But Smith pointed out that he has researched the subject tirelessly, and that he enjoys discussing the topic with his professors. "The creation/evolution debate is something that lights my
fire," he said. "I enjoy it, and I'm really passionate about that."

—From "The Age-Old Debate: Creationist Students in the
Science Classroom" by Chase Mitchell, page 381

G. B. TRUDEAU

Doonesbury, "Uh-Oh . . ."

[THE BOSTON SUNDAY GLOBE / December 18, 2005]

Before You View

Think about the means by which a cartoonist can convey a message compared to a writer. Are there any liberties or restrictions that a cartoonist has to keep in mind? What is Trudeau's take on creationism in the following piece?

G. B. TRUDEAU *developed the comic strip* Doonesbury *while he was a student at Yale University. In 1973 he earned his MFA in graphic design from the Yale School of Art and in 1975 became the first comic strip artist to win a Pulitzer Prize for editorial cartooning—a prize that previously had been awarded only to editorial page cartoonists. Trudeau has been quoted in Richard Saul Wurman's* Follow the Yellow Brick Road *(1992) as saying, "Whether revered or reviled in their lifetimes, history's movers framed their questions in ways that were entirely disrespectful of conventional wisdom. Civilization has always advanced in the shimmering wake of its discontents."*

 See It Now: Check out *Slate*'s archive of *Doonesbury* cartoons at bedfordstmartins.com/americanow, Chapter 11.

Discussing Main Point and Meaning

1. Why does the cartoonist place the evolution versus creation debate in the context of the doctor's office?
2. Where do you think Trudeau stands on the evolution debate? Why?

Examining Details, Imagery, and Design

1. Consider the attitude of the patient. What does it tell you about him?
2. What impression do you have of the doctor? What does that tell you about his position in the matter of the evolution debate?

Thinking Critically

1. Why do you think Trudeau uses TB (tuberculosis) as a means to showcase evolution?
2. What is the doctor implying with his offer to use an older treatment as opposed to a newer one? Why does he say this?

In-Class Writing Activities

1. Consider the points that Trudeau raises in his cartoon. Would these points have been as effective in an essay? Why or why not?
2. Irony is a powerful tool for pointing out problems in arguments. What is irony, and how is it used in this cartoon?

Discussing the Unit

Suggested Topic for Discussion

Do you think that it is possible to have a productive dialogue between both sides of the evolution versus creation debate, or will the same talking points be repeated? What is your opinion on the matter, and how does it fit into the discussion that you have read here and experienced so far? Would you be willing to discuss your opinion with someone who held a different one?

Preparing for Class Discussion

1. The opinions held by the two sides in this debate are not only different sides, they are supported in different ways. Consider how the writers on each side in this argument support their stance. Is there a middle ground for discussion?
2. Why has this debate reached new levels of visibility lately? Do you think that this has made it more or less difficult for professors, scientists, and teachers to engage in it? Does the publicity help or hurt it?

From Discussion to Writing

1. What does *theory* mean, as the term is commonly understood? What is a *scientific theory*? Are the two different? After comparing them, why do you think that this distinction might be important in terms of this debate?
2. What do you think it means for the debate that the popular cartoonist Gary Trudeau chose to make it the subject of one of his Sunday morning pieces? Do you think that it is possible to inject humor into the discussion without offense? Why might this be a good or bad idea?

Topics for Cross-Cultural Discussion

1. Consider the essays in this chapter, as opposed to the cartoon. Can these be thought of as targeting different cultures, appealing to them differently? What are the differences between the two mediums that might be used to appeal to different cultures, and what different cultures might they be targeting?
2. Would you consider the scientific community and the religious community to be different cultures? Why or why not? Do you think that it is possible to bridge the gap between these two groups with essays and cartoons such as those shown in this chapter? What problems do you see between the two?
3. Are countries other than the United States debating creationism versus evolution? If so, what are the main arguments surrounding the debate? What groups hold what positions? How does the climate of the debate compare to that in the United States?

12

Torture: Can It Ever Be Justified?

Americans were shocked in April 2004 when stories and images of prisoner abuse at Iraq's Abu Ghraib prison suddenly exploded in the news after the *New Yorker* magazine broke the story. The abuses at Abu Ghraib stimulated a national debate on torture: Had the United States overstepped the basic humanitarian behavior normally granted toward enemies captured in combat? Did the rights of prisoners of war guaranteed by the Geneva Conventions apply to nonuniformed terrorists? What are permissible and impermissible methods of obtaining information from prisoners? The debate will continue to resonate for some time, as the issues apply not only to the war in Iraq but to future wars that are likely to involve the ambiguous military status of terrorist combatants. The issue goes well beyond politics to the heart of what constitutes moral behavior.

A basic statement forbidding the use of torture in any way, shape, or form was released by the prominent U.S. senator from Arizona, John McCain, in November 2005 (see p. 393). In "Say No to Torture," Dan Mollison, a University of Illinois columnist, examines McCain's proposed amendment to specifically ban "cruel, inhuman, or degrading treatment or punishment" against anyone in the custody of the United States. The Bush White House, which opposed the measure on grounds of national security, backed down when it was obvious the Senate would approve the bill by an overwhelming majority (its final vote was 90 to 9). Although Mollison recognizes the potential military benefits of torture, he ultimately concludes that the "practices raise far too many problems and inconsistencies for them to be continued by the U.S."

The Senate voted on October 5, 2005. On November 21, McCain (who had been a victim of military torture when he was captured by the North Vietnamese during the Vietnam War) published a lead essay in *Newsweek* that fully expressed his views on the illegitimacy of torture. A supporter of the war in Iraq, McCain nevertheless took a critical view of the Bush administration's tolerance for the aggressive interrogation of captured enemy combatants. McCain appeals to both the moral and pragmatic values of Americans, pointing out that torture is unlikely to provide reliable intelligence and that it seriously injures the image of the United States throughout the world. "The mistreatment of prisoners," McCain argues, "harms us more than our enemies."

Few people support the routine use of torture, but how should we behave if faced with the so-called ticking bomb? The noted columnist and TV news commentator Charles Krauthammer says: "Let's take the textbook case." In "The Truth about Torture," he sides with McCain on banning torture in most instances. But he doesn't want to go as far as McCain in making torture absolutely impermissible. Here's how he views Ethics 101: "A terrorist has planted a nuclear bomb in New York City. It will go off in one hour. A million people will die. You capture the terrorist. He knows where it is. He's not talking." In such extreme circumstances, Krauthammer maintains, torture would not only be acceptable, it would be a "moral duty."

"Most people agree that desperate times call for desperate measures," claims the columnist Cathy Young in "Torturing Logic." "But just how desperate can we get?" she wonders as she examines the arguments put forward by McCain and Krauthammer. Although she discovers flaws in both arguments, she believes that it is a better safeguard against the possibility of any form of torture to be absolutely against it than to be prepared to use it in dire circumstances: "If we start with the idea that torture is sometimes acceptable, that slippery slope is going to take us pretty low."

McCain Amendment No. 1977
From SourceWatch
Defense Appropriations Act of 2006; Amendment 1977
From the 2005 Congressional Record; October 5, 2005, Page S11061

The amendment text

(Purpose: Relating to persons under the detention, custody, or control of the United States Government)

At the appropriate place, insert the following:

SEC. __. UNIFORM STANDARDS FOR THE INTERROGATION OF PERSONS UNDER THE DETENTION OF THE DEPARTMENT OF DEFENSE.

(a) In General.—No person in the custody or under the effective control of the Department of Defense or under detention in a Department of Defense facility shall be subject to any treatment or technique of interrogation not authorized by and listed in the United States Army Field Manual on Intelligence Interrogation.

(b) Applicability.—Subsection (a) shall not apply to any person in the custody or under the effective control of the Department of Defense pursuant to a criminal law or immigration law of the United States.

(c) Construction.—Nothing in this section shall be construed to affect the rights under the United States Constitution of any person in the custody or under the physical jurisdiction of the United States.

SEC. __. PROHIBITION ON CRUEL, INHUMAN, OR DEGRADING TREATMENT OR PUNISHMENT OF PERSONS UNDER CUSTODY OR CONTROL OF THE UNITED STATES GOVERNMENT.

(a) In General.—No individual in the custody or under the physical control of the United States Government, regardless of nationality or physical location, shall be subject to cruel, inhuman, or degrading treatment or punishment.

(b) Construction.—Nothing in this section shall be construed to impose any geographical limitation on the applicability of the prohibition against cruel, inhuman, or degrading treatment or punishment under this section.

(c) Limitation on Supersedure.—The provisions of this section shall not be superseded, except by a provision of law enacted after the date of the enactment of this Act which specifically repeals, modifies, or supersedes the provisions of this section.

(d) Cruel, Inhuman, or Degrading Treatment or Punishment Defined.—In this section, the term "cruel, inhuman, or degrading treatment or punishment" means the cruel, unusual, and inhumane treatment or punishment prohibited by the Fifth, Eighth, and Fourteenth Amendments to the Constitution of the United States, as defined in the United States Reservations, Declarations and Understandings to the United Nations Convention Against Torture and Other Forms of Cruel, Inhuman or Degrading Treatment or Punishment done at New York, December 10, 1984.

The Senate voted on the Amendment October 5, 2005, and the result was—yeas 90, nays 9. . . .

DAN MOLLISON

Say No to Torture

[THE DAILY ILLINI, University of Illinois at Urbana–Champaign/December 7, 2005]

Before You Read

Is torture ever justified? What arguments can be used for or against torture? What argument does the author of the following essay put forth, and who might he have in mind as his audience?

Words to Learn

endorse (para. 2): to give approval or support to (v.)

degrading (para. 2): lowering in dignity, dishonoring, or disgracing (adj.)

veto (para. 2): to refuse; to override (as in the president's power to prevent the enactment of a legislative bill) (v.)

despicable (para. 3): deserving of contempt or scorn (adj.)

inmate (para. 4): a person who is confined or held prisoner (n.)

intelligence (para. 5): information (in this case, information useful to the government) (n.)

recanted (para. 5): made a formal retraction of a statement (v.)

DAN MOLLISON *is a senior at the University of Illinois at Urbana–Champaign majoring in English and a frequent contributor to the* Daily Illini. *He was a weekly opinion columnist for the paper when it published "Say No to Torture." Mollison, who wrote in response to the news of the prisoner abuse at Abu Ghraib, says, "I wanted those who read this column to think about what justice means to them, and to consider the responsibility that is entailed in maintaining it." His advice to fellow writers: "Learn how to think for yourself, how to critically examine what you perceive, and the rest will flow easily and effortlessly. Never stray from doing what you think is right."* For a "Student Writer at Work" interview with Mollison, see page 400.

In our twelve years of school, many of us have begun each school   1
day by reciting the Pledge of Allegiance. The words of the Pledge
have been drilled into us. But given the recent debates over U.S. torture practices against terrorists, it seems that its message of "liberty
and justice for all" has not stuck.

Senator John McCain (R-Arizona), a former victim of torture at   2
the hands of the North Vietnamese, refused on December 4 [2005] to
back down from his demand that the White House endorse his proposed ban on the use of torture against terrorists. McCain's measure,
which is attached as an amendment to a defense bill, includes specific
language banning "cruel, inhuman, or degrading treatment or punishment" against any person in U.S. custody. The White House first
responded by threatening to veto the bill, citing the importance of national security. But after the Senate approved McCain's measure by a
vote of 90 to 9, the White House began to seek a compromise.

While it can be difficult to see how torture can be justified, it's   3
understandable that Bush would be hesitant to expand torture laws.
The U.S. has used torture as a means of extracting information from
war prisoners for decades, and these meth-
ods have proven to be very successful. Like it

There's no question that or not, there's no question that America's
America's use of torture use of torture has strengthened our national
has strengthened our security. It's also important to remember
national security. that the victims that we're talking about here
aren't exactly following the same "rules of
war" as the rest of the international community; they have had no
hesitation in targeting and killing innocent people, including children.
But regardless of torture's benefits for Americans and of the despicable nature of terrorists, these practices raise far too many problems
and inconsistencies for them to be continued by the U.S.

One of torture's fundamental issues is that it occurs in uncon-   4
trolled environments by government agents who might not always act
in the interests of the people. Because torture is never "officially endorsed" by the government, the U.S. can't have ultimate authority
over who is tortured, why they're tortured, and what methods are
being employed against them. The lack of protocol over torture practices leaves serious room for abuse by U.S. agents. How can we know
that a soldier isn't choosing to torture an inmate out of racism or a
feeling of religious superiority rather than a desire to extract information from him? Allowing U.S. regulations on torture practices to continue to remain ambiguous makes torture for reasons other than national security far too easy to achieve.

There is also some doubt regarding how much we can trust the va- 5
lidity of information gathered through torture. As McCain noted, some
of the intelligence "used in one of the presi-
dent's speeches . . . concerning the threat of
weapons of mass destruction . . . was later recanted." This apparent reference to the false
WMD intelligence gathered from a detainee
at Guantanamo Bay is not only poignant but
has some logic behind it. Part of the training
included in terrorist training camps is brainwashing. Terrorists are led to believe that the
West is evil, and that the holiest act they can
perform is to sacrifice their own lives in an effort to kill Westerners.
Would a terrorist—who is so willing to sacrifice his life for America's
destruction—give reliable information while being tortured? In his
eyes, to do so would mean "siding with the devil." I'm not an expert
on intelligence gathered through torture, but it seems to me that it
would be very difficult to achieve reliable results.

> *It is entirely
> hypocritical for
> a nation founded
> on freedom and
> equality to torture
> those in custody.*

Despite the significant advantages that the torture of terrorists can 6
offer us, it is entirely hypocritical for a nation founded on principles of
freedom and equality to torture those in its custody. Holding ourselves
to a higher standard than terrorists may be
frustrating, especially when we remember the
innocent lives that have been lost at their
hands, but to do otherwise only lowers us to
their level. America needs to stay true to the
ethical principles we so openly embrace.

> For an annotated excerpt of
> this essay that highlights
> Mollison's writing strategies,
> see page 399.

 Read It Now: Read more editorials by Mollison and other University of
Illinois students at **bedfordstmartins.com/americanow**, Chapter 12.

Vocabulary / Using a Dictionary

1. What does it mean to *justify* something (para. 3)? What does the
   word *justify* have to do with the word *justice?*
2. What is a *sacrifice* (para. 5)? What does this word have to do
   with holiness?
3. How is the word *extract* (para. 3) different from the word *obtain?*

Responding to Words in Context

1. What does it mean to have something *drilled into* you (para. 1)?
   What does it mean to say this about the Pledge of Allegiance?

2. What makes something *poignant* (para. 5)? Why does Mollison distinguish poignancy from logic (para. 5)?
3. What words does Mollison use in relation to terrorists? How do these choices affect his argument?

Discussing Main Point and Meaning

1. What are the core arguments that Mollison makes against using torture? What are they based on?
2. How often does the author mention ethics in the essay? Where is it mentioned, and in what context?

Examining Sentences, Paragraphs, and Organization

1. Consider the use of quotations in the essay. How are they used? Are they used differently throughout?
2. Why does the author open his essay with a reference to the Pledge of Allegiance?
3. How does the author organize the arguments that he uses? Are they handled well? Were you surprised by his concluding paragraph? Why or why not?

Thinking Critically

1. Why do you think that the author uses quotations around the phrase *rules of war* (para. 3)? What does this imply?
2. How does the author reconcile the statement that torture has been used successfully in the past with the thesis that it cannot be used now?
3. Is it true, as Mollison states, that "torture has strengthened our national security" (para. 3)? Explain.

In-Class Writing Activities

1. Do you find the arguments raised in this essay compelling? Why or why not?
2. Given that the main body of the essay contains entirely pragmatic (as opposed to moral or ethical) arguments, why do you think the author closes the essay by appealing to an ethical point of view? Is this effective?

ANNOTATION: Establishing a Main Point

As we learn to express our opinions clearly and effectively, we need to ask ourselves a relatively simple question: Will my readers understand my *main point?* In composition, a main point is sometimes called a *thesis* or *thesis statement.* It is often a sentence that summarizes our central idea or position. It need not include any factual proof or supporting evidence — that is supplied in the body of the essay — but it should represent a general statement that clearly shows where we stand on an issue. Although main points are often found in opening paragraphs, they can also appear later in an essay, especially when the writer wants to set the stage for his or her opinion by opening with a relevant quotation, a topical reference, or an emotional appeal. This is the way University of Illinois student **Dan Mollison** decides to express his main point in **"Say No to Torture."** He begins his essay with a well-known quotation and then turns in the next paragraph to a specific political incident before clearly stating his position at the end of his third paragraph. Note that before he states his position, he first acknowledges two arguments made by those who would support the use of torture in time of war. By claiming that (a) even if torture can help us and (b) even if our enemies themselves are guilty of it, the United States should not continue the practice, Mollison makes his position clear and adds considerable weight to his central point. Once he establishes his point, he then goes on to discuss the "problems and inconsistencies" raised by the practice of torture.

In his first two paragraphs Mollison notes differing views held by Senator McCain and the White House.

He then acknowledges "benefits" of torture before offering his anti-torture stance.

While it can be difficult to see how torture can be justified, it's understandable that Bush would be hesitant to expand torture laws. The U.S. has used torture as a means of extracting information from war prisoners for decades, and these methods have proven to be very successful. Like it or not, there's no question that America's use of torture has strengthened our national security. It's also important to remember that the victims that we're talking about here aren't exactly following the same "rules of war" as the rest of the international community; they have had no hesitation in targeting and killing innocent people, including children. But regardless of torture's benefits for Americans and the despicable nature of terrorists, these practices raise far too many problems and inconsistencies for them to be continued by the U.S.

— From "Say No to Torture," by Dan Mollison, Page 395

Student Writer at Work: Dan Mollison
On Writing "Say No to Torture"

Q: What motivated you to write this column?

A: I wrote this piece as the nation was grappling with news about the torture practices taking place at Abu Ghraib — I thought that it might be helpful to offer a balanced look at the national dialogue that was happening at that time. This subject intrigued me because it revolves around how willing we are as a nation to abide by our own principles of freedom and justice when temptation arises.

Q: How would you describe your political opinions?

A: In recent years extremist political ideologies have been widely adopted on both ends of the spectrum. Because I believe that many of the solutions to our nation's problems lie in the center, I have made an effort in my columns to fully understand both sides of an issue before developing my own view. It's sad that efforts to "bridge the gap" in this way have been dwindling, because both liberals and conservatives have very valid arguments to offer regarding most of the major issues that we debate as a nation.

Q: Describe how you went about writing this piece.

A: This column took me about six hours to write. I tend to write very slowly, sentence by sentence, without continuing to a new idea until the one I'm working on feels "tight" enough to me. When I completed the first draft of the column, I e-mailed it to the opinion editor, and then we met to go over it.

Q: What were your goals when you revised?

A: I knew that the more strongly I crafted my argument, the more people would be engaged to think about the issue I was addressing. And that's aside from the fact that it was being published in the *newspaper:* imagine what it's like to have your intimate opinions revealed to everyone you know, and thousands of others that you don't?! I wanted to be sure that readers of my column knew exactly what I was saying, because if I screwed up I could have ended up looking like a real moron!

Q: Do you generally show your writing to friends or bounce your ideas off others?

A: At the time I wrote this, I had a poor unfortunate roommate that I bothered occasionally with initial drafts of my columns. Other than that, I mainly worked alone, and then waited until after my columns were published in the paper to ask my friends, "So, what did you think?" I do recall, however, that I had some e-mail correspondence with my father as I was gathering information for this column. This discussion really helped me develop my point of view about American-endorsed torture, because my father (who is conserva-

tive) was able to offer his differing perspective regarding why torture is important for national security. He helped me understand how our country
gains from torture, which then enabled me to create the balance in my column I was looking for.

JOHN McCAIN

Torture's Terrible Toll

[NEWSWEEK/MSNBC.COM/November 21, 2005]

Before You Read

How does knowing that John McCain was a prisoner of war affect
your reading of his argument against torture? On what points does
he agree with the current administration? With what points does he
take issue?

Words to Learn

partisan (para. 1): devoted to or
biased toward a group or cause
(adj.)
tenacious (para. 1): holding persis-
tently to something (adj.)

atrocity (para. 1): an appalling or
atrocious act (n.)
vigilance (para. 1): watchfulness (n.)
latitude (para. 2): freedom from
normal restraints (n.)

JOHN MCCAIN, *U.S. senator from Arizona since 1987 and Republican presidential candidate in the 2000 election, is a veteran of the Vietnam War. While
serving as a pilot in the Navy, McCain was shot down and, for over five years,
held as a prisoner of war (POW) and tortured in North Vietnam. Although his
captives offered to release him when they found out that McCain was the son of
the Pacific Command Admiral in charge of the U.S. war effort in Vietnam,
McCain refused to be sent home because of his belief that no POW should go
home unless all POWs could. He was finally released in 1973. In an effort to
prohibit the inhumane treatment of prisoners, McCain sponsored the McCain
Detainee Amendment to the Department of Defense Authorization bill.*

nefarious (para. 2): extremely
wicked (adj.)
imperatives (para. 2): obligations;
duties (n.)
coerced (para. 3): forced (v.)
Geneva Conventions (para. 3): a
series of agreements first formulated at an international convention held in Geneva, Switzerland,
in 1864, establishing rules for the
treatment of prisoners of war, the
sick, and the wounded. (n.)
reciprocity (para. 4): mutual depen-
dence, action, or influence; an
understanding between countries
or institutions that if one party
acts a certain way, the others will
too (n.)
malevolence (para. 5): ill will; mal-
ice; hatred (n.)

disseminated (para. 5): spread
about; dispersed (v.)
valiant (para. 6): brave; heroic (adj.)
inalienable (para. 7): absolute;
incapable of being surrendered
or transferred (adj.)
abhorrent (para. 8): disgusting;
loathsome; detestable (adj.)
imminent (para. 10): likely to occur
at any moment (adj.)
in extremis (para. 11): in extreme or
grave circumstances (Latin) (adv.)
contingency (para. 11): an event,
such as an emergency, that is
possible but not certain (n.)
onerous (para. 15): oppressive;
excessively burdensome (adj.)

The debate over the treatment of enemy prisoners, like so much 1
of the increasingly overcharged partisan debate over the war in Iraq
and the global war against terrorists, has occasioned many unserious
and unfair charges about the administration's intentions and motives.
With all the many competing demands for their attention, President
Bush and Vice President Cheney have remained admirably tenacious
in their determination to prevent terrorists from inflicting another
atrocity on the American people, whom they are sworn to protect. It
is certainly fair to credit their administration's vigilance as a substan-
tial part of the reason that we have not experienced another terrorist
attack on American soil since September 11, 2001.

It is also quite fair to attribute the administration's position— 2
that U.S. interrogators be allowed latitude in their treatment of
enemy prisoners that might offend American values—to the president's and vice president's appropriate concern for acquiring actionable intelligence that could prevent attacks on our soldiers or our al-
lies or on the American people. And it is quite unfair to assume some
nefarious purpose informs their intentions. They bear the greatest responsibility for the security of American lives and interests. I understand and respect their motives just as I admire the seriousness and
patriotism of their resolve. But I do, respectfully, take issue with the

position that the demands of this war require us to accord a lower station to the moral imperatives that should govern our conduct in war and peace when they come in conflict with the unyielding inhumanity of our vicious enemy.

Obviously, to defeat our enemies we need intelligence, but intelligence that is reliable. We should not torture or treat inhumanely terrorists we have captured. The abuse of prisoners harms, not helps, our war effort. In my experience, abuse of prisoners often produces bad intelligence because under torture a person will say anything he thinks his captors want to hear—whether it is true or false—if he believes it will relieve his suffering. I was once physically coerced to provide my enemies with the names of the members of my flight squadron, information that had little if any value to my enemies as actionable intelligence. But I did not refuse, or repeat my insistence that I was required under the Geneva Conventions to provide my captors only with my name, rank and serial number. Instead, I gave them the names of the Green Bay Packers' offensive line,

3

> *The abuse of prisoners harms, not helps, our war effort.*

knowing that providing them false information was sufficient to suspend the abuse. It seems probable to me that the terrorists we interro-
gate under less than humane standards of treatment are also likely to
resort to deceptive answers that are perhaps less provably false than
that which I once offered.

Our commitment to basic humanitarian values affects—in
part—the willingness of other nations to do the same. Mistreatment
of enemy prisoners endangers our own troops who might someday be
held captive. While some enemies, and Al
Qaeda surely, will never be bound by the
principle of reciprocity, we should have concern for those Americans captured by more
traditional enemies, if not in this war then in
the next. Until about 1970, North Vietnam
ignored its obligations not to mistreat the
Americans they held prisoner, claiming that
we were engaged in an unlawful war against them and thus not
entitled to the protections of the Geneva Conventions. But when their
abuses became widely known and incited unfavorable international
attention, they substantially decreased their mistreatment of us.
Again, Al Qaeda will never be influenced by international sensibilities
or open to moral suasion. If ever the term "sociopath" applied to
anyone, it applies to them. But I doubt they will be the last enemy
America will fight, and we should not undermine today our defense
of international prohibitions against torture and inhumane treatment
of prisoners of war that we will need to rely on in the future.

To prevail in this war we need more than victories on the battlefield. This is a war of ideas, a struggle to advance freedom in the face
of terror in places where oppressive rule has bred the malevolence
that creates terrorists. Prisoner abuses exact a terrible toll on us in
this war of ideas. They inevitably become public, and when they do
they threaten our moral standing, and expose us to false but widely
disseminated charges that democracies are no more inherently idealis-
tic and moral than other regimes. This is an existential fight, to be
sure. If they could, Islamic extremists who resort to terror would destroy us utterly. But to defeat them we must prevail in our defense of
American political values as well. The mistreatment of prisoners
greatly injures that effort.

The mistreatment of prisoners harms us more than our enemies. I
don't think I'm naive about how terrible are the wages of war, and
how terrible are the things that must be done to wage it successfully.

> Mistreatment of enemy
> prisoners endangers our
> own troops who might
> someday be held
> captive.

4

5

6

It is an awful business, and no matter how noble the cause for which it is fought, no matter how valiant their service, many veterans spend much of their subsequent lives trying to forget not only what was done to them, but some of what had to be done by them to prevail.

I don't mourn the loss of any terrorist's life. Nor do I care if in   7
the course of serving their ignoble cause they suffer great harm. They have pledged their lives to the intentional destruction of innocent lives, and they have earned their terrible punishment in this life and the next. What I do mourn is what we lose when by official policy or official neglect we allow, confuse, or encourage our soldiers to forget that best sense of ourselves, that which is our greatest strength—that we are different and better than our enemies, that we fight for an idea, not a tribe, not a land, not a king, not a twisted interpretation of an ancient religion, but for an idea that all men are created equal and endowed by their Creator with inalienable rights.

Now, in this war, our liberal notions are put to the test. Ameri-   8
cans of good will, all patriots, argue about what is appropriate and necessary to combat this unconventional enemy. Those of us who feel that in this war, as in past wars, Americans should not compromise our values must answer those Americans who believe that a less rigorous application of those values is regrettably necessary to prevail over a uniquely abhorrent and dangerous enemy. Part of our disagreement is definitional. Some view more coercive interrogation tactics as something short of torture but worry that they might be subject to challenge under the "no cruel, inhumane or degrading" standard. Others, including me, believe that both the prohibition on torture and the cruel, inhumane and degrading standard must remain intact. When we relax that standard, it is nearly unavoidable that some objectionable practices will be allowed as something less than torture because they do not risk life and limb or do not cause very serious physical pain.

For instance, there has been considerable press attention to a tac-   9
tic called "waterboarding," where a prisoner is restrained and blindfolded while an interrogator pours water on his face and into his mouth—causing the prisoner to believe he is being drowned. He isn't, of course; there is no intention to injure him physically. But if you gave people who have suffered abuse as prisoners a choice between a beating and a mock execution, many, including me, would choose a beating. The effects of most beatings heal. The memory of an execution will haunt someone for a very long time and damage his or her psyche in ways that may never heal. In my view, to make

> To make someone believe that you are killing him by drowning is no different than holding a pistol to his head and firing a blank.

someone believe that you are killing him by drowning is no different than holding a pistol to his head and firing a blank. I believe that it is torture, very exquisite torture.

Those who argue the necessity of some abuses raise an important dilemma as their most compelling rationale: the ticking-time-bomb scenario. What do we do if we capture a terrorist who we have sound reasons to believe possesses specific knowledge of an imminent terrorist attack?

In such an urgent and rare instance, an interrogator might well try extreme measures to extract information that could save lives. Should he do so, and thereby save an American city or prevent another 9/11, authorities and the public would surely take this into account when judging his actions and recognize the extremely dire situation which he confronted. But I don't believe this scenario requires us to write into law an exception to our treaty and moral obligations that would permit cruel, inhumane and degrading treatment. To carve out legal exemptions to this basic principle of human rights risks opening the door to abuse as a matter of course, rather than a standard violated truly *in extremis*. It is far better to embrace a standard that might be violated in extraordinary circumstances than to lower our standards to accommodate a remote contingency, confusing personnel in the field and sending precisely the wrong message abroad about America's purposes and practices.

The state of Israel, no stranger to terrorist attacks, has faced this dilemma, and in 1999 the Israeli Supreme Court declared cruel, inhumane and degrading treatment illegal. "A democratic, freedom-loving society," the court wrote, "does not accept that investigators use any means for the purpose of uncovering truth. The rules pertaining to investigators are important to a democratic state. They reflect its character."

I've been asked often where did the brave men I was privileged to serve with in North Vietnam draw the strength to resist to the best of their abilities the cruelties inflicted on them by our enemies. They drew strength from their faith in each other, from their faith in God and from their faith in our country. Our enemies didn't adhere to the Geneva Conventions. Many of my comrades were subjected to very cruel, very inhumane and degrading treatment, a few of them unto death. But every one of us—every single one of us—knew and took great strength from the belief that we were different from our enemies, that we were better than them, that we, if the roles were reversed, would not disgrace ourselves by committing or approving such mistreatment of them. That faith was indispensable not only to our survival, but to our attempts to return home with honor. For without our honor, our homecoming would have had little value to us.

The enemies we fight today hold our liberal values in contempt,   14
as they hold in contempt the international conventions that enshrine them. I know that. But we are better than them, and we are stronger for our faith. And we will prevail. It is indispensable to our success in this war that those we ask to fight it know that in the discharge of their dangerous responsibilities to their country they are never expected to forget that they are Americans, and the valiant defenders of a sacred idea of how nations should govern their own affairs and their relations with others — even our enemies.

Those who return to us and those who give their lives for us are   15
entitled to that honor. And those of us who have given them this onerous duty are obliged by our history, and the many terrible sacrifices that have been made in our defense, to make clear to them that they need not risk their or their country's honor to prevail; that they are always — through the violence, chaos and heartache of war, through deprivation and cruelty and loss — they are always, always, Americans, and different, better and stronger than those who would destroy us.

Web **Read It Now:** Read more essays by Senator McCain and learn his views on a full range of issues at **bedfordstmartins.com/americanow**, Chapter 12.

Vocabulary / Using a Dictionary

1. What does the word *nefarious* (para. 2) have to do with *divinity*?

2. What is the Latin root of the word *disseminate* (para. 5)? What does each part of the root term mean when you take it apart?

3. The word *ignoble* (para. 7) first emerged some time between the years 1400 and 1450. Why do you think this word may have become common at that time?

4. What does the word *alienable* (para. 7) have to do with the concepts of selling and ownership?

5. What is the relationship between the word *onerous* (para. 15) and *onus*?

6. What does it mean to *enshrine* (para. 14) something? What is the root of this word?

Responding to Words in Context

1. What does McCain mean by *actionable intelligence* (para. 2)? Why do you think he chooses those words?

2. Why would McCain use the phrase *vicious enemy* (para. 2) as opposed to just *enemy*? Is there a difference between the two terms?

3. What is the effect of McCain's use of the word *respectfully* in paragraph 2? What might this indicate about the primary audience he wants to reach with the essay?

4. Make a list of the words that McCain associates with democracy and fair treatment of prisoners. How do these terms contrast with those he uses to describe torture and abuse? Where does he echo the Declaration of Independence and the Gettysburg Address?

5. In paragraph 8, what does McCain mean by *liberal notions*?

6. How can a disagreement be *definitional* (para. 8)?

Discussing Main Point and Meaning

1. What does McCain mourn for (see para. 7)? What doesn't he mourn for? Why would he choose to phrase his feelings in such a way?

2. What specific evidence does McCain offer for his arguments?

3. Is McCain sympathetic or unsympathetic to the position of the president and the vice president in terms of their level of responsibility? Explain.

4. Why does McCain choose to describe and discuss the tactic known as waterboarding (para. 9)?

5. Does McCain think torture is ever justifiable (see para. 11)? Explain.

6. Based on this essay, what is McCain's attitude toward religion?

7. According to McCain, what should set American soldiers apart from enemy soldiers?

Examining Sentences, Paragraphs, and Organization

1. How does McCain work his personal experiences into the essay? Does he do so effectively?

2. Locate the thesis statement in each of McCain's paragraphs. Is his presentation of thesis sentences consistent? How do these statements contribute to the overall clarity of the essay?

3. Describe McCain's tone in this essay and identify a sentence that supports your description.

4. How does McCain close his essay? What points does he end on, and how do they relate to the rest of the piece?

5. How are the arguments that McCain uses organized? Are they arranged well? Why or why not?

Thinking Critically

1. Consider why McCain might feel the need to speak out on this topic. Do his experiences cause you to lend his words more or less weight? Explain.

2. What message does McCain send by bluntly referring to Al Qaeda using the term *sociopath* (para. 4)? What other terms might he have used?

3. Based on your reading of this essay, how does McCain see the United States's role in the world? Support your answer with specific evidence from the essay.

4. Do you believe that the United States is engaged in a "war of ideas," as McCain writes in paragraph 5?

In-Class Writing Activities

1. Discuss the range of arguments that McCain raises to prove his point. What kind of range do they have? Why do you think he chose the arguments that he did?

2. McCain specifies that adhering to our values and refraining from torture will not have the same effect on Al Qaeda that it did on the North Vietnamese. What arguments does he use to convince readers that we should refrain from torture regardless of this? Are they convincing enough to surmount this problem?

CHARLES KRAUTHAMMER

The Truth about Torture

[THE WEEKLY STANDARD/December 5, 2005]

Before You Read

Can torture yield useful information? In what circumstances, if any, should the use of torture be considered?

Words to Learn

pieties (para. 1): statements or acts that seem to be motivated by goodness but are in fact hypocritical or marked by falseness; affectations of devotion, saintliness, holiness (n.)

conviction (para. 2): firmly held viewpoint (n.)

humane (para. 4): characterized by compassion and sympathy (adj.)

hors de combat (para. 4): French for "out of the fight"; disabled (adj.)

combatant (para. 5): fighter; a person who takes part in armed strife (n.)

detainees (para. 6): people held in custody or confinement (n.)

deterrent (para. 6): hindrance; impediment (n.)

scrupulousness (para. 8): conforming to high standards (n.)

tentativeness (para. 11): hesitancy; uncertainty (n.)

miscreant (para. 11): a vicious or depraved person; villain (n.)

dereliction (para. 17): deliberate or conscious neglect (n.)

mellifluent (para. 17): smooth-talking (adj.)

metastasized (para. 18): spread destructively (v.)

countenance (para. 22): to permit or tolerate (v.)

ghoulish (para. 24): strangely diabolical or cruel; morbid; showing a fascination with death, disease, and so on (adj.)

posit (para. 25): to suggest; to propose as an explanation (v.)

CHARLES KRAUTHAMMER, *a well-known neoconservative, is a prize-winning weekly columnist for the* Washington Post. *His writing also appears in* Time *magazine, the* Weekly Standard, *and the* New Republic, *and he is a regular guest commentator on Fox News. In the following piece written in response to the controversy surrounding the McCain Detainee Amendment, Krauthammer argues that a ban on torture must allow for some necessary exceptions.*

Rubicon (para. 29): point of no
return (n.)
jihadist (para. 30): a fighter in a
holy war; a person involved in an
emotional crusade for an idea or
principle (n.)
sadomasochism (para. 32): an interaction in which one person enjoys inflicting pain on another
who enjoys experiencing pain (n.)
post facto (para. 32): Latin for
"after the fact" (adj.)
superfluous (para. 35): unnecessary
or excessive (adj.)
preening (para. 41): showing off;
gloating (n.)

During the last few weeks in Washington the pieties about tor-   1
ture have lain so thick in the air that it has been impossible to have a
reasoned discussion. The McCain amendment that would ban "cruel,
inhuman, or degrading" treatment of any prisoner by any agent of
the United States sailed through the Senate by a vote of 90–9. The
Washington establishment remains stunned that nine such retrograde, morally inert persons—let alone senators—could be found in
this noble capital.

Now, John McCain has great moral authority on this issue, hav-   2
ing heroically borne torture at the hands of the North Vietnamese.
McCain has made fine arguments in defense of his position. And
McCain is acting out of the deep and honorable conviction that what
he is proposing is not only right but is in the best interest of the
United States. His position deserves respect. But that does not mean,
as seems to be the assumption in Washington today, that a critical
analysis of his "no torture, ever" policy is beyond the pale.

Let's begin with a few analytic distinctions. For the purpose of   3
torture and prisoner maltreatment, there are three kinds of war
prisoners:

First, there is the ordinary soldier caught on the field of battle.   4
There is no question that he is entitled to humane treatment. Indeed,
we have no right to disturb a hair on his head. His detention has but
a single purpose: to keep him hors de combat. The proof of that
proposition is that if there were a better way to keep him off the
battlefield that did not require his detention, we would let him go. Indeed, during one year of the Civil War, the two sides did try an alternative. They mutually "paroled" captured enemy soldiers, i.e.,
released them to return home on the pledge that they would not take
up arms again. (The experiment failed for a foreseeable reason: cheat-
ing. Grant found that some paroled Confederates had reenlisted.)

Because the only purpose of detention in these circumstances is to   5
prevent the prisoner from becoming a combatant again, he is entitled
to all the protections and dignity of an ordinary domestic prisoner—

412   Torture: Can It Ever Be Justified?

indeed, more privileges, because, unlike the domestic prisoner, he has committed no crime. He merely had the misfortune to enlist on the other side of a legitimate war. He is therefore entitled to many of the privileges enjoyed by an ordinary citizen—the right to send correspondence, to engage in athletic activity and intellectual pursuits, to receive allowances from relatives—except, of course, for the freedom to leave the prison.

Second, there is the captured terrorist. A terrorist is by profession, indeed by definition, an unlawful combatant: He lives outside the laws of war because he does not wear a uniform, he hides among civilians, and he deliberately targets innocents. He is entitled to no protections whatsoever. People seem to think that the postwar Geneva Conventions were written only to protect detainees. In fact, their deeper purpose was to provide a deterrent to the kind of barbaric treatment of civilians that had become so horribly apparent during the first half of the 20th century, and in particular, during the Second World War. The idea was to deter the abuse of civilians by promising combatants who treated noncombatants well that they themselves would be treated according to a code of dignity if captured—and, crucially, that they would be denied the protections of that code if they broke the laws of war and abused civilians themselves.

Breaking the laws of war and abusing civilians are what, to understate the matter vastly, terrorists do for a living. They are entitled, therefore, to nothing. Anyone who blows up a car bomb in a market deserves to spend the rest of his life roasting on a spit over an open fire. But we don't do that because we do not descend to the level of our enemy. We don't do that because, unlike him, we are civilized. Even though terrorists are entitled to no humane treatment, we give it to them because it is in our nature as a moral and humane people. And when on rare occasions we fail to do that, as has occurred in several of the fronts of the war on terror, we are duly disgraced.

> Even though terrorists are entitled to no humane treatment, we give it to them because it is in our nature as moral and humane people.

The norm, however, is how the majority of prisoners at Guantanamo have been treated. We give them three meals a day, superior medical care, and provision to pray five times a day. Our scrupulousness extends even to providing them with their own Korans, which is the only reason alleged abuses of the Koran at Guantanamo ever became an issue. That we should have provided those who kill innocents in the name of Islam with precisely the document that inspires their barbarism is a sign of the absurd lengths to which we often go in extending undeserved humanity to terrorist prisoners.

Third, there is the terrorist with information. Here the issue of torture gets complicated and the easy pieties don't so easily apply. Let's take the textbook case. Ethics 101: A terrorist has planted a nuclear bomb in New York City. It will go off in one hour. A million people will die. You capture the terrorist. He knows where it is. He's not talking.

Question: If you have the slightest belief that hanging this man by his thumbs will get you the information to save a million people, are you permitted to do it?

Now, on most issues regarding torture, I confess tentativeness and uncertainty. But on this issue, there can be no uncertainty: Not only is it permissible to hang this miscreant by his thumbs. It is a moral duty.

Yes, you say, but that's an extreme and very hypothetical case. Well, not as hypothetical as you think. Sure, the (nuclear) scale is hypothetical, but in the age of the car- and suicide-bomber, terrorists are often captured who have just set a car bomb to go off or sent a suicide bomber out to a coffee shop, and you only have minutes to find out where the attack is to take place. This "hypothetical" is common enough that the Israelis have a term for precisely that situation: the ticking time bomb problem.

And even if the example I gave were entirely hypothetical, the conclusion—yes, in this case even torture is permissible—is telling because it establishes the principle: Torture is not always impermissible. However rare the cases, there are circumstances in which, by any rational moral calculus, torture not only would be permissible but would be required (to acquire life-saving information). And once you've established the principle, to paraphrase George Bernard Shaw, all that's left to haggle about is the price. In the case of torture, that means that the argument is not whether torture is ever permissible, but when—i.e., under what obviously stringent circumstances: how big, how imminent, how preventable the ticking time bomb.

There are circumstances in which torture not only would be permissible but required.

That is why the McCain amendment, which by mandating "torture never" refuses even to recognize the legitimacy of any moral calculus, cannot be right. There must be exceptions. The real argument should be over what constitutes a legitimate exception.

Let's take an example that is far from hypothetical. You capture   15
Khalid Sheikh Mohammed in Pakistan. He not only has already killed
innocents; he is deeply involved in the planning for the present and future killing of innocents. He not only was the architect of the 9/11 attack that killed nearly three thousand people in one day, most of them
dying a terrible, agonizing, indeed tortured death, but as the top Al
Qaeda planner and logistical expert he also knows a lot about terror
attacks to come. He knows plans, identities, contacts, materials, cell
locations, safe houses, cased targets, etc. What do you do with him?

We have recently learned that since 9/11 the United States has   16
maintained a series of "black sites" around the world, secret detention centers where presumably high-level terrorists like Khalid Sheikh
Mohammed have been imprisoned. The world is scandalized. Black
sites? Secret detention? Jimmy Carter calls this "a profound and radical change in the . . . moral values of our country." The Council of
Europe demands an investigation, calling the claims "extremely worrying." Its human rights commissioner declares "such practices" to
constitute "a serious human rights violation, and further proof of the
crisis of values" that has engulfed the war on terror. The gnashing of
teeth and rending of garments has been considerable.

I myself have not gnashed a single tooth. My garments remain   17
entirely unrent. Indeed, I feel reassured. It would be a gross dereliction of duty for any government not to keep Khalid Sheikh
Mohammed isolated, disoriented, alone, despairing, cold and sleepless, in some godforsaken hidden location in order to find out what
he knew about plans for future mass murder. What are we supposed
to do? Give him a nice cell in a warm Manhattan prison, complete
with Miranda rights, a mellifluent lawyer, and his own website? Are
not those the kinds of courtesies we extended to the 1993 World
Trade Center bombers, then congratulated ourselves on how we
"brought to justice" those responsible for an attack that barely failed
to kill tens of thousands of Americans, only to discover a decade later
that we had accomplished nothing—indeed, that some of the
disclosures at the trial had helped Osama bin Laden avoid U.S.
surveillance?

Have we learned nothing from 9/11? Are we prepared to go back   18
with complete amnesia to the domestic-crime model of dealing with
terrorists, which allowed us to sleepwalk through the nineties while
Al Qaeda incubated and grew and metastasized unmolested until on
9/11 it finished what the first World Trade Center bombers had
begun?

Let's assume (and hope) that Khalid Sheikh Mohammed has been 19
kept in one of these black sites, say, a cell somewhere in Romania,
held entirely incommunicado and subjected to the kind of "coercive
interrogation" that I described above. McCain has been going around
praising the Israelis as the model of how to deal with terrorism and
prevent terrorist attacks. He does so because in 1999 the Israeli
Supreme Court outlawed all torture in the course of interrogation.
But in reality, the Israeli case is far more complicated. And the complications reflect precisely the dilemmas regarding all coercive interrogation, the weighing of the lesser of two evils: the undeniable inhumanity of torture versus the abdication of the duty to protect the
victims of a potentially preventable mass murder.

In a summary of Israel's policies, Glenn Frankel of the *Washing-* 20
ton Post noted that the 1999 Supreme Court ruling struck down secret guidelines established 12 years earlier that allowed interrogators
to use the kind of physical and psychological pressure I described in
imagining how KSM might be treated in America's "black sites."

"But after the second Palestinian uprising broke out a year later, 21
and especially after a devastating series of suicide bombings of pas-
senger buses, cafes and other civilian targets," writes Frankel, citing
human rights lawyers and detainees, "Israel's internal security service, known as the Shin Bet or the Shabak, returned to physical
coercion as a standard practice." Not only do the techniques used
"command widespread support from the Israeli public," but "Israeli
prime ministers and justice ministers with a variety of political
views," including the most conciliatory and liberal, have defended
these techniques "as a last resort in preventing terrorist attacks."

Which makes McCain's position on torture incoherent. If this 22
kind of coercive interrogation were imposed on any inmate in the
American prison system, it would immediately be declared cruel and
unusual, and outlawed. How can he oppose these practices, which
the Israelis use, and yet hold up Israel as a model for dealing with terrorists? Or does he countenance this kind of interrogation in extreme
circumstances — in which case, what is left of his categorical opposition to inhuman treatment of any kind?

But let us push further into even more unpleasant territory, the 23
territory that lies beyond mere coercive interrogation and beyond
McCain's self-contradictions. How far are we willing to go?

This "going beyond" need not be cinematic and ghoulish. (Jay 24
Leno once suggested "duct tape" for Khalid Sheikh Mohammed.)
Consider, for example, injection with sodium pentathol. (Colloquially

known as "truth serum," it is nothing of the sort. It is a barbiturate whose purpose is to sedate. Its effects are much like that of alcohol: disinhibiting the higher brain centers to make someone more likely to disclose information or thoughts that might otherwise be guarded.) Forcible sedation is a clear violation of bodily integrity. In a civilian context it would be considered assault. It is certainly impermissible under any prohibition of cruel, inhuman, or degrading treatment.

Let's posit that during the interrogation of Khalid Sheikh Mohammed, perhaps early on, we got intelligence about an imminent Al Qaeda attack. And we had a very good reason to believe he knew about it. And if we knew what he knew, we could stop it. If we thought we could glean a critical piece of information by use of sodium pentathol, would we be permitted to do so?   25

Less hypothetically, there is waterboarding, a terrifying and deeply shocking torture technique in which the prisoner has his face exposed to water in a way that gives the feeling of drowning. According to CIA sources cited by ABC News, Khalid Sheikh Mohammed "was able to last between 2 and 2½ minutes before begging to confess." Should we regret having done that? Should we abolish by law that practice, so that it could never be used on the next Khalid Sheikh Mohammed having thus gotten his confession?   26

> Khalid Sheikh Mohammed "was able to [withstand waterboarding] between 2 and 2½ minutes before begging to confess." Should we regret having done that?

And what if he possessed information with less imminent implications? Say we had information about a cell that he had helped found or direct, and that cell was planning some major attack and we needed information about the identity and location of its members. A rational moral calculus might not permit measures as extreme as the nuke-in-Manhattan scenario, but would surely permit measures beyond mere psychological pressure.   27

Such a determination would not be made with an untroubled conscience. It would be troubled because there is no denying the monstrous evil that is any form of torture. And there is no denying how corrupting it can be to the individuals and society that practice it. But elected leaders, responsible above all for the protection of their citizens, have the obligation to tolerate their own sleepless nights by doing what is necessary—and only what is necessary, nothing more—to get information that could prevent mass murder.   28

Given the gravity of the decision, if we indeed cross the   29
Rubicon—as we must—we need rules. The problem with the McCain
amendment is that once you have gone public with a blanket ban on all
forms of coercion, it is going to be very difficult to publicly carve out
exceptions. The Bush administration is to be faulted for having attempted such a codification with the kind of secrecy, lack of coherence,
and lack of strict enforcement that led us to the McCain reaction.

What to do at this late date? Begin, as McCain does, by banning   30
all forms of coercion or inhuman treatment by anyone serving in the
military—an absolute ban on torture by all military personnel everywhere. We do not want a private somewhere
making these fine distinctions about ticking
and slow-fuse time bombs. We don't even
want colonels or generals making them. It
would be best for the morale, discipline, and
honor of the Armed Forces for the United
States to maintain an absolute prohibition,
both to simplify their task in making deci-
sions and to offer them whatever reciprocal treatment they might receive from those who capture them—although I have no illusion that
any anti-torture provision will soften the heart of a single jihadist
holding a knife to the throat of a captured American soldier. We
would impose this restriction on ourselves for our own reasons of
military discipline and military honor.

Begin by banning all forms of coercion or inhuman treatment by anyone serving in the military.

Outside the military, however, I would propose, contra McCain,   31
a ban against all forms of torture, coercive interrogation, and inhuman treatment, except in two contingencies: (1) the ticking time
bomb and (2) the slower-fuse high-level terrorist (such as KSM). Each
contingency would have its own set of rules. In the case of the ticking
time bomb, the rules would be relatively simple: Nothing rationally
related to getting accurate information would be ruled out. The case
of the high-value suspect with slow-fuse information is more complicated. The principle would be that the level of inhumanity of the
measures used (moral honesty is essential here—we would be using
measures that are by definition inhumane) would be proportional to
the need and value of the information. Interrogators would be con-
strained to use the least inhumane treatment necessary relative to the
magnitude and imminence of the evil being prevented and the importance of the knowledge being obtained.

These exceptions to the no-torture rule would not be granted to   32
just any nonmilitary interrogators, or anyone with CIA credentials.

They would be reserved for highly specialized agents who are experts and experienced in interrogation, and who are known not to abuse it for the satisfaction of a kind of sick sado-masochism Lynndie England and her cohorts indulged in at Abu Ghraib. Nor would they be acting on their own. They would be required to obtain written permission for such interrogations from the highest political authorities in the country (cabinet level) or from a quasi-judicial body modeled on the Foreign Intelligence Surveillance Court (which permits what would ordinarily be illegal searches and seizures in the war on terror). Or, if the bomb was truly ticking and there was no time, the interrogators would be allowed to act on their own, but would require post facto authorization within, say, 24 hours of their interrogation, so that they knew that whatever they did would be subject to review by others and be justified only under the most stringent terms.

Exceptions to the no-torture rule would be reserved for highly specialized agents.

One of the purposes of these justifications would be to establish   33
that whatever extreme measures are used are for reasons of nothing but information. Historically, the torture of prisoners has been done for a variety of reasons apart from information, most prominently reasons of justice or revenge. We do not do that. We should not do that. Ever. Khalid Sheikh Mohammed, murderer of 2,973 innocents, is surely deserving of the most extreme suffering day and night for the rest of his life. But it is neither our role nor our right to be the agents of that suffering. Vengeance is mine, sayeth the Lord. His, not ours. Torture is a terrible and monstrous thing, as degrading and morally corrupting to those who practice it as any conceivable human activity including its moral twin, capital punishment.

If Khalid Sheikh Mohammed knew nothing, or if we had reached   34
the point where his knowledge had been exhausted, I'd be perfectly prepared to throw him into a nice, comfortable Manhattan cell and give him a trial to determine what would be fit and just punishment. But as long as he had useful information, things would be different.

Very different. And it simply will not do to take refuge in the   35
claim that all of the above discussion is superfluous because torture never works anyway. Would that this were true. Unfortunately, on its face, this is nonsense. Is one to believe that in the entire history of human warfare, no combatant has ever received useful information by the use of pressure, torture, or any other kind of inhuman treatment? It may indeed be true that torture is not a reliable tool. But that is very different from saying that it is never useful.

The monstrous thing about torture is that sometimes it does   36
work. In 1994, 19-year-old Israeli corporal Nachshon Waxman was
kidnapped by Palestinian terrorists. The Israelis captured the driver
of the car used in the kidnapping and tor-
tured him in order to find where Waxman
was being held. Yitzhak Rabin, prime minis-
ter and peacemaker, admitted that they tortured him in a way that went even beyond
the '87 guidelines for "coercive interroga-
tion" later struck down by the Israeli Supreme Court as too harsh.
The driver talked. His information was accurate. The Israelis found
Waxman. "If we'd been so careful to follow the ['87] Landau Com-
mission [which allowed coercive interrogation]," explained Rabin,
"we would never have found out where Waxman was being held."

The monstrous thing about torture is that sometimes it does work.

In the Waxman case, I would have done precisely what Rabin did.   37
(The fact that Waxman's Palestinian captors killed him during the Israeli
rescue raid makes the case doubly tragic, but changes nothing of
the moral calculus.) Faced with a similar choice, an American president
would have a similar obligation. To do otherwise—to give up the
chance to find your soldier lest you sully yourself by authorizing torture
of the person who possesses potentially lifesaving information—is a
deeply immoral betrayal of a soldier and countryman. Not as cosmically
immoral as permitting a city of one's countrymen to perish, as in
the Ethics 101 case. But it remains, nonetheless, a case of moral abdication—of a kind rather parallel to that of the principled pacifist. There is
much to admire in those who refuse on principle ever to take up arms
under any conditions. But that does not make pure pacifism, like no-torture absolutism, any less a form of moral foolishness, tinged with moral
vanity. Not reprehensible, only deeply reproachable and supremely im-
practicable. People who hold such beliefs are deserving of a certain respect. But they are not to be put in positions of authority. One should be
grateful for the saintly among us. And one should be vigilant that they
not get to make the decisions upon which the lives of others depend.

Which brings us to the greatest irony of all in the torture debate.   38
I have just made what will be characterized as the pro-torture case
contra McCain by proposing two major exceptions carved out of any
no-torture rule: the ticking time bomb and the slow-fuse high-value
terrorist. McCain supposedly is being hailed for defending all that is
good and right and just in America by standing foursquare against
any inhuman treatment. Or is he?

According to *Newsweek*, in the ticking time bomb case McCain   39
says that the president should disobey the very law that McCain

seeks to pass—under the justification that "you do what you have to do. But you take responsibility for it." But if torturing the ticking time bomb suspect is "what you have to do," then why has McCain been going around arguing that such things must never be done?

As for exception number two, the high-level terrorist with slow-   40
fuse information, Stuart Taylor, the superb legal correspondent for *National Journal,* argues that with appropriate legal interpretation, the "cruel, inhuman, or degrading" standard, "though vague, is said by experts to codify . . . the commonsense principle that the toughness of interrogation techniques should be calibrated to the importance and urgency of the information likely to be obtained." That would permit "some very aggressive techniques . . . on that small percentage of detainees who seem especially likely to have potentially life-saving information." Or as Evan Thomas and Michael Hirsh put it in the *Newsweek* report on McCain and torture, the McCain standard would "presumably allow for a sliding scale" of torture or torture-lite or other coercive techniques, thus permitting "for a very small percentage—those High Value Targets like Khalid Sheikh Mohammed—some pretty rough treatment."

But if that is the case, then McCain embraces the same exceptions I   41
do, but prefers to pretend he does not. If that is the case, then his much-touted and endlessly repeated absolutism on inhumane treatment is merely for show. If that is the case, then the moral preening and the phony arguments can stop now, and we can all agree that in this real world of astonishingly murderous enemies, in two very circumscribed circumstances, we must all be prepared to torture. Having established that, we can then begin to work together to codify rules of interrogation for the two very unpleasant but very real cases in which we are morally permitted—indeed morally compelled—to do terrible things.

Web **Read It Now:** Read more opinion articles by Krauthammer at bedfordstmartins.com/americanow, Chapter 12.

Vocabulary / Using a Dictionary

1. What does *retrograde* (para. 1) mean? What do its Latin roots have to do with walking?

2. What is the difference between *conviction* (para. 2) and *convict*?

3. Look up the origins of the word *scrupulousness* (para. 8). What does it have to do with weight?

4. How is the word *miscreant* (para. 11) connected with religious beliefs?

Responding to Words in Context

1. What does it mean to be "beyond the pale" (para. 2)?
2. Explain what Krauthammer means by *moral calculus* (para. 13).
3. What is *moral preening* (para. 41)? Is this intended as a positive term? How does this word choice affect the tone of what Krauthammer is saying?
4. What is the impact of the phrase *ticking time bomb* (para. 12), which Krauthammer repeats several times in the essay?
5. Krauthammer writes that Al Qaeda "incubated and grew and metastasized" (para. 18). What images does the phrase bring to mind?

Discussing Main Point and Meaning

1. What is Krauthammer's main argument about torture? How does it compare to the views held by McCain (see p. 401)?
2. According to Krauthammer, for what "deeper purpose" (para. 6) were the Geneva Conventions created?
3. What are the main ways that the author differentiates between soldiers and terrorists? Why does he spend time describing these differences?
4. Under what circumstances does the author describe torture as "a moral certainty"?

Examining Sentences, Paragraphs, and Organization

1. Consider the opening paragraph. What does the author immediately establish in his introduction?
2. How does the author organize the examples he uses to support his arguments?
3. How effective are Krauthammer's paragraphs on what he sees as three types of war prisoners (see paras. 4–11)? Explain.
4. Consider these sentences: "The gnashing of teeth and rending of garments has been considerable" (para. 16) and "I myself have not gnashed a single tooth. My garments remain entirely unrent" (para. 17). What is Krauthammer referring to? What is the effect of these sentences on you as a reader?

Thinking Critically

1. What specific arguments about torture does the author try to refute? Does his overall argument work? Explain.

2. Consider Krauthammer's take on the torture of Khalid Sheikh Mohammed. Do you agree with his perspective? What do you think of his view of the "ticking time bomb" scenario? Are there instances when torture is necessary? Explain.

3. If torture is to take place, would assigning this task to "highly specialized agents who are experts and experienced in interrogation," as Krauthammer suggests in paragraph 32, cut down on abuses? In other words, can torture be controlled? How might a government ensure that expert interrogators would not act sadistically as soldiers did at Abu Ghraib?

4. In closing this essay, Krauthammer points out that McCain does indeed allow for exceptions to a hard-line "no torture" law, although he does not publicize this. Why would Krauthammer point this out?

In-Class Writing Activities

1. Consider the arguments that the author uses to justify torture. Are they pragmatic? Ethical? Both? Why do you think this?

2. What claims made by Krauthammer, if any, do you take issue with? Be specific in your response, citing particular passages and explaining your critique.

3. What problems might lawmakers have in legislating when torture is acceptable and when it is not?

CATHY YOUNG

Torturing Logic

[REASON/March 2006]

Before You Read

What is the logic behind arguments used for or against torture? How does Cathy Young's logic compare to that of other writers in this unit?

Words to Learn

ushered in (para. 1): led; introduced (v.)

disclosures (para. 2): facts and details that are made public (n.)

caved (para. 2): an informal term for gave in, yielded, surrendered (v.)

depravity (para. 3): moral corruption (n.)

pundits (para. 3): critics (n.)

sodomizing (para. 6): in this context, the crime of forcing anal sex (v.)

gestating (para. 7): conceiving and developing (v.)

internment (para. 17): the confirement of people or property, especially during wartime (n.)

CATHY YOUNG *is an author, a public speaker, and a columnist for the* Boston Globe *and* Reason *magazine. She writes on a variety of issues including gender, education, and politics. The Russian-born writer describes herself on her Web site as a libertarian/conservative and states, "One of my goals in my writing is to cut through left/right stereotypes and focus on the issues from an independent perspective." She writes, "I am a strong believer in individual rights and limited government. I believe in judging people as individuals, not on the basis of membership in a group. I believe that reality trumps ideology, left or right. I believe Western democracy, flawed though it is, is worth defending. Perhaps most important, I believe that it should be possible for honest and intelligent people to disagree on political issues and respect each other."*

I never imagined, immediately after 9/11, that four years later we   1
would be having a debate on whether and how much the United
States should torture prisoners—or that the Bush administration
would wage a losing battle against anti-torture legislation sponsored
by a Republican senator. Maybe I should have seen it coming, after
the attacks on New York and Washington ushered in a new culture
of fear. Most people agree that desperate times call for desperate
measures. But just how desperate can we get?

The disclosures of detainee abuse at Abu Ghraib were followed   2
by revelations that such tactics had also been used in interrogations of terror suspects at Guantanamo Bay, with high-level government approval. The issue finally came to a head in 2005 with the
anti-torture legislation spearheaded by Senator John McCain
(R-Arizona), himself a survivor of torture at the hands of the North
Vietnamese. The White House found itself in the curious position of
arguing, simultaneously, that "we do not torture" and that the
McCain bill (which clarifies that the ban on "cruel, inhuman and degrading treatment" applies to all U.S. personnel and all persons in
U.S. custody) would tie our hands in the war on terror. In December
the administration finally caved and dropped its opposition to the
legislation, whose passage seemed inevitable.

Torture is the ultimate depravity. Fittingly, the torture debate has   3
featured some new lows in depravity of the rhetorical kind. Leading conservative pundits, including Charles Krauthammer, Jonah
Goldberg, and Thomas Sowell, have derided opposition to torture as
"moral preening" or "moral exhibitionism." Others made an issue of
the homosexuality of journalist Andrew Sullivan, who has emerged
as one of the most vocal critics of torture. After Sullivan condemned
a notorious incident in which a female interrogator pretended to
smear an al Qaeda suspect with her menstrual blood in order to
make him unclean in the eyes of his God, the *Wall Street Journal*'s
James Taranto suggested that Sullivan's reaction came from disgust
at female physiology related to a lack of sexual experience with
women.

The *Journal* editorial page also distinguished itself by taking the   4
peculiar position that so-called "waterboarding," a technique in
which a tightly bound detainee has water poured over his face in a
way that induces a sensation of drowning, was not really torture but
a "coercive interrogation" tactic relying on "psychological pressure."

The *Journal* just as bravely dismissed exposure to extreme heat   5
and extreme cold, just short of causing fatal hypothermia, as mere

"discomfort." The columnist and Council of Foreign Relations fellow Max Boot (a *Journal* editorial page alumnus) pronounced in the *Los Angeles Times*—on the very day the Bush administration dropped its opposition to the McCain bill—that the torture scandal was vastly overblown because a lot of this so-called torture was quite similar to what millions of U.S. soldiers have to endure in boot camp.

Of course, when those trainees are subjected to waterboarding, it's precisely to prepare them to withstand torture. Besides, one could use a similar analogy to argue that sodomizing a prisoner with a plastic tube is no big deal because it's quite similar to the colonoscopies voluntarily endured by millions of Americans every year. 6

The most nuanced "anti-anti-torture" case was made by Charles Krauthammer in the *Weekly Standard*. Krauthammer agreed that "torture is a terrible and monstrous thing, as degrading and morally corrupting to those who practice it as any conceivable human activity," and he did not try to excuse practices like waterboarding as "nontorture." But he also argued that some forms of this monstrous activity must remain permissible in extreme circumstances, and that our leaders must take this burden of conscience in order to save lives. He outlined two exceptions: the "ticking time bomb" scenario and the high-value, high-level terrorist who possesses a treasure trove of information about the terror network and the plots it's gestating. 7

But Krauthammer's argument has several weaknesses. He greatly overestimates the plausibility of the "ticking time bomb" scenario. If the attack is to take place within minutes, coercive or painful methods ought to be useless: The captive will tell the interrogators a fake story—possibly preplanned in the event of capture—and by the time they realize they've been duped the bomb will have gone off. 8

The captive will tell the interrogators a fake story—and by the time they realize they've been duped the bomb will have gone off.

The reliability of torture-extracted information aside, allowing what Krauthammer calls "torture-lite" (stress positions, heat and cold, probably waterboarding) with the goal of saving lives raises a disturbing question: What if the "lite" version doesn't break the detainee? Do we start pulling fingernails and administering electric shocks to genitals? Use "coercive" techniques on a terrorist's child? Where on the slippery slope do we stop? 9

Curiously, Krauthammer also argues that McCain's anti-torture position is more flexible than it's made out to be. The senator has said that the president may authorize illegal techniques in an 10 emergency such as a hostage rescue or an imminent attack; and legal experts, including the *National Journal*'s Stuart Taylor, suggest that his bill would likely be interpreted so that the harshness of allowed interrogation techniques could increase depending on the urgency of the situation.

This should trouble real anti-torture purists, but why does it   11
bother Krauthammer, who concludes that "McCain embraces the same exceptions I do"? Because he thinks that McCain's anti-torture crusade is dishonestly moralistic, a claim to the moral high ground based on false pretenses. Krauthammer wants us "to be honest about doing terrible things." But what, from Krauthammer's point of view, do we have to gain from being honest?

I am more strongly opposed to torture than Krauthammer is, but   12
I'm enough of a realist to recognize that any "no torture" stand will likely be qualified with some tacit acknowl-

If we start with the idea that torture is sometimes acceptable, that slippery slope is going to take us pretty low.

edgment that, under some very bad circumstances, some very bad things will happen. That's far better than a Krauthammer-style declaration that "we must all be prepared to torture." If we start with a "thou shalt not torture" absolute, we are likely to be extremely vigilant about lapses from this commandment. If we start with the idea that torture is sometimes acceptable, that slippery slope is going to take us pretty low.

Already, we've reached the point of seriously debating why torture is bad. On *National Review*'s staff blog, Goldberg wonders what makes it so much worse than killing people in combat or putting them in prison.   13

Actually, there are a lot of reasons. Torture robs the individual of   14
all control of his or her body and mind. It's quite possible to maintain one's human dignity and selfhood while imprisoned; not so with torture, which, as Sullivan put in the *New Republic*, "takes what is animal in us and deploys it against what makes us human."

Imprisonment does not do that. Nor does death; it simply ends   15
the individual's existence. Many people have chosen death over severe pain — not only because of the suffering involved, but because of the loss of dignity.

On the giving end, the evil of torture is unique as well. It inflicts   16
systematic severe suffering on a helpless human being. It also creates

the danger that at least some of the torturers will enjoy it, particularly if they have been primed to see the one being tortured as an evil, sub-human creature getting his just deserts. Every pro-torture (or anti-anti-torture) argument, including Krauthammer's, relies on the assumption that terrorists are entitled to no humane treatment.

Anti-torture absolutists often point out that we were able to beat   17
Hitler without resorting to torture. On the other side, there is the valid point that America did not really win that war with clean hands: Consider the internment of Japanese-Americans and the large-scale bombing of civilians. That we no longer do such things is surely a sign of moral progress. If the War on Terror brings us regression on the issue of torture, it will be a tragedy—and, in all likelihood, one as unnecessary as internment was during World War II.

 Read It Now: Read more of Young's perspectives published in the *Boston Globe* and *Reason* at **bedfordstmartins.com/americanow,** Chapter 12.

Vocabulary / Using a Dictionary

1. What does it mean to do things *simultaneously* (para. 2)?

2. What are the positive and negative meanings of the word *notorious* (para. 3)?

3. If something is *systematic* (para. 16), what is it?

4. What are some synonyms for *regression* (para. 17)?

Responding to Words in Context

1. What are *revelations* (para. 2)? Why might the author have chosen this word and not one of its synonyms?

2. What does Young mean by the term *slippery slope* (paras. 9, 12)?

3. The journalist Andrew Sullivan is quoted as saying that torture "'takes what is animal in us and deploys it against what makes us human'" (para. 14). Why does he choose the word *deploys*? What imagery does this word bring to mind?

4. What does it mean to be *subhuman* (para. 16)? What other words include the *sub-* prefix? How is this term different from *inhuman* (para. 2)?

Discussing Main Point and Meaning

1. What is Young's main argument about the use of torture?
2. How does Young characterize the editorials on torture in the *Wall Street Journal*? Does she agree with them? Explain.
3. What does Young think of Charles Krauthammer's argument about torture in the *Weekly Standard*? Of Jonah Goldberg's argument posted at the *National Review* blog?

Examining Sentences, Paragraphs, and Organization

1. Young writes that "desperate times call for desperate measures" (para. 1). Are you bothered by this cliché? Why or why not?
2. Paragraph 8 begins, "But Krauthammer's argument has several weaknesses." Is this transition effective? Explain. Identify other transitions in Young's essay and evaluate them.
3. How does the author use quotation marks in the essay? What do they indicate?
4. How does Young reference other writers to help prove her point? What are the benefits and disadvantages of this?
5. On what point does the author close the essay? Is this effective?

Thinking Critically

1. What is the difference between "pro-torture" and "anti-anti-torture"? Why might the author use one in preference to the other?
2. The author admits that the possibility for torture exists in the future. Does this weaken her argument? Explain.
3. Young notes that journalist Max Boot has said that "the torture scandal was vastly overblown because a lot of this so-called torture [is] quite similar to what millions of U.S. soldiers have to endure in boot camp" (para. 5). What does Boot mean? What do you think of this comment?
4. In paragraph 17, Young indicates that the United States did not win World War II with "clean hands." Can wars be fought with "clean hands"? Should they be? Explain.

In-Class Writing Activities

1. Why might an author pay special attention to the arguments used in a debate, rather than simply participating in the debate itself? Discuss some of these ideas.

2. Young notes that current debates on "why torture is bad" are themselves a bad thing. What does she mean?

Discussing the Unit

Suggested Topic for Discussion

When considering the arguments for or against torture, examine the ways that the writers in this chapter try to bring you around to their points of view. This is a complicated topic, and the means by which the arguments are made can be as important as the arguments themselves. What do you think of torture? Why? Which authors in this chapter do you most identify with?

Preparing for Class Discussion

1. How are moral and ethical arguments used in the various selections in this unit? Do you believe it is important for a nation to impose on itself higher ethical values than its enemies possess? Why or why not?

2. Some arguments presented in this unit are direct attempts to refute the statements of others. Point out some of these, and discuss how they are handled by their authors. Identify what you consider the most persuasive refutations. Which do you think are the weakest?

From Discussion to Writing

1. Compare and contrast the arguments made by Mollison and McCain. Are there similarities? Differences? Are both of these authors on the same side of the debate, and how does this affect the means by which they argue their sides?

2. Every selection in this chapter attempts to define what acceptable behavior is for soldiers and policymakers. Discuss the range of acceptable behavior. What are some of the behavioral extremes discussed in the readings?

Topics for Cross-Cultural Discussion

1. What do the arguments used in the various essays in this chapter tell you about the perceived audience of each essay? Do you think the essays were written with specific cultural audiences in mind?

2. The debate about torture has grown out of an international conflict. How do other nations view the debate taking place in the United States? Are there similar debates taking place elsewhere?

Information for Subscription

Periodicals

Adbusters (adbusters.org): six issues yearly. Features and critical commentary on the news, media, and popular culture. Subscription address: Adbusters Subscriptions, 1243 West 7th Avenue, Vancouver, British Columbia, V6H 1B7, Canada; subscriptions@adbusters.org; or call (604) 736-9401.

The Boston Globe (boston.com/news/globe): daily. General newspaper covering local, national, and international news, business, sports, and arts for Boston, MA. Subscription address: Boston Globe, P.O. Box 55819, Boston, MA 02205-5819; or call (800) 622-6631.

The Chronicle of Higher Education (chronicle.com): weekly. A news and career-information source for college and university faculty, administrators, and students. Subscription address: Circulation Department, The Chronicle of Higher Education, 1255 23rd Street, NW, Washington, DC 20037; circulation@chronicle.com; or call (800) 728-2803.

The Cincinnati Enquirer (enquirer.com): daily. General newspaper covering local, national, and international news, business, sports, and arts for Cincinnati, OH. Subscription address: Circulation Department, The Cincinnati Enquirer, 312 Elm Street, Cincinnati, OH 45202; or call (800) 876-4500.

The Columbia Journalism Review (cjr.org): six issues yearly. Analysis of the business of journalism. Subscription address: Columbia Journalism Review, Journalism Building, 2950 Broadway, Columbia University, New York, NY 10027; subscriptions@cjr.org; or call (888) 425-7782.

DoubleTake (doubletakecommunity.org): biannual. Liberal arts journal featuring narratives, stories, essays, and photography. Subscription address: The Johns Hopkins University Press Journals Division, DoubleTake / Points of Entry, P.O. Box 19966, Baltimore, MD 21211-0966; or call (800) 548-1784.

Harper's Bazaar (harpersbazaar.com): monthly. Fashion and beauty articles. Subscription address: Harper's Bazaar, P.O. Box 7178, Red Oak, IA 51591-0162; or call (800) 888-3045.

Los Angeles Times (latimes.com): daily. General newspaper featuring local, national, and international news, business, sports, and arts for Los Angeles, CA. Subscription address: Circulation Department, Los Angeles Times, 202 W. 1st Street, Los Angeles, CA 90012; or call (800) 252-9141.

National Geographic (nationalgeographic.com): monthly. Photo features on history, geography, and current events. Subscription address: National Geographic Society, P.O. Box 98199, Washington, DC 20090-8199; or call (800) 647-5463.

The New Republic (tnr.com): weekly. Analysis of American politics, foreign policy, and culture. Subscription address: The New Republic, 1331 H Street, NW Suite 700, Washington, DC 20005; or call (800) 827-1289.

Newsweek (newsweek.com): weekly. News and commentary on the week's events in national and international affairs. Subscription address: Newsweek Subscriptions, P.O. Box 59967, Boulder, CO 80322; or call (800) 631-1040.

The New Yorker (newyorker.com): weekly. Feature articles on politics and culture, fiction, poetry, and humor. Subscription address: The New Yorker, P.O. Box 37684, Boone, IA 50037-0684; or call (800) 825-2510.

The New York Times (nytimes.com): daily. Definitive source for national and international news, business, and arts reporting; includes the weekly *New York Times Magazine* on Sundays. Subscription address: The New York Times, 229 W. 43rd Street, New York, NY 10036; or call (800) NYTIMES.

The New York Times Magazine (nytimes.com/pages/magazine): weekly. Features on national and international news, arts, and fashion; included in the Sunday edition of *The New York Times*. Subscription address: The New York Times, 229 W. 43rd Street, New York, NY 10036; or call (800) NYTIMES.

Open Spaces (open-spaces.com): quarterly. Features on politics, culture, science, arts, and travel. Subscription address: Open Spaces Publications, Inc., PMB 134, 6327 C SW Capitol Highway, Portland, OR 97239-1937; or call (503) 227-5764.

Orion (oriononline.org): six issues yearly. Features and commentary with an awareness of ecological and social issues. Subscription address: The Orion Society, 187 Mail Street, Great Barrington, MA 01230; orion@orionsociety.org; or call (888) 909-6568.

Parade Magazine (parade.com): weekly. Weekly entertainment magazine included in selected Sunday newspapers across the country.

Subscription address: Parade Publications, 711 3rd Avenue, New York, NY 10017-4014; readerservices@parade.com; or call (212) 450-7000.

The Philadelphia Inquirer (philly.com): daily. General newspaper featuring local, national, and international news, business, sports, and arts for Philadelphia, PA. Subscription address: The Philadelphia Inquirer, P.O. Box 8263, Philadelphia, PA 19101; or call (215) 854-2000.

PMS (pms-journal.org): yearly. Women's literary journal of poetry, memoir, and story. Subscription address: PMS, University of Alabama at Birmingham, Spencer Honors House, 1190 10th Avenue South, Birmingham, AL 35294-4450.

Reason (reason.com): monthly. Politically independent magazine of news, analysis, and reviews. Subscription address: Reason, 3415 S. Sepulveda Boulevard, Suite 400, Los Angeles, CA 90034; subscribe@reason.com; or call (310) 391-2245.

Smithsonian (smithsonianmagazine.com): monthly. Features on arts, history, sciences, and popular culture. Subscription address: Smithsonian Information, P.O. Box 37012, SI Building, Room 153, MRC 010, Washington, D.C. 20013-7012; smithsmt@palmcoastd.com; or call (800) 766-2149.

Townhall.com: online source. Conservative political commentary, analysis, and activism from 120 contributing sources. Contact information: Townhall.com, 1901 N. Moore Street, Suite 205, Arlington, VA 22209; info@townhall.com; or call (703) 294-6046.

USA Today (usatoday.com): daily. Nationwide newspaper covering current events, business, and entertainment. Subscription address: USA Today, National Customer Service, 7950 Jones Branch Drive, McLean, VA 22108; or call (800) USA-0001.

The Wall Street Journal (wsj.com): daily. Business and financial news, managerial trends, and politics. Subscription address: *The Wall Street Journal*, 200 Burnett Road, Chicopee, MA 01020; wsj.service@dowjones.com; or call (800) 568-7625.

The Washington Post (washingtonpost.com): daily. National newspaper featuring national and international news, politics, business, sports, and arts. Subscription address: The Washington Post, P.O. Box 17370, Arlington, VA 22216; or call (800) 627-1150.

The Weekly Standard (weeklystandard.com): weekly. Political features on foreign policy, national news, and arts. Subscription address: The Weekly Standard, P.O. Box 96127, Washington, DC 20077-7767; or call (800) 283-2014.

Wired (wired.com): monthly. Technology news, culture, and politics. Subscription address: Wired, P.O. Box 37706, Boone, IA 50037-0706; subscriptions@wiredmag.com; or call (800) SO WIRED.

Student Sources

The Auburn Plainsman, Auburn University (theplainsman.com): daily. Student newspaper featuring campus, city, and state news for Auburn, AL.

The Columbia Spectator, Columbia University (columbiaspectator .com): daily. Independent student newspaper providing local news and features to the Columbia University and Morningside Heights communities in New York, NY.

The Daily Campus, The University of Connecticut (dailycampus .com): daily. Independent student newspaper covering news and sports for the University of Connecticut at Storrs, CT.

The Daily Illini, University of Illinois (dailyillini.com): daily. Independent student newspaper featuring local and national news.

The Daily Pennsylvanian, The University of Pennsylvania (dailypennsylvanian.com): daily. News and sports for the University of Pennsylvania and the Philadelphia area.

The Daily Reveille, Louisiana State University (lsureveille.com): daily. National, international, technology, and sports news for Louisiana State University.

The Digital Collegian, Pennsylvania State University (collegian .psu.edu): daily. Independent student newspapers covering campus news, sports, and arts.

Diskord/Campus Progress, University of Chicago (diskord.uchicago .edu): monthly. Progressive student journal with features on international, domestic, and cultural issues for the University of Chicago.

The Emory Wheel, Emory University (emorywheel.com): twice weekly. Independent student-run newspaper reporting news, sports, and entertainment for Emory University in Decatur, GA.

Facebook.com. Social Web site connecting people through high school, college, corporate, and regional networks.

MySpace.com. Social networking Web site featuring interactive profiles, photos, and search engines.

Pacific News Service (pacificnews.org). Nonprofit media organization featuring commentary, news analysis, and investigative reporting by often unheard voices, such as artists and young writers of color.

The Reflector, Mississippi State University (reflector-online.com): daily. News, entertainment, and sports for Mississippi State University in Starkville, MS.

The State News, Michigan State University (statenews.com): daily. Independent student newspaper covering campus, national, and world news to Michigan State University.

Studentsagainstsweatshops.org. International student organization dedicated to fighting for sweatshop-free labor and workers' rights.

The Tufts Daily, Tufts University (tuftsdaily.com):daily. News, arts, and sports for Tufts University in Medford, MA.

U. Magazine (colleges.com/Umagazine): quarterly. National magazine for prospective and current college students about college, technology, and entertainment news.

Acknowledgments

Adbusters (poster). "Buy Nothing Day." Courtesy of www.adbusters.org.

American Civil Liberties Union (advertisement). "The man on the left is 75 times more likely to be stopped by the police while driving than the man on the right." Reprinted by permission of the ACLU and DeVito/Verdi.

American Indian College Fund (advertisement and screen capture). "If I Stay on the Rez" and American Indian College Fund "History and Mission." Reprinted by permission of the American Indian College Fund.

America's Army: The Rise of a Soldier game (Web screen). © 2005 Ubisoft Entertainment. All Rights Reserved. Courtesy of the United States Army.

Charles Atlas ® "The Insult That Turned a 'Chump' into a Champ©" Copyright 2007, under license from Charles Atlas, Ltd. (www.CharlesAtlas.com).

Jaclyn Barbarow. "Queering the Campus, Loud and Clear." The Emory Wheel, Emory University, October 14, 2005. Reprinted by permission of the author and The Emory Wheel.

Isra Javed Bhatty. "Reppin' Islam." Diskord/Campus Progress, May 2005. This article was published in Diskord magazine at University of Chicago, and online at CampusProgress.org, a Center for American Progress publication. Reprinted by permission of the Center for American Progress.

Jason Browne. "If You Don't Have an Opinion, Relax." The Reflector Online, Mississippi State University, April 19, 2005. Reprinted by permission of the author and The Reflector.

Michael Bugeja. "Facing the Facebook." The Chronicle of Higher Education, February 27, 2006. Reprinted by permission of the author.

John Angus Campbell and Stephen C. Meyer. "Evolution: Debate It." USA Today, August 14, 2005. Reprinted by permission of the authors.

Art Carey. "Men's Faces Go Under the Knife." The Philadelphia Inquirer, February 19, 2006. Reprinted by permission of the author.

Kevin Collins. "Acknowledging the Gray Area in Rape Dialogue." The Daily Pennsylvanian, University of Pennsylvania, March 29, 2004. © 2004 The Daily Pennsylvanian, Inc. Reprinted with permission of The Daily Pennsylvanian and the author.

Alan Diaz (photograph). "Armed federal agents seize Elian Gonzalez" by Alan Diaz appears by permission of AP/Wide World Photos.

Elissa Englund. "Good Grammar Gets the Girl." The State News, Michigan State University, September 14, 2005. Reprinted by permission of the author and The State News.

Facebook.com. Facebook (Web screen). Courtesy of Facebook.com.

Food Force game (Web screen). © United Nations World Food Program.

Angela Adair Fowler. "The Facebook Addiction Spreads." The Reflector, Mississippi State University. Reprinted with permission.

Thomas E. Franklin (photograph). "Three Firefighters Raising the Flag." © 2004 Getty Images. Photo by Thomas E. Franklin/The Bergen Record/Getty Images.

Henry Louis Gates Jr. "My Yiddishe Mama." The Wall Street Journal, February 1, 2006. Copyright © 2006 by Henry Louis Gates, Jr. Reprinted by permission of the author. Reprinted from The Wall Street Journal © 2006 Dow Jones & Company. All rights reserved.

438   Acknowledgments

Sarah J. Gernhauser. "The Morality of Designer Knock-Offs." *The Daily Reveille*, Louisiana State University, January 18. 2005. Reprinted by permission of the author and *The Daily Reveille*.

Getty Images (photographs). "John Scopes" photograph by New York Times Co. "Clarence Darrow and William Jennings Bryan" photograph from Hulton Archive. "Anti-Evolution League" photograph from Topical Press Agency. "John McCain" photograph by Getty Images/Alex Wong. "Western Union Telegram" photograph by Getty Images/Mario Tama.

Jan Goodwin. "The Human Cost of Fakes." *Harper's Bazaar*, January 2006. Reprinted by permission of the author.

The Granger Collection (advertisement). "Automobile ad, 1904." Reprinted by permission of The Granger Collection, New York.

The Granger Collection (photograph). "Thorstein Veblen." Reprinted by permission of The Granger Collection, New York.

William Haefeli (cartoon). "You must be this tall to have an opinion." © The New Yorker Collection 2006 William Haefeli from cartoonbank.com. All Rights Reserved.

Rebecca Hagelin. "Video Game Violence and Our Sons." Townhall.com, March 28, 2006. Reprinted by permission of the author. www.homeinvasion.org.

Grace Hsiang. "'FOBs' vs. 'Twinkies': The New Discrimination is Intraracial." Pacific News Service, April 15, 2005. Reprinted by permission of the author, New American Media, and Pacific News Service.

Adam Jacot de Boinod. "Global Wording." Originally published in *Smithsonian*, March 2006. From *The Meaning of Tingo* by Adam Jacot de Boinod, copyright © 2005 by Adam Jacot de Boinod. Used by permission of The Penguin Press, a division of Penguin Group (USA) Inc.

Michael Kinsley. "The Twilight of Objectivity." *The Washington Post*, March 31, 2006.

Judith Kleinfeld. "What's Going On ... and What's Going Wrong ... with Our Boys?" *Open Spaces*, August 2006, Vol. 8, Issue 2. Reprinted by permission of the author.

Kobal Collection (images). "Peyton Place" 20th Century Fox/Kobal Collection. "Roots" Warner Brothers TV/David Wolper Prods/Kobal Collection. "Death Race 2000" The Kobal Collection.

Charles Krauthammer. "The Truth about Torture." *The Weekly Standard*, December 5, 2005. Reprinted by permission of the author.

Daphne Myrto LaBua. "My Brain Has a Sex?" *The Tufts Daily*, Tufts University, October 26, 2005. Reprinted by permission of the author and *The Tufts Daily*.

Jhumpa Lahiri. "My Two Lives." From *Newsweek*, March 6, 2006. © 2006 Newsweek, Inc. All rights reserved. Reprinted by permission.

Peter Law. "A Call for More Sweatshop Labor." *Columbia Daily Spectator*, Columbia University, January 26, 2005. Reprinted by permission of the author and the *Columbia Daily Spectator*.

John Leo. "Awash in Euphemisms." Townhall.com, February 27, 2006.

Mike Luckovich (cartoon). "You've got a monkey on your back." Published in the *Atlanta Journal Constitution*, June 16, 2006. By permission of Mike Luckovich and Creators Syndicate, Inc.

Doug Marlette (cartoon). "That does it—Tell Iran this will be their last warning!" Published September 25, 2006. Reprinted by permission of Doug Marlette. www.dougmarlette.com.

John McCain. "Torture's Terrible Toll." From *Newsweek*, November 21, 2005. © 2005 Newsweek, Inc. All rights reserved. Reprinted by permission.

Charles McGrath. "The Pleasure of the Text." *The New York Times Magazine*, January 22, 2006. Copyright © 2005 by The New York Times Co. Reprinted with permission of The New York Times Agency.

Bill McKibben. "Pie in the Sky." *Orion*, March/April 2006. Reprinted by permission of the author.

Chase Mitchell. "Age-Old Debate: Creationist Students in the Science Classroom." *The Auburn Plainsman*, Auburn University, October 13, 2005. Reprinted by permission of the author and *The Auburn Plainsman*.

Dan Mollison. "Say No to Torture." *The Daily Illini*, University of Illinois. December 7, 2005. Reprinted by permission of the author and *The Daily Illini*.

MySpace.com. "MySpace Tour" Web screen. Courtesy MySpace.com.

Brandon Nadeau. "Video Games Make Society Less Violent." *The Daily Campus*, University of Connecticut, October 21, 2005. Reprinted by permission of the author and *The Daily Campus*.

National Retail Federation. "Top Toys for Tots." Survey conducted by BIGresearch for the National Retail Federation. Reprinted by permission of the National Retail Federation.

The New York Times Editorial Board. "Debunking the Concept of 'Race.'" *The New York Times*, July 30, 2005. Copyright © 2005 by The New York Times Co. Reprinted with permission.

Camille Paglia. "The Pitfalls of Plastic Surgery." *Harper's Bazaar*, May 1, 2005. Reprinted by permission of the author.

Lucia Perillo. "Definition of Terms." Originally published in *PMS poemmemoirstory*, Volume 5/2005.

Steven Pinker. "Sex Ed: The Science of Difference." The New Republic, February 14, 2005. Reprinted by permission of *The New Republic*, © 2005, The New Republic, LLC.

Random House Permissions (cover). "Roots." Jacket cover from *Roots* by Alex Haley. Used by permission of Dell Publishing, a division of Random House, Inc.

RCA/Thomson (advertisement). RCA telegram ad. Reprinted by permission of Thomson/RCA.

Darcy Richie. "Calling for a New Dialogue on Rape." *The Daily Pennsylvanian*, March 17, 2004. © 2004 The Daily Pennsylvanian, Inc. Reprinted with permission of *The Daily Pennsylvanian* and the author.

Annie Bradford Rispin. "Here's Looking at You: Is Body Image Being Taken Too Seriously?" *U. Magazine*, Fall 2005. Reprinted by permission of *U. Magazine*.

Joe Rosenthal (photograph). "Flag Raising at Iwo Jima, February 23, 1945" by Joe Rosenthal appears by permission of AP/Wide World Photos.

Megan Rundle. "Unearthing Family Roots." *The Digital Collegian*, Pennsylvania State University, December 5, 2005. Reprinted by permission of the author and *The Digital Collegian* at Pennsylvania State.

William Safire. "Changing Warming." *The New York Times Magazine*, August 14, 2005. Copyright © 2005 by The New York Times Co. Reprinted with permission of The New York Times Agency.

Eugenie C. Scott and Glenn Branch. "Evolution: Just Teach It." *USA Today*, August 14, 2005. Reprinted by permission of authors.

Jerry Scott and Jim Borgman (cartoon). "When Guys Hang Out." © Zits—Zits Partnership. Kings Features Syndicate.

Index of Authors and Titles

Need help with writing and research?
Visit the Re:Writing Web site

bedfordstmartins.com/rewriting

Re:Writing is a comprehensive Web site designed to help you with the most common writing concerns. You'll find advice from experts, models you can rely on, and exercises that will tell you right away how you're doing. And it's all free and available any hour of the day. You can find help for the following situations at the specific areas of bedfordstmartins.com/rewriting listed below.

- Need help with grammar problems? **Exercise Central**

- Want to see what papers for your other courses look like? **Model Documents Gallery**

- Stuck somewhere in the research process? (Maybe at the beginning?) **The Bedford Research Room**

- Wondering whether a Web site is good enough to use in your paper? **Evaluating Online Sources Tutorial**

- Having trouble figuring out how to cite a source? **Research and Documentation Online**

- Confused about plagiarism? **Avoiding Plagiarism Tutorial**

- Want to get more out of your word processor? **Using Your Word Processor**

- Trying to improve the look of your paper? **Designing Documents with a Word Processor**

- Need to create slides for a presentation? **Preparing Presentation Slides Tutorial**

- Interested in creating a Web site? **Mike Markel's Web Design Tutorial**